014229791 Liverpool Univ

PLANNING • ENVIRONMENT • CITIES

Series Editors: Yvonne Rydin and Andrew Thornley

The context in which planning operates has changed dramatically in recent years. Economic processes have become increasingly globalized and new spatial patterns of economic activity have emerged. There have been major changes across the globe, not just changing administrations in various countries, but also the sweeping away of old ideologies and the tentative emergence of new ones. A new environmental agenda emerged from the Brundtland Report and the Rio Earth Summit prioritizing the goal of sustainable development. The momentum for this has been maintained by continued action at international, national and local levels.

Cities are today faced with new pressures for economic competitiveness, greater accountability and participation, improved quality of life for citizens and global environmental responsibilities. These pressures are often contradictory and create difficult dilemmas for policy-makers, especially in the context of fiscal austerity. New relationships are developing between the levels of state activity and between public and private sectors as different interests respond to the new conditions.

WITHDRAWN FROM STOCK

In these changing circumstances, planners, from many backgrounds, in many different organizations, have come to re-evaluate their work. They have had to engage with actors in government, the private sector and non-governmental organizations in discussions over the role of planning in relation to the environment and cities. The intention of the *Planning, Environment, Cities* series is to explore the changing nature of planning and contribute to the debate about its future.

The series is primarily aimed at students and practitioners of planning and such related professions as estate management, housing and architecture as well as those in politics, public and social administration, geography and urban studies. It comprises both general texts and books designed to make a more particular contribution, in both cases characterized by: an international approach; extensive use of case studies; and emphasis on contemporary relevance and the application of theory to advance planning practice.

PLANNING • ENVIRONMENT • CITIES

Series Editors: Yvonne Rydin and Andrew Thornley

*Published*

Philip Allmendinger
**Planning Theory (2nd edn)**

Ruth Fincher and Kurt Iveson
**Planning and Diversity in the City: Redistribution, Recognition and Encounter**

Patsy Healey
**Collaborative Planning (2nd edn)**

Ted Kitchen
**Skills for Planning Practice**

Peter Newman and Andrew Thornley
**Planning World Cities**

Michael Oxley
**Economics Planning and Housing**

Yvonne Rydin
**Urban and Environmental Planning in the UK (2nd edn)**

Geoff Vigar, Patsy Healey and Angela Hull with Simin Davoudi
**Planning, Governance and Spatial Strategy in Britain**

*Forthcoming*

Cliff Hague, Euan Hague and Carrie Breitenbach
**Regional and Local Economic Development**

Patsy Healey
**Making Better Places: People, Planning and Politics in the 21st Century**

*Other titles planned include*

**Introduction to Planning**
**Urban Design**

**Planning, Environment, Cities**
**Series Standing Order**
**ISBN 0-333-71703-1 hardback**
**ISBN 0-333-69346-9 paperback**
(*outside North America only*)

You can receive future titles in this series as they are published. To place a standing order please contact your bookseller or, in the case of difficulty, write to us at the address below with your name and address, the title of the series and one of the ISBNs quoted above.

Customer Services Department, Macmillan Distribution Ltd
Houndmills, Basingstoke, Hampshire RG21 6XS, England

# Planning Theory

## Second Edition

Philip Allmendinger

palgrave
macmillan

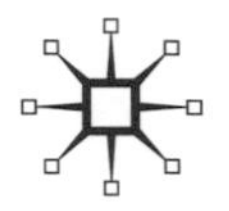

© Philip Allmendinger 2002, 2009

All rights reserved. No reproduction, copy or transmission of this publication may be made without written permission.

No portion of this publication may be reproduced, copied or transmitted save with written permission or in accordance with the provisions of the Copyright, Designs and Patents Act 1988, or under the terms of any licence permitting limited copying issued by the Copyright Licensing Agency, Saffron House, 6-10 Kirby Street, London EC1N 8TS.

Any person who does any unauthorized act in relation to this publication may be liable to criminal prosecution and civil claims for damages.

The author has asserted his right to be identified as the author of this work in accordance with the Copyright, Designs and Patents Act 1988.

First published 2002
Reprinted twice
Second edition 2009

Published by
PALGRAVE MACMILLAN

Palgrave Macmillan in the UK is an imprint of Macmillan Publishers Limited, registered in England, company number 785998, of Houndmills, Basingstoke, Hampshire RG21 6XS.

Palgrave Macmillan in the US is a division of St Martin's Press LLC, 175 Fifth Avenue, New York, NY 10010.

Palgrave Macmillan is the global academic imprint of the above companies and has companies and representatives throughout the world.

Palgrave® and Macmillan® are registered trademarks in the United States, the United Kingdom, Europe and other countries

ISBN 978-0-230-22364-6 hardback
ISBN 978-0-230-22365-3 paperback

This book is printed on paper suitable for recycling and made from fully managed and sustained forest sources. Logging, pulping and manufacturing processes are expected to conform to the environmental regulations of the country of origin.

A catalogue record for this book is available from the British Library.

A catalog record for this book is available from the Library of Congress.

10 9 8 7 6 5 4 3 2 1
18 17 16 15 14 13 12 11 10 09

Printed and bound in China

*For Claudia, Hannah, Lucia and Eleanor*

# Contents

# List of Tables and Figures

## Tables



## Figures



## Acknowledgement

The author and publishers would like to thank Patsy Healey for permission to use Figure 2.1, originally published in Healey *et al.* (1982) *Planning Theory: Prospects for the 1980s* (Oxford: Pergamon).

# 1 What is Theory?

## The nature of theory

Before we embark on any exploration of theory it is necessary to define what we mean. The word theory is used widely and can cover a variety of meanings depending on the context or use. For example, it can be used in a pejorative way to dismiss something as being impractical or unrelated to reality as in 'this is all too theoretical'. At the other extreme it can be used in a more positive way to criticize a piecemeal or knee-jerk reaction as in 'this has no theoretical grounding'. Beyond its rhetorical use the word can also be used to cover a wide range of ideas or propositions from Einstein's theory of relativity to the theory that the relationship between birth and the relative position of stars will influence daily experiences. The notion of theory then is a diffuse phenomenon. Regardless of problems with use and definition there are some general ideas of what is meant:

> Theory is an *explanatory* supposition which can be defined broadly or narrowly. (McConnell, 1981, p. 20)

> . . . a theory is not a theory at all, until it has been used in practice over a considerable period of time. (Reade, 1987, p. 156)

> The main concern of social theory is the same as that of the social sciences in general: the illumination of concrete processes of human life. (Giddens, 1984, p. xvii)

In addition to the above, theory is normally required to include some element of prediction or prescription so as to guide action. Accordingly, theory could be seen as having a number of elements; *it abstracts a set of general or specific principles to be used as a basis for explaining and acting, with the theory being tested and refined if necessary.*

While this definition would seem broadly uncontentious, I would argue that it does not take us as far as we need to go. For a start, under this definition theory could cover a multitude of situations; for example, it does not tell us what distinguishes theory from conjecture or from ideas. Neither does it distinguish between the different uses and levels of theory; for example, can all theories be used in different situations? This is particularly important in planning where it has long been argued that there are theories *of* planning (why it exists and what it does) and theories *in* planning (how to go about it). Second, the definition ignores the context of theory, particularly the social construction of knowledge. The idea that theories or ideas are 'objective' or privileged views upon 'reality' has been queried and rejected by philosophers for centuries. This is something that we will come to later but suffice to say here that theories can be regarded as part of a discourse formation, that is, words, statements, symbols, similes, etc. that all mean different things in different contexts and are dependent upon their context and wider understanding. Words are contentious and ambiguous, and interpretations of meaning will inevitably vary. This has important implications for the formation, interpretation and evaluation of theory in different places. Finally, and linked in some ways to the last point, theory in the social sciences is not immune from the influence of power and its wider social context, that is, there are *political* and *temporal* elements to theories. Some theories have been advanced to protect or further expand the influence of powerful interests. Systems theory, for example (covered in Chapter 3), is not just a way of thinking about how cities 'work'. It also has significant implications for the ways in which planning should be undertaken that empowers certain groups (planners) over others. This points to a need to examine the disciplinary and historically variable relations of power and its influence upon theories.

What we need therefore is an approach to theory that goes beyond broad definitions and addresses the points above.

### *The differences between the natural and social sciences*

The first distinction that is usually made in theory is between the natural and social sciences. This may seem like an obvious difference to some but there is a strong tradition that argues that social science theory should follow the same apparently logical positivist approach as the natural sciences in trying to uncover general deductible laws and truths. In 1996 the journal *Social Text* published an article by the physicist Alan Sokal entitled 'Transgressing the Boundaries – Toward a Transformative Hermeneutics of Quantum Gravity', which reflected upon recent developments in physics from the standpoint of postmodern cultural theory. The article was a hoax that aimed to expose what Sokal and others saw as the nonsense paraded by cultural theorists (some of which we cover later on in this book). The point of the article was to expose some of the differences between the understandings and methodologies of the natural and social sciences by satirizing them. As Weinberg pointed out in a response to Sokal's 'paper':

> There are those 'postmoderns' in the humanities who like to surf through avant garde fields like quantum mechanics or chaos theory to dress up their own arguments about the fragmentary and random nature of experience. There are those sociologists, historians, and philosophers who see the laws of nature as social constructions. There are cultural critics who find the taint of sexism, racism, colonialism, militarism, or capitalism not only in the practice of scientific research but even in its conclusions. (Weinberg, 1996)

The gap between the natural and social sciences is one that is as broad as ever. While Weinberg and others attack the relativism of some social science, social scientists respond with criticisms of the reductionism of natural scientists. The problem, as with many of these 'debates', is that both sides were talking past each other. The realms of quantum physics and postmodern philosophy have little to say or contribute to each other. However, these are extremes. In planning, we deal with both social and natural sciences. The justification for many early planning controls was the relationship between physical conditions (e.g., slum housing) and its social implications (e.g., ill health).

Early sociologists such as Auguste Comte, Emile Durkheim and Max Weber attempted to put studies of society on a more 'scientific' footing. However, it was the logical positivists typified by the 'Vienna Circle' who argued that if something was not observable then it was not verifiable and if it was not verifiable then it was metaphysical and meaningless. While logical positivism as an approach has been largely abandoned it continues to have an influence upon social sciences through the focus upon empiricism. The idea of both science and social science being linked by a search for general laws and causal explanations has in some ways made social science appear inferior by comparison. For example, there is no equivalent in the social sciences of a law explaining and predicting the influence of gravity. While there are still proponents of naturalism (the view that, with adaptation, the methodologies of the natural sciences are appropriate for the social sciences), the majority view is that society cannot be explained in the same way that we can explain the workings of gravity, it can only be provisionally understood. The social sciences are also dominated by what appear to be numerous conflicting theories based on fundamentally different views of the world, for example, Marxism and liberalism. Giddens (1984) argues there will never be any universal laws in social science because of difficulties with empirical testing and validation. One problem is separating theory from the society that is being conceptualized or theorized. Society has a habit of shifting values, meaning and actions. It would be difficult if not impossible to test an idea or theory of society that has been taken up by society thereby shifting the original grounds upon which it could be tested. Another issue concerns the extent to which our worldview shapes what we see: observing and measuring various dimensions of class, for example, requires us to believe that such a phenomenon exists even though this is disputed. Measuring class presupposes that we believe it exists, which is itself a political position. There is an issue, therefore, of context and distance. The social sciences can never fully divorce themselves from the subject that is being studied. Ideas that seem radical and new at one time can be now accepted as being ordinary and familiar. Social theory, therefore, not only reflects upon society but can also shape it in a way that natural sciences cannot. This is sometimes referred to as the difference between an 'open' system (e.g., society) and a 'closed' system (e.g., natural laws such as gravity). But this is not to elevate the natural sciences to a superior position where science holds a monopoly on truth or reason. It is to say, however, that science and social science study different manifestations of reality in different ways. Nor is it to say that there are not issues with scientific theory and methodology.

In the eighteenth century, the Scottish philosopher David Hume examined the inductive basis of science. Induction is an approach that examines the available evidence and uses it as a basis for formulating laws and theories. For example, if I observe 500 white swans I could conclude, on the basis of induction, that the next swan I see will be white. However, the 501st swan may well be black thereby undermining my prediction. Induction uses past information as a basis for the future and is the basis of most scientific research. Generalizations or theories based on inductive reasoning go beyond what is known and observable and as such can never be 'true', or even probably true and therefore much of science is based on conjecture. This situation has come to be known as 'Hume's puzzle'. Hume and his eighteenth-century colleagues did not consider this situation was anything more than an interesting philosophical point. After all, they were living in an age where Newton's newly discovered laws of motion had opened up much of the natural world to human study and control and were themselves based on the inductive approach. These laws 'worked' so why question the approach used to generate them?

Actually, they did not work in all situations. Following the discovery of quantum mechanics, Einstein's theory of relativity and the newly emerging sciences of chaos and complexity, Newton's laws were shown to be wrong in some circumstances. While for everyday purposes the differences between the theories of Newton and Einstein are irrelevant (Newton's laws were good enough to take man to the moon and back) they have been jumped upon by some social scientists as proof that the natural sciences seek to grasp an objective reality that simply does not exist. This led Karl Popper and others to conclude that no part of scientific reasoning is above question, particularly if based on inductivism. Instead of induction Popper developed an account of science based on fallibility. Popper believed that there was no need for induction beyond the basic human search for patterns and regularities. But as long as we are aware that patterns and regularities can be wrong then the puzzle holds no problems. Good conjectures or theories should therefore be outlandish and provocative in order to test and falsify current theories. Falsification rejects the idea that theories are true and instead sees them as speculative or provisional truths that stand for as long as they are not disproven. Using the swan example again, a fallible approach would be to devise a hypothesis 'all swans are white'. That hypothesis would be tested through observation and would remain a 'provisional truth' until disproven. Using this approach human knowledge could progress through a series of ever more falsifiable and accurate theories that can never be proven.

Popper's ideas have been extremely influential, though they have not been without their own critics. One of the main problems with falsification (as with logical positivism) is observation. According to falsificationists, theory rejection is based on observation. So if observation refutes a theory then the theory should fall. But, as many writers including Popper himself have realized, observation statements are themselves fallible. Take a look at Figure 1.1. Do you see a staircase from beneath or from above? It may not be a theory that is wrong, it may be the observation. In modern physics much experimentation at the sub-atomic level can only be achieved through the medium of instruments, making observation itself subject to the accuracy of human-made forms of measurement. Consequently, according to this view theories cannot be conclusively falsified because the observation statements that form the basis for falsification may themselves prove to be false (Couvalis, 1997, p. 63).

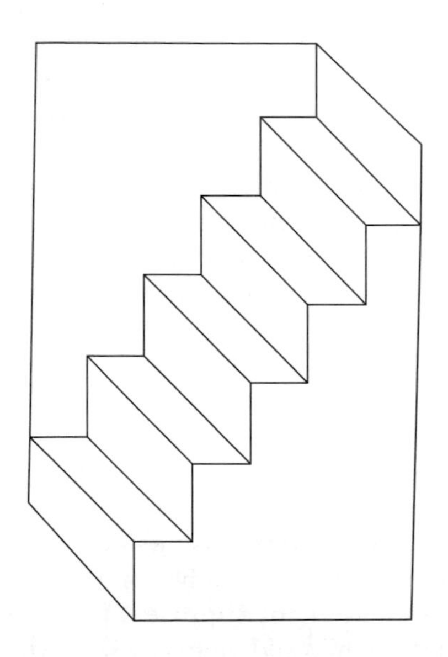

**Figure 1.1** The problem of perception
*Source*: based on Chalmers, 1994, p. 24.

A further problem has been explored by Imre Lakatos. He argues that a theory should not be refuted simply because it is counterintuitive or falsified. Many theories, as pointed out earlier, are a product of their time. Both Copernicus and Newton battled to have their theories accepted, as they were radical departures from contemporary thinking. The problem, according to Lakatos, is that science will never abandon a theory unless there is a better one to replace it. So, falsification is not enough. Refutation on its own appears to leave a vacuum, whereas scientists will actually continue to use a theory even if it has been falsified until a better explanation emerges.

This is an idea that has been most famously associated with Thomas Kuhn (1970). Rather than the logical and abstract falsification view of Popper, which saw science as a cumulative growth of knowledge, Kuhn argued that science proceeds on the basis of revolution. Science works with *paradigms* or views of reality that encapsulate current knowledge of a subject. Once established a paradigm begins to be challenged when researchers probe its limits. Problems then emerge that cannot be explained by the paradigm and cannot be resolved until a new paradigm emerges and the old one is abandoned. Different paradigms will have very different worldviews often making them incomparable. A classic example used by Kuhn to illustrate this concerns what is generally termed the 'Copernican Revolution'.

The idea that the earth is at the centre of the universe had first been advanced by Aristotle in the fourth century BC. This idea dominated science and was reinforced by Christian doctrine. However, in the sixteenth century the Polish astronomer Nicolaus Copernicus developed a heliocentric (sun-centred) theory that addressed some of the less convincing aspects of the geocentric (earth-centred) approach. The problem was that Copernicus could not prove some aspects of his theory and it did not gain much support from the scientific community, who were still locked in the geocentric paradigm. For over 100 years the ideas of Copernicus remained a minority paradigm. It took the Italian physicist and astronomer Galileo to confirm the Copernican theories through observation. Galileo observed that the motions of planets and stars changed in the ways predicted by Copernicus. The scientific establishment were unconvinced and still wedded to the Aristotelian geocentric view. A more serious challenge was to come when

Galileo's ideas were denounced as heretical and he was forced to renounce his theories. The heliocentric view could not be reconciled with the Bible and therefore it was wrong (this decision was reversed by the Pope in 1992). Galileo's ideas were to influence Isaac Newton and others, though it was not until the late seventeenth century that the heliocentric view of the universe was broadly accepted by science – over 200 years since Copernicus first advanced it.

Kuhn uses the Copernican example as an illustration of the ways scientific paradigms work. The geocentric and heliocentric views of the universe belonged to different worldviews – recourse to 'evidence' made little difference. Again, Kuhn's ideas have been highly influential not only in terms of the explanation but also in terms of the criticisms and avenues he has opened up. There is still a widespread assumption that the scientific community in general and scientists as individuals are rational beings, that is, that they will act in a way that will reject or choose theories on the basis of evidence. As a result of Kuhn's revolutionary view of scientific progress attention began to be paid to the subjective or normative aspects of science. This turn to the subjective has been termed the *relative* view of science:

> Since for the relativist, the criteria for judging the merits of theories will depend on the values and interests of the individual or community entertaining them, the distinction between science and non-science will vary accordingly. (Chalmers, 1994, p. 103)

Such relativism allows for different theories to exist side by side each claiming with equal validity that their view is just as correct or legitimate as the next. This is not only true of, for example, Marxist versus liberal views, but also of the dominance of science against other areas of knowledge. Central to this relativist view of science is Paul Feyerabend (1961, 1978, 1981, 1988). Much of Feyerabend's writings are motivated by a concern with freedom and in particular the need to question the dominant role given to science and the way in which it is perceived and presented:

> Thus, while an American can now choose the religion he likes, he is still not permitted to demand that his children learn magic rather than science at school. There is a separation between state and church, there is no separation between state and science. (1988, p. 299)

The ongoing debate between evolution and creationism in the USA is a similar situation of competing worldviews that both appeal to different legitimacies. In planning such relativism is characteristic of postmodernism and postmodern planning (see Chapter 8), though advocacy (Chapter 7), also argues for a plethora of plans based around multiple and competing viewpoints. In a similar vein, others have also focused attention on Kuhn's questioning of the objective nature of scientists themselves. As Couvalis (1997) points out, scientists often appear to have been influenced by external factors that have nothing to do with evidence and more to do with whether a theory should bolster a particular social group to which they belong. Barnes and Bloor (1982), for example, claim that scientists always accept theories partly because of factors other than purely scientific ones. They identify what they term a 'strong programme' that, rather like Kuhn's paradigm, dominates thinking, methodology, interpretation and results. So, for example, students who want to pass exams regurgitate the strong programme and, as science has been given a dominant position in society, the public accept a 'strong programme' as 'truth'. Barnes and Bloor do not claim that a 'strong programme' is always wrong, but that it can be wrong. Scientists, researchers, students and society come to accept it as a 'truth' or dominant discourse regardless of its validity.

Others, such as Longino (1990), have also persuasively argued that the ways in which data are formulated and interpreted are also affected by social values. Any number of theories can be logically consistent with the same data. So if one theory is chosen over another there must be a reason for this that has less to do with objective science and more to do with social factors.

Although many of these views of science have been questioned and are by no means uncritically accepted I have discussed them to demonstrate two things. First, that the natural sciences are not necessarily superior to the social sciences in terms of knowledge accumulation. This is not to say that a broad social constructivist view of science is itself correct – gravity is not asymmetrical depending upon your culture. Rather than being anti-scientific, relativist views emphasize and highlight the social dimension of theories and methodologies. Second, that the critique of natural science is equally applicable to the social sciences and helps us understand why we find a multitude of competing theories and views of planning. In particular, it has relevance to grey areas between the two and, specifically, for fields such as planning, which involve aspects of both natural science and social science.

*Unpacking 'theory'*

After identifying and questioning the distinction between theory in the social and natural sciences, as well as problematizing the idea of theory in both, we can now turn to some other questions set out earlier, for example, are all theories the same? Judge, Stoker and Wolman (1995) provide a useful starting point and identify six broad categories in the assessment of different kinds of theory (Table 1.1 and below).

*Normative theory* says how the world *ought* to be and provides ideas about how to achieve this state. Traditionally, these could be regarded as theories *of* planning and could, for example, include Marxist, liberal and communicative or collaborative planning approaches.

*Prescriptive theories* concern themselves with *how* to go about things or the means. Traditionally, this has been termed theories *in* planning and includes, for example, cost–benefit analysis, mixed scanning, etc.

*Empirical theory* explains and interprets reality and focuses on causal relationships and dependent and independent variables. Hypotheses form part of empirical theory that allows it to be tested and adjusted. Examples could include theories concerning the impact of out of town retail upon town centres.

*Models* are more simple representations and pictures of reality that do not always include hypotheses but are still testable.

*Conceptual frameworks or perspectives* are really a linguistic analysis of situations and ideas leading to perspectives and critiques that might otherwise be lost. Some Marxist perspectives can be seen to fall into this category (though into others too) and can lead to a perspective on, for example, class or freedom that questions assumptions, practices and theories.

*Theorizing* generally is a catch-all category that covers thinking and debating ideas and other theories as to their suitability and applicability.

These six categories provide a useful *way in*, going beyond the general idea of theories described at the beginning of this chapter. We can see how theories are not homogeneous, perform different roles and come in different shapes and sizes. However, this categorization still raises a number of questions. First, as social constructivists would argue, to what extent are *all* theories normative, for example, in undertaking empirical work (e.g., looking for evidence to confirm or refute a theory) can you escape a particular view of the world in choosing what to study and how to study it? Similarly, in putting together a prescriptive theory you will be choosing what to include and exclude. Many prescriptive theories implicitly include normative elements, for example, reducing inflation through controlling the money supply or punishing crime by locking criminals up. All include some *a priori* assumptions and prescriptions about how the world operates or should be. This builds on the work of Kuhn, etc. above – we are 'programmed' to see things in certain ways in both the natural and social sciences. Thus, whether we consider Al Qaeda to be terrorists or freedom fighters points to a socially constructed framework or paradigm

***Table 1.1*** **Categories of theory**

| *Type of theory* | *Characteristics* |
|---|---|
| Normative | Concerns how the world ought to be |
| Prescriptive | Concerned with best means of achieving a desired condition |
| Empirical | Concerned with explaining reality |
| Models | Representations or stylized and simplified pictures of reality |
| Conceptual frameworks or perspectives | Ways of looking at or conceiving an object of study |
| Theorizing | Thinking about some aspect of a phenomenon |

*Source*: based on Judge, Stoker and Wolman (1995).

with which we view the world. This adds a further dimension to our idea of theory – to what extent is science a random trawl or a deliberate process in which the scientist sets out to find data to confirm or refute expectations?

At the very least, the boundaries between different kinds of theory are not black and white. At worst, and this is what I argue, *all theory is to greater and lesser degrees normative.* Ernest Alexander (2003) comes to a similar conclusion when he rejects the possibility of a 'general theory' of planning:

> I have gone so far as to assert that, for any practical purposes, there is no 'planning'. Rather, there is a diversity of practices in planning (as there is everywhere), and different kinds of planners in different contexts should (and do) enact different models or theories of planning. (Alexander, 2003, p. 181)

Highlighting the normative dimension of theories is not a particularly new position, as I have outlined above, but it is one that has been traditionally more implicit than explicit. This perspective does not undermine the concept and usefulness of theory or the use of any specific research technique. What it does do is point to a more political and contestable approach to theory. This brings us to the view of theory as discourse.

### *Theory as discourse*

At the heart of this understanding of theory as being socially constructed is the relationship between power and discourse. Such an approach rejects the idea that there is such a thing as 'truth' as an absolute or objective concept. If social science theory is a search for understanding rather than explanation and prediction then we must accept the normative element of methodology. This relates to fundamental debates in philosophy that need not concern us here. What writers such as Hume, Hegel and Nietzsche advance to greater and lesser degrees and with different emphases is the idea of truth as a relative concept, that is, the idea that truth varies from context to context, relative to language and culture. Central to this is the widely held view that rationality and science have hijacked and dominated the idea of truth in an absolute or objective sense since the Enlightenment. Modern philosophy is sceptical of such views and critical of the implications. For example, Lyotard questions the whole Enlightenment basis of objective scientific knowledge:

> Science has always been in conflict with narratives. Judged by the yardstick of science, the majority of these prove to be fables. But to the extent that science does not restrict itself to stating useful regularities and seeks the truth, it is obliged to legitimate the rules of its own game. It then produces a discourse or legitimation with respect to its own status. (1984, p. xxiii)

In Lyotard's relativistic view, science has no more claim to objective knowledge than what he terms 'narratives' or stories. Instead, science is itself based on higher-level narratives or 'meta-narratives' that involve values and assumptions. We can see this through the ways in which there has developed a symbiotic relationship between science and the state. For example, scientific progress is often seen as a necessary and crucial part of the drive for industrial and commercial growth. However, Marxists for example, would argue that science ultimately serves, or ought to serve, the liberation of humanity from exploitation. Others would ascribe a different ultimate goal for science: 'many supposedly objective aspirations to science inevitably tend to be framed by some kind of metanarrative involving distinctly value laden notions of social progress and human emancipation' (McLennan, 1992, p. 332). According to this view the ability of science to 'uncover' the truth was dealt a severe blow with the discovery of relativity and quantum mechanics, which imply that science can at best approximate rather than pinpoint. Scientists strongly reject this argument and invite those who think that they can defy the laws of gravity to do so. This postmodern view of rationality and truth poses a number of questions for 'facts' and processes as well as any approach to objective and absolute ideas of right and wrong. Under this view truth is *socially* produced: 'Truth is to be understood as a system of ordered procedures for the production, regulation, distribution, circulation and operation of statements' (Fontana and Pasquino, 1991, quoted in Richardson, 1996, p. 282). One example has been explored by Michel Foucault and concerns the treatment of madness throughout history. The contemporary theory that we should exclude the mad from society is a relatively recent phenomenon. According to Foucault, the treatment of mental illness in the west is a particularly cultural condition in contrast to many primitive societies where the mad are often the centre of religious or other social activities: 'Such a comparative, historical approach highlights both that madness has no pre-social essence and also that there is nothing natural or inevitable about the strategies through which, in modern society, the mad are confined or socially excluded' (McNay, 1996, p.17). Therefore, the answer to the question of 'What is mad?', as well as the theory of treating the mad through excluding them from society, is built not upon some scientific or objective truth but upon changing social attitudes. Such attitudes act in a similar way to Kuhn's paradigms or what are also termed discourses. The concept of discourse is notoriously difficult to pin down, though van Dijk (1997) identifies three main dimensions: discourse as *language use,* as the *communication of beliefs* (cognition) *and interaction in social situations.* Insofar as it is possible to separate these aspects we are mainly concerned here with the second area, namely discourse as cognition, in both written and verbal communication. Through the choice of words, style, nuance, emphasis, inflection, etc., users of language express opinions and ideologies. Written and spoken language is consequently an inherently political act based on a unique individual interpretation of a situation *and* a socially shared stock of meaning. This social stock of meaning is itself founded on the premise that ideas or theories are generated by the social forces dominant in and characteristic of their age. They are a framework that provides a system of meaning, which in turn influences the way people understand their role in society and how they act. It should be clear how the idea of discourse relates to and helps 'flesh out' the social nature of theories discussed earlier through helping identify the inputs of society and mechanisms such as language.

Discourses are historically contingent and politically constructed, as we saw in Foucault's example of the treatment of madness. The contemporary social perspective on madness created 'knowledge' of the mad as being different from other people and a threat that should be excluded from society. But this knowledge was politically produced, that is, there were different perspectives on madness that were possible, as Foucault demonstrated, but this particular one became dominant. Foucault argues that confinement was presented as being benevolent. However, he goes on to claim that it was actually a way of discouraging idleness and sloth in society where cheap labour was necessary. In recent years we can see that confining the mad is far less prevalent in many places where community-based care is now the current approach.

To take an example from planning, we can see ideas such as 'green belts' as discourses. They emerged to tackle perceived problems of urban growth and are used, with different labels, throughout the world. One hundred years ago people would not have know what a green belt was, though now they are one of the most well-known aspects of planning practice. This is not to say that they are uncontentious or have not developed, but green belts have become a *symbol* of planning and carry meanings and significance. For some they represent a desirable attempt to limit urban sprawl, for others they are the basis for ensuring cities are sustainable and for others still they are a reflection of middle-class Nimbyism (Not In My Back Yard). And yet they only exist as social constructions to represent a vision or idea that cities should not grow indefinitely and carry with them enough of a common vision that people know that they exist. Some have tried to explore the implications of green belts upon a range of factors, to appeal to evidence and study the implications. Evans and Hartwich (2006), for example, highlight the detrimental impact green belts have had on land and house prices, travel to work times, carbon emissions and access to recreational facilities. Yet despite this 'evidence' successive governments remains as committed as ever to them. Why is this? The main reason is that the data and evidence selected by Evans and Hartwich (and others who have criticized green belts) has been chosen and used to fit a position that is critical of planning regulations *per se*. Other organizations, such as the Campaign to Protect Rural England (2006) choose very different evidence or use similar evidence in different ways to argue for the 'success' of green belts. Again, their position helps define what evidence and theories are used to support it. Without a hint of irony (and providing a good example of how heated such debates can get on planning matters), the CPRE respond to Evans and Hartwich's position:

> Several of the claims made in them are mere assertions. A few can only be described as bizarre. But CPRE has also uncovered misuse of statistics to make a false comparison between the UK's housing and cities and those of other European nations. A few politicians and commentators appear to have swallowed this nonsense whole. In this rebuttal we expose the confusions, the lack of evidence and the dodgy statistics

> underlying the Policy Exchange's ill-conceived attack on planning, housing and the environmental movement. (CPRE, 2006, p. 2)

There is no appeal to objective evidence in the same way that exists in the natural sciences. So the discourse of green belts includes certain ideas and elements that are commonly understood but are also very personal; restraining urban growth, protecting the countryside etc. The combination of social and personal interpretation allows them to be described both positively and negatively, depending on a point of view. And in expressing that view (or ideology) a person is constructing or changing the discourse of green belts.

The term 'green belt' is highly evocative and conjures up images that people will understand and in doing so includes certain ideas and excludes others. The discourse of green belts 'makes sense' of the term, though it is changeable and socially constructed. Green belts become a 'norm' and such norms represent truth and knowledge in modern society. But what are the influences upon norms, knowledge, truth and discourse? According to this analysis, power is posited as *the* influence. Traditionally, power was exercised visibly in society, for example, the authority of the king being exercised through public executions. In modern societies, however, power is far more hidden and surreptitious. For example, Michel Foucault rejects the idea that power is uni-directional (i.e., the orthodox Marxist view of class and economic power being dominant), but instead argues that power is found at all levels of society and social existence. It is invisible and 'flows' through the complex web of networks that make up modern life. His argument is that centralized power (e.g., absolute monarchies) are no longer necessary to maintain discipline as modern power is insidiously disciplinary. This form of discipline overcame a central weakness of centralized power whose effects were uneven and dysfunctional. Changes to a more democratic system of government did not therefore aim to create a more equitable system but, 'to set up a new economy of power which was better distributed, more efficient and less costly in both economic and political terms' (McNay, 1994, p. 92). Instead of centralized power, we now have 'social control . . . produced by a complex network of rules, regulations, administrative monitoring and the management and direction of people's daily lives' (Painter, 1995, p. 9).

Monitoring and regulating these internalized rules of behaviour are various 'judges of normality' such as doctors, social workers, teachers and planners. Power is consequently disciplinary and such discipline is crucial to the growth of capital and the search for new forms of accumulation. In this sense Foucault's analysis has some strong parallels with Marxist and Weberian approaches.

Here, then, we can see the link between disciplinary power, 'judges of normality' and discourse. It is the judges of normality who generate discourses such as green belts and regulate them. Here also we can begin to see wider arguments concerning knowledge, power and truth. We should not be asking whether an argument or theory is true, but instead, 'ask how, why and by who, truth is attributed to particular arguments and not to others' (Richardson, 1996, p. 283). Power is legitimized in the name of scientific 'truth', which is valued above other forms of knowledge because the discourse around science has granted it a valuable status. Because of this, society has a 'will to truth', valuing scientific truth, which masks power: 'A vast range of social practices, such as economies or punishment, seek to justify themselves by reference to a true discourse, yet should be subject to a politically motivated critique' (Simons, 1994, p. 43). We could, therefore, conclude that the thrust of the argument so far in this chapter is that theory can be seen as discourse and could be argued to be a mask for power and politics. The recognition of theory being another discourse used and open to abuse by powerful policy analysts has been investigated by Richardson: 'theoretical perspectives are called upon in a selective and arbitrary way, to suit a given situation. Clearly this tendency bestows significant power in the policy analyst, who informs the selection of perspectives, theories and ultimately methods' (1996, p. 286). For 'policy analyst' we could insert 'planner'. The use of theory as discourse by planning practitioners has been explored by Grant (1994, p. 74) who confirms the political and power laden nature of theory, as well questioning its empirical basis: 'People promote theories that fit their normative perspectives. Theories that become part of popular culture meet community needs and expectations.'

We can see, therefore, that there are two major inputs into theory; normative elements (societal and individual) and discursive elements, both of which are influenced by power. In planning there are a variety of influences upon both normative and discursive aspects of theory formation, but one that we will focus on in particular is the role of what Foucault termed 'agents of norms', or planners themselves, and their relative autonomy in society.

*Theory, structure and agency*

To better understand the role of 'agents of norms' we need to appreciate the influence upon such actors. Many ideas and theories contain implicit notions of the relationship between structure and agency that reflect deeper understandings about the relative autonomy of actors and agents in the settings in which they find themselves (Hay, 1995). We discussed the idea of planners as 'agents of norms' above, which implied an autonomous role for them. But there has been a prolonged debate in the social sciences about the extent of this autonomy; what influences come to bear on them? The main question that we should concern ourselves with is: *to what extent are individuals (agents) autonomous in their thoughts and actions and how much does society (structure) influence them?* In planning terms, we could ask whether a plan was a reflection of the local desires and needs of an area or whether it was directed far more by the influence of central government or powerful economic forces. In planning theory, the relationship between structure and agency is equally important for a number of reasons. First, the use of theory by planners may be limited by the role of structure. Second, some theories ignore this relationship, particularly theories of planning (i.e., how to go about it) and thereby limit their usefulness. An understanding of the two is essential for an appreciation of the use and limits of theory.

The social sciences have witnessed two broad approaches to this relationship: structuralism and intentionalism. Structuralism is often associated with Marxism and emphasizes the role of structure (e.g., the capitalist mode of production) in dictating and shaping actions and events (Hay, 1995, p. 194). As such, structuralism has been heavily criticized for ignoring the role and influence of actors and portraying them as automatons. An alternative approach, termed 'intentionalism', takes the polar extreme in focusing on individual action and the micro-politics of interaction and underpins approaches such as Public Choice Theory (see Chapter 5). Criticism of intentionalism has been levelled at the sometimes 'illogical' nature of human behaviour and the importance of unintended consequences of action. There have been a number of attempts to fuse structuralism and intentionalism and overcome the apparent dualism. The most influential of these attempts has been advanced by Anthony Giddens through what he terms structuration. Structuration replaces this dualism with a duality; for example, instead of two coins, structuralism and intentionalism, Giddens sees them as two sides of the same coin. It attempts to switch attention to the interrelationship between structure and agency and:

> 1. to recognize the *duality of structure*: that is, the manner in which structures enable behaviour, but behaviour can potentially influence and reconstitute structure; and
> 2. to recognize the *duality of structure and agency*: that is, to transcend the dualism of deterministic (structuralist) views of structure and voluntaristic (intentionalist) views of agency. (Cloke, Philo and Sadler, 1991, p. 98)

There is then mutual dependence and clear link between structure and agency: 'social structures are both constituted by human agency, and yet at the same time are the very medium of this constitution' (Giddens, 1976, p. 121). Both structure *and* agency are important – people make structures and structures influence people. Another broadly similar attempt that seeks to fuse structure and agency is the critical realism of Bhaskar (1979, 1998) and the strategic relational approach of Jessop (1990). As Hay (1995) points out, Jessop's approach takes a more structuralist starting point, claiming that there are layers of structure that influence agents and limit the range of options that are open to them. Jessop (1990) also adds a strategically selective element that implies that political and economic structures of the state, such as capitalism, are more open to certain strategies of agents than others.

While Giddens, Bhaskar and Jessop all place different emphases on the fusion of structure and agency, the general conclusions we can draw from their work is of action producing:

1. *Direct effects* upon structural contexts within which it takes place and within which future action occurs – producing a partial transformation of the structural context (though not necessarily as anticipated).

2. *Strategic learning* on the part of actors involved, enhancing awareness of structures and the constraints/opportunities they impose, providing the basis from which subsequent strategy might be formulated and perhaps prove more successful. (Hay, 1995, p. 201)

Other perspectives, particularly those aligned around Actor Network Theory, highlight the importance of social relations and power as the main constituency of agency. Post-structuralist perspectives (see Chapter 8) argue that we cannot distinguish between structure and agency. According to this position structures are indistinguishable from the actions within them. This doesn't help us a great deal, particularly as communicative planning theory (see Chapter 9), which, as Watson (2008) points out, is the dominant paradigm in planning theory, is explicitly based upon the notion of structure and agency. These theories have two uses for our understanding of planning theory. First, the relationship between structure and agency potentially helps us understand the relationship between theory and practice in planning. As I discuss further on in this chapter, there is a long-standing debate in planning concerning the relationship between theory and practice and how the two influence each other. Academics claim that practitioners ignore theory, while practitioners claim academics are divorced from reality. Yet both clearly influence each other. Planners do not turn up to work each day without any knowledge or preconceived ideas. A critical realist approach as set out above potentially helps us understand this relationship. If we associate theory with structure and practice with agency we can draw parallels between the ways in which theory is formed in a complex symbiotic relationship. In some ways it backs up the discursive arguments earlier but adds an important dimension of existing structures (theories) being more influential than pure agency. The implications of this are that agents (e.g., planners) create and interpret theories in the light and knowledge of existing theories. Thus, in trying to tackle issues of homelessness the planner might have in mind neo-liberal theories on the supply and demand of housing as well as Marxist theories on surplus labour (these theories are both covered in more detail later in this book). Neither may be directly applicable to the situation in a certain place but they may help direct or formulate thinking along a particular path.

Second, the critical realist perspective also helps us comprehend the relative autonomy of individual planners and the way they use, interpret and develop theory for their jobs. Planners do not operate in a vacuum devoid of structural influences. There are rules, existing processes and norms, for example, that limit what they can do. When planners say they are acting in a 'professional' way, that implies they are in some way detached from other influences and they are, perhaps, underestimating the pervading influence of society upon them. What planner could honestly claim that issues such as their upbringing, societal norms or even the impact of a decision upon a career would not, even implicitly, have an impact upon a decision? Similarly, when planners, as they sometimes do, try to shrug their shoulders and blame 'the system' or factors beyond their control it is worth remembering that they and others like them created that system or set of ideas. A collection of decisions creates a precedent or even 'policy by decision' that amounts to a structure. Planners are influenced by structure, as well as creating that structure.

### *Theory, time and space*

I have looked at the ways in which planners and society influence the development, use and interpretation of theory. It is now necessary to add two further dimensions to this: time and space. It is often tempting to take what has been termed the 'Whig view of history': 'the argument that human history has been leading up to the present day and that past forms of social and political organisation should be evaluated according to how far they advanced or retarded that process of development' (Painter, 1995, p. 34). I argued above that theory was normative and discursive, that is, produced by individuals within a wider social context. As such, theory is historically contingent and dependent upon cultural, social and political circumstances. But can a normative and discursive view of theory be seen as consistent with the evolutionary, linear Whig theory of history? As Giddens (1984, p. 237) points out, human beings make their history in cognisance of that history, that is, they are aware of time and give it meaning as well as simply 'living it'. The evolutionary/Whig view implies that history and theory develop into higher and higher levels of sophistication and understanding. It is difficult, writes Gellner, to 'think about human affairs without the image . . . of an all embracing upward growth' (Gellner, quoted in Giddens, 1984, p. 237). The danger that Giddens identifies with this view is the inclination to identify superior power with moral superiority. In terms of theory, we could see certain ideas that have current ascendancy as being in some ways superior to theories that were more dominant at some other time. Theories sometimes build upon each other, developing ideas that have been criticized and tested, but the terms of their development, as I discussed above, are dictated by changes in society and the grounds upon which they can be tested often change. Theories also develop and emerge in response to changes in society. One example of this, which I cover in more detail in Chapter 4, concerns the development of the classical tenets of Marxist theory. Marxist theory predicted the fall of capitalism. However, a century or so after Marx developed his ideas capitalist economies were still flourishing in many parts of the world. To account for this some theorists began to rework Marxism in the late 1960s and develop it to tackle new values, the cultural dimension of Marxism and modes of behaviour in society. In the natural sciences there tends to be progress as theories are tested and refined to better explain and predict a natural phenomenon. In the social sciences such linear progress is replaced by a much more crowded and contingent landscape of theories and ideas. As I discuss in Chapter 2, there is no *one* planning theory that we can assimilate and take into practice. Instead, there are a range of competing ideas and theories that will, to greater or lesser degrees, correspond to our values and views of their world.

Turning to the spatial aspects of theory we can see that its discursive basis raises the possibility of different discourses existing in different places. For example, it would not be controversial to suggest that at the level of the nation state ideas will be interpreted differently because of the historical, cultural, economic and political windows through which theories are seen. But, beneath the nation state, different locales also interpret ideas and theories differently. A number of studies have pointed to what they term the 'locality effect', where every locality is a unique configuration of economic activities, divisions of labour, cultural traditions, political alignments, spatial arrangements and physical form (e.g., Healey *et al.*, 1988). This has been dubbed the 'geological metaphor' (Warde, 1985) because of the way that various 'layers' of influence form a unique social geology in different areas. So, for example, the industrial employment background to a particular area may have influenced historic political attitudes that may have led to a pro-active local stance on cooperative banking, allowing the growth in small businesses. But the economic is not always the most important factor. Religion, immigration, geography etc. can all have a major impact on place.

The uniqueness of place can influence the formulation, interpretation and modification of ideas and theory. So theory is not 'fixed' nationally or sub-nationally. The extent to which this is the case will vary, depending on such factors as the 'level' of theory; for example, more general theories such as Marxism are more likely to be interpreted similarly in different areas than those dealing with the relationship between government and society. This may seem of little importance until you realize that planning is practised at different levels of government where often the local interprets planning policies formulated nationally and generates local policies and plans. Discretion or choice is inherent to planning and governments throughout the world and allows for some autonomous interpretation and formulation of theory. I do not want to over-emphasize this dimension to theory, but merely highlight that when we talk of theory we must not assume that what we mean will necessarily be understood in different contexts or will even be used or interpreted in a similar fashion.

I have argued that all social science theory should be seen as more or less normative, that is, not value-free. Theories, like truth, are socially created and can be seen as discourses that 'make sense' of society at a particular time. Because of their power-laden nature, theories can and do have a highly political role. They are not 'objective' or in some way separate from society; they are part of that society. Such a society itself is not homogeneous; it varies through time and space, allowing for different formulation, interpretation and uses of theory. This brings us to a recurrent theme in all assessments of planning theory – the so-called 'theory–practice gap', or how theory is or is not used in planning practice.

## The theory–practice gap

To bemoan the theory–practice gap is now *de rigueur* for any exploration of planning theory. Watson (2008) complains about the lack of a 'good fit' between planning theory and contextualized planning practice. A further dimension is that there is a mismatch between theory that largely originates in English language-based journals (what Watson terms the 'metropole') and other contexts of planning, particularly in the developing world. As I briefly mentioned above, academics argue that they think up new theories for planners to use and to justify planning which are totally ignored by practitioners. Practitioners on the other hand claim that academic theory has no bearing or meaning for practice that is based on 'common sense'. The whole situation still echoes Glass (1959) and Reade's (1987) view that the legitimation of planning came too easily and too soon and that planning has no endogenous body of theory. Alexander (1997) asks some pertinent questions of the situation.

First, he asks, is there really a divorce between planning theory and practice? Second, if the gap exists, so what? If the gap exists and it matters, what can be done to bridge it? Alexander comes to the conclusion that each development in planning theory fills a gap in retrospect, that is, practice develops apace and different theories emerge with 'champions' who say, 'No, *this* theory best explains planning's *raison d'être and* how to do it.' There is a gap then and, according to Alexander, it is unbridgeable because there is a 'market' in theories. As I mentioned above, this allows planners to 'pick and choose' theories to justify their actions or approaches. As Cliff Hague puts it, planners have been magpies across the disciplines, picking relevance where they found it (Thomson, 2000, p. 127). This is a dimension to theories that I have explored elsewhere (Allmendinger and Tewdwr-Jones, 1997). The argument in this chapter is that, in answer to Alexander's second question, 'If the gap exists, so what?', practising planners actually find the diversity and abundance of theory an advantage. They can never aspire to 'truth', and they would not want to.

If we see planning and planners as being involved in a continuous power 'game', as portrayed earlier, then the absolute claim to 'truth' in planning theory would involve a loss of power and discretion by planners. Planners and others who 'use' theory (even if implicitly) benefit from being able to advance theories that cannot be 'proved' but nevertheless are to their benefit. So, as well as Alexander's claim that the theory–practice gap is ontologically unbridgeable we can also add that there are strong practical reasons for making it so – nobody seems to have considered *why* there has been little interest in bridging the 'gap' by practitioners.

We can also begin to see, therefore, why it is that some current theories, such as those based on communicative rationality or collaborative planning (covered in Chapter 9) which Alexander (1997) claims have so much potential, have not largely been adopted by practising planners (Tewdwr-Jones and Thomas, 1995). The problems are not only in translating the principles of communicative rationality into practice (though this itself is a significant difficulty); it is simply that such an approach involves a loss of power for planners by challenging their expert status and current dominant discourses. This perspective presents planning theory as a battleground; a battle over the creation of knowledge and theory, a battle over the distribution and (mis)use of power and a battle over the translation of theory into practice. This is not to take a totally nihilistic view of theory. On the contrary, it is to locate theory in a political context.

But why should planners 'pick and mix' theory? Is it a deliberate ploy to concentrate power or is there another reason? The view of planning and theory as power is only one aspect of why there is a theory–practice gap. There is another aspect that needs to be explored to fully appreciate the role of the planner. To understand it further we need to look at some theories of the state and professions. Planning practice the world over is a highly bureaucratized function carried out, on the whole, by planners working for public authorities. Although some have argued that planners could potentially include 'the planned' (e.g., the public), and planners themselves are increasingly working for private companies, we will stick to the public sector planner in this analysis.

Most countries that have public-led planning have a professional organization to represent them and their profession. In the USA, the American City Planning Institute (ACPI) was established in 1917; in the UK, the Town Planning Institute was formed in 1913. Such organizations projected a self-image of planning as one of rational, apolitical and universal 'problem solving'. The notion of an identifiable and achievable 'public interest' abounded. As Evans (1995, p. 55) points out, one could expect such newly formed organizations to claim altruism and political neutrality if they wanted to professionalize, but the feeling of neutrality and public interest is actually implicit in the ethos of planning. Much of this belief can be traced back to the early philanthropic or reforming views of planning, but what is of interest to us is the way in which it has been perpetuated and the impact it has had.

Once planning had a professional institute distinct from the engineering and architectural professions it followed the same path as other professions in establishing a symbiotic (or corporate in Reade's [1987] terms) relation between itself, its members and the government or state. We can now begin to see the basis of a reciprocal relationship. Government needs planners to undertake its policies. Planners and their professional body need the government as an employer and to legitimize their claim to professionalism (and associated status and benefits). This relationship also extends to private sector planners. While planners in consultancies bemoan regulations and bureaucracy, they also realize that such processes provide them with the ability to sell their time and expertise to clients. Parts of the requirements of professionalism are neutrality and expert status. So planners, through their professional status, are unlikely to take political stances or perspectives that are overtly anti-status quo. This does not preclude them from taking stances that are political and justifying them from the perspective of 'professionalism'.

But an even more subtle relationship exists within this trinity of planner, profession and state. Planning is dominated by chartered planners, that is, members of the ACPI or the Royal Town Planning Institute (RTPI). While you can still be a planner without being a member, it is certainly more difficult without membership. As a member, the institute's codes and ethics bind you. For the planners' institute to maintain its privileged (or corporate) status with government it needs to assure the state that it can maintain a regulated and educated membership capable of implementing centrally directed policies, processes and systems. Therefore, government does not negotiate with planners – it does this with their professional body. And the professional body in turn fulfils its side of the bargain by regulating its membership and ensuring they cooperate and implement government objectives.

The situation is a little more complicated than the stark outline above especially because of the autonomy and discretion offered to planners who work for local public bodies. There is evidence to suggest that planners can and do implement policies differently than envisaged by government (Allmendinger, 1997). However, the professional status of planners limits the extent to which they can act as reflective individuals and the extent to which they are subject to the normal influences of social science approaches, as their views, opinions and options are limited. As Evans (1995, p. 46) puts it:

> The process is obviously two-way. Professional groups are granted a high level of influence on policy matters in their respective areas and . . . the state legitimises professional knowledge and credentials. In exchange, the professionals are expected to participate in achieving policy goals which fit within certain parameters and limits.

The relationship between planners, their professional body and the state ensures that planners are not 'free agents' able to objectively investigate, explore or challenge existing discourses or theories. In addition, a number of writers (e.g., Reade, 1987; Thornley, 1993; Evans, 1993, 1995, 1997) have pointed to what are termed 'contradictions' in the planners' role. Though planners still portray themselves as apolitical and technically expert, roughly 80 per cent of them are employed in the public sector in the UK, through which they are charged with carrying out preferred policies of central and local government. Although the RTPI code of conduct, for example, clearly states that planners shall, 'fearlessly and impartially exercise their independent professional judgement to the best of their skills and understanding' (1994, p. 1), it would be a brave (foolish?) person who did not appreciate the relationship to their employer as being of equal importance. The ACPI code has similar provisions (Howe, 1994). As a result, planners are constantly mediating at least three potentially contradictory influences: their own personal and professional feelings, their employers objectives and the code and ethics of their professional institute. I cover this in more detail in Chapter 7.

Another issue is the extent to which planners can claim to be acting in the 'public interest'. Apart from the difficulties in defining the 'public interest', in acting as mediator for development proposals planners must cooperate with private interests to, for example, meet the requirement for housing land supply or to ensure that enough land is available for industrial expansion and growth. There is no point in allocating land for the future development needs of a community if the owner has no intention of developing it. There is, necessarily, a close relationship between the planner as regulator of development and the development industry itself. While many planners recognize the skewed nature of 'public interest', there is still a widespread claim to impartiality (Evans, 1995).

We can see some close parallels between the foregoing discussion and the structure and agency debate earlier. As we have seen, Giddens attempted to overcome the duality of structure and agency and argue that, 'social structures are both constituted by human agency, and yet are the same time the very medium of this constitution' (Giddens, 1976, p. 121). Bhaskar and Jessop went further and argued that certain economic and social theories proposed by actors are more likely to be acceptable to the state structure than others., specifically, those that supported existing structures such as capitalism or the centrality of government. We can see how the triad of bodies relevant here (planners, professional institute and state) emphasizes and reinforces the status quo and acts as a constraint upon change.

We can also see *why* planners pick and choose theory. Because of the conflicting pressures upon them (personal/professional, employee, professional body, state) it is hardly surprising that different justifications and approaches are required in different circumstances. It is not the individual planner's fault *per se*; they are caught in an unresolvable dilemma. But before we feel too sorry for the planner we must remember three things. First, that a large proportion of planners actually believe that they are neutral and apolitical. Second, that they receive significant benefits from their 'professional' status (jobs, social standing etc.). Finally, that there is little if any pressure from planners to change the situation.

What we are concerned with here, however, is the extent to which these influences upon planners affect the formulation, interpretation and use of theory. This perspective recognizes that theory formulation is not confined to academia and that planners can and do formulate theories themselves based upon a variety of influences including, but not exclusively, those from educational and research institutions.

What I have attempted to do in this chapter is 'problematize' the idea of theory and outline and explore its social basis. It should be clear that when we are talking of planning theory there is far more to it than a simplistic notion of modelling, predicting or understanding causes and effects. By these measures, much of planning theory would fail to be classified as theory at all. Theories are tools that mask as much as they reveal. Attention is normally paid to whether or not a particular theory corresponds with reality or how accurately it might tell us something. The view taken here questions what philosophers call the 'correspondence view of truth' and instead argues for a more relativistic and socially embedded perspective. Instead of asking whether a theory 'works', we should be asking questions about *why* this particular theory was used, *who* is using it and for *what* purpose. The answer to these questions will tell us as much (if not more) of importance as whether the theory corresponds to reality.

# 2 The Current Landscape of Planning Theory

## Introduction

In Chapter 1 I attempted to 'problematize' the idea of theory and question some basic assumptions with a perspective that emphasized a much more discursive and socially constructed basis to the notion of theory. What I intend to do in this chapter is turn my attention to how the perspectives of Chapter 1 help us better understand different kinds of theories and how they relate to each other through a typology.

As I touched upon in Chapter 1, there is an assumption that planning as a profession needs some form of theory or thinking to underpin its claim to have specialist knowledge (one of the prerequisites of being a profession). But what are planning theories? Do we need them? Maybe the idea of theory is unhelpful? One leading planning theorist introduces a book on collaborative planning (see Chapter 9) without even mentioning the word 'theory':

> Every field of endeavour has its history of ideas and practices and its traditions of debate. These act as a store of experience, of myths, metaphors and arguments, which those within the field can draw upon in developing their own contributions, either through what they do, or through reflecting on the field. This 'store' provides advice, proverbs, recipes and techniques for understanding and acting, and inspiration for ideas to play with and develop. (Healey, 1997, p. 7)

This perspective is more in line with the argument developed in Chapter 1. If planning can exist without 'theories', can we talk about planning theory and, if so, what are planning theories? For some, such as Robin Thompson, 'traditional' planning functions are being subsumed into a more 'issue'-based focus. The need to think across professional boundaries to deliver, for example, regeneration or economic development requires new skills and knowledge. This makes the idea of a core of planning theory even less sustainable than it has been in the past. Nevertheless, the notion of theory in such a dynamic and fluid context is even more important:

> [Theory] offers a means by which the regular infusion of new ideas can be understood by practice. Theory can be an early warning system preparing planners for new influences. It can also help to consider how these new influences can be absorbed into current practice, what the consequences could be, and what alternative responses are available. (Thompson, 2000, p. 130)

There was a time when discussion of planning theory could be undertaken confidently. For Andreas Faludi, planning was 'the application of scientific method – however crude – to policy making' (1973, p. 1). This perspective saw planners as technocrats who focused upon procedures or processes – the means – while politicians and others set the ends. This inevitably led to a paternalistic and patronizing idea of 'them' (the public) and 'us' (the planners):

> one of the most forceful arguments for placing primary responsibility for goal formulation on the planner ... [is] the assumption, traditional to professionals, that, in some way, they 'know more' about the situations on which they advise than do their clients. (Chadwick, 1971, p. 121)

For Chadwick and others, planning practice was underpinned by a 'unified planning theory'. In the past 30 years or so, such confidence and arrogance has been replaced by uncertainty and introspection. This situation has come about for two reasons. The first is the perceived failure of such technocratic approaches to address the problems that planners and others were attempting to address. Sandercock (1998, p. 4), for example, accuses planning in its technocratic mode of being anti-democratic, race- and gender-blind and culturally homogenizing. The various 'problems' planning set out to address were either untouched (e.g., poverty and homelessness), exacerbated (e.g., wealth inequality) or added to by some of the solutions themselves to create new problems (e.g., urban motorways and high-rise tower blocks). A unified planning theory was a chimera. For Wildavsky, if planning was everything, then perhaps it was nothing (1973).

The second reason is less specific and relates to broad changes in understanding and theory that have been ongoing in the past three decades or so. Such changes are related to some of the issues I discussed in Chapter 1 concerning Kuhn's paradigms, the relativist views of Feyerabend, the rejection of 'master-narratives' and over-arching theories by Lyotard and the role of power and discourse in the formation, interpretation and application of theory. The term for this broad shift is post-positivism. The phrase itself derives from the recognition that social theory has moved beyond the search for universal truths and, instead, recognizes that the contexts of theory, including their social and historical background, shape not only theories but also what we count as evidence to assess them.

This change is in direct conflict with traditional views of planning that saw it based upon, 'the neutrality of observation and the givenness of experience; the ideal of unequivocal language and the independence of data from theoretical interpretation; the belief in the universality of conditions of knowledge and criteria for theory choice' (Bohman, 1991, p. 2; Flyvbjerg, 2001). In place of this we have a post-positivist recognition of indeterminacy, incommensurability, variance, diversity, complexity and intentionality in some routes of theoretical development – traits that question the very notion of 'planning'. A post-positivist approach requires 'shifting from causal reasoning as a basis for plan-making to discovering and confirming meaning' (Moore Milroy, 1991, p. 182) (see Chapters 8 and 9).

What is positivism and how did it influence planning? Positivism sought 'the discovery of a set of general methodological rules or forms of inference which would be the same in all sciences, natural and social' (Bohman, 1991, pp. 16–17). It sought to systematize human life based on real (positive) as opposed to imagined knowledge or myths, much in the same was as naturalism discussed in Chapter 1. Thus, positivists base knowledge upon empirical or mathematical observations, trying to uncover 'truths' or relationships between objects. In planning, the high point of positivism was to be found in the systems and rational approaches of the 1960s (see Chapter 3). Values or politics were downplayed to provide the objectives, such as 'reduce traffic congestion'. Once set, such objectives provided the end point for a positivist investigation of the means towards such ends (conveniently ignoring the role that positivism had in setting such objectives themselves through the use of observations on the nature of the 'problem').

The ability to separate facts from values was itself a problem with positivism. In Chapter 1 this was highlighted through the issues I identified with observation and the social context of theory. Such problems were partly the reason for the search for alternative approaches that sought not to suppress values but to recognize and expose them. Thus post-positivism emphasizes:

- A rejection of positivist understandings and methodologies and embraces instead approaches that contextualize theories and disciplines in larger social and historical contexts.
- Normative criteria for deciding between competing theories;
- The ubiquity of variance in explanations and theories.
- An understanding of individuals as self-interpreting, autonomous subjects. (Bohman, 1991)

The post-positivist conception sees planners as fallible advisors who operate, like everybody else, in a complex world where there are no 'answers', only diverse and indeterminate options. Rather than recourse to 'objective' evidence or reality, the emphasis in post-positivist planning is on language and 'making meaning' through language. This takes the perspective of theory as being discursively created and tries to understand it as such. Fischer and Forester, for example, term this new understanding and its relation to planning the 'linguistic turn' in twentieth-century philosophy (1993). Some schools of planning theory now draw directly upon post-positivist ideas. Collaborative planning (Chapter 9) and post-structuralist/postmodern planning (Chapter 8) are the two clearest examples, though some forms of pragmatism (Chapter 6) also entail a post-positivist perspective.

This is not to say that there has been a clear shift in planning theory from positivist-based theories to post-positivist. Instead of a shift, we have a cluttered landscape of ideas and theories that makes any book about planning theory a less than straightforward affair. Malcolm Grant points to the eclectic nature of planning and its theories:

> Planning has not developed as an intellectual discipline in its own right. It has no original disciplinary foundation. It has no first principles of its own, but rather draws upon certain foundation disciplines including law, architecture, design, geography, sociology and economics. The balance between these foundation disciplines is shifting all the time, so the intellectual basis of planning is exceptionally flexible or fluid. This is an important part of the richness of planning, but it means that there is less certainty than with other professions about what planning 'owns' and what, therefore, it should be developing. (Quoted in Thompson, 2000, p. 130)

The main question that arises is: what theories should be included? Another issue is how to provide a way of conceptualizing or understanding planning theory in such a fragmented landscape. Traditionally, this latter question has been addressed through what is termed a typology of planning theory that identifies and classifies different epistemologies. I believe, however, that the means to address the issue of what to include in a book on planning theory follows from how we conceptualize or 'frame' the subject.

## Typologies of planning theory

A typology has three basic functions, it:

- Corrects misconceptions and confusion by systematically classifying related concepts.
- Effectively organizes knowledge by clearly defining the parameters of a given subject.
- Facilitates theorizing by delineating major subparts of distinct properties and foci for further research. (Yiftachel, 1989)

Typologies provide a 'frame' or a common understanding of subject area, methodologies, language and history of the development of ideas and practice beyond the random. Typologies are therefore useful, if not essential, to anyone involved in the subject area. Planning is no different in this respect. The multi-faceted and eclectic nature of planning and its theories has been extensively commented upon (e.g., Reade, 1987). Unlike other areas of the social sciences, such as economics, or other professions, such as medicine, planning has no endogenous body of theory (Sorensen, 1982). The reasons for this are open to debate, though Reade (1987) argues that there are two main explanations. The first is that planning as a state activity was legitimized by government before it developed any justification for itself. Planning was supported by some influential groups in society for a variety of reasons, which did not amount to a coherent theory as to why planning existed and how it should be approached. The second reason Reade advances is that planners themselves are not interested in theory or theorizing, but focus on the technical aspects of planning – what I outline as systems and rational planning in Chapter 3 (Reade, 1987, p. 157). Instead of having its own set of theories, planning draws upon a wide range of theories and practices from different disciplines. Consequently, planning typologies have had an important role in helping to understand often diverse influences, ideas and theories.

Up until the early 1980s the dominant typology of planning theory had been provided by Faludi (1973), who based on his approach on the distinction between substantive and procedural theory: 'Procedural theories define and justify methods of decision making whereas substantive theories pertain to interdisciplinary knowledge relevant to the content of planning: that is urban land use' (Yiftachel, 1989, p. 24). Procedures, or means, were to be the business of planning and planners. Theory was dominated by the systems and rational approaches, both of which emphasized process above substance. The substantive–procedural distinction (see Chapter 3) was attacked by, among others, Thomas (1982), Paris (1982) and Reade (1987) for portraying planning as apolitical and technical. Subsequent developments by Faludi (1987) to account for these criticisms merely accepted that different kinds of substantive theory existed, but the proper concern of planning was procedural theory. Notwithstanding these criticisms, the substantive–procedural distinction remained a popular typology with which to approach and understand planning theory (Alexander, 1997). This was in part due to its symbiotic relationship with rational and systems theory, both in the academic literature and by the architects, engineers and surveyors who dominated practice (Sandercock, 1998).

The dominance of the substantive–procedural foundation to planning theory and practice was at its height until the late 1970s when 'the post-war consensus on planning thought, as in many other fields, had blown apart into a diversity of positions' (Healey, 1991, p. 12). The different positions were outlined by a number of studies (e.g., Underwood, 1980; Friedmann, 1987; Healey, McDougall and Thomas, 1982). Nevertheless, the early fragmentation of positions was seen in relation to (either a development of or an opposition to) Faludi's substantive–procedural typology. Healey's map of the theoretical stances in planning theory in the 1970s, for example, defined the new and emerging positions by reference to procedural planning theory (Healey, 1991). Thus, social planning and advocacy planning is portrayed as a development of procedural planning theory through the view that, 'Procedural Planning Theory should be orientated to social welfare goals' (1991, p. 13) (Figure 2.1). This incremental perspective on the development of theory *vis-à-vis* the substantive–procedural typology missed the depth of the rupture that occurred with the shift to a post-positivist understanding and basis to some theories. In many fundamental ways, new or rediscovered fields of theory had irrevocably broken with the positivist past and the substantive–procedural distinction that had been used to frame it. In the absence of an alternative typology with which to analyze these changes, theorists generally retained the substantive–procedural distinction. As a consequence, analyses of the changing nature of planning theory could not account for why such a fragmentation of planning was occurring, nor fully appreciate the changes or their implications.

Nevertheless, some theorists did attempt to develop new typologies or perspectives. One of the first attempts to account for the increasing pluralization of theory and relate to a framework for understanding it was advanced by Nigel Taylor (1980). Taylor attempted an alternative conception in an attempt to shift away from both Faludi's substantive–procedural distinction and his normative preference for process as the subject of planning. In rejecting Faludi's dualism, Taylor replaced it with another that highlighted the difference between sociological theories (empirically based) and philosophical questions (ideological and normative). Taylor's approach was developed by Cooke (1983), who also argued that the substantive–procedural distinction was false. In place of a dualism, Cooke posited three theories of planning and spatial relations: theories of the development process, theories of

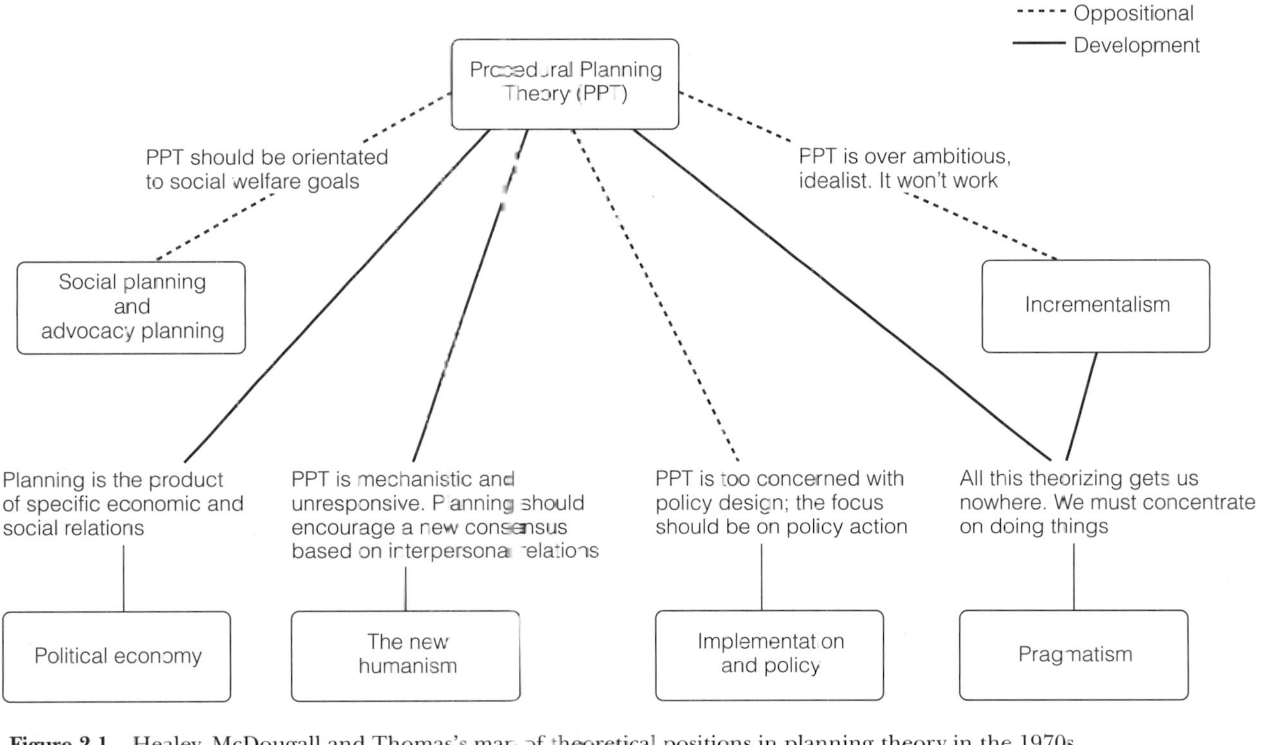


**Figure 2.1** Healey, McDougall and Thomas's map of theoretical positions in planning theory in the 1970s

*Source*: Healey, McDougall and Thomas, 1982, p. 7.

the planning process and theories of the state. While accepting their approaches were significant developments of Faludi's approach, Yiftachel criticized both Taylor and Cooke for i) failing to deal with the procedural–substantive and explanatory–prescriptive axes, ii) inaccurately treating most theories, as if they were competing explanations for a common phenomenon, and iii) not setting clear boundaries for the field of planning inquiry.

In attempting to address these points, Yiftachel's typology sought to frame planning theory around the three questions – the analytical debate (what is urban planning?), the urban form debate (what is a good urban plan?) and the procedural debate (what is a good planning process?). Yiftachel claimed that these three forms of theory had developed more or less alongside each other and were often complementary as they operated 'on different levels of social processes' (1989, p. 28). Notwithstanding Yiftachel's threefold distinction, he sets his own interpretation firmly within the substantive–procedural framework: 'it is still useful to separate between the two types, mainly because (a) procedural theories are mostly prescriptive whereas analytical theories are explanatory, and (b) the two types do not, in the main, relate to the same phenomenon' (Yiftachel, 1989, p. 29). As Hillier and Healey (2008, p. x) highlight, despite attempts to escape the procedural–substantive framework debate in planning, theory regularly returns to it. The distinction between substantive and procedural theories is reinforced by Faludi (1987) and Yiftachel's acceptance that both procedural and substantive theories are required for planning and that neither has any dominance over the other.

At this point, around 1990, debate and development in the assessment of the growing theoretical pluralism and its implications for understanding and classifying planning theory came to a halt. This is surprising given the explosion in theoretical thinking that has occurred in the meantime (see Hillier and Healey, 2008). Is the substantive–procedural distinction still 'fit for purpose'? Few contemporary accounts of planning theory address it beyond dismissing its relevance (e.g., Forester, 1989; Sandercock, 1998). Healey's (1997) account of collaborative planning, for example, avoids any discussion of it at all. One could conclude that has been overtaken by developments in theory that I have already outlined.

Rather than the bifurcation of procedural and substantive theory, post-positivism emphasizes a more normative dimension that diffuses such a duality. Substantive and procedural theories blur into one as they both exhibit prescriptive and analytical elements – as I discussed in Chapter 1, there is no value neutral way of understanding theory. The ability to separate facts and values is rejected, as is the positivist basis to the distinction between substance (analysis) and procedure (process).

Most of the current developments in planning theory (e.g., collaborative, neo-pragmatism, postmodern), as well as new perspectives on planning, such as feminism, are derived from a largely post-positivist perspective. Post-positivism, as a gross generalization, has a suspicion of 'closure' or definition. But this does not or should not be used as a reason for rejecting classifications as a basis for understanding *per se*. The problem is not one of a principled rejection, but the difficulty of seeing a way through myriad positions (Murdoch, 2006). The indeterminacy characteristic of many aspects of post-positivist social and planning theory does not undermine Yiftachel's argument that typologies correct misconceptions and confusion by systematically classifying related concepts and effectively organize knowledge that helps facilitate theoretical development. I believe, however, that it does undermine Yiftachel's approach. There are two reasons for this. First, Yiftachel's typology is based on a linear and progressive view of developments in planning theory. With a timescale running from 1900–80 along a vertical axis, he traces the evolution of different schools of theory in relation to each other. Thus, Weberian analysis evolves into pluralism and finally neo pluralism. A post-positivist perspective would problematize such a teleological view. While there is a lineage at a crude and abstract level, it could be argued that this no longer captures the essence of what is a much more fluid and (at times) non-linear development of theory. There is now a much more eclectic 'pick and mix' basis to theory development and planning practice that is better seen as relating to issues, time and space *in a linear and non-linear manner*.

One example of this is the way in which current theories can be distinguished in terms of the above three criteria. Collaborative planning, pragmatism and post-stucturalist/postmodern planning theory all owe something to the development and evolution of different theories and ideas that could be traced on a linear model. But what does this tell us exactly? Let us take the issue of relativism on which all three schools of theory have something important to say. While post-positivism hints at a form of relativism (in this sense relativism could be taken as a tolerance and acceptance of different values and opinions to the point of being unwilling to judge others), all three schools have different positions on this issue *within and between them.* As I mentioned in Chapter 1, relativism has been a theme of philosophers from Plato onwards. At different periods there have been equally valid and competing ideas on it.

Plato advanced the idea that concepts such as beauty were highly relative in his 'argument of opposites' – objects or ideas never possess their properties in an absolute or unqualified way. For Plato, absolute knowledge did exist but only in the abstract. Such knowledge could not be verified by recourse to some reality and was accessible through intellect. Aristotle fundamentally disagreed and instead argued that an empirical or experiential perspective would reveal the true nature of something. This debate between relativists and absolutists has involved philosophers such as Descartes, Spinoza, Leibniz, Kant, Lock, Hume, Hegel, Russell and Wittgenstein, to name a few. What is important to note is not that there has been linear progress or evolution, but that at different times and in different places over the past 2,500 years or so the basic positions have been held simultaneously as they still are now. So Yiftachel's typology tells us little beyond the existence of various schools of theory over a (relatively) short period of time. Further, while time is important in terms of identifying a dominant school of thought it is not necessarily or even ordinarily related to progress in the social sciences (i.e., theories evolve into 'better fits' of reality). Some extreme forms of postmodernism, for example, take an Aristotelian perspective celebrating and working towards difference (Chapter 8). On the other hand, collaborative theorists (Chapter 9) accept difference while seeking to reach consensus based upon interpersonal discourse.

A related criticism of Yiftachel's typology from a post-positivism perspective concerns the issue of space. Different theories and ideas can be located in time (linear and non-linear). But there is also a spatial dimension that helps explain *why* these ideas were emphasized or de-emphasized at different periods and in different places, as I pointed out in Chapter 1. The point is that a two-dimensional perspective that emphasizes time in a linear sense tells us little about the origin, development or application of theory in differing social, economic and political contexts – does advocacy planning mean the same in Scotland as it does in San Francisco? The missing key is space and its relation to varying social, economic and political contexts.

The second reason why Yiftachel's approach is no longer useful as a typology relates to his categories of planning theory. Yiftachel's three categories outlined earlier are in turn based upon Faludi's distinction between procedure and substance in planning theory. Such a distinction has been widely criticized, as I outlined earlier. In relation to planning typologies, I believe that there is another important problem: to what extent can we now (if ever) distinguish between theories 'of' and 'in' planning? This fixation with prepositions has diverted attention away from the extent to which all theory, to greater or lesser degrees, is normative (i.e., suffused with values and embedded within a social and historical context). A post-positivist perspective would argue that the procedural–substantive distinction is a false dichotomy. Taking any one of the current schools of theory, it is impossible to separate substance and procedure. Postmodern planning theory, for example, starts from the premise of incommensurability between private languages, as well as the notion of consensus as 'terror'. Both are normative positions but both could clearly influence any procedures or approaches to planning (though it could be argued that postmodernism precludes planning at all – see Allmendinger, 2001).

Does such a view on the redundancy of the substantive–procedural distinction make typologies themselves redundant? In such a contextualized understanding of planning theory is it possible to map a spatially sensitive, temporally linear and non-linear landscape? I believe that a post-positivist perspective not only provides a powerful critique of current planning typologies but can also provide the basis for an alternative. In the remainder of this chapter, I attempt to account for why there has been an explosion in theoretical thinking and provide a new understanding or typology of planning theory with which to understand it. Such an understanding rejects the distinction between substantive and procedural planning theory and instead posits a much more socially embedded and historically contingent understanding. Before offering an alternative planning typology, it is first necessary to explore the thinking behind post-positivism in more detail and its manifestations in planning, as well as previous attempts and critiques of planning typologies.

What does a post-positivist perspective mean for a typology of planning theory? There are a number of ways of interpreting such a broad approach, but I would offer an interpretation of post-positivism that emphasizes a number of principles:

- All theory is, to greater or lesser degrees, normative, that is, suffused with values and embedded within a social and historical context.
- Given such a social and historical context, the application or use of theory cannot be 'read off' from the principles or tenets of that theory derived from a more abstract understanding.
- Theory is mediated through space and time, allowing for its differential formulation, interpretation and application.
- If theories are normative, variable through time and space and contextualized through social and historical mediations (of which planning is one), there is no distinction between substance and procedure, but a complex iterative relationship between ideas and action.

One route for a post-positivist planning typology to take in the light of these principles is to emphasize influences upon theory rather than a substantive–procedural distinction. Identifying and tracing influences and how theories are transformed, mediated and used in a linear and non-linear way and different contexts, including time and space, provides both an explanation of why we have experienced such a fragmentation of theories in the past two decades and why some theories seem incommensurable. Implicit within the concept of influences is the idea of planning drawing upon debate and ideas from a variety of fields. Also implicit is the distinction between different kinds of theory and the uses to which they are put.

This is not an attempt to reintroduce a substantive–procedural distinction by the back door, but to recognize that some theories contribute to planning in different ways. Neither does it run contrary to the post-positivist principle that all theory is, to greater or lesser degrees, normative. Conceptual frameworks or perspectives such as regulation theory may be normative but make a qualitatively different contribution to planning theory than, say, theories of policy networks. One may therefore see theories as being drawn upon and used in different ways – which is actually what happens in practice. Collaborative planning, as interpreted by Healey (1997), draws upon critical theory, structuration theory, as well as elements of cognitive psychology. Critical theory is itself built upon the foundations of hermeneutics and elements of political economy, while structuration builds upon a plethora of theories and ideas from a variety of sources. Healey's interpretation differs from that of Forester (1989, 1999) and others who broadly subscribe to the collaborative or communicative position.

This approach avoids the two drawbacks of Yiftachel's typology identified earlier, that is, it is not based upon a linear view of time and theoretical development and it also avoids the false substantive–procedural distinction. In the light of such an approach, I identify five broad categories of theory below that provide a typological framework to help identify and map theory in planning:

- *Exogenous theory*. Planners have always drawn upon various theories that, while not being a specifically concerned with planning *per se*, have a relevance for space, policy processes or governance. Such exogenous theories include, for example, theories of democracy, cognitive psychology, regime and regulation theory, implementation theory, central–local relations, nationalism and a host of other 'meso-level' theoretical constructs. Some of these theories, such as central place theory, have been developed into indigenous planning theory (see below) at certain times, while others, such as regime theory and regulation theory, remain in the 'background' providing an understanding of planning and space. Exogenous theories differ from social theory mainly in their level of abstraction. Exogenous theories do not provide a holistic or general theoretical understanding of society but focus instead on a particular element of society, for example, the relationship between observed phenomena such as car-usage and the decline of town centres. Thus they are *generally* more empirically based and testable than social theories (see below).
- *Framing theory*. Drawing upon a variety of different forms of theory and seeking to occupy 'a similar semantic space as concepts such as paradigm, schema and conceptual complex' (Alexander and Faludi, 1996, p. 13) is a discrete

and unique form of theory that seeks to frame our understanding of planning. Planning doctrine is an obvious example of framing theory, though other more macro and abstract forms of framing include whether one frames an understanding of planning from a modern or postmodern perspective. Other kinds of framing approach include the assumptions and directions taken in any writing or discussion of planning itself – how we perceive its purpose and what goals we give it. As Alexander and Faludi have demonstrated in their understanding of doctrine, the origins of any frame used are a complex accretion of cultural and historical understanding and practice. Framing theory, therefore, draws on empirical and metaphysical bases and can be seen to be akin in some respects to the idea of paradigms developed by Thomas Kuhn.

- *Social theory*. Social theory has developed from sociology generally to a related though discrete set of reflections upon and understandings of society. Two broad categories of social theory exist: the 'top-down' structuralist approaches (e.g., structuralism, functionalism, Marxism), which examine the structuring forces upon individuals, and the more 'bottom-up' interpretative understandings (e.g., symbolic interactionism, ethnomethodology, phenomenology), which emphasize the reflective nature of individuals and their ability to choose. In recent years a third category has been added that seeks to overcome the duality of structural and intentional approaches, including the structuration theory of Giddens and Habermas's critical theory, by theorizing a relationship between the two. Social theory has been highly influential in indigenous planning theory. Four areas have had particular influence recently: critical theory, rational choice theory, Foucault's archaeology and genealogy and structuration theory. Apart from rational choice theory, the emphasis has been upon the more interpretative turn in social theory and indigenous planning theory, for example, postmodern planning theory (e.g., Sandercock, 1998), collaborative planning (e.g., Healey, 1997), neo-pragmatism (e.g., Hoch, 1984, 1995, 1996).
- *Social scientific philosophical understandings*. These come under the broad categories of, for example, positivism, falsification,

realism, idealism, etc. Social scientific philosophy is distinct in subtle ways from social theory and requires a separate understanding. All social theories make a number of assumptions regarding philosophical arguments. In some ways these understandings are linked to social assumptions regarding, for example, whether they are based upon a realist understanding of the primacy and open nature of reality (e.g., structuration) or a more closed system of reality (e.g., Public Choice Theory). Consequently, a philosophical understanding and perspective on social science can reveal the foundations of social theory. This has two benefits. The first is that, on surface appearances, some aspects of social theory appear very similar and proponents of each may appear to be arguing past each other or about aspects that have little relevance. One example of this is the understanding of the relationship between structure and agency within collaborative planning theory. The structure–agency perspectives of Giddens and Bhaskar (as discussed in Chapter 1) appear so similar as to essentially be the same. However, the different positions each take have significant though subtle implications for an understanding of the relationship between the planner and the structures within which she works.

- *Indigenous planning theory.* From all of the above comes a peculiar kind of theorizing that is planning-specific. Most books on planning theory list various perspectives, including the usual suspects of Marxism, New Right, advocacy, systems, rational comprehensive, design, collaborative and neo-pragmatic theories among others. These are schools of planning theory that in a variety of ways draw upon the other four forms of theory outlined above. For example, New Right planning theory is constructed from philosophical understandings of closed systems, positivist outlooks concerning naturalism, a Lockean conception of the human mind as a devoid of *a priori* structuring, rational choice theory concerning the maximization of individual utility and an understanding of humans as individuals who create society through aggregate actions. But indigenous planning theory cannot be simply 'read off' from a combination of other kinds of theoretical understanding in a post-empirical perspective. Space, time, the institutional and government context and other important influences also play an important role in the formulation of indigenous theory. This means, for example, that not only is neo-liberal planning theory an amalgam of different understandings, it is also mediated through current institutional and spatial arrangements that mean it is modified to suit not only the UK but the planning arrangements in the UK.

## The approach

From the typology I develop above it becomes clear that there are different kinds of theory that could be covered in this book. Previous attempts have taken a variety of approaches depending upon their emphasis. Books on planning theory are broadly divided into polemical texts (e.g., Faludi, 1973; Healey, 1997; Sandercock, 2003; Hillier, 2002) that draw upon a variety of different kinds of theory from the five categories above, and broad approaches that focus upon what I have termed indigenous planning theory. This book will take the latter form. Within the two broad approaches to theory books there are two further models: the historically driven narrative (e.g., Freidmann, 1987, Taylor, 1998; Hall, 1988, 1998 ) or those that emphasize the origins and philosophical foundations of theory (e.g., Cooke, 1983; Friedmann, 1987; Hillier and Healey, 2008). Obviously this is a somewhat artificial distinction. It is difficult to write about systems theory without drawing upon positivism, for example. The difference, therefore, comes down to one of emphasis.

There are advantages and disadvantages in any model. The 'cross-cutting' approach provides a theoretical and philosophical lineage of ideas that in a post-positivist framework or understanding is required to avoid the idea of linear developments in theory. It does, however, tend to underplay the temporal and spatial elements that provide a necessary understanding to why a particularly theory became popular in practice at one time or another. It is difficult to see why advocacy planning developed without some idea of the civil unrest at the time. Similarly, the historically driven approach provides an exciting and easily digestible context but often sacrifices subtlety or non-historical concepts that do not easily fit into the 'big picture'.

I have chosen to follow an approach that is basically organized around what I have identified as indigenous planning theory (an unattractive phrase, admittedly). There are a number of reasons for this. First, it is more easily understood by the person who wants to know about planning theory rather than the history of philosophy. Second, it is still possible to draw upon other aspects of theory such as structuration, although these will be necessarily dealt with in a superficial way. The most important reason, however, is that provided by the spirit of post-positivism. Although this highlights space and time as being important elements in the understanding of ideas, it also requires us to be wary of approaches that seek to explain an issue or subject in a linear and progressive framework.

For students of planning it is worth mentioning another dimension to understanding planning theory. Regular questions from students include 'Why is there so much planning theory?' and 'Why is planning theory writing so incomprehensible?'. In recent years, with the turn to postmodernism and post-structuralism in particular, it has become more difficult to answer such questions satisfactorily. One explanation that is worth keeping in mind concerns what is termed 'the social production of knowledge'. Academics are driven to publish by a range of pressures (institutional, promotion etc.). The process for of publication in books or journals involves peer review. One is likely to get published if the paper or book is original and advances ideas but not too groundbreaking in that it advances knowledge to the point where it leaves existing theory behind. If a particular paper or book advances new ideas that discredit existing ideas then the advocates of the existing ideas are unlikely to take it well. It's a fine balancing act: there is encouragement to publish, but in an incremental way. This helps explain both the sheer amount of material and the seeming complexity around different epistemologies. The upshot is that planning theory, like other fields of social science, can seem to generate more heat than light (which is, in part, a justification for this book though others will decide on how much light it has generated).

So, the typology I have chosen points to focusing upon what I have termed indigenous planning theories. The issue of which theories to include is still outstanding. The choice is made easier by the clear identification of a number of schools or epistemologies of theory that have traditionally been the subject of previous books on theory. The reader who is familiar with planning theory will therefore not be surprised by my choice. For others, the selection is divided between largely positivist and post-positivist positions that have been influential in planning over the past 40 years or so.

In the chapters that follow I have sought to provide an overview of such schools of planning theory. This involves a familiar path of context, history/development, main themes, critiques and conclusions, emphasizing the themes and ideas outlined in Chapters 1 and 2.

# 3 Systems and Rational Theories of Planning

## Introduction

As Taylor (1998) points out, there has been a tendency to conflate systems and rational planning into a broad category of Procedural Planning Theory (PPT). There are some overlaps between the two areas that allow us to consider them in the same chapter. Like rational theories of planning the systems approach is concerned with the generation and evaluation of alternatives prior to making a choice (Faludi, 1987, p. 43). Both, however, are also distinct in important respects. According to Faludi (1987) rational planning makes the crucial distinction between formal (means) and substantive (ends) rationality that systems planning fails to do. Nevertheless, PPT is the label given to both systems and rational planning approaches.

Both the systems and rational views rose to prominence in the 1960s and early 1970s and saw planning as a general societal management process (Healey, McDougall and Thomas, 1982). The approach contrasted sharply with the dominant 'planning as design' paradigm. As a reaction against PPT and for other reasons driven by wider social and economic change a number of other positions emerged that both built upon PPT and opposed it. Those that developed from PPT came from the policy sciences and focused on, for example, implementation. Those that opposed it included political economy perspectives such as Marxism (Healey, McDougall and Thomas, 1982).

Notwithstanding these developments the influence of PPT on planning theory and practice in the 1970s and beyond cannot be overestimated. Systems theory still has a stranglehold on the way contemporary planning is approached through its emphasis on modelling and the interrelated nature of towns and cities. Retail Impact Analysis, Traffic Impact Analysis and Environmental Impact Analysis as current planning techniques are all, to greater or lesser degrees, part of and build upon the systems approach. Rational planning equally has a strong current influence through its claim to underpin planning with 'scientific' and 'objective' methods that can be applied to all aspects of planning practice. The continued good currency of rational process planning lies in its claims that planning can be a scientific enterprise with the associated kudos and respectability that accompanies it. It also provides a simple and highly structured view of the world and how to act in the face of inherent complexity despite the quantum shift in theoretical thinking that rejects it as 'contentless' and 'contextless' (Thomas, 1982).

What has changed is the way in which both systems and rational theories relate to more political and value-laden dimensions of planning practice and theory. Andreas Faludi (one of the foremost advocates of the rational process view of planning) followed Max Weber's concern that means should be separated from ends in planning. Planning was a generic activity that could be applied to any situation where rational procedures for decision-making were appropriate. Further, planners' concern with means would envelope the more political and messy world of ends or values – once the ends were decided they were to be 'fed into' the rational process model. Thinking in planning theory and practice (e.g., collaborative planning) now largely reverses this and instead sees both ends and means as being much more closely linked. Planning is now not seen as a generic, discrete activity separate from political processes but as part of such processes. Rationality in planning is now embedded within such processes.

A further development that I cover in Chapter 9 on collaborative planning regards the nature of rationality itself. The kind of rationality that Faludi and others talked of was of an instrumental variety that was based on a particular view of objective knowledge. Jürgen Habermas and those who have interpreted his work in the field of planning argue that there are other forms of rationality. Communication based on agreed standards of behaviour is one important and currently popular alternative that underpins the communicative or collaborative planning theory approach. Such different conceptions of rationality do not seek to replace instrumental forms of rationality but complement and envelope them so as to provide alternative ways of agreeing and implementing means and ends in planning.

## Systems theory

> Any community consists of a wide variety of geographic, social, political, economic and cultural patterns which both act and interact to form the nature and condition of society. The relationship between these various patterns is constantly changing, giving rise to new and different conditions, some beneficial to the community, some deleterious. It is the planner's function to comprehend this tangled web of relationships, and where necessary, to guide, control and change their composition. To do this planning is concerned with prediction, not only of population size and land use in isolation, but also of human and other activities as well. It has been said that planners are now the prisoners of the discovery that in a city everything affects everything else. (Ratcliffe, 1974, p. 104)

A systems view of planning arose in the mid- to late 1960s in the UK largely through the work of Brian McLoughlin (1969) and George Chadwick (1971). They had been influenced by the development of systems thinking in the biological sciences where it was argued that i) systems existed in all areas of the natural and human environment and, ii) that systems could be controlled through regulating the communication between the various constituent parts.

The heart of the systems approach to planning is an acceptance that cities and regions are complex sets of connected parts, which are in constant flux. Planning, as a form of systems analysis and control (Taylor, 1998, p. 62), must itself be dynamic and concerned with change. Such a view of planning contrasted sharply with the (then) design tradition of planning that dominated and, in the words of one of the leading exponents of systems planning, differed 'considerably from what most town planners have, so far, thought of as being relevant to their subject' (Chadwick, 1971, p. xi).

What is a system? McLoughlin (1969), Ratcliff (1974) and Taylor (1998) all point to the dictionary definition of a system as a useful starting point. According to the *Oxford English Dictionary*, a system is understood as a 'complex whole', a 'set of connected things or parts' and a 'group of objects related or interacting so as to form a unity'. Commonly referred to systems such as eco-systems emphasize the mutual relationship between different but reliant organisms. In systems planning, cities, towns, regions etc. are seen as comprised of different but related components. Employment is different to housing but there is a relationship between the two so that when employment levels rise demand for housing will be expected to rise too. Similarly, this will also have an impact upon transport, retail and other connected systems. There is a 'ripple effect' at work where a change in one part of the system leads to implications and feedback from others, which may well also have an impact upon the original initiator. Figure 3.1 demonstrates the relationship between a number of systems as they are nestled, embedded or related to each other.

Where did such a view arise? Both McLoughlin and Chadwick make strong links between essentially human systems such as cities and ecological or natural systems – we can learn from the latter about what to expect in the former. As McLoughlin says at one point 'The image of planning in the future must be drawn not so much from building as from gardening' (1969, p. 24). In particu-

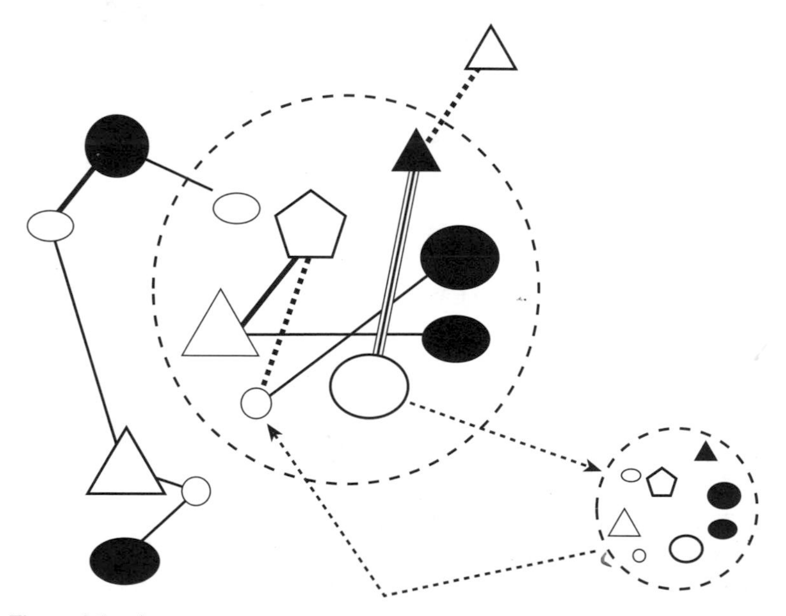

**Figure 3.1** A system

*Source*: based on McLoughlin, 1969, p. 76.

lar, there are three facets of ecological processes that can be seen as equally relevant in our attempt to understand human affairs. First, the successive diversification and increasing complexity of rules and functions and the contexts within which these are performed. Second, adaptation *to* physical space or the adaptation *of* space (e.g., building) creates habitats for a wide range of activities. Finally, the evolution of a rich variety of communications that are used to connect the locations of such activities.

Systems are dynamic. They change through the competitive behaviour of those involved who act in an optimizing way (e.g., attempt to earn more money, get to work quicker, move to a bigger house, etc.). But the actions of those involved will also have an impact upon other individuals and the relations within the system. If I decide to build a supermarket it will (I hope) have an impact upon shopping patterns, traffic flows, etc. Systems adapt, shift and evolve. Very large numbers of decisions are being made by multitudes of individuals and groups – sometimes in response to the consequences of decisions made by others. The emphasis upon such a systems view of the world is complexity. Planners and others must find ways in which they can classify and predict such decisions in order to be able to manage change. This is not as difficult as it might sound. Decisions and actions are not made anew each time. There are constraints upon action. For example, market constraints (e.g., we cannot all afford to move to an area we would like) mean that we can focus on effective demand. Legal and social constraints add a further dimension – we must act within the norms and rules of society.

A further crucial aspect of a systems or cybernetic understanding is that of rational utility. We act either individually or collectively in predictable ways that aim to maximize personal utility. A firm needs to minimize transport costs, for example, while individuals want to live in safe, accessible and healthy environments. The combination of such constraints and rational behaviour mean that systems *can* be theorized, modelled and predicted. Planning's role in this is to anticipate the dynamics of a system such as a city or region in an holistic way and plan accordingly:

> Planning seeks to regulate or control the activity of individuals and groups in such a way as to minimise the bad effects which may arise, and to promote better 'performance' of the physical environment in accor-

> dance with a set of broad aims and more specific objectives in the plan. (McLoughlin, 1969, p. 59)

Here, we have some strong links with the debates and trajectory of geography around the same time. Both geography and planning were attempting to model complex, interconnected systems. Both required quantitative analysis that was driven by the developments in computing power. Attempts to model cities and regions had been around for quite some time. Models such as those developed by Christaller or von Thünen, for example, analyzed cities and regions in a systematic way and sought immutable laws about ordered location. However, in the eyes of systems theorists such models lacked sophistication and were to understanding modern urban systems what Columbus's instruments were to flying an aeroplane (McLoughlin, 1969, p. 66). More sophisticated models were required that did not abstract reality to the point of over-simplicity.

As well as greater sophistication offered through increased computing power, a further dimension was also required in any future model: evolution. 'What would happen if . . . ?' was the basis of modelling complex, evolving systems. McLoughlin points to wind-tunnels, water-tanks and even experiments on animals as ways in which man tries to model and better understand such complexity. Such models were based on 'closed systems' that could be more easily understood than a changing and evolving city. A systems approach to city planning would need to shift from the discrete modelling of 'closed systems' to more holistic understandings that allowed for feedback and evolution. As McLoughlin points out, however:

> The trouble is that when we try to take into account the inter-relations of more than about a dozen or so of these issues, their scores of immediate side-effects, their hundreds of indirect effects all merging and overlapping with different time-lags, we find the human brain cannot cope without assistance. We cannot model the city in our heads – its complexity overwhelms us. (1969, p. 82)

It is difficult to disagree with this point. Where one goes from here has shaped at least two fields of planning theory. Friedrich von Hayek, for example, argued that such complexity meant that state planning was impossible *and* undesirable. If one cannot possibly comprehend the extent of such a system then it should left to the market – the aggregate of many individual decisions within constraints such as the rule of law. This perspective formed the basis of neo-liberal or New Right thinking on the role of the state and planning, which I cover in Chapter 5. System planning theorists such as McLoughlin, however, came to different conclusions. Cities could be modelled if only we had enough understanding and computational power. There are two implications of such a systems perspective that I am going to focus on here. The first is the attitude towards plans and the second is methods for forecasting and modelling.

Plans should not be seen as static documents but rather as dynamic and changing as the systems themselves. According to McLoughlin:

> The basic form of plans should be statements which describe how the city should evolve in a series of equal steps – of say, five years at a time. These statements would be a series of diagrams, statistics and written matter, which would set out for each five-yearly interval the intended disposition of the principal activities – agricultural, industrial, commercial, residential – together with the intended communication and transport networks . . . Such plans are the necessary description of the course or trajectory we wish a dynamic system to follow. They bring together land use and communications at all times; they show where the city should go and how it can get there. (1969, pp. 83–4)

This is a form of planning that is high on regulation and central control. The planner is 'a helmsman steering the city' (McLoughlin, 1969, p. 86). Once a model of the system is developed and forms a basis for the plan it can also be used to evaluate proposals (Figure 3.2). The heart of the evaluation of a proposal is the model of the system into which there are clear inputs (the proposal) and outputs (the predicted impact). It should be noted that the dynamism or evolving nature of the system is accounted for in the 'feedback loop' as the proposal (if approved or refused) will have an impact that needs to be taken into account. Note, however, that the feedback loop does not stretch to the model of the system itself. This is presumably because the model is comprised of immutable laws that will be not be influenced by changes. Whether or not this is a weakness of the systems approach will be discussed below.

The second implication of the systems approach that I want to focus on concerns methods for forecasting and modelling. I have

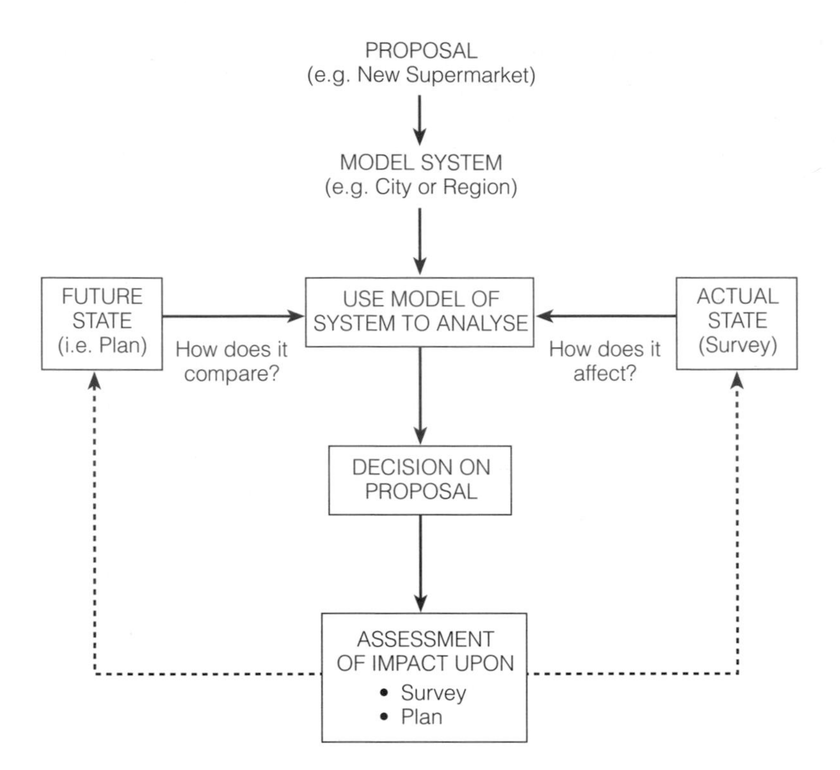


**Figure 3.2** Methodology for planning proposals
*Source*: based on McLoughlin, 1969, p. 86.

already mentioned the recognition of complexity and the enormous number of individual and group decisions with the various permutations. Planning has for too long tried to overcome such complexity through intuition and hunch (see Chapter 6 on such methods in planning). These tools or attitudes do not meet up to the needs of complexity (though why not, exactly, is not clear). McLoughlin argues for a number of changes in the approach of planners to better model cities. The first is the obvious one of increasing the amount of data and the inputs to methods such as projections and forecasts. Investigations of causal mechanisms, in particular, will help develop more accurate and robust models because they 'allow us to account for or assume differing patterns of change in the components of a situation' (1969, p. 169). Thus, it is not enough to focus on simply population trend projections, but we need to understand the influence and significance of birth and death rates and the influences upon them such as health, affluence, migration etc.

The second systems approach involves taking different forecasts and bringing them together through models. The models that were used in planning were too descriptive and simple to capture the complexity of a city. A cybernetic approach involves mathematic models that seek 'to make statements about the environment (the location of activities and the pattern of flows in urban and regional systems) which enable [the model-maker] to understand and cope with it' (McLoughlin, 1969, p. 223).

The first step in any modelling of complex systems is the recognition of patterns through observations. This leads to a hypothesis that involves a causal sequence of events, e.g., pedestrianizing a road leads to an increase in retail rental levels though causes congestion elsewhere. But a crude cause and effect relationship is insufficient. A model must be able to predict that if x is changed by 1 it will lead to a change in y of 5. What happens, however, when numerical values are not possible? This could arise with, say, attempting to tackle homelessness. How can such qualitative issues be tackled through mathematical modelling? Here the logic of a mathematical model can be followed even if numbers themselves are not used.

The third implication of a systems approach concerns how to choose those projected or simulated future states of the system that yield optimum conditions. This is essentially how to choose which of the multitude of simulations to follow. This is done through a combination of pragmatism (the availability of resources such as time and people) and relating the simulation to objective optimization. If the objective was to maximize economic growth then different trajectories or simulations will be tested against criteria, such as rates of growth, or different methods of achieving faster rates of growth, such as improving communications links, allocating land for industrial growth.

A fourth and final implication is the choice of plan itself. Like the evaluation of different models or simulations, the guiding principle here is 'how far each plan satisfies all the objectives which have been adopted for the planning exercise' (McLoughlin, 1969, p. 265). Three techniques are suggested as methods for undertaking such an evaluation: cost–benefit analysis, a planning balance sheet and a goals achievement matrix. All three vary in their method but broadly employ a combination of quantitative and qualitative analysis. The goals achievement matrix quantifies, for example, the different impacts of plans and weighs them according to how desirable in terms of goals and objectives they are. The result is a rather subjective matrix of costs and benefits that points to a 'best' solution.

The systems approach is not simply a method for planning that can be 'picked off the shelf' by planners. It also has implications for issues such as the organization of planning functions within public bodies, teaching and skills. There is not the space here to develop many of these themes but it is worth mentioning a few. The first implication is of a more centralized organization of planning in public bodies. A 'core group' or central information unit will develop 'the model' or system that will be the focus for other functions such as development control. Other departments will use the model and feed back information to the central information unit to allow the model to be further developed. The development of the model will primarily be an activity for professional planners who will not only build the model but also have primary responsibility for setting objectives and goals:

> one of the most forceful arguments for placing primary responsibility for goal formulation on the planner . . . [is] the assumption, traditional to professionals, that, in some way, they 'know more' about the situations on which they advise than do their clients. (Chadwick, 1971, p. 121)

Models will be mathematically based. In a moment of future gazing, McLoughlin predicts that

> Most planning offices now and in the future will need access to at least a small or medium-sized computer as well as more modest equipment such as automatic electronic calculating machines. (1969, p. 300)

The second implication regards the kind of planners that systems planning requires. McLoughlin argues that the traditional functional divisions in planning based around development planning, development control etc. will need to be replaced by a division of labour that reflects the requirements of systems planning. Thus, planning as a function of public bodies could be organized around five divisions:

1. 'Activities' contributors: demographers, economists, persons with knowledge of special activities such as extractive industries, recreation, tourism, shipbuilding, etc.
2. 'Space' contributors: architects, landscape architects, engineers, land surveyors, valuers, agriculturalists, geographers, geologists, etc.
3. 'Communication' contributors: transport engineers, specialists in air traffic, telecommunications, public transport, etc.
4. 'Channels' contributors: engineers of many kinds, also architects, landscape architects, etc.
5. Contributors providing a general service to the organization:

    a. goal-setting: sociologists, political scientists, etc.
    b. simulation, modelling and 'information services': systems analysts, mathematicians, programmers, etc.
    c. evaluation: economists, sociologists, psychologists, etc.
    d. implementation: public administrators, public work experts, etc. (McLoughlin, 1969, p. 309)

Criticisms of systems planning have been aimed both at its pretensions and at its assumptions and implications. Rittel and Webber (1973) for example, saw systems planning as a failed attempt at self aggrandizement on the part of planners:
With arrogant confidence, the early systems analysts pronounced themselves ready to take on anyone's perceived problem, diagnostically to discover its hidden character, and then, having exposed its true nature, skilfully excise its root causes. Two decades of experience have worn the self-assurance thin (quoted in Faludi, 1973, p. 43):

> Faludi concentrates on two broad criticisms of his own. The first is that, following Batty (1982), systems planning was already outdated, inappropriate and impossible when McLoughlin and Chadwick wrote their books. During the 1960s planning as a function of the state became far more complicated and politicized, leading to the rise of the planner as advocate rather than objective policy analyst (see Chapter 7 for more on this). McLoughlin's image of the planner as helmsman failed to appreciate the complexity of the competing and conflicting objectives of the growing multitude of actors involved. As Faludi puts it, planning in the 1970s became a 'complicated political game which probably defies coordination' (1987, p. 46). In other words, system theorists did

> not appreciate the extent of the complexity involved nor did they appreciate how some forms of complexity (e.g., conflicting political objectives) would make the systems approach unachievable. There is also the question of the extent to which the systems approach was undesirable as well as unachievable. Should we be planning in a way that is technical rather than political? Should planners be determining means and ends?

Faludi's second point (following Webber, 1983) regards the legacy that the systems approach left for planning as a profession. The problem was less that systems planning was doomed to failure and more about the illusions that it gave planners about eventually being able to achieve something akin to understanding and control:

> [the] attractiveness of the idea of scientific planning has been hard to resist, for it held out the promise of right answers, of revealing what we should want, and of saying what we need to do. It seduces with the prospect of certainty, and thus with the prospect of relief from the discomforts of ambiguity and of having to decide things in the face of conflicting evidence and competing wants. But scientific planning is a mirage. Science and planning are very different sorts of enterprise . . . scientists seek to observe, describe, and explain . . . Planners are quite the opposite; their purposes are to change whatever it is they are confronting, preferably, of course, to improve it. (Webber, 1983, quoted in Faludi, 1987, p. 46)

There is little to add to this passionate and accurate summing up of the impact of systems planning on the profession. While we might question the assumption of planning as control we should equally not reject the need of planning to project, understand and model. The whole approach of attempting to model and predict impacts, therefore, has rightly remained part of planning. There is a danger of dismissing systems planning as a tool within planning with systems planning *per se*. This has been helped by systems planners themselves. There was a confusion by the advocates of systems planning concerning ends and means. Cities can be treated like systems and undoubtedly they are complex adaptive systems. This can be useful in helping our understanding of how cities and regions work – retail impact assessments are a clear example of current ways in which we see impacts of planning decisions being more than simply local and physical. But an acceptance of cities and regions as systems does not necessitate an approach that plans them in such a way with the various implications that entails. Where, for example, is the role of public participation in a systems view? McLoughlin (1969, pp. 120–2) believes that goals should be formulated through a 'dialogue between professionals and politicians'. He goes on to list who he considers to be 'politicians' and includes such groups as trade unions, churches, etc., 'and, in certain instances, the public at large' (1969, p. 121). A systems perspective is highly 'planner-centric' in that it places a great deal of emphasis upon professional opinion in an abstracted and technical process where goals flow from analysis of problems – congestion requires more roads, poor-quality housing requires wholesale clearance and the erection of tower-blocks. In this respect it shares some of the criticisms that have been aimed at rational process planning discussed below.

As Faludi rightly points out, McLoughlin came to criticize his systems work for these very reasons: 'The system approach, operational research, mathematical models and cybernetics provided at the end of the 1960s a wonderful justification for a bureaucratised profession and its academic counterpart' (quoted in Faludi, 1987, p. 45). The legacy of systems planning has been a feeling that, given enough computing power, cities can be modelled. There is a tendency in planning theory, particularly in the post-positivist era, to dismiss such ideas in favour of a more collaborative or communicative approach (see Chapter 9). In practice, systems approaches still have an important role to play through, for example, Environmental Impact Assessment (see Wilson, 2000). I cover more recent developments in Chapter 8.

There is one further development that is worth mentioning. Although Faludi and others dismissed systems planning as being unachievable, the idea of systems and, in particular, complex adaptive systems in nature and human society began to take off again in the late 1980s. In the face of the inability of models to understand and predict complex behaviour, a number of fields in the natural and human sciences have begun to develop more sophisticated conceptions. The two areas that are currently being developed involve ideas around chaos and complexity. Both fields of theory have sought to address the more involved and intricate dimensions of systems. As opposed to the more rational and utility-maximizing aspects of the 1970s understanding of systems, complex systems are characterized by:

- a great many independent agents interacting with each other in a great many ways
- spontaneous self-organization
- adaption and (co)evolution
- dynamism. (Waldrop, 1992, p. 11)

The main difference is that McLoughlin's conception of a city was what would be now termed 'simple', that is, based on linear and predictable behaviour. Complexity theory instead emphasizes a great deal more irregular behaviour (Table 3.1).

This does not necessarily mean that we cannot 'plan' or model. It does, however, emphasize a more modest and contextualized approach that recognizes that aggregate human behaviour is not always reducible to a simple formula. It also raises the point that we should not put too much hope on computing power being able to one day model the city.

The notions of complexity and chaos have acted as a stimulus to the resurgence in systems-based understandings and models of places. Using methods such as cellular automata, researchers have begun to model the dynamics and interactions of cities and the consider the impact of policy interventions, including planning (Byrne, 1998; Batty, 2005).

***Table 3.1* Characteristics of complex and simple systems**

| Complex | Simple |
|---|---|
| Counterintuitive, acausal behaviour (i.e., it did not turn out as expected) | Reducible behaviour |
| Adaptive behaviour through constant and varied feedback | Few interactions or feedback/feedforward loops |
| Diffusion of power and authority | Centralized decision-making and concentrated power |
| Irreducible. Breakdown of aspects does not lead to total collapse | Decomposable. Weak interactions among components |

*Source*: based on Casti, 1994, p. 269.

**Rational process theories of planning**

Just as McLoughlin and Chadwick are synonymous with a systems view of planning, so Andreas Faludi's name is closely associated with rational process theories of planning. But, as Faludi points out, this is to forget the significant contribution made by the 'Chicago School' of planning theory and research in the immediate postwar years. Even though the work done by those such as Banfield, Perlof etc. in Chicago was influential, it was itself built upon earlier foundations laid by, among others, Max Weber and Karl Mannheim. Even then, there are debates in rationality that go back to Plato and Aristotle.

The term 'rational' has an etymological root to the Latin *ration*, meaning 'reason'. A rationalist is normally taken to be someone who emphasizes logical capacities and can give reasons for a particular view. This is normally contrasted with more emotive or intuitive reasoning. Art is an area where analytical skills or reason are not required – you like a painting or film for a variety of personal reasons that are sometimes difficult to express. As Healey, McDougall and Thomas (1982, p. 8) characterize it, rationality typically involves 'the clarification of policy goals, systematic analysis, logical generation of policy alternatives, systematic evaluation of these alternatives and monitoring performance'.

Such concerns with rationality were the preoccupation of the German economist and social historian Max Weber who, while appreciating that subjective judgements or 'sense data' would always influence decisions to greater or lesser degrees, sought to analyze and prescribe a form of bureaucracy and rational decision-making that separated facts and values. The proper concern of rational decision-making should be with facts. Values, ends, goals etc. were the realm of politics. This dualism led Weber to make a distinction between *formal* and *substantive* rationality. Formal rationality is concerned with means and efficiency. It is not related to ends. When given ends or objectives, a formally rational approach will seek to meet those ends in the most efficient and effective way. If the end is to travel between A and B then a straight line is the formally most rational way of doing it. Such means are based on logic or reason. Substantive rationality concerns ends and their evaluation. Reason and logic are still employed at the expense of, say, instincts or tradition but clearly involve more than simply efficiency or effectiveness. One example might be poverty. The existence of poverty would not be disputed (by most people). What to do about it is another issue that is substantively rational. A market-led solution and state intervention are two extremes and both could be and are argued for and against. This is the realm of politics.

Planning should concentrate on formal rationality or the means. In dealing with formal rationality:

> Weber was extremely careful to set forth the conditions for objective analysis. He argued passionately for an intellectual asceticism in which factual statements would be held rigidly apart from statements of value. He contended that a social science had to adhere to the same formal standards as the physical sciences, specifically to the principle by which personal inclinations and preferences were to be brutally excised from analysis. Values judgements, he asserted, had a non-scientific origin. They were the result of culture, tradition, social position, and personal preference, and they had no place in scientific discourse. (Friedmann, 1987, p. 99)

The irrational forces of life – politics in particular – needed to be tamed through rationality and the rules of science.

Planning was part of the means by which this could be achieved. Those who worked in public organizations such as planning had the responsibility to act rationally in an impartial and single-minded way towards the organization's goals. In return, they received status and rewards such as secure tenure and public esteem. As Low (1991, p. 69) points out, however, bureaucrats such as planners were not just concerned with serving politicians whose responsibility it was to devise ends or substantive rationality – they were actually opposed to democracy. While politicians desire their legitimacy through periodic elections, bureaucracies, such as those in local government desire their own form of legitimacy from technical expertise, 'objectivity' and impartiality: 'both the complexity of technical knowledge and the secrecy with which the bureaucracy guards the superiority of the professionally informed tend to diminish the capacity of the political leader to exercise control' (Low, 1991, p. 72).

This conflict hints at the tensions that Friedmann claims Weber thought existed between formal and substantive rationality: 'Human beings strive for formal rationality in their action, but the more they try, the more they run headlong into trouble: society is not a logical structure designed by engineers but rather consists of logical and illogical elements and relations' (1987, p. 98). Although some have tried to reconcile formal and substantive rationality, they are based upon different values. Functional rationality is akin to efficiency, substantive rationality to equality.

Weber's ideas were (and are) highly influential and were broadly translated into planning (in its broadest sense) through the work of Karl Mannheim. Mannheim famously said that planning is the rational mastery of the irrational. The 'irrational' he had in mind was broadly akin to substantive rationality – politics, democracy, mass opinion etc. Like Weber, Mannheim distinguished between functional and substantive rationality and like Weber he argued for planning to be objective and unbiased in the face of inevitable social and personal influences. To minimize such influences, planners need to think strategically and interdependently. Strategic thinking would help lift them above their immediate context to 'higher levels' of thinking about principles. Interdependent thinking would involve what we would now recognize as formal rationality, that is, it concerns itself with the best means of achieving set ends. As Friedmann (1987) points out, however, such formally rational thinking was to be set within the context of and related to concrete situations. Thus, Mannheim's rationalism is less dogmatic and more practice-orientated than Weber's.

Notwithstanding these differences, there are common features and implications of rationalism for planning in the work of Weber and Mannheim. The first is what Friedmann (1987, p. 105) terms the 'rift between politics and planning'. A crude interpretation might be that planning was the formally rational foil to the grubby and self-serving institution of politics. This attitude of technical competence and political neutrality still remains in the minds of many planners. The Royal Town Planning Institute's *Code of Professional Conduct* (RTPI, 1994, p. 1), for example, states that planners,

- shall act with competence, honesty and integrity, and
- shall fearlessly and impartially exercise their independent professional judgement to the best of their skill and understanding.

The second implication and legacy has concerned attitudes, methods and theories of planners towards planning. One of the main centres that developed and popularized thinking around rationality for planning was to be found in the Chicago School (Faludi, 1987; Friedmann, 1987).

The Chicago School was a degree course offered at the University of Chicago in the 1940s and 1950s. The attitude and motivation for the course and those involved in it emerged from two major events. The first was the depression of the 1930s and the New Deal response to it, which involved significant and massive planned public intervention in the economy. The second motivation was the experience of World War II, which again required significant central planning of the economy. One of the leading exponents of a more planned economy and interventionist state at the time was Rexford Tugwell, who (as well as holding high political office) was involved in the Chicago School. Tugwell championed both economic and land-use planning, believing that it 'would achieve a clear vision of the future, above the din of petty politics, by becoming institutionalised as a fourth branch of government, with its own autonomous sphere' (Friedmann, 1987, p. 109). Planning would provide a counter to the petty and disreputable nature of politics through the power of experts and their technical, objective abilities.

Rationality was at the heart of Tugwell's vision of planning. Through a bureaucracy, planning:

> surveys, for understanding, the whole organism of which it is a part, . . . it appraises most carefully the operation of the parts as they affect the functioning of the whole, . . . it undertakes a meticulous study of the resources and the developing direction of the organism . . . and it produces the Development Plan which it will propose for public examination. (Tugwell, 1940, quoted in Friedmann, 1987, p. 111)

Note here the use of the term 'organism', which Tugwell, like systems analysts and Faludi (see below), felt was a useful metaphor for the complex system of society.

Tugwell's visions and ideas were influential in the development of other thinkers of the Chicago School. The overall thrust of the rational approach and the influence of Tugwell was a programme designed to use the methods and tools of science towards social ends in order to ensure that public decision-making was based on facts rather than hunch:

> In this conception, planners came close to representing the free-floating intelligentsia which played such an important role in Karl Mannheim's writings. Their social science training would establish a basis of a scientific kind of politics, but their personal qualities . . . would prevent them from usurping the traditional decision-making functions in a democracy on the basis of technical expertise. (Sarbib, 1983, quoted in Faludi, 1987, p. 24)

Planning, according to the Chicago School, was a generic term. This meant that it involved various methods that could be applied to a variety of situations and disciplines. The output from such a rational process was an explicit and objective form of decision-making. This was the subject of Meyerson and Banfield's book *Politics, Planning and the Public Interest* (1955). Both Meyerson and Banfield had been involved in the Chicago School and applied its theme of rational decision-making to detailed areas of public policy, including planning and housing. The two themes of rationality so far discussed, that is, the formal-substantive rational split and the generic nature of planning, were at the core of their argument, which saw a rational decision as one where:

> 1. The decision-maker considers all of the alternatives [courses of action] open to them; i.e., he considers what courses of action are possible within the conditions of the situation and in the light of the ends he seeks to attain.
> 2. He identifies and evaluates all of the consequences which would follow from the adoption of each alternative, i.e., he predicts how the total situation would be changed by each course of action he might adopt.
> 3. He selects that alternative the probable consequences of which would be preferable in terms of his most valued ends. (Meyerson and Banfield, 1955, quoted in Faludi, 1987, p. 30)

Such criteria have been translated into a process of rational action for planning. Andreas Faludi's approach to rational planning is both a clear interpretation of rational process planning and a heuristic that provides a benchmark against which other forms of planning now seem to be judged. Faludi's main work on planning as a rational process was simply entitled *Planning Theory* (1973). The actual content clearly follows the trajectory set by the Chicago

School and work by, among others, Meyerson and Banfield. Planning, according to Faludi, is about the best way of producing results (1973, p. 5). To achieve this, planners should act much in the same way as research scientists in searching for the best methodology. In trying to decide from a vast array of information and views which course of action to take a planner must use rational criteria. Like Weber and Mannheim, Faludi views the planner as taking a non-ideological and objective stance:

> the information provided by ideological criticisms is a useful signpost to what may underlie a proposal, but it must not paralyse them lest they should become defunct as a decision-taker. They are more likely, therefore, to evaluate arguments as they are manifestly made . . . judging premises for their acceptability and conclusions for whether proper inferences have been drawn . . . In short, they will combine particular demands and proposals into one overall rational choice. (Faludi, 1973, p. 37)

In his earlier work Faludi compared this rational approach to that which underpins systems analysis of the kind followed by McLoughlin and Chadwick above (Faludi, 1973, p. 38) though he was to later recant this (Faludi, 1987, p. 42–4). Nevertheless, there are some overlaps with the joint emphasis upon process and rationality. Where the two schools diverge is in the systems inclusion of substantive rationality.

Like McLoughlin, Faludi felt that rational process planning influenced not only individual decisions but also organizational structures. A planning agency, as Faludi termed them, was simply a bureaucracy for the identification and solving of problems in an effective way. It should therefore be organized in a way that allowed this to happen. The way in which Faludi approaches this is through drawing parallels between a model planning agency and the workings of the mind:

> Planning agencies have components serving the same purposes as the components of the human mind engaged in operational thinking, and that the information processes occurring in a planning agency show patterns similar to those of operational thinking. (Faludi, 1973, p. 58)

Although Faludi could be accused of making a little too much of this analogy (though he does recognize some drawbacks of it), the core of the comparison is simple. The memory is comprised of discrete functions. It takes in information and inputs through a *receptor*, which is linked to both *memory* and a *selector* that have the function of choosing between alternative responses. An *effector* then produces changes in the environment as a result. Basically, we take information in through our senses, decide what reaction we should have to it and then act. The analogy with planning comes alive when memory is complemented with what Faludi terms 'images' – pictures or visions of the future. This future vision, which we could also term goal (hence the link to substantive rationality), is used as an ideal with which we can compare what is currently the case. Adjustments can then be made through the *effector* to ensure that the vision is achieved. The vision, according to Faludi, can be a community one, though there are issues of how to gather such a single vision from disparate interests.

The link to agency organization arises from identifying discrete functions that correspond to the way in which a mind operates. The receptor is now called the survey unit that undertakes research on aspects of planning. The development plan section becomes the image or vision drawing upon information from the receptor or research unit. The selector becomes the planning committee or those who make decisions and, finally, the *effector* can be seen as akin to the development control section, who make decisions on proposals and how they relate to the vision or plan. This is a simplified presentation of Faludi's ideas, but they give an indication of the extent to which formal rationalism provides a basis for decision-taking or decision processes. It also demonstrates the extent to which such a way of thinking about planning (or any other decision-making procedure, such as collecting taxes or running a hospital) can be applied to more than simply a decision-making procedure but also the structure and organization itself. It is worth noting a couple of points at this stage.

The first is the way in which Faludi's conception of rational decision-making also clearly includes reference to ends or substantive rationality. Planning as a rational process envelopes substantive rationality or the vision that drives formal rationality. Values, vision or plans become almost secondary to the means of getting there. The second is the fuzzy nature of the relationship between ends (substantive) and means (formal) rationality. Although Faludi accepts that there is no clear demarcation between the two, the model seems to present them as distinct. As many critics of the rational approach have pointed out, there are strong arguments that such a distinction cannot and should not be maintained. Finally, there is the implicit attitude towards inputs and outputs in each of the distinct parts of Faludi's model. There are clear and identifiable inputs such as a wider public vision and environmental concerns but these are treated as largely unproblematic and where there are possibly areas of conflict these are brushed over and seen as being 'technical' problems to be 'fed into' the rational process and organization.

One answer to these issues, however, is that the rational model as presented by Faludi is not a description of how things are done but a model or heuristic, as well as a way of justifying decisions that have been made. There are two important points here. Faludi has been accused by some of creating a model of planning as a decision-making process that is unrealistic. He accepts this. Second, Faludi also argues that going through a decision-making process in a less than rational way, that is, using intuition, hunches, etc., matters less than justifying that process in a rational way afterwards:

> A person wishing to present conclusions convincingly outlines rational considerations that might have led to them in an orderly fashion. He does not normally claim that this is the actual process he used, but only that others should agree with his conclusions because they appear to be derived from reasoned argument. (Faludi, 1973, p. 81)

This may seem a curious stance given the emphasis upon process and organization in contributing towards rationality. What it does do is emphasize the 'ideal–reality' gap, as well as clarifying what Faludi actually means by the term 'rationality'. Faludi's idea of rationality would seem to lie in an ideal process *and* in a justification of decisions that have not actually followed that process.

The process to be followed, according to Faludi, helps clarify the issue of what it is to be rational. Like the systems view, the rational planning process has a series of steps to be followed which, in many respects, appear similar to McLoughlin's approach above. The rational process begins with the identification and definition of a 'problem' that needs to be addressed. This might be a vision of a 'better world' or more immediate issues such as finding the best land to allocate for industrial expansion. Again, Faludi is less than clear on what problems are, where they emerge from and how to resolve conflicts between them to arrive at an agreed position. The only advice is that, 'Objectives describe possible worlds, not fantasies' (Faludi, 1973, p. 89).

Once objectives have been set, a programme is then devised that involves, 'intentions concerning the type and intensity and the timing of actions aimed at manipulating the control variables of a problem situation so as to achieve a set of objectives' (Faludi, 1973, p. 89). Faludi admits that in the complex world of planning there are likely to be a number of programmes that could meet given objectives. The task of choosing between alternative programmes becomes one of achieving objectives while minimizing expenditure or resources. This is the ideal – setting objectives, exploring programmes to achieve them, choosing a programme and implementing it. In reality there are problems of ill-defined issues and objectives, uncertainties concerning external influences such as the decision-making of other agencies, economic stability etc. Nevertheless, the rational process method still provides the best way of approaching such environments of uncertainty because, even if the programme chosen will not fully meet the objectives, at least it is moving public action in the right direction.

This hint at reality being removed from the idea of rational planning is explored further by Faludi. How can decisions be made and programmes chosen in an environment as complex as planning? Faludi advances a number of decision-making approaches that seek to tackle such issues:

- *Routinization.* In most bureaucracies 'short-cuts' emerge that speed up decision-making and allow attention to be focused on important rather than trivial issues. Faludi argues that such automated rule-based systems also have an important role to play in arriving at the right programmes for particular objectives consistently. Consequently, provided automated rule-based systems are well thought out and justifiable, they can provide useful ways of coming to a decision on which programme to employ without using an inordinate amount of resources to do so each time.
- *Sequential decision-making.* In situations where it appears there is an overload of information or programmes to be assessed to meet a given objective then one way of ensuring that the different programmes are properly evaluated in terms of

impact and resources is through a sequential matrix-based scoring mechanism. Unlike routinization, this approach does evaluate different programmes on an *ad hoc* basis, thereby ensuring that the most appropriate programme is chosen each time. It does, however, take more time and resources.

- *Mixed scanning.* It may be obvious that some approach between routinization and sequential decision-making is a sensible compromise. Etzioni (1967) developed an approach he termed 'mixed scanning', which involves identifying and imposing patterns on information. A broad scanning of the problem is complemented with a detailed examination of aspects that arise from the larger scan. Mixed scanning highlights that we do not approach an issue or problem without a picture of what to expect or how to 'frame' it. We are predisposed through experience to recognize more and less important aspects. Thus mixed scanning is a compromise approach to the choosing of a programme of action that is likely to fit in well with how people actually work.

These three options for how to proceed rationally highlight some of the criticisms that have been aimed at the rational-process view of planning. There are clearly trade-offs between a formulaic approach that emphasizes distinct and idealized stages to be followed and the 'real world', which is often more messy and less straightforward. This criticism has led to a number of other approaches being developed the most influential of which was Lindblom's Disjointed Incrementalism (see Chapter 6 on pragmatism for more on this).

There are broadly two further schools of criticism concerning the rational-process approach. The first comes from a broadly Marxist perspective. There are two aspects of such criticisms. The first is that Faludi's approach assumes a division in rationality that *does* not exist. As Chris Paris puts it:

> Faludi has taken an *analytical* distinction and treated this as a real division in the nature of planning as a human activity . . . he takes the simplifying device too far and by so doing obscures the reality of the interaction between the social context of planning, the theories that planners hold (consciously and unconsciously) and the internal procedures of planning practice. It is thus argued that he wrests the practice

> of planning from its social, political and economic context and consequently operates on a mythical patient of his own making. (1982, p. 3)

I have covered this criticism in some detail above so will not revisit it here. The second broadly Marxist concern is built upon the foundations of the first and says that Faludi's distinction between different kinds of rationality *should* not exist. A typical perspective argued that 'procedural theory is essentially "contentless" in that it specifies thinking and acting procedures but does not investigate what is the context of these' (Thomas, 1982, pp. 13–14). This 'contentless' nature divorces rational planning from the normal political economy concerns of historically real and contextualized situations while positing a view of society as being based upon individual rather than class conflict (see Chapter 4). Instead, we have a pluralist perspective with a high degree of societal consensus and planning as a process that depoliticizes planning and eventually seeks to remove politics altogether. This is obviously a red rag to the Marxist bull, particularly as procedural planning provides no standpoint from which to criticize society or capitalism but aligns itself with the rationality of dominant economic forces.

The second school of criticism concerns other forms of rationality and has provided a way forward for planning under the communicative school of theory. Within this perspective are a wide range of positions that could be labelled postmodern or neo-modern. The more postmodern perspective was highlighted by Friedrich Nietzsche, who championed what he termed the Dionysian element in human nature – the darker, more emotional side that contrasted with our more calculating and rational behaviour. D. H. Lawrence put this well:

> Real knowledge comes out of the whole corpus of the consciousness; out of your belly and your penis as much as out of your brain and mind. The mind can only analyse and rationalise. Set the mind and the reason to cock it over the rest, and all they can do is to criticise, and make deadness. (1998, chapter 4)

This may be taking things a little too far – we need to make and justify collective decisions on the basis of more than intuition – but Lawrence's more general point about the need to balance the rational with the intuitive is one that has echoes with the critiques of many others. Sandercock (1998, pp. 4–5), for example, claims that planning became too infused with narrow, technical rationality and missed out on the more spontaneous aspects of humanity:

> In the post-war rush to turn planning into applied social science much was lost – the city of memory, of desire, of spirit; the importance of place and the art of place-making; the local knowledges written into the stones and memories of communities. Modernist architects, planners, engineers – Faustian heroes, all – saw themselves as experts who could utilise the laws of development to provide societal guidance.
>
> The social sciences have been dominated by a positivist epistemology which privileges scientific and technical knowledge over an array of equally important alternatives – experiential, intuitive, local knowledges; knowledges based on practices of talking, listening, seeing, contemplating, sharing; knowledges expressed in visual and other symbolic, ritual, and artistic ways rather than in quantitative or analytical modes based on technical jargons that by definition exclude those without professional training.

Another broad-side at rational and systems planning has been fired by Patsy Healey. She claims that

> Technical and administrative machineries advocated and created to pursue goals are based on narrow and dominatory scientific rationalism. These machineries have further compromised the development of a democratic attitude and have failed to deliver the goals promoted. (1993b, p. 233)

Assessment of the actual impact of such planning approaches also points towards issues of a blindness towards processes and criteria that cannot be easily assimilated into either quantifiable methods or logical processes. Oren Yiftachel (1994) in Israel and Mark Oranje (1996) in South Africa have looked at the ways in which a more technical rationality has been used and abused by planning for ends that are dominatorily oppressive. Bent Flyvbjerg (1998) has explored issues of rationality and power in relation to planning in the Danish town of Aalborg. Flyvbjerg follows Nietzsche and Michel Foucault's argument that rationality is a way of creating and reinforcing power relations. He argues that political decisions that have significant implications for 'who gets what' are then rationalized afterwards as being rational. Planning is used as an ideology to present a rational and logical front to powerful relations between economic and political interests. This sounds similar to the arguments presented by political economy interpretations regarding the 'real' role of planning in propping up and reproducing relations of production (see Chapter 4).

Flyvbjerg draws upon Niccolò Machiavelli's *The Prince* as a guide to understanding the motivation of actors to suppress formal rationality. Power is the key theme as Machiavelli argues: 'We must distinguish between . . . those who to achieve their purpose can force the issue and those who must use persuasion. In the second case, they always come to grief' (Machiavelli, 1984, quoted in Flyvbjerg, 1998, p. 37). Flyvbjerg questions the use of 'always' (it must be remembered that *The Prince* is a work of fiction), but nevertheless agrees with the sentiments of Nietzsche that 'the greater the power, the less the rationality' (1998, p. 37).

This is an important perspective on rationality which basically says that we use the term rationality as a smokescreen for decisions that have already been taken and which mask powerful economic or political relations. Some might regard this as a cynical view, though work by Jill Grant (1994) in Canada has shown how planners can rationalize action after the event (as Faludi suggested) but also after decisions have been taken. Faludi argued that it was perfectly acceptable to rationalize largely irrational decision-making processes in a *post hoc* manner. Thus a decision taken based on intuition is acceptable in a world that favours rational processes providing that it can be justified and explained rationally afterwards. What Faludi was saying here is that the mind does not necessarily work in a common-sense way but we can still achieve rational decisions and action. What Faludi did not say or envisage, however, is the way that planners and others rationalize decisions in a *post hoc* fashion to validate their own legitimacy or to choose processes and methods that fit what they intuitively or ideologically think should happen: 'A persuasive theory corresponds to reality as the actor sees it. People promote theories that fit their normative perspectives' (Grant, 1994, p. 74). Faludi has responded to some of these criticisms (1982, 1987). He considers the broad political economy thrust to be 'thorough, competent and fair' (1982, p. 28). By 1987 he was less ready to cede ground (probably because in the intervening period there had been far more criticism and planning theory had developed in new directions). His defence is based on four propositions that he claims were already accounted for in his original text. On the matter of rational planning being 'contentless', he argues that goals as well as means can be subject to a rational process. On the issue of different underlying views of society, for example, pluralism versus political economy, he simply agrees to disagree with his critics. He claims that rational planning does not seek to replace politics but complement it: 'political and planning choices are one and the same in the sense that all public choices have an element of both' (1982, p. 31). Finally, on the issue of not being 'critical', he claims that rational planning highlights important elements and choices of public debate that can then be discussed in a critical way.

Faludi's defence is in some ways unconvincing – I have little doubt that his approach would lead to a depoliticization of planning and a rise in the power and influence of technical and professional decision-making mechanisms. Yet, as Stephenson (2000) has highlighted in his study of the preparation of plans, there are some elements, housing and transport in particular (with retailing to a lesser degree), that remain 'technical' and largely planner-led. Nevertheless, this study concluded that purely rational and technical analyses did not exist in isolation from the political:

> The original identification of the problems that the plans sought to address did not arise in the first place from formal technical analysis. Rather, the problems were identified from experience, day-to-day observation, and matters raised by the public, politicians and outside agencies. The acquisition of technical information was important as a means to conform the nature of the problems, and also reflected the planners' own understanding of them. (Stephenson, 2000, p. 102)

What is important, however, is the need to separate what Faludi says and the interpretation of where it places him and his ideas in the wider political and normative arena. Some criticize the rational approach for being 'contentless', though I seriously doubt whether a more critically aware planning could do without a methodology for making and implementing decisions. Faludi is caught up in a much wider normative debate about positions. As such he is often castigated for being 'part of' something that others oppose.

This is not to say that there are not legitimate criticisms of the rational approach. The recent shift towards a more communicative form of rationality, in theory characteristic of the collaborative or communicative approaches, has provided both a strong indictment and a way of embedding formally rational approaches within a more discursive and political arena (see Chapter 9). The growing societal rejection of 'top-down' solutions and the distrust of professionals has added to the feeling that formally rational and systems approaches are, at best, tools rather than ends in themselves.

## Conclusions

The systems and rational approaches are the apex of positivist planning theory. The common characteristics of control and prediction echo the concerns of those who criticize the applicability of natural scientific method to the more messy and open nature of society. But they also highlight many of the themes discussed in Chapters 1 and 2. The expert planner versus the layperson was a battle about more than simply access to computer models: it was about control. The ways in which the issues were presented concentrated control in the hands of planners and a select group of others. Those not privy to such expert knowledge were excluded. In the phraseology of Chapter 1, planners were the 'agents of norms'. Truth, in the systems and rational approaches, was absolute, not relative.

The attractiveness of such 'scientific' approaches to those hungry for skills and knowledge perhaps explains the endurance of systems and rational theories of planning. But, like most theories, the interface with reality often proves to be the downfall:

> I recall my first job on the Leicester and Leicestershire Sub-Regional Planning Study. This was directed by Brian McLoughlin whose teaching of the impact of systems theory upon planning had interested me and other students of his at Manchester University. The Study attempted to apply the systems approach to a specific task of planning practice. Systems theory offered a valuable methodological framework for developing strategic planning policies, but at every turn compromises had to be made to accommodate the real world of political expectations, existing commitments and so on. I recall us trying for example to use queuing theory and deciding that it actually bore no relationship to real behaviour. The Study was a success, but entirely because McLoughlin was able to jettison idealized or formulaic application of his theory and to apply it pragmatically to the needs of practice. (Thompson, 2000, p. 131)

It was also clear how theorists such as McLoughlin and Chadwick took theories from other disciplines and fields and turned them into indigenous planning theories. Their approaches were unique to planning given the ways in which ideas such as systems, taken from the biological sciences, were shaped to fit institutions such as local authorities, urban form, existing political realities and the needs of a profession. Time and space were similarly significant. It is no coincidence that the systems approach developed around the same time as computer power became cheaper and more accessible in the 1960s. Neither is it a coincidence that the reactions against the top-down perspective of both approaches emerged at a time when the broader public were questioning the role of the government generally. This practical reaction was mirrored by a theoretical reaction particularly at the apolitical nature of systems and rational approaches. Most powerful in this critique was the renewed interest in political economy approaches.

# 4 Critical Theory and Marxism

## Introduction

The essence of critical theory* is to change society rather than simply understand and analyze it. While there are many positions within the broad school of critical theory, particularly those related to the Frankfurt School of thought, we will focus in the first instance upon one main dimension, namely Marxist theory. I go on to highlight later critical theory, developed out of the shortcomings of Marxist thought, to come to terms with later incarnations of capitalist society and the failure of Soviet-style interpretations to protect and develop individual freedom. The key proposition of Marxist theory is that urban areas and planning cannot be treated as objects of study separate from society. They are produced by that society and, more fundamentally, have an internal logic and function that is primarily derived from the economic structuring forces within that society – in most cases capitalism. Put simply, cities and planning (including planning theory) are reflections of capitalism and at the same time help constitute it. Such a perspective poses serious challenges to many cherished concepts, particularly in approaches such as those described in the previous chapter. For example, planners often justify planning by reference to the 'public interest'. According to critical and Marxist perspectives, there is no such public interest but only an interest of capital that projects or creates a state mech-

• Critical theory is often used synonymously with the terms Marxism and political economy. There are differences between the different schools of thought, most notably the role of positivism and the cultural dimensions of capitalism. Important similarities concern the rejection of superstition and dogmatism and the desire to change society, not simply analyze it.

anism such as planning to help it continue and give the impression of public control. This amounts to what Nicholas Low (1991, p. 4) has termed a dissenting theory of planning because it is highly critical and yet provides few alternatives to the status quo beyond dismantling it.

It may seem anachronistic to even include a chapter on Marxist and critical theory. Surely, the collapse of communism in Eastern Europe and the Soviet Union between 1989 and 1991 finally demonstrated the redundancy of radical alternatives to the neoliberal hegemony? Andrew Gamble and others believe that such approaches still have an important role to play:

> There is an intellectual core to Marxism which is worth preserving and which is capable of further development. Marxism continues to pose key questions about the origins, character and lines of development of economic and social systems of the modern world. (Gamble, Marsh and Tant, 1999, p. 4)

I would agree with this. Critical and Marxist analyses raise important issues about planning and help, in the words of Law-Yone, to 'expose [planning's] complicity with state and nation and capitalism' (2007, p. 317). And while the context may have changed, the system Marx described and the critique he provided, though developed to new levels of sophistication and understanding under critical theory, remains essentially the same and relevant today.

## Critical theory and Marxism

Like most schools of thought, there are a variety of perspectives within Marxism and critical theory. Any attempt to provide even an overview is, therefore, bound to be incomplete. However, key to understanding the approach is the work of Karl Marx. In Marx's time (even more than today), the economy and the market was the fundamental regulating and structuring mechanism. The founder of the political economy approach, Adam Smith, had written of this and the 'invisible hand' in his *The Wealth of Nations* and helped define the relationship between capital and labour that was central to Marx's later work. Marx began from the broadly agreed principle that people needed to produce the material means of life (e.g., food, shelter, etc.) in order to survive. To do this they entered into social relations with others that were a division of labour, for example, farming, tool-making, etc. The difference under capitalism was that while previously workers had produced enough to survive and reproduce they now produced more than they needed and not for themselves but for payment.

Marx distinguished between what he termed necessary labour and surplus labour. What workers were paid was what workers and their families needed to survive. What they produced over and above this (the surplus labour) went to the employer. This relationship between employer and worker was *the* fundamental division in society. The two groups – those who owned the means of production and those who sold their labour – represented capital and labour. Theirs was an asymmetrical relationship based on exploitation where capitalists gained more through their appropriation of surplus labour. Both represented diametrically opposed groupings or classes – the bourgeoisie and the proletariat. Both, equally, had fundamentally different interests – the bourgeoisie to increase profit and the proletariat to increase wages and living conditions.

The fuel for this relationship was capital and its aim was profit. Capital, in Marxist terms, is 'congealed labour'. Labour had produced more than it required and the result was 'locked up' in banknotes, buildings, machines, etc. As such, capital is more than an inanimate object; *it is a socially produced relation.* This may seem rather obscure but it is an important characteristic. Marx spent much time and energy trying to pin down what capital is. He saw it not as a cash amount but as a means of production and thereby part of a process. This dynamic property of capital is related to a circulation where capital is used to purchase commodities such as materials, the means of production and labour. Surplus value or profit is then created allowing the process to continue.

The circuit of capital requires one more important dimension; that of consumption. Somebody has to purchase the commodities to enable the process to continue. That someone is the exploited worker. We therefore have a complete circuit. There are some obvious problems to this, however. If the worker is expected to consume what he produces but is paid less than the total value of their work then surely there must be an excess of goods? Here we have another dimension of Marxist thinking; that of crises. Marx claimed that there was a tendency for capitalism to undergo periodic crises which arose because it over-produced goods. Not all of these goods could be consumed by workers leading to 'under consumption'. A related reason for a crisis to occur is that of a falling rate of profit. Capitalists need to maximize surplus value by either reducing real wages, increasing the working day or introducing mechanized forms of production. All things being equal, and at a gross simplification, the outcome in the longer term is a falling rate of profit as workers have less to spend. In all circumstances, the result is a crisis.

Crises have occurred in capitalist economies as predicted by the Marxist interpretation, most notably the depression of 1929–41. But capitalism can avoid or displace crises through a number of mechanisms. These include capitalists consuming part of their profits rather than investing them and thereby reducing the demand deficit. International expansion in the search for new markets or cheaper materials, wars and new technological developments all provide other opportunities for capitalism *as a whole* to stave off crises. But perhaps the most important factor is the role of the state. Keynesianism, for example, was based on the premise that capitalism could be 'managed' by manipulating supply and demand. Urban planning, as I shall detail further on in this chapter, is arguably another state mechanism that is complicit in this state role of avoiding crises.

Marx argued that not only were crises inevitable but they also held out the opportunity for a different mode of production, that is, socialism. Such a revolution would not be a reformulation of capitalism but a sequel to capitalism and involve a 'forcible overthrow of the whole extant social order' and require, *inter alia*, the expropriation of landed property, and the application of all land rents to public purposes, centralization of the means of communication and transportation and the common ownership of the means of production (Marx and Engels, 1985, p.133).

This is a very basic outline of Marxist thought. What it does not include, and what makes Marxist thought and the core of critical theory both relevant and applicable to planning, are its assumptions and implications. One characteristic is that of alienation. Workers are not only commodities to be bought and sold but are subject to a dehumanizing alienation from satisfaction in their work because their output belongs to their employer. Further, workers increasingly undertook specialized tasks and never produced a single whole product. Marx's solution was the common ownership of property and means of production. But if workers were alienated from power and dissatisfied with their lot, why did they not do something about it; in short, what was stopping the revolution?

Marx developed his theory of false consciousness to help explain this. Workers knew that they undertook the work and capitalists made the profits but could not and did not fully grasp the intricacies, dimensions and full implications of this. Consequently, people considered capitalism fair (after all, they sold their labour and were not coerced into doing so) and the rewards of capitalists to be just for the risk taken. Such a consciousness operated at an individual and class level. Marx did not develop the idea of false consciousness very far, although this was done by the Italian Antonio Gramsci. Gramsci explored the ways in which the bourgeoisie establishes and maintains its rule. To this end, Gramsci introduced the idea of hegemony (authority over others): 'With this [the idea of hegemony] he demonstrated that a dominant class, in order to maintain its supremacy, must succeed in presenting its own moral, political and cultural values as societal norms, thereby constructing an ideologically engendered *common sense*' (Hay, 1999, p. 163). Hegemony must rest upon active consent and a common agreement that capitalism works in everybody's favour This common agreement or hegemony involves various state mechanisms of which planning, as I shall discuss below, is generally regarded as being one.

Regardless of the hegemony, the manifestation of state activity only formed what Marxists term the superstructure that is built upon the base of the capitalist mode of production. Marx introduced the concept of base and superstructure thus:

> In the social production of their life, men enter into definite relations that are indispensable and independent of their will; relations of production that correspond to a definite stage of development of their material productive forces. The sum total of these relations of production constitutes the economic structure of society, the real foundation, on which rises a legal and political superstructure and to which correspond definite forms of social consciousness. The mode of production of material life conditions the social, political and intellectual life process in general. It is not the consciousness of men that determines their being, but, on the contrary, their being that determines their consciousness. (Marx, 1971, Preface)

What Marx is saying here (and there has been considerable controversy over this) is that the economic structure of society (capitalism) conditions the existence and forms of the state and what we think about it. So while we may tinker with the day-to-day operations and forms of state activity this will be within limits set by the needs and manifestations of capitalism.

## The link to planning

All this talk of the circulation of capital, hegemony and crises etc. sounds fine in theory, but what does it have to do with planning? There has been a plethora of studies that have sought to apply and develop political economic and Marxist approaches to urbanization and planning. Richard Foglesong (1986) identifies a number of different perspectives on how land use planning can be 'explained' through a Marxist interpretation. All have built upon voluminous writings concerning the role of the state under capitalism. Central to any Marxist understanding of planning is this role of the state. Hay (1999) identifies four broad Marxist conceptions of the state:

- *The state as the repressive arm of the bourgeoisie.* Basically, the state exists as an expression of the repressive might of the ruling class.
- *The state as an instrument of the ruling class.* This conception sees the state as an instrument of the ruling class for enforcing and guaranteeing the stability of the class structure itself. The attention of Marxists focuses upon the influence of those in power and the network of relations between them.
- *The state as an ideal collective capitalist.* Under this understanding the state is seen as providing necessary interventions and conditions for capitalism to reproduce itself.
- *The state as a factor of cohesion.* Here, the state is understood as providing a unity and cohesion of social formation by sanctioning class domination.

Whatever the justification, the state is a crucial focus of Marxist attention because it is a 'key nodal point in the network of power relations that characterise contemporary capitalist societies' (Hay,

1995, p. 156). The most influential Marxist perspective on the state takes the *state as an ideal collective capitalist* position above – also known as structuralism. This position argues that although capital is diverse and often in competition it nevertheless depends upon certain basic factors to enable it to create surplus value and profit. Capitalism, according to Marxists, is inherently unstable. It has inbuilt contradictions related to over-production. The state is therefore required to provide this stability; in particular, it provides:

- General infrastructure that cannot be provided profitably by private businesses.
- The capacity to defend militarily national economic space.
- The provision of a legal system that establishes and protects private property.
- Systems for regulating and ameliorating class struggle and conflict between capital and labour. (Hay, 1999, p. 157)

These roles displace the crises inherent within capitalism to the state. 'The implications of this for a Marxist theory of the state are profound. For the state is revealed, once again, as playing a crucial role in safeguarding the circuit of capital' (Hay, 1999, p. 158). Marxist views of the state have evolved over time. Two particularly important developments that are significant to an understanding of planning have been made by Gramsci. As I outlined above, Gramsci tried to understand how capital managed to continually stave off crises and what role the state had in this. Such an understanding provides us with a view of the state not so much as a repressive force, but as part of a *persuasive* force that seeks to convince subordinate classes that there is no alternative to the status quo. Thus, the state acts through various mechanisms that present it as legitimate in the eyes of the many and does not need to resort to violence to maintain capitalism. The various forms that such influence could take have been explored by, among others, Michel Foucault and I discuss Foucault's work in Chapter 8.

So the state has a critical role in Marxist theory. Planning, as part of the state, is presented in a completely different light to the apolitical and technocratic view of the systems and rational approaches. Following the arguments above, planning potentially seeks to help sustain capitalism and even persuade people that it is acting on their behalf (through public participation, etc.), while in reality it is merely a façade for powerful interests. As Scott and Roweis put it:

> the specific interventionist sphere of urban planning . . . emerges, like all State intervention, out of a web of concrete, historically determinate conflicts and problems embedded in the social and property relations of capitalist society generally, and out of capitalist urbanisation in particular. (1977, p. 1103)

Such a crude analysis has been the subject of a number of Marxist interpretations of planning that have sought to explore in more detail how planning functions within capitalism.

One such interpretation has been developed by the geographer David Harvey (1973, 1989). Starting with the basics, Harvey argues that there is a spatial dimension in labour and commodity markets. People live, eat and work in 'places' – mostly cities – and, consequently, capitalism is associated with such patterns. At a simple level, one can see the 'reflection' of the urban in capitalism or, as he puts it, 'Capital accumulation and the production of urbanisation go hand in hand' (Harvey, 1989, p. 22). Factories, houses, roads etc. are largely to be found in places determined by the needs of capital, for example, factories near sources of material, houses near factories. But Harvey goes further than this. Capitalism is about profit and profit is surplus value created in production. The creation of profit is related to time (the speed at which surplus value is created). Speed is also related to space because movement across space (labour, goods, information etc.) takes time. Competition puts pressure on capitalism to reduce both these temporal and spatial impediments upon the creation of surplus value or profit. Here we have the crux of the Marxist interpretation of the urban and its implications for planning – urban areas will be constantly under pressure from the dynamic of capitalism to respond to the need to increase profit through being more 'efficient'. Efficiency here refers to the 'annihilation of space by time' (Harvey, 1989, p. 22). In other words, *capitalism will constantly seek to reduce physical barriers to the production of surplus value or profit.* It is worth reflecting upon this point particularly as it has significant implications for what planners actually do.

One example close to planners' hearts will help illustrate this. Towns and cities function as centres for the production and consumption of labour and goods. One particular product that has always been important is food. Markets (in the sense of an area for buying and selling food) have been traditionally associated with town centres. Location was driven by access (the agglomeration of points of sale reduced the time between production and consumption and thereby increasing the profit that could be made) and consequently markets were normally found in areas that were easily accessible, for example, crossroads.

In medieval times, markets normally dealt in surplus produce, that is, what the grower decided was not needed to sustain a family. Around the time of the industrial revolution high streets shops evolved as a later development as more commodities were produced beyond the staples of life. Capitalism was looking for ways of disposing of surplus goods and realizing profit. Accessibility of the consumer to these goods was still paramount and was also still determined by foot or horse. Nevertheless, competition had created a different urban form than simply a temporary central market. We now had the development of permanent shops, typically in a linear form along what we know as a high street. Dear and Scott refer to such areas as 'concentrated clusters', which are located around raw material sites or transport nodes 'where the costs of assembling and processing basic inputs is at a minimum' (1981, p. 9).

Later still, the popularity of the car has again created a new urban form. Accessibility is still the driving force behind the location of markets. However, the car (a technological innovation) allowed larger stores to develop on the edge or even out of towns. So urban form in most towns and cities reflects the dynamic of capitalism and its legacy can be seen in an urban form typified by the declining high street and the mushrooming of retail sheds on bypasses and ring roads. As Harvey states:

> Considerations derived from a study of the circulation of capital dictate, then, that the urban matrix and the 'rational landscape' for accumulation be subject to continuous transformation. In this sense also, capital accumulation, technological innovation and capitalist urbanisation have to go together. (1989, p. 23)

This 'rational landscape' applies to all areas of production and consumption in urban areas, leading to a hierarchy of centres of different functions and sizes (Dear and Scott, 1981, p. 9).

This is not the whole story, however, in the relation between urban areas and capitalism. Towns and cities are not simply a reflection of the dynamics of capitalism, they are also its pre-requisite. The relation between labour and capital is at the heart of the Marxist analysis. According to Braudel (1984) urban areas played a vital role in bringing both together so that they could be mobilized by capitalism for further rounds of accumulation. The spatial concentration of communication, markets and physical infrastructure were required before capital accumulation could begin. Urban areas provided this concentration. Such areas also provided an efficient and effective means of concentrating labour in one place, ensuring its availability and maintaining its compliance with the system through civil controls such as the police and military.

Harvey argues that a further implication of the concentration of labour in urban areas was the need for urban politics to develop mechanisms through which labour could be reproduced and remain available when required. Thus education, healthcare and habitable environments became the priority of urban politicians such as Joseph Chamberlain in Birmingham (Harvey, 1989, p. 30). However, different regimes approached the social reproduction of labour in different ways. Some followed a more ruthless minimalist approach, while others sought to take a more interventionist line. The varying success or failure of approaches to urban governance adds a further dimension to the relation between dynamics of capitalism and urban areas. Relative success or failure could relate to conscious decisions concerning how an urban area adapts to capital accumulation. For example, a more interventionist approach might add impediments that inhibit the free circulation of capital, such as tax to pay for education and welfare. Such urban areas might not necessarily be less attractive to capital because of such measures, however, as skilled labour, for example, might be more attracted to these areas because of such provision.

Providing the conditions for capitalist accumulation does not necessarily mean that such accumulation will occur. Harvey (1989) argues that the more likely scenario (borne out by experience) is a persistent condition in urban areas of a shortage of capital and a surplus of labour. This arises because dominant power relations favour capital (those in power are usually capitalists) and that capital can take advantage of technological innovation by investing in new products or can shift to other areas of production or other urban areas where profits are higher.

This raises the issue of the dynamics of capitalism impacting at an *intra*-urban, as well as an *inter*-urban, scale. Just as a city is continually subject to the dynamics of accumulation, regions are also influenced by such processes. We can therefore envisage why some cities or regions might do better than others and why we have the emergence of an international urban hierarchy (Cohen, 1981). This has two implications. The first is that we can see the distribution and fortune of different urban areas and regions as being historically constituted by the dynamics of capitalism. Second, that urban areas and regions are in competition with each other to maintain or attract future rounds of accumulation.

In summary, a Marxist analysis looks at cities as being both *constituent* and *reflective* of capitalism. Urban areas:

- reflect the dynamics of capital accumulation.
- are under constant pressure to reduce spatial differences.
- provide the conditions for the concentration of capital and labour for continued future accumulation.
- are an arena for state regulation and control over labour, particularly in times of labour surplus.

This symbiotic relationship between the urban and capital will have given some strong clues as to why some form of state intervention in land and property is required. There are basically two reasons. The first is that capitalism cannot provide all of the conditions that it needs to continue. In particular, infrastructure such as roads, bridges etc. are not commodities like land or labour that can be bought and sold because they involve a great deal of capital investment with little or no return. Other services and commodities such as parks, refuse collection and low-cost housing also fall into this category.

Second, the dynamic of capitalism will mean that land uses will change and, at some time, conflict between land uses will emerge. As Dear and Scott put it:

> As capitalist society finds expression in urban form and process, so it encounters limits to its own further development and viability. In the

> urban system these limits are due less to external physical restrictions on the progress of society than they are to internal contradictions in the spatial dynamics of production and reproduction. (1981, p. 12)

Residential areas may be affected by smoke and noise from incoming industry, while retail uses may be disadvantaged by congestion caused by new office developments. The point is that rapid change in one area may impact upon another where a reaction to such change is *relatively* slower. This creates asymmetry. One cannot or maybe would not want to simply move house because a factory located nearby. The house would have to be sold (perhaps at a cost lower than the outstanding mortgage); children may have to move school; family, friends, employment and a host of social networks may be close by. Over the long term, such a shift is more likely to occur but in the short term the emergence of conflicting uses is very disruptive.

This understanding of why planning exists sounds similar to the justification of planning from a neo-liberal perspective. There are some important differences, however. First, according to neo-liberals capitalism is self-regulating – supply and demand will reach equilibrium eventually. Marxists, on the other hand, argue that capitalism is inherently unstable and prone to crises that may eventually overturn it. Neo-liberal theorists begrudgingly accept a minimal role for state intervention to help the market work more efficiently. Marxists perceive of a much more fundamental role. Planning is 'a means of collectively readjusting the spatial and temporal development of urban land use' (Dear and Scott, 1981, p. 13). Planning is an extension of the state and changes its imperatives (goals, emphases and theories etc.) in response to the needs of capital. There is no such thing as an apolitical planning or Faludi's procedural planning based on objective technical or professional ethics and standards. It is, on the contrary,

> an ever-changing historical process that is continually shaped and re-shaped by broad systems of urban tensions. Thus urban planners in Europe and North America have not turned their attention now to zoning procedures, now to urban renewal, now to expressway construction, simply as a result of the appearance of 'new ideas' within an abstract and self-propelling planning theory. It is only when urban development begins to produce *real* problems and predicaments that planners attempt to counteract them. (Dear and Scott, 1981, p. 13)

This is Dear and Scott's Gramscian interpretation of planning under which professional objectivity, techniques, methods and public participation are a placebo that convinces the public that the impacts and injustices of the market are being treated, while in reality planning is actually helping to perpetuate those symptoms.

Harvey (1985) interprets the role of planning and the idea of ideology in more detail. Planners are taught the tools of social reproduction, for example, zoning the 'best' configurations of investment. But the planner also needs authority and power to intervene and enforce such ideas. This authority rests upon the idea of a utopian 'harmonious' society – the 'public good' argument and the public respect and deference to 'professionals'. Harvey argues that this public good, far from being an objective and professional balance of competing claims, is actually an ideology that perpetuates the existing social order and facilitates social reproduction. As Harvey points out, this does not mean that planners are mere defenders of the status quo. On the contrary, they have to be dynamic and anticipate problems and potential crises.

This may seem a rather depressing assessment but it is actually bleaker than it first appears. Planning is perceived by capital to be both necessary, in the sense of providing the necessary conditions for the continuation of accumulation, and as a palliative to provide a feeling of control or 'public good'. But the actual scope of planning and its effectiveness are curtailed by the begrudging attitude of capital, which wants to minimize any intervention, and by the location of planning within the state apparatus. Because the state serves the interests of capital so will planning:

> The very raison d'être of planning is bound up in the mutual accommodations of the political and the economic. The state is in need of the institutionalization of planning in order to prepare the ground for the development and reproduction of capitalist relations, and the needs of capital are that the interventions of the state are necessary for a smoother functioning of the market. Hence, modern planning makes its appearance as an institutionalized mechanism for the good of the general public. (Law-Yone, 2007, p. 319)

This limits the scope for planning intervention to a market-supportive role (behind a façade of intervention in the public interest). Planning is therefore indispensable but restrained (Dear and Scott, 1981, p. 14; Fogelsong, 1986). However, because it is restrained, the outcome of planning can actually compound further rounds of capital accumulation by creating problems as well as attempting to solve them. Here, Dear and Scott (1981) become rather vague about what they consider to be the problems that have arisen as a result of planning and depend instead on the general point that planning is both a cure and a sickness in one.

Dear and Scott go on to make the point that such failures (whatever they may be) are not the result of planners' shortcomings or inadequate theories. 'The failures of planning in practice are less failures of knowledge than they are inevitable concomitants of collective intervention in a society that at once clamours for and yet restrains such intervention' (Dear and Scott, 1981, p. 14). As a consequence:

> Urban planning interventions are, by their very nature, remedial measures generated as reactive responses to urban land use and development pathologies. Planners are frequently able to control the outer symptoms of these pathologies, but they can never abolish the capitalist logic that produces them. (Dear and Scott, 1981, p. 15)

One may be forgiven for feeling that the relationship between capital and planning seems to be so contingent and abstract as to be of little practical use.

There is one more dimension that is worth mentioning. Both Harvey (1985) and Foglesong (1986) try to disaggregate the idea of capital and identify different dimensions and interests. For example, 'property capital' (e.g., developers, builders, mortgage lenders etc.) is crucially different to manufacturing capital. The former might resist an expansion of state activity into its realm that the latter might welcome. Reasons for this are not hard to find. Regulation can help maintain and even create profit at a local scale by restricting competition or regulating the flow of land or property that can be used for accumulation purposes. In the UK, for example, local authorities are bound to identify five years' supply of housing land. This helps property capital plan and maintains a degree of certainty. Manufacturing capital, on the other hand, might welcome regulation if it restricts competition in an area or protects adjacent sites from noxious developments. Thus, there is not a homogeneous conception of capital and, at certain times and in certain places, alignments between different aspects of capital will vary.

One further important implication of the Marxist perspective related to Dear and Scott's perspective above concerns theories generally and planning theory specifically. The overall view is that planning theory, like planning, is subject to the dynamics and manifestations of the foundations of society, that is, the capitalist mode of production and its various social corollaries such as the class system. There is no autonomous planning theory. Instead, all planning theory (except, presumably, Marxist interpretations) arises and evolves in response to the needs of capitalism: 'urban planning acquires and changes its specific targets and emphases as well as its supportive ideologies (including planning theory, professional codes of behaviour, and so on)' (Scott and Roweis, 1977, p. 1105). As they go on to state:

> Urban planning is not (and cannot be) the homeostatic phenomenon of conventional planning theory, but it is an ever changing historical process that is being continually shaped and reshaped by reference to a broad system of social tensions of which it eventually itself becomes a part. (Scott and Roweis, 1977, p. 1105)

This does not mean that planning theory is fixed. Harvey (1985) argues that what he terms planning ideologies change through crises. Although he does not elaborate on this point it seems that Harvey's crises of ideology can be seen to be akin to Kuhn's conception of paradigms (see Chapter 1). However, a major difference would be the reason and justification for such changes. While Kuhn talks of revolutions occurring because existing paradigms could not explain something, Harvey claims that changes occur because of crises of accumulation and the role of planning in it.

One consequence of this perspective is that it is rather scornful of all existing planning theories, distinctions (e.g., procedural and substantive) and justifications (e.g., acting in the 'public interest'). Thomas, for example, is particularly scornful of systems theory, which he describes as 'contentless' (1982), while Scott and Roweis damn planning theory generally as 'trivial' and 'vacuous' (1977). Approaches such as systems planning treat the whole process as ahistorical and apolitical, thereby masking planning's true function. In this role, planning theory and planning generally act as an ideology in the Marxist sense of disguising and legitimizing the role of the state by providing a semblance of intervention and public interest while in reality making little, if any, difference.

Manifestations of capitalism such as urban deprivation or poverty are thereby seen as bureaucratic problems rather than treated as a direct outcome of capitalism. This depoliticizes the capitalist mode of production while politicizing planning and other state functions by pointing to their failures. Thus, planning itself takes the blame for the consequences of capital, thereby distracting attention from the 'problem' itself, that is, the inequities created by capitalism.

This politicization of planning has another dimension. As well as focusing attention upon planning (which is, after all, only a small part of state activity), it also encourages different aspects of state activity to look to each other as impediments or facilitators, allies or enemies. Thus intra-state (different departments, different professions, different levels of government) conflict also occurs.

## From Marxism to critical theory

A related field or stance that has developed out of Marxist analysis is critical theory. Marxists began to rethink Marxism when it became clear from the experience of Soviet-style communism that socialism did not lead to freedom and democracy. Further, a crisis of capitalism in Germany had led to the rise of fascism not socialism and, in other parts of the west, capitalism was much more resilient in surviving crises than Marxists had assumed. Consequently, a new understanding of political economy was required.

Critical theory developed as a result, largely through the work of what is known as the Frankfurt School, which could be described as being broadly anti-capitalist and anti-Soviet-style socialism. I shall be dealing in more detail with critical theory and its relationship to planning in Chapter 9. Here, I want to mention the relationship with Marxist thought. As Low (1991) points out, the difference between Marxism and the Frankfurt School lay in the former's struggle for communism and the latter's struggle for freedom. Critical theorists do not want to undermine Marxism but attempt to reinvigorate and develop it to account for a range of phenomena such as Soviet socialism, fascism, domination in all forms and the continued existence of capitalism.

Two figures that helped develop such ideas were Theodor Adorno and Herbert Marcuse. Adorno pursued a number of ideas, though a dominant theme was his desire to undermine closed systems of thought (including orthodox Marxism) and the ways such thoughts, even with good intentions, become uncritically dominant. He argued for constant critique against such closed systems (a theme that prefigured a central tenet of postmodern thinking – see Chapter 8) in order to sustain capacities for criticism. Marcuse engaged more with Marxism and, in particular, authoritarianism and bureaucratization. Socialist societies, like capitalist ones, reduced individual autonomy and freedom because they were still organized around production and technology. They were no more free in practice than capitalist ones.

Marcuse also turned his attention to how capitalism had managed to stave off crises and avoid unrest and revolution. He argued that capitalism had managed this by creating a cultural solidarity (in some ways similar to Gramsci's hegemony). This solidarity used images, myths and other techniques to shape mass attitudes towards accepting, for example, inequality, unemployment or inflation. This cultural dimension to Marxist analysis was a crucial development that was taken forward by the French philosopher Jean Baudrillard (see Chapter 8 on postmodernism for more on Baudrillard). Baudrillard, like the Frankfurt School, was disenchanted with Marxist analysis. Following the failed student protests in Paris in 1968, he and a number of other thinkers also began to rethink why capitalism had continued to survive.

Like Marcuse, Baudrillard focused on the cultural dimensions of capitalism and argued that capitalism has led to a technological explosion, the death of 'authenticity' and its replacement with simulacra that bear no relation to any reality whatever. Simulacra refer to an image or representation of reality. What Baudrillard is arguing is that we cannot see or perceive reality any more because capitalism creates so many images of reality. One example that is often referred to is Disneyland. There, we can 'see' an idealized reality of urban form where streets have no poverty, danger and dirt. The streetscape is 'packaged' with various references to an idealized past and present often using images that are cherished as being somehow desirable (e.g., low-rise, car and litter-free streets).

The postwar explosion in consumerism and products has in turn led to the development of new values, modes of behaviour and relations to objects and to other people (Kellner, 1989, p. 10) replacing Marxist-inspired class based classification and structuring systems. Objects, such as consumer durables, now confer status through socially constructed signification. This adds an important cultural dimension to Marxist critiques of political economy accompanying the standard view of consumption as satisfaction of needs. As Kellner (1989, p. 18) points out, if everything in society can now be seen as a commodity to be bought and sold separate from any fixed meaning, then there can be no individual realization of the individuals' plight at the hands of capitalism. If there is no individual consciousness then there can be no group consciousness without which collective group revolt is impossible. This places Baudrillard, the former Marxist, in an ambivalent position *vis-à-vis* Marxism itself. Baudrillard's attempts to update Marxist thought into a neo-Marxian framework have the effect of undermining it and adding a powerful addition. Unlike the Frankfurt School writers, however, Baudrillard is disenchanted with and moved away from Marxist analysis, towards a much more nihilist, postmodern perspective (see Chapter 8).

## Critical and Marxist planning

Critical and Marxist interpretations have been the foundation for both attacks and defences of planning. One area where there has been less debate or influence is alternatives. Chapter 3 of this book deals with systems and rational planning theory – procedural planning theory (PPT) as it is generally known. Historically, PPT reached its high-water mark in the early to mid-1970s with the publication of Andreas Faludi's *Planning Theory* (1973). Here was a state of the art interpretation of a substantive and procedural basis for planning. Crudely, planning was presented as a decision-making process within which political objectives and public participation could be absorbed. This perspective came under increasing criticism from the emerging Marxist interpretations of planning. Thomas, for example, argued that PPT and, in particular, instrumental rationality, 'produces an attitude within the actors [planners] which is abstracted from qualitative, historically real situations they are in' (1982, p. 14). Camhis similarly was concerned that 'too much preoccupation with procedure or method in the abstract tends to push aside the real issues' (1979, p. 6). According to this perspective, Faludi and others have wrested 'the practice of planning from its social, political and economic context' (Paris, 1982, p. 3).

This growing criticism was fuelled by two major studies though neither were Marxist themselves. The first, entitled *The Containment of Urban England* (Hall *et al.*, 1973), claimed that the postwar planning system had had three main impacts. First, it had successfully contained urban sprawl through tools such as green belts. Second, it had achieved increased suburbanization, that is, increased distance from home to work. This had mostly occurred because new developments had 'leap-frogged' the green belt. Third, urban containment had also led to an increase in land and property prices. This had arisen because containment had better fixed the supply of land and, with fixed or even increasing demand, had thereby inevitably led to a rise in price. Looking in more detail at the distributional impacts of planning, the report also claimed that planning had actually contributed to wealth inequality. This had arisen because land and property inflation had disproportionately hit the poorer.

*The Containment of Urban England* seemed to be an indictment of postwar planning and PPT. One Marxist interpretation could see it as highlighting the role of planning in projecting a value-free, public interest activity while simultaneously aiding class-based capital accumulation. Another Marxist analysis could claim that planning was merely ineffective, with little actual impact upon property prices, the allocation of land and inequality. This latter position was advanced by Pickvance:

> According to the conventional interpretation of post-war urban development in Britain physical planning is the determining factor and hence physical planners must shoulder the blame for 'failures' such as 'soulless' housing estates, high-rise flats, or the decline of inner-city areas. (1982, p. 69)

Pickvance argued that such a perspective was erroneous and that the determining factor in urban development was the operation of market forces that were, despite planning, subject to very little constraint. Pickvance advanced this claim based on an argument thus: planning has no positive powers to enforce change to happen, only negative powers to stop development from happening. Consequently, it has to plan with the market, not against it. This can be tested by assessing whether the allocation of development land is very different from what would have been expected. If this is so then planning is a powerful regulatory force. If not, then market forces determine land use planning allocations. Not surprisingly, Pickvance argued that most planning is *trend planning* – following market decisions, for example, allocating city centres for office development (see also Brindley, Rydin and Stoker,1996 and Chapter 10 for more on this). Intervention planning such as green belts and new towns are untypical of planning *per se.*

This is a classic Marxist interpretation of planning – land use regulation is only a shop-front of rational, public-interest decision-making that hides the logic of market mechanisms. But it is limited. The problem with this interpretation is that it ignores the change in both planning and the market as a result of the existence of both. To illustrate this with an example, let us suppose that a local planning authority issues guidance on the design of houses to help developers in understanding what is and is not acceptable. Although it may take time (and a number of refusals and appeals), if a local planning authority maintains this stance architects and builders will eventually begin to submit proposals that correspond with it. Pickvance's interpretation of this may be that the planning authority is legitimizing designs and layouts of the market. A more holistic interpretation might be that market designs have been influenced by largely negative powers *over time.* At certain periods, when development pressure is more or less, the influence of planning will vary. It is therefore difficult, if not impossible, to test a 'with and without' situation, as Pickvance argues. The two are inextricably linked.

This is not to seriously question the argument that planning is largely market-led. It is. However, this is less a point about the ineffectiveness of planning and more about what planning is for. The much criticized and vague 'public interest' defence/justification of planning can as easily be used to argue that the public interest is largely coterminous with the market. This is a marginalist view of planning – it exists to make small not large differences. If one accepts this perspective (as neo-liberals or public choice theorists would), then they would respond to Pickvance with a shrug of the shoulders. What is not in doubt is the implicit point of Pickvance that planning and the market work in collaboration not conflict and that, consequently, the state (including planning) regulates capitalism – we should not *expect* outcomes from planning that are significantly different to that of the market.

The second study that helped illuminate the relationship between planning and the market and added to our understanding was entitled *Land Use Planning and the Mediation of Urban Change* (Healey *et al.*, 1988). While Hall *et al.* (1973) and Pickvance (1982) focused attention upon the distributional consequences of planning Healey *et al.* examined whether the system itself was biased in favour of certain interests over others. They found that

> despite the [planning] system's very considerable malleability, it embodies constraints which systematically privilege certain groups and interests. These reinforce the interests of powerful groups . . . Planning practice is thus 'structured' by the dominant power relations of society, most noticeably the economic drive to secure profitability and safeguard future production conditions. (1988, p. 244)

Rather than a class-based analysis, Healey *et al.* were specific in their identification of those interests that were more powerful than others:

- The agriculture industry.
- The mineral extraction industry.
- Some industrial firms.
- Knowledgeable property developers.
- All land and property owners interested in the appreciation of their property holdings.
- Well-organized community and environmental pressure groups. (1988, p. 245)

Damningly, they concluded that

> the state thus serves to safeguard the interests in land of activities essential to continued production (agriculture and mining). It promotes the interests of some producers in their search for production sites, and in particular has given attention to safeguarding the exchange value of land and property as an investment, and has thus facilitated the use of the built environment as a store of value for capital. (1988, p. 245)

Here was a study that had looked at the operation of planning and backed up the Marxist's case (though the study itself was not a Marxist perspective by any means).

Some might claim that analyses that demonstrate planning favours certain interests over others are highlighting the obvious:

all political systems are biased. This is certainly the view of Healey *et al.*, who argue that it is not that planning favours landowners or developers but that such biases are hidden behind a front that purports to be even-handed. This takes us to the alternatives advanced by Marxists.

As I noted earlier, the area of alternatives from a Marxist perspective is not a fruitful one. This partly derives from the contradictory position held by planners in the eyes of Marxists:

> Viewed as 'problem solvers', planners may adopt ends of equality and social justice but, in order to serve these ends, they must adopt means (such as encouraging investment) that serve capital . . . planners are also workers and members of a class themselves. They are not outside the class struggle or simply servants of the bourgeoisie. They have some choice in the use of what power and knowledge they possess. (Low, 1991, p. 211)

Are planners part of or a solution to the problem? They can be both, according to Marxists and critical theorists. Two broad approaches typify the stance on the contradictory role of planners. The first approach assumes that planners cannot achieve much, even working with the market, and therefore the solution is stronger, more positive planning (e.g., Boddy, 1982, 1983; Reade, 1987). For example, Evans argues that

> The current land-use planning system in Britain is mainly characterised by what has been termed 'trend planning'. In other words, its predominant feature is the tendency to accommodate and support market trends. If sustainability is to be a real policy goal, a much more positive, proactive planning approach will be required which will inevitably need to offer strong opposition to market forces. (1997, p. 10)

Similarly, Boddy (1982) argues that land in the UK should be nationalized to ensure a more efficient supply of building land and greater control over the form of development. This, he argues, would not be problematic, as 'private landownership is not essential to the appropriation of the surplus by the exploiting class (bourgeoisie) from the producing class (proletariat)' (1982, p. 92).

The second Marxist and critical perspective concerns the roles and values of planners and their ability to affect change from within the planning system. This involved a more pragmatic acceptance of the status quo and the market-led role of planning. This position is broadly allied to the collaborative school discussed in Chapter 9. Taylor argues that theorists such as John Forester seek

> to combine the insights of those neo-Marxist political economists who maintained a critical distance from capitalism with the more pragmatic implementation theorists who accepted the need to work with capitalist land developers (and other interest groups) in order to secure at least some planning gains. (1998, pp. 127–8)

Even the more strident critics of planning do not necessarily want to see it abolished or replaced by more positive and strengthened intervention. Marcuse, for example, thought that plans should not be forced upon people but arrived at through free agreement. Such critical theorists seek a more radical version of democracy that will challenge capital from the grass roots.

The danger of this approach is that in order to achieve something the bigger picture is lost or ignored. Planners could become complicit rather than critical and aware of their role *vis-à-vis* capitalism. For more committed Marxists, planners who work with capitalism are simply serving to perpetuate it through compromises and deals. Allmendinger (2004), for example, argues that Planning Aid (a charity that provides free planning advice in the UK) exists to help cover up biases within planning. The argument goes that what Planning Aid does is postpone crises in and challenges to planning by helping assure those dissatisfied or excluded from the system that they eventually had 'a voice' or a 'fair say'. Planning Aid acts to divert attention away from the close relationship between planning and capital.

As Taylor points out, whether one subscribes to the 'critical distance' or 'work from within' school of thought comes down to personal values. Current thinking, through 'critical pragmatism' (see Chapters 6 on pragmatism and 9 on collaborative planning), seeks to reconcile both, encouraging planners to be 'reflective practitioners'. Inevitably, the practice of planning becomes more embedded within practice than reflection as the day-to-day pressure and fire-fighting dominates.

## Conclusions

The Marxist and critical interpretations of planning are powerful and raise many important questions and posit original and provoking theses about the role and outcome of land use intervention. One must be particularly careful, however, in drawing upon these ideas not to confuse critique with ideology. As Taylor (1998, p. 127) points out, so-called analyses are often little more than arguments for less capitalism and more collective planning.

One of the main criticisms of such interpretations is that they are reductionist. Castells (1977, p. 62) was particularly guilty of this when he argued that the urban was not a separate area of study distinct from the economic and social processes of capitalism. Dear and Scott were early advocates of the logic of capitalism being a major determining factor upon the physical, economic and social characteristics of urban areas, but such characteristics '*cannot* be automatically read off from the over-arching capital–labour relation' (1981, p. 6). In other words, there are influences other than the mode of production. They go on to add that

> Contemporary capitalism is by no means simply reducible to a rigid model, consisting of a binary social structure of opposing capitalist and proletarian classes . . . there exist many different social groups which enormously complicate the patterns of social and political alliances in capitalism . . . one of the significant expressions of this complexity is the modern city, where territorial divisions and conflicts consistently breach class divisions and conflicts. (1981, p. 7)

Individuals, as Scott and Roweis (1977) argue, have substantial control over the purchase, sale and development of land, but no one person has control over the aggregate outcomes from this process. This less reductionist approach touches upon a question that is at the heart of much modern social theory: the relation between structure and agency (see Chapter 1).

The politicization of planning rather than capitalism and the role of planners and planning in it lead to a distinct Marxist or critical theory attitude towards planners. Like the scorn for theories other than their own, Marxists and critical theorists have a dismissive and at times patronizing attitude towards the daily function of planners themselves. Whatever their role or function, planners are perceived as dupes to the real functioning of capitalism, social reproduction and their role in it. They not only defend the existing capitalist social order but actively seek to clear a path for it by anticipating problems and working through their professional and public interest role to avoid them. Even recourse to 'rational' planned orderings is questioned – any rational order is one that is rational for social reproduction. Those who question such an order are accused of being 'irrational'. Planners, therefore, are encouraged to present deeply political issues in a technical way if they are to progress with least resistance. The impact of an out-of-town supermarket is assessed through a technical and largely professionally determined retail impact study that examines technical issues such as yields, footfall and trade diversion rather than, for example, questioning whether large supermarkets are actually good for society through their monopolistic control.

Planners and planning cannot escape the logic of such an argument. Even if they are radical planners, they are merely 'helping capitalism'. As Harvey (1985) admits, all planners do not subscribe to the same worldview; some are less technical and more political than others. But the fusion of technical planning and a necessary ideology (necessary to justify the technical view), according to Harvey, means that planners' capacity to 'understand' and 'act' are limited. Planners have learnt 'little or nothing' about the true nature of their work (Harvey, 1985). Harvey uses the example of population dispersal as an example of the duplicity of planning and planners.

Two strategies have been employed by planning and planners to order the population in such a way as to avoid riots and conflict in areas of low wages and unemployment. The first is dispersal – employed through the new towns in the UK after World War II – which lowered densities and created 'social stability'. The second was the policy of attempting to recreate a 'spirit of community' in urban areas that sought to create greater harmony between the classes around an idea of common community values. This included changes such as environmental improvements, which Harvey claims are not aimed at enhancing the lives of residents but at improving the efficiency of labour by making residents 'happier'.

Here, it will be useful to differentiate between the combative (one might also add paranoid) Marxist rhetoric, which seems to paint with a very broad brush, and some more fundamental and illuminating points. Again, planners and planning cannot escape the logic of such an understanding. *Whatever* is done can be construed as contributing to the functioning of capitalism. Marxist theory constitutes what I termed social theory in my typology (Chapter 2). It provides a holistic though largely abstract body of thought that seeks to explain and explore the dimensions and operation of society. It also has predictive elements (e.g., crises and the rise of socialism). Clearly, it is also normative in that the interpretation of evidence to support it is value-driven.

The interpretation of Marxist and critical thought to provide an indigenous planning theory was relatively straightforward, given the role of the state in such thinking and the role of planning as a state activity. But the mediation of this in time and space provide an interesting dimension. As a reaction against the bureaucratic and state-led approach of the 1960s it provided an explanation at a time when some where looking for one of why the state was acting in such a high-handed and arrogant way – Marxist theory had been around for nearly 100 years before then, so why now? Similarly, the questioning of orthodox Marxism and its development are also related to such issues. Paris, May 1968, is a date and place etched into the social scientific conscience, as it is here that many former Marxists saw the limits to such analyses. Student riots against the state and capitalism had a much wider intellectual impact. One result was to seek a development of these ideas that ultimately led to other forms of social theory, such as regulation and regime theory (Chapter 10). Another response was to reject Marxism altogether and this ultimately led to postmodern theory (Chapter 8). One more practical response was to strengthen the hand of capital itself through a return to classic liberalism and it is to this development that we now turn.

# 5 Neo-Liberal Planning

## Introduction

Neo-liberal theory has been highly influential in planning and other areas of state activity over the past three decades. While many would not agree with Fukuyama's triumphalism (1989, pp. 3–4), there is little doubt that the combination of neo-liberal economic and social authoritarian policies has become almost hegemonic. Primarily, this has arisen because of the political ascendancy and popularity of right of centre governments in countries such as the United Kingdom, the USA, Denmark, Norway, the Netherlands, Belgium, Canada and Japan and an acceptance of many of the right's economic policies by left wing governments in France, Spain, Australia and New Zealand. Nevertheless, the term neo-liberal is a broad one that encompasses a multitude of different emphases and positions. There are significant differences between these schools of theory. Such differences come down to an evolution of thinking, the differences between theory and practice and the variation of theory, interpretation of theory and policy in different places. This highlights one of the more interesting dimensions of this particular school of theory, which is that it has been applied to land use planning in a more or less wholesale way. Thus, in the UK the neo-liberal Conservative governments of the 1980s took aspects of neo-liberal thinking and used it as a basis to attempt to restructure all aspects of land use and planning controls – the aims of the system, the institutions within which planning operated, the processes it followed and the outcomes that were expected. Every aspect of land use planning was affected by the neo-liberal approach even down to the attitude of the planners themselves. Neo-liberal thinking challenges the very notion of planning. Yet, significantly, there is a gap between theory, policy and outcome – what was meant to happen did not happen. Despite over a decade of attempted reforms of planning based on neo-liberal principles, the UK still found itself with a system more or less unchanged. Other countries that have gone down the neo-liberal route have had similar experiences (e.g., Spain and Australia – see Gleeson and Low, 2000; Cladera and Burns, 2000). This gives us a unique insight into the application of a school of planning theory that other theories examined in this book cannot claim to match.

Nevertheless, we should be cautious. There are problems as well as opportunities associated with the study of putting theory into practice on such a scale. I have already mentioned the first – that is, the difference in intended outcomes; was this a result of the theory itself, its implementation, other factors or all or none of the above? Linked to the discussion on closed and open systems in Chapter 1, how do we to separate neo-liberal theory from the practice of governments having to juggle with issues such as electoral popularity, internal party strife and complex social and economic problems?

The issue of 'testing' a theory through practice – a generally accepted dimension of 'theory' as set out in Chapter 1 – was also argued to be problematic in the social sciences. The experiences of neo-liberalism across the globe reinforces this view. There is not a simple causal relationship between neo-liberal theory and practice – both have influenced each other. Although this has occurred to certain degrees in other areas of planning theory, neo-liberalism had a highly political and almost missionary zeal to challenge the status quo. As Mrs Thatcher, the prime minister of Britain during the 1980s and a leading proponent of neo-liberal thinking, used to say, 'There is no alternative.' An important consequence was a lack of monitoring and a reluctance to accept that theory could in any way have been 'wrong' or based on invalid assumptions, even in the face of evidence to the contrary.

This is not the only problem. It is by no means agreed that such a thing as neo-liberalism exists (Marsh and Rhodes, 1989). The influential Conservative writer Irving Kristol (1996) has written of the important differences between American and British neo-liberal thinking, for example. The specific social, economic and political contexts of each country combined with evolution in practice mean that there is no one neo-liberalism. While the term 'neo-liberalism' does not explain the phenomenon, it does provide is a starting point in any investigation of its identify and coherence (Gamble, 1988). Notwithstanding these differences of opinion regarding the existence of the neo-liberalism, we can follow the majority view and say that the neo-liberalism encompasses two approaches that have a variety of labels (Gamble, 1984, 1988; Edgar, 1983; King, 1987; Kerr and Marsh, 1999). Whatever the title, it is broadly agreed that neo-liberalism is based on a combination of a market-orientated competitive state (liberalism) and an authoritarian strong state (conservatism). This is why the prefix 'new' or 'neo' has been applied – both liberalism and conservatism are traditional *separate* approaches of the political right but their fusion is a genuinely new approach.

These ideas have been applied to public policy in theory and practice. Planning has been no exception to this. Planning in Australia, for example, has been subject to the neo-liberal approach. Here, 'entrenched anti-planning conservatism has been revitalised by the increasing political authority of neo-liberalism' (Glesson and Low, 2000, p. 133). However, it has been the liberal strand in particular that has had a strong influence on the neo-liberal approach to planning. This is not to discount the conservative element and its emphasis on centralization and minimization of discretion. The fusion of these two strands not only characterizes neo liberalism, but has also provided its nemesis through the difficulties, ambiguities and contradictions their combination brings.

Neo-liberal theory sees planning as wrapped up in the hopes and beliefs of a better society, characterized by the Enlightenment. However, as discussed later, it has been argued that their prescriptions are as much a product of modernity as planning. According to this view, planning is not a natural feature of a free-enterprise society. It requires a mandate of the people to intervene in the market and must demonstrate its worth. This is not to say that neo-liberals consider the market to be perfect. But any problems that emerge from the operation of markets are preferable to trying to intervene in them and allocate resources in other ways. In other words, the liberal view is that there is nothing wrong with markets that cannot be put right by what is right with markets.

This chapter will explore both the theory and practice of planning under neo-liberalism, with particular emphasis on the liberal component. As there is a strong link between neo-liberal theory and practice in the UK, this chapter will concentrate on the

Thatcher government's approach to planning, while acknowledging the contribution of US theory. Various writers have sought to translate neo-liberal ideas into neo-liberal planning theory and there is little doubt that the Thatcher governments attempted to translate these ideas and others into planning practice during the 1980s (Thornley, 1993; Allmendinger and Thomas, 1998). It will be clear that the ideas behind neo-liberalism, whether they are liberal or conservative, are hostile to planning *per se* and if any planning is required under a neo-liberal world it would be to support the market not supplant it. The Thatcher governments give us a unique insight into the neo-liberal relationship between theory, policy and practice, enabling us to reflect on how ideas were realized in government and evaluate policy outcome and implementation against theory.

## Liberalism

Liberalism covers a range of ideas and theories concerning the primacy of the markets mechanisms, individual freedom and the role of the state. Many of the these theories have their origins in the writings of people like Smith, Burke, Mill and de Tocqueville, though its main political proponents – Margaret Thatcher in the UK and Ronald Reagan in the USA – have popularized the ideas of two figures in particular, Milton Friedman and Friedrich von Hayek, the latter being the ideological inspiration behind much of the New Right's thinking. Hayek has been somewhat demonized as 'anti-planning' (Cherry, 1988; Faludi, 1973) and, as Lai (1999) points out, he did criticize the UK's planning legislation when it was first introduced. Nevertheless, Hayek's arguments against planning are normally aimed at central economic planning and consequently these ideas have been interpreted as a basis for attacking other kinds of planning, including town planning.

At the heart of Hayek's writings is the primacy of the market. It is axiomatic that markets are a superior way of organizing societies and the problem is seen to be creating the conditions in which markets can function more efficiently (Gamble, 1988, p. 38). Writing against the backdrop of fascism in Europe and Stalin's dictatorship in the Soviet Union, Hayek's primary concern was with personal and political freedom. He argued that state intervention in the market should be far less than it is. Hayek's works can be organized around four main themes (Kavanagh, 1987). First, central planning (though not all planning) is dangerous and inefficient. It interferes with the market, reduces personal liberty and undermines the rule of law by creating discretion within the state apparatus. Further, the logic of intervention invariably leads to demands for more state control (see the discussion on public choice school below). He also attacks the vagueness of values underpinning such intervention and concepts such as 'social welfare':

> To direct all our activities according to a single plan presupposes that everyone of our needs is given its rank in order of values which must be complete enough to make it possible to decide between all the different courses between which the planner has to choose. (Hayek, 1944, pp. 42–4)

Inequality, which is the basis of concepts such as welfare and state intervention, is the driving force behind the market. While the immediate benefits of inequality are hidden and diffuse, its impact on declining areas, for example, is more apparent, leading to calls for intervention (Thornley, 1993, p. 65). Such intervention challenges freedom; in a free society individual attributes such as initiative and skill determine who gets what.

Second, Hayek claims society is irreducibly complex. Market interactions lead to a spontaneous order that stratifies society. Such an order is not the outcome of a plan or design but human action. Planners cannot hope to replicate this, as they can only know a tiny part of society. Third, there is an overriding importance attached to markets and market mechanisms in allocating resources. While the complexity of society has made it impossible to coordinate activities through a conscious plan, the coordination of activities for the benefit of society does take place through free and competitive markets using knowledge held throughout society. Price mechanisms are the key to this and allow a collective coordination of individual actions (Low, 1991, p. 169).

Finally, government and state intervention is given a limited role, for example, to ensure the rule of law is maintained, provide infrastructure and national defence and act as the arbiter of disputes. In these circumstances government should intervene in the market by imposing rules that are set out and agreed in advance:'Within the known rules of the game the individual is free to pursue his personal ends and desires, certain that the powers of government will not be used to deliberately frustrate his efforts' (Hayek, 1944, p. 54). Government would then ensure that the rule of law is maintained and the courts would arbitrate in any disputes. Discretion and *ad hoc* decisions would therefore not exist.

As Lai (1999) and others have pointed out, notwithstanding Hayek's antipathy for central planning, he was not against planning *per se.* Neither was he against town planning:

> In *The Constitution of Liberty* Hayek made a distinction between (a) 'town planning' as practical measures to correct an imperfect land market, and (b) 'town planning' aimed at displacing the market mechanism altogether. Hayek rejected the latter but accepted the former. (Lai, 1999, p. 1571)

While Hayek argued that market failures are best dealt with through market forces, this did not apply to planning. Hayek acknowledges the unique role of property, urban areas and 'neighbourhood effects' in relation to the market (Thornley, 1993, pp. 69—74; Sorenson and Day, 1981; Lai, 1999) and accepts that conflicts between owners and users of land will inevitably emerge in urban areas. As Hayek put it:

> The usefulness of almost any piece of property in a city will in fact depend on what one's immediate neighbours do and in part on the communal services without which effective use of the land by separate owners would be nearly impossible. (Quoted in Thornley, 1993, p. 73)

In a perfect market situation such problems could be resolved through the courts by aggrieved parties, but the large number of cases that would arise and the likelihood of more than two parties being involved would make such a solution impractical. Developers would face uncertainty when making decisions and the courts would find it difficult to assess damage from, for example, pollution or noise:

> The general formulas of private property or freedom of contract do not . . . provide an immediate answer to the complex problems (neighbourhood effects) which city life raises . . . Some division of the right of control [is needed] between the *holders of a superior right* to determine the character of a large district to be developed and the *owners of inferior right* to use the smaller units. (Quoted in Lai, 1999, p. 1572)

Above, 'superior right' is a clear hint at the need for some kind of planning. 'Inferior right' refers to individual landowners or users. Holders of 'superior right' are to be given the responsibility for controlling uses over a larger district through, for example, zoning. This justifies the opportunity for state-initiated organizations or mechanisms, such as planning, to emerge to improve and support the market, but only, according to Sorenson and Day, where there are such effects and not as a right: 'there is a clear implication that where neighbourhood effects either do not exist, are positive or are detrimental but trivial, owners should be free to develop their property as they see fit' (1982, p. 392).

While Hayek and other libertarian philosophers broadly agree about the need for some kind of intervention in urban land markets there is less agreement on the mechanisms by which this should be achieved. Hayek advances the argument that market failure in urban areas does not mean that markets should be abandoned altogether. The principles upon which markets are based can and should still provide the mechanisms and tools for any state intervention. Indeed, an understanding of markets and price mechanisms is vital to any form of planning.

Spatially, planning should only be undertaken at a local level according to Hayek. National or regional planning cannot be justified because they do not directly relate to 'neighbourhood effects'. The concept of a 'rule of law' is central to any system of intervention because of its minimization of bureaucratic interference and discretion. For markets to operate efficiently as much information as possible must be known before any decision is taken. Where decisions that affect markets are taken by bureaucrats on an *ad hoc* basis it adds to uncertainty. The role of bureaucrats and discretion is of particular importance to neo-liberals. There is a feeling that the presumption in favour of markets has been reversed and that planning and intervention generally is now the 'norm' in society. This is a particular concern of the Public Choice School (PCT) (see Pennington, 2000). PCT applies the methods of economic analysis to political activity and bureaucrats and provides a theoretical argument against the notion that public agents or bodies are disinterested and neutral (Gamble, 1988). The assumption behind PCT is that individuals are rational, self-interested actors and that these characteristics shape political behaviour in voter, politician or bureaucrat (King, 1987, p. 92). Like neo-liberalism itself, PCT is not a coherent theory and three main strands can be identified.

First, developing Hayek and Friedman's idea of an irreducibly complex society, Arrow (1951) concludes that it is impossible to aggregate individual preferences into a 'common good' that the state can use to justify intervention. The best way to maximize public good as a whole is through maximizing freedom for individuals to make their own choices. Second, Downs (1957) took the idea of the selfish individual and applied it to political parties and voters. He argued that political parties develop policies to achieve political success and that there was no reason to believe that voters or consumers would act radically differently in the two environments. The problem is that voters do not realize the full economic cost of their actions and there is no real constraint on what politicians can offer to induce people to vote for them. There is a tendency, therefore, for politicians to offer vote inducements to the electorate that may not be of long-term benefit. Finally, Tullock (1978) develops similar themes in relation to bureaucrats, portraying them as self -interested budget maximizers. While politicians try to 'buy' votes, this creates the capacity for bureaucrats to expand budgets and increase their own standing. Government consequently becomes 'over supplied' with bureaucrats who intervene in the market for their own ends and without regard to long-term consequences.

Public Choice theorists argue that political institutions must be designed to facilitate individual liberty by placing limitations on the activities of self-interested politicians and bureaucrats (King, 1987, p. 104). Echoing Hayek and Friedman, market principles are the best basis for any decisions, but where political inputs are required a unanimous decision should be necessary (Buchanan, 1975). The status quo then becomes preferable to any decision harming even one person.

PCT has been used to analyze planning by, among others, Poulton (1991) and Pennington (2000):

> Consumers as voters desire planning insofar as they perceive it as improving their personal well-being; planners as advisors and administrators, seek to maximise their personal return from their employment; and politicians seek to utilise planning as a means to help attain or retain political power. (Poulton, 1991, p. 266)

Planning is another way of gaining political and personal advantage and its 'proper', that is, market-supportive role will be secondary to that. Pennington takes this one step further and uses PCT to help explain why planning has not met its postwar aims of protecting the environment and being part of the welfare state, but has instead helped redistribute wealth from the poor to the middle classes.

Although disparate, the liberal tenet of the neo-liberalism can be summed up by a begrudging two cheers for limited and local intervention in the urban areas: 'The issue is therefore not whether one ought not to be for town planning but whether the measures to be used are to supplement and assist the market or to suspend it and put central direction in its place' (Hayek, quoted in Lai, 1999, p. 1573).

## Conservatism

Although of far less influence than its liberal partner in the neo-liberal approach to planning, the conservative strand of theory has served to modify liberal market instincts. There is little doubt that in some areas of public policy, such as law and order, conservatism has been more important than liberalism in neo-liberal thinking. There is far less coherence to the conservative tenet of neo-liberalism than liberalism *per se*, though its core ideas have been an integral aspect of the political right for longer than the market-orientated element. One consequence of a lack of general agreement is that there is more abstraction and poeticism in the language of conservative writers, which the more economics-based liberal theory lacks. Conservatism, according to one of its most eloquent proponents Michael Oakeshott, is about being disposed to think and behave in certain ways:

> To be conservative, then, is to prefer the familiar to the unknown, to prefer the tried to the untried, fact to mystery, the actual to the possible, the limited to the unbounded, the near to the distant ... the convenient to the perfect, present laughter to utopian bliss. (Quoted in Kristol, 1996, p. 10)

The problem with liberalism, according to conservatives, is its atomistic nature – it requires inequality and poverty and therefore undermines social stability and authority:

'A truly liberal model can never satisfactorily be accommodated by Conservatism precisely because it lacks any conception of order and authority not dictated by individual reason' (Norton and Aughey, 1981, p. 41). King (1987) argues that as such conservatism is secondary to liberalism because it arises primarily in response to the consequences of liberal economic policies. But Aughey (1984) regards it as being far closer to neo-liberal thinking than liberalism. This debate is a distraction as far as we are concerned, but the relative importance of either strand has been significant in policy development as we shall see later. For now, two aspects of conservatism concern us: the emphasis upon the authority of the state and its distaste for democracy.

The authority of the state is paramount in the conservative strand of the neo-liberalism and particular contempt is reserved for any activity or organization that may undermine that authority, which includes most aspects of the postwar social democratic consensus and the welfare state. The provision of universal welfare is seen as decreasing self-reliance and responsibility and questioning the role of the family. Closely allied with this breakdown of tradition and traditional roles in the eyes of conservatives are social consequences such as rising crime, disorder, vandalism etc. The answer is to reassert the state's authority; providing the power to command and coerce those who would otherwise reform and destroy (Thornley, 1993: 40): 'there can be no freedom without order. There can be no order without authority; and authority that is impotent or hesitant in the face of intimidation, crime or violence, cannot endure' (Thatcher, quoted in Eccleshall, 1994, p. 85). To achieve this the state must appeal to innate feelings of custom and a respect for law and order. It is not unnatural, then, that conservatives also have a natural suspicion of democracy. Parallels can be drawn here between the Public Choice theorists' distaste for 'vote buying' and utility maximizing by the electorate. The outcome according to both critiques is the dictatorship of the masses, as opposed to the preference of the market (liberal) or a strong state (conservative): 'society depends on the cooperation of unequals – of the few who lead and give orders, and of the many who follow and obey' (Mallock, quoted in Eccleshall, 1994, p. 80). Another link between the liberals and conservatives can be found in the latter's suspicion of bureaucrats or the 'new class' as Kristol (1978) terms them. Again, such bureaucrats are seen as not being neutral, but acting on behalf of the forces of social democracy and encouraging concepts such as welfare and democracy.

Why and how the fusion of these two sets of ideas emerged has not been satisfactorily explained. What is clear is that neo-liberalism was and is a phenomenon not restricted to any particular state and its ideas have, to greater and lesser degrees, been picked up and used throughout the world. What is clearer is that neo-liberalism was mainly Anglo-American in origin. In both countries the market has long held a primacy over the role of the state. Both countries (in different ways) dabbled with interventionist policies both before and after World War II and both 'suffered' what the political right perceived as an excess of personal freedom in the 1960s and afterwards, which began to question the traditional role of the state as guardian of the public good. The election of the Conservative Party in the UK in 1979 and the Republicans in the USA in 1981 heralded similar approaches to the state and the market. As Ronald Reagan said during his first year of office, 'Government is not the solution to our problems. Government is the problem.'

How these two contradictory strands have been brought together in neo-liberalism may not be as difficult to grasp as it appears, though it has led to a great deal of confusion not only from observers but in government as well. The main problem in exploring the coherence of the New Right beyond theory is that we need to examine the practice of government. Government actions and policies are influenced by a variety of factors, including electoral popularity, inherited policies etc., all of which can sway an ideological approach. In addition, various commentators have questioned the coherence of liberalism and conservatism within the New Right (Riddell, 1983; Hirst, 1989; Levitas, 1986). There is little doubt that different elements within the New Right, and especially within the New Right governments in the UK and USA, approach policy in different ways. Beesley (1986) distinguishes between the two strands by claiming liberalism stresses the individual, freedom of choice, market security and minimal government, while conservatism emphasizes strong government, social authoritarianism, disciplined society, hierarchy and subordination. As Kavanagh (1987, p. 107) points out, the political practice of the New Right combines both sides. Therefore, there must be some common ground between the two. First, there is significant overlap between the two strands concerning the role of the state, including its role in security and law and order which requires centralization of power in government. Second, both strands are suspicious of democracy, as we have seen; the liberals because of its 'vote buying' potential and the conservatives because of its permissiveness. Third, there is a degree of symbiosis between the two. Liberals need a strong state to contain dissent and police the market. Conservatives need the potential for material wealth offered through the market to justify a more authoritarian state.

However, the real test of consistency in the New Right can only be gauged through it implementation. Can you combine liberalism and conservatism both in planning theory and in practice?

## Neo-liberalism and planning

Although we can identify the two central tenets of neo-liberal thinking, it was not clear how these would apply to land use planning. One of the series editors of this book, Andy Thornley, has questioned whether neo-liberalism is a school of planning theory in the same way that, say, the collaborative school is. He has a point in that there are fewer planning theorists writing from a neo-liberal perspective. This is partly explained by the broadly collectivist mindset of planners generally – to become a planner or planning academic is to enter into a world where the common good is raised above that of the individual. As we have seen, neo-liberalism is hostile to many aspects of the state and is not, ordinarily, attractive to an interventionist mindset. Nevertheless, there are some writers on planning theory from a neo-liberal perspective, such as Mark Pennington, Alan Evans, Anthony Sorensen and Martin Auster to name a few. But I think this is to ignore the nature of planning theory, which, as I pointed out in Chapters 1 and 2, lacks broad theoretical thinking in any case and certainly far less than, say, economics or politics. Neo-liberalism is more diffused than other schools of planning theory but it is still a school of theory. What gives it added significance, and the reason why I have chosen the broader field of neo-liberalism rather than classical liberal theory, is that it has been applied to planning.

Planning has not been immune from a variety of approaches seeking to interpret and alter it in line with neo-liberal philosophy.

Apart from the wide-ranging criticism of the principles and practice of postwar planning, all the works that have attempted to translate neo-liberal theory into an approach to planning have one common feature. All agree that there is a need for *some* form of land use control and all believe that control should be centrally directed and orientated to help rather than hinder the market.

Regardless of the system or country, the broad criticisms are similar. The UK system, according to the neo-liberals is probably best summed up by Jones (1982): 'Planning policy in Britain is ill conceived and poorly administered. The aims of it are obscure and there is little evidence that they are achieved even where they can be discerned' (Jones, 1982, p. 25). The answer in relation to the USA, according to Siegan (1972), is not to tinker with the system: 'Better zoning is no more the answer to no zoning than better censorship is to no censorship' (quoted in West, 1974, p. xii). But this does not mean a bonfire of planning controls. Nearly all critics recognize what Hayek termed externalities such as pollution, noise etc. in urban living. Pearce *et al.* (1978) maintain that it would perhaps be the planners' most important contribution to efficient and just resource allocation if they were able to communicate the importance of externalities (Pearce *et al.*, 1978, p. 86). Pennance (1974) goes on to call for planning to concentrate on, 'The establishment of precisely what are the important kinds of externality generated by urban existence, how they call for planning intervention and how they might be handled by general modifications to our system of property control' (Pennance, 1974, p. 19). Common arguments put forward regarding the impact of a lack of land use controls and alternative systems are usually based on the approach found in the works of Jacobs (1961). According to the former, the aim of planning should be to encourage the diversity that normally springs naturally from the operation of the market. Current planning regulations do not contain the necessary degree of flexibility to allow the myriad of uses inherent within urban areas to develop. What is required, therefore, is a system that does not classify businesses into strict categories and zone land accordingly.

Many of the critics of postwar planning draw upon Siegan's work to justify alternative approaches to regulation (see, for example, West, 1974; Jones, 1982; Walters, 1974). Jones is one of many who claim that the lack of land use controls would not be the nightmare planners would have us believe:

> Defenders of planning are apt to conjure up visions of the hideous and garish free-for-all which would result if it were removed. It is quite possible, though, that the resultant order might be more popular to tastes and convenience than the environment imposed by the planning class. (Jones, 1982, p. 21)

Anthony Steen (1981) concurs with the notion that market mechanisms are best left to allocate land uses. Discussing bringing new life back to cities he considers, 'This means abandoning a rigid zoning policy, doing away with all manner of planning restrictions and burying structure plans' (Steen, 1981, p. 62–3). As well as criticizing current practice, most writers offer constructive alternatives broadly following two types. The first is concentrated on wholesale structural reform of land use control with a renewed emphasis on the market. The second also involves structural reform, though recognizes differing degrees of control to address differing spatial requirements. These two types of alternative, major structural reform and spatial differentiation, both contain a combination of liberal and conservative perspectives on planning though to differing degrees. It is clear that the general concerns upon which these alternatives are based fall into three categories:

- the relationship between the state and the market;
- administrative discretion as a basis for decision-making;
- the cost of the planning system in terms of administration of the system and the opportunity cost of delays and refusals of permission to develop.

The first form of alternative put forward is based on market mechanisms and a rule of law covering nuisance and restrictive covenants limiting the scope of development. Typical of this approach is that of Jones (1982), who suggests a five-point plan. First, a major structural reform would replace the entire planning system with land use tribunals, which would decide on cases of noise and pollution between uses and what should be done. Second, private covenants would replace conditional planning permission, which would be drawn up on an individual or area basis. Third, there would be direct ministerial control over politically sensitive proposals in rural or environmentally sensitive areas. Fourth, third-party insurance would be required for all private building to cover claims against externalities such as loss of light and, fifth, there would still be the need for public inquiries for large proposals such as power stations. This wholesale replacement based on market mechanisms is popular throughout the critics of planning (see, for example, Bracewell-Milnes, 1974, p. 92; West, 1974, p. 29). However, Jones's (1982) work came to a different conclusion with regard to their alternative and this forms the basis of the second approach: there should be major structural reforms that simplify the planning system and remove unnecessary restriction.

An alternative system based on spatial differentiation would be founded on three zones. The first type of zone, the 'restricted' zone, would still have controls as now, although procedures would be simplified and administration would be central (Thornley, 1993). The second type of zone would be for industrial areas in inner cities, where the only regulation would be on the grounds of safety, public health, pollution and nuisance control. The third type of zone would cover the remaining areas – general zones for residential estates etc. – and, according to Thornley's (1993) interpretation, would occupy the middle ground between strict conservation and planning-free 'industrial zones'.

Similarities between all the proposals for alteration can be seen to exist and include a move away from discretionary planning towards 'blueprint' or 'zoning'-based planning, a shift from the accepted role of public participation to a more limited arena for input with more clearly defined criteria, a greater reliance on the market and a tiered approach to planning involving a 'horses for courses' approach to the needs of different areas. According to Thornley (1993), the ideas of the critics of planning differ at the level of detail:

> In general terms there seems to be agreement that the planning system has enormous faults and that the process of determining the use and control over land should be shifted away from the planning system, and its political context, into the market and legal arena. (Thornley, 1993, p. 117)

It is possible to draw out three common principles from the critics in their alternatives for planning that closely follow the liberal and authoritarian tenets of neo-liberalism. These principles, in whole or in part, form the basis of a theoretical neo-liberal approach to planning (Table 5.1).

*Table 5.1* **Common principles in alternative approaches to planning**

| Principle | Manifestation |
|---|---|
| Rule of law | System based on tribunals, covenants, third-party insurance |
| Centralization | Centrally directed approach with no local discretion |
| Market orientation | Minimal regulation and the provision of information to help the market make investment decisions |

*Source*: based on Allmendinger and Thomas, 1998.

It is obvious from Table 5.1 that the extent to which these three principles are germane depends on the different approaches of the individual critics of planning. So, whereas Jones (1982) has a distinct emphasis on a rule of law and market orientation, the Adam Smith Institute pursue spatial differentiation (a three-tiered system). This gives a wide scope of possible change from a wholesale replacement of the system to a modified existing system. The obvious question is: what are the criteria that justify the use of, say, a rule of law, in one circumstance and centralization in another?

The critics of planning clearly reflect the two tenets of neo-liberalism. The most obvious parallel lies in the emphasis on liberal market mechanisms. A major emphasis in the work of authoritarian and liberal strands is on the threat not of planning but of democracy itself and the emergence of what Kristol (1978) and others regarded as a 'class' of bureaucracy as described by Poulton above. Obviously, authors such as Jones (1982) and Walters (1974) consider that planners are among such a class and many of the alternative systems remove this perceived deficiency from land use regulation.

Along with criticism of planners themselves, there is also a general resistance to change from society, which is recognized in the authoritarian strand of neo-liberalism (Hirst, 1989). Many of the references within the alternative options for planning recognize the existence of externalities concerned with the land market and point towards the need for a (modified) system addressing issues such as conservation etc. These concessions could be seen to be a response to pressure from voters normally sympathetic to deregulation. However, the strong state of the authoritarians would be necessary to resist pressures to retain planning controls in most areas.

Another authoritarian strand concerns the need to do more than simply 'roll back the frontiers of the state' – people need to be forced to become more enterprising. Incomes from the land market have, since the war, been to a large extent guaranteed by supply-side deficiencies, including the need to obtain planning permission. The removal of this constraint would lead to competition and the necessity for landowners and users to adjust to maintain their position, leading to a greater efficiency of land use. Perhaps the most important overall relationship between neo-liberal theorists, such as Hayek and those who have sought to translate these ideas into an alternative for planning, lies in the assumption upon which their proposals are based. Planning is perceived as a supply-side constraint to economic growth. The demand side of the equation, according to this theory, is coiled and waiting to take advantage of a freeing up of regulations.

The first question we addressed concerned whether liberal and conservative principles could be applied to planning and the answer would seem to be yes, but a qualified yes. Clearly of the three common principles (Table 5.1) the liberal emphasis on market orientation and rule of law has been paramount. But can you combine a liberal rule of law with conservative centralization? Jones's (1982) approach discussed above manages both but this is theoretical. Can this be sustained in practice? Evidence from studies of neo-liberal governments, such as those of Margaret Thatcher in the 1980s, suggest not. We now turn our attention to the second question: can there be a practical neo-liberal approach to planning? To answer this we will examine a UK example, simplified planning zones (SPZs).

## Simplified planning zones: neo-liberal planning in practice?

Simplified planning zones are arguably the most radical attempt by the Thatcher Conservative governments to reorientate UK planning along neo-liberal lines (Allmendinger, 1997). Since its inception in the 1947 Town and Country Planning Act, the UK planning system has been based on regulation supported by guidance and information (Healey *et al.*, 1988). Decisions on development proposals are made 'on their merits' with regard being had to a development plan where appropriate. Unlike other systems, the plan itself does not confer permission and there is no guarantee that decisions will even follow the plan. A considerable degree of discretion is built into the system to grant or refuse permission. Although the weight given to the plan in determining applications was altered in 1990, this approach characterized the postwar years.

SPZs promised to do away with this by introducing a combination of plan and permission. The 1984 proposals saw SPZs as being suitable in most parts of the country with no limit on their size. They could, in effect, be adopted by local planning authorities to cover their whole area. At this time they clearly involved a combination of all three aspects of neo-liberal thinking contained in Table 5.1. They minimized discretion and introduced a rule of law by granting planning permission in advance. They had a clear market orientation in opening up the kinds of developments that would be allowed and ceding centralized control to the Secretary of State through reserve powers to direct local planning authorities to adopt a zone and even impose one if necessary.

Reaction to the 1984 proposals was mixed. While some private companies and landowners welcomed deregulation in principle, many local planning authorities and other public bodies heavily criticized both the assumptions behind the zones and the proposals themselves. Nevertheless, the government proceeded with the idea and introduced it in the 1986 Planning and Housing Act. As the Act progressed through Parliament various debates were held on the concept. It was here that the divisions within the neo-liberal approach began to emerge.

Although not all of the Conservative Members of Parliament (MPs) at the time could have been described as neo-liberal, many were. Tensions began to emerge between the government's approach and that of many of its own MPs, particularly on the question of the balance between the liberal and conservative elements. It became obvious that some members did not agree with the liberalization of planning and argued instead for retention of the system but with less local and more central control: 'Many local authorities are hostile to development ... therefore it might be wise for the government [to take the decision to have such a zone] and not leave it to the local authorities themselves' (Richard Alexander,

*Hansard*, 4 February 1984). Others thought that SPZs did not go far enough. What they wanted was a complete deregulation of the system with only a minimal structure retained 'Rather than tinkering with the system we need outright radical reform' (Anthony Steen, Hansard, 13 March 1986). This left the government in an awkward position. After following both liberal and conservative strands they now had to defend a neo-liberal approach against the more exclusive positions of both tenets. The result was that to gain the support it needed from its own MPs the government had to tone down and alter its proposals. Assurances were given to some MPs that they would not have SPZs forced upon them in rural (mostly Conservative-voting) areas. Others were assured that local planning authorities would not be able to avoid the zones and could not frustrate them through attaching too many conditions. In the end, after various changes, one Opposition MP was moved to comment, 'It occurred to me that this was not quite the mad dash for freedom that some Conservative members were looking for from SPZs' (John Cartwright, Hansard, 13 March 1986). The result has been less than successful. Considering that SPZs could have changed the face of planning in the UK there are actually only a handful in existence covering a few hundred hectares in total. They have proved to be unpopular both with the public and private sectors for a variety of reasons. First, following the fudge over liberal and conservative pressures the guidelines that accompany SPZs are very vague about what they are meant to achieve and in what areas they are suitable. The effect has been that local planning authorities and others are unsure about where they are appropriate and have consequently avoided them. Second, some of the liberal deregulatory assumptions behind them have been questioned. Firms, landowners and developers did not want the kind of certainty offered by market mechanisms as in the rule of law – they preferred the certainty of the current system, which allowed them to comment on the proposals of others. Third, practice has exposed the fragility of terms such as 'certainty and flexibility'. In practice, the zones have demonstrated that you cannot have both at the same time. Flexibility requires a range of uses and developments to be permitted; but this created uncertainty for adjoining landowners and users within the zones and immediately adjacent to them. Finally, it is not clear why some powers have been centralized while others have been based on a rule of law approach and why certain degrees of discretion have been kept. If discretion is anathema, then why didn't the government remove it altogether? The answer lies in the application of theory. While liberalism would call for the removal of discretion, conservatism and its centralizing ethic requires some to be maintained. In addition, the planning system itself was electorally popular, particularly in protecting those rural areas from the pressure of development.

## Critiques of neo-liberalism

As Low (1991) points out, whatever the practical outcome of neo-liberal planning theory, it leaves little comfort for planners, whose proper role under such a regime is likely in most approaches to be radically different than at present. Similarly, few would disagree that many of the criticisms of planning by the neo-liberals have not been without some foundation – blueprint planning, bureaucratic decision-making etc. But this is not to say that the balance between freedom and intervention introduced by the neo-liberalism is without criticism. In particular, neo-liberal theory can be criticized at two levels: theoretical and practical.

Klosterman (1985) has pointed to the inefficiencies of markets, particularly in relation to land. For markets to work they require a number of preconditions, including large numbers of buyers and sellers, broadly identical goods, sufficient information and perfect mobility for production, labour and consumption. The land market is not a commodity like any other and does not meet these criteria: 'The numerous obvious divergencies between markets in the real world and economists' competitive market ideal justify a range of government actions fully consistent with private property, individual liberty and decentralised market choice' (Klosterman, 1985, quoted in Campbell and Fainstein, 1996, p. 152). As well as difficulties in applying the market principle to land, Lindblom (1977) takes up a more fundamental stance, attacking the idea that markets support liberty. People without property are not free and are excluded from any benefits that such 'freedom' may bring. It is also not the case that people have always 'earned' their property in some efficient market exchange. The current distribution may have involved coercion in a previous age and much property is still inherited. Similarly, the idea that markets are not coercive is false.

Markets can exclude participation or favour people or groups, for example, those without access to the resources to participate or those with greater access to power respectively.

In addition to these criticisms of markets, much more fundamental points are raised by Gray (1993). According to his analysis, the irony of neo-liberalism is that it damned planning as imperfect and the product of modernity, but applied its own rationalism as a solution – rationalism that was as much a product of modernity and the Enlightenment. While imperfectability was recognized within institutions of government it was not recognized in the institutions of the market. The neo-liberal fascination with the market supposes that the functions and limits of state activity can be specified once and for all, by a theory, instead of varying with the history, traditions and circumstances that people and government inherent (Gray, 1993, p. xii). Further, markets are not institutions that are independent and products of a spontaneous order. Instead, they are sustained by cultural traditions and created by government. In a forerunner to Hutton's (1995) critique, Gray argues that markets and institutions are actually based on trust and integrity, hardly faceless and purely logical: 'rationalist tradition [has] infected the political presumptions of the New Right, which also has the characteristics of technical, or constitutional fixes (1993, p. xiii). Mechanisms such as negative income tax to tackle poverty or the removal of discretion in planning assume the solution to problems by a single institutional rule or device. What SPZs demonstrated was that many other factors were important in creating an environment where development could take place; knowledge about what others were doing on land next to your own, certainty that your investment was not going to be adversely affected by another's decision – all things derived from the erstwhile planning regime. There can be too much uncertainty in markets, which can be counterproductive, a point that Hutton (1995) makes clearly. As Gray (1993, p. xv) concludes, 'The political thoughts of the New Right . . . suppresses recognition of the institutions of the market as being fallible, as frail and as obdurately perfect as any other human institution.'

In addition to the theoretical problems, there are also practical problems in applying neo-liberal theory to planning. As Thornley (1993) points out, it is not at all clear how neo-liberals define externalities that justify intervention. Throughout the 1980s, in the UK at least, the definition of externalities seemed to shift until it eventually included matters originally excluded, such as design. As in the case of SPZs, other neo-liberal approaches to planning in the UK exhibited the conflict between economic and environmental criteria, as well as conflicts between a rule of law and centralization. As Eccleshall puts it, 'Conservatives will continue to squabble over the legitimate activities of government while agreeing about the need for social inequality and a strong state' (1994, p. 86). Planning exhibited this confused approach. While few would doubt that the planning policies and politics that emerged under neo-liberalism constituted a distinctive change (Savage and Robins, 1990), it would seem that, apart from anti-planning rhetoric, the approach of neo-liberalism in the UK has been characterized by a degree of confusion and inconsistency. This brings us to another point. As Levitas (1986) ponders, perhaps too much emphasis has been placed on the coherence of neo-liberalism. Or, as Rutherford (1983) argues, perhaps it has intellectual consistency that cannot be sustained in practice. Kavanagh (1987) tends to side with the Rutherford's view. Divisions within neo-liberalism run deep, but this does not preclude common approaches as discussed earlier. Problems arise dues to what Bulpitt (1986) calls 'statecraft' – or the art of politics.

## Conclusions

Despite Fukuyama's 'end of history' thesis, it would appear that the form of neo-liberalism typical of the Thatcher and Reagan years has had its day in the UK and USA. Apart from some die-hards who claim, like Marxists, that their ideas were incorrectly applied or wilfully distorted (Gray, 1993), the agenda seems to have moved, and planning is no exception to this (Allmendinger and Tewdwr-Jones, 1997). Hutton's (1995) analysis combined with the search for alternatives among many neo-liberals seem to back up Gray's point about context being important. Economic globalization and environmental concerns are now driving national policies on land use planning. The former requires less intervention, while the latter requires a more active state. The search is now on for a smarter planning. This includes, as one UK government inquiry into planning put it, efficiency and effectiveness in planning:

> while planning policies and processes aim to address market failures, there can also be costs associated with government intervention. Where information is imperfect, plans may under- or over-provide for certain non-market goods, while the transaction costs of intervention may be high. There may also be unintended consequences of policy. The planning system therefore needs to ensure it tackles market failures in an efficient and effective manner. (Barker, 2006, para. 1.5)

There is a realization that just as markets do not achieve optimal results neither does planning. Temporally, neo-liberalism emerged at a time of crisis and rethinking of the role of the state during the economic crises of the 1970s. Like Marxism, the central ideas had been around for at least a century until they and their proponents found their niche. Spatially, it emerged in the Anglo-Saxon economies, which were more open to free-market ideas than the more centre-left social-democratic countries of continental Europe. As the economic crisis has passed, so have many of the justifications and demands for a more radical and minimalist role for the state.

Overall, neo-liberal theory helped identify many of the problems of civil society, be it the economy, bureaucracies, the role of the state or whatever. As an explanation, like Marxism, it gave us a useful critique. But its application demonstrated its inherent contradictions and shortcomings. Luckily for planners, the practical application of theory was hampered by these contradictions.

# 6 Pragmatism

## Introduction

Pragmatism and neo-pragmatism are highly practical approaches to planning. Pragmatism emphasizes direct action regarding specific problems – what works best in a given situation or circumstance. This has led some to accuse pragmatism of being conservative and blind to the deeper forces and structuring influences in society. In that respect it is the antithesis of the political economy approach discussed in Chapter 4. Pragmatism has its roots in an historical philosophical dispute regarding the nature of reality and experience. These debates need not concern us too much here. What is of relevance for planning is the ways in which a pragmatic stance is about 'getting things done':

> Given the theoretical pluralism in planning, and the evident failings of most of the (theoretical) positions discussed to get to grips with the specific practice of planning anti-theoretical reactions are no surprise. Many planners are now desperately concerned to demonstrate their 'relevance' to local councils, to central government and to a highly critical public. The emphasis is on 'getting things done' . . . producing visible results. This is no doubt a commendable objective, but the creation of products in isolation from questions of purposes and values is ultimately a socially dangerous activity. It also makes planners more than usually vulnerable to the charge that they are nothing more than blind operators of the system within which they find themselves. (Healey, McDougall and Thomas, 1982, p. 10)

As with all the theories and positions discussed in this book, time and space are as central to an understanding as the theory itself. Action and 'getting things done' were a dominant theme of planning during the 1980s in the UK. As I discuss in Chapter 5, a neo-liberal government pursued an anti-state and -planning approach throughout that decade. Many in the public sector found themselves having to justify their existence and an action-orientated approach helped that. In the USA, 'getting things done' has always been a more dominant philosophy behind land use regulation. It is not surprising, therefore, that pragmatism itself and its interpretation as a theory or approach to planning largely originated there. Pragmatism is the one major philosophical movement to originate and remain more or less completely in the USA. The flavour of pragmatism reflects an American concern for practical and 'common sense' solutions within an agreed liberal-democratic framework. It is often impatient and dismissive of grand or abstract theorizing.

Despite developments in pragmatism, particularly in recent years, the basic philosophy and core remain the same. It is now clear that pragmatism as a philosophy of practice is not simply about 'getting things done'. It has developed into an approach to complex and intractable problems based around the role of the planner and the use of language. In this respect it has some close parallels with the collaborative approach. But it is also has some links with postmodern thinking, especially through the work of Richard Rorty (Rosenfeld, 1998). It was Rorty who first claimed that pragmatism was postmodernism ahead of its time as it too rejected what postmodern theorists term meta-narratives or foundational truth (see Chapter 8). There is also an element of post Marxist thinking rolled in. Neo-pragmatism, as some call it, accepts that an incremental approach that focuses upon action misses inequality and powerful relations in society. What is now called for is a more critical perspective that still focuses upon action but seeks to do so in a way that is inclusive rather than (by default) perpetuating inequality.

The result is a potent mix of philosophy, theory and practice that on the surface appears simple but is, in fact, much deeper, particularly in the light of recent developments. There are also some unresolved tensions in a pragmatic approach to planning. Such tensions have led to criticisms that rightly point to pragmatism's power blindness. As philosophers and planning theorists have developed the core ideas of pragmatism to take on board these criticisms it now begins to resemble a cross between postmodernism and collaborative planning, taking elements of both. This may be over-simplistic. There are some important differences, as I discuss below, but it is worth flagging up that pragmatism is not as straightforward as it may appear. This is compounded by the different emphases that various philosophers of pragmatism stress.

## What is pragmatism?

The dictionary definition of pragmatism usually involves the idea of a practical approach to problems. But what is meant by 'practical' is more fundamental to pragmatism as a movement or philosophy. Pragmatists such as John Dewey, Richard Rorty, Charles Peirce or William James argue that we have an incremental and pragmatic view of the world devoid of *a priori* theorizing. We decide what to believe not because it corresponds to the reality of the world, but because an idea or belief makes sense to us and helps us act. We change our beliefs not because we have been given a new or privileged view of the world, but because new beliefs make more sense of it or resolve inconsistencies. Rather than philosophizing about problems, Dewey and Rorty argue instead for an intellectually practical approach. 'Doing and making' as activities both alter the problem as perceived and provide a solution. Knowledge, argued Dewey, is only one aspect of experience. Dewey also 'emphasises praxis and the application of critical intelligence to concrete problems, rather than *a priori* theorising' (Festenstein, 1997, p. 24). This is a more fluid and (some would argue) relativistic perspective than found in many philosophies. As William James puts it:

> the great assumption of the intellectuals is that truth means essentially an inert static relation. When you've got your true idea of anything, there's an end of the matter. You're in possession: you know; you have fulfilled your thinking destiny. You are where you ought to be mentally; and nothing more need follow on that climax of your rational destiny. Epistemologically you are in stable equilibrium.
>
> Pragmatism, on the other hand, asks its usual question, 'Grant an idea or belief to be truth,' it says, 'what concrete difference will its being true make in anyone's actual life? How will the truth be realised? What experience will be different from those which would obtain if the belief were false? What, in short, is the truth's cash-value in experimental terms?' (James, 1878, quoted in Soloman, 1997, p. 207)

This is almost the response many academics get when trying to explain what they do – *that's all very fine, but what use is it to me?* The pragmatists' frustration with abstraction and theorizing is clearly evident. Truth is not something that can be proven as such; it is the outcome of using an idea. If I choose one theory from a number of options that to me seems right and the outcome is successful then, as far as pragmatists are concerned, that is good enough. This raises the issue of how to choose between competing ideas or theories. Pragmatists emphasize cultural or social influences upon thought. Such influences provide us with what could be termed a 'mass' of ideas that help structure our thoughts. These also help us act on the basis of intuition – what we think is best or might happen. We develop instincts and a 'nose for the possible'.

Such a mass is difficult to alter even in the face of evidence that undermines it – we tend to believe things regardless of other views that dispel or ridicule it. This is because such beliefs are not simply a matter of weighing up evidence. Pragmatists argue that we cannot be expected to give reasons for such beliefs or answer every conceivable doubt, only those that we have ourselves. But, while we know that we must be sceptical about the future as we cannot guarantee it, we need to act and do so on the basis of our instincts – we are pragmatic in the everyday sense of the word. If there is a conflict between rationalism and intuition, then intuition is likely to be convincing.

This question of taking risks or acting on intuition is best exemplified by religion. William James argued that the existence of God could not be proven. It was a leap of faith. Yet many people either believe or do not believe. They do not withhold their support simply because it cannot be proven scientifically. As James put it:

> Just as a man who in a company of gentlemen made no advances, asked a warrant for every concession, and believed no one's word without proof, would cut himself off by such churlishness from all the social rewards that a more trusting spirit would earn – so here, one who would shut himself up in snarling logicality and try to make the gods extort his recognition willy-nilly, or not get it at all, might cut himself off forever from his only opportunity of making the god's acquaintance. (Quoted in Soloman, 1997, p. 322)

In other words, it costs us nothing to believe, particularly if there is a chance that it might be true. If we did not believe and God's existence was true we might have lost salvation. It is a wager or bet not based on evidence but a calculation of the odds and rewards.

A related aspect of this idea of a 'mass' of ideas is the issue of bias. If we have an 'apperceptive mass' of beliefs and values then the consequence is evidence of an attitude or bias. Pragmatists do not use the term 'bias' pejoratively, but as an inherent part of acting and thinking. Thinking back to Chapter 1, such a perspective is similar to Kuhn's concept of paradigm in some ways. Rather than a paradigm structuring thoughts and practices, pragmatists look at both the individual and social as structuring influences or biases, as they term them. One implication of this emphasis on the individual is that as we cannot get outside our own beliefs then certain views will be incommensurable and conflict therefore inevitable (again, a theme of Kuhn's concept of paradigms). There can be no recourse to an outside 'truth' with which to resolve differences.

The only way around such difference is through discourse or language. As Rorty puts it, 'Disagreements between disciplines and discourses are compromised or transcended in the case of conversation' (quoted in Mounce, 1997, p. 194). The central role given to language has some superficial parallels to the collaborative emphasis (see Chapter 9). But the big difference (and the overlap between pragmatism and postmodernism) is the rejection of absolutes, consensus or transcendental truths. Collaborative theorists advocate certain absolute truths about, for example, openness, freedom from oppression, etc. While pragmatists do not deny the desirability of such values, they argue that they are provisional, that is, they may be revised and examined through conversation and open discourse. It is the role of planners and philosophers to help facilitate such discourses by suggesting new ways of looking at an issue or being provocative and, sometimes, ironic.

Another implication of the idea that we cannot get beyond a highly personal perspective is the breakdown of the concept of theory and practice. We cannot empirically or objectively 'test' theories (for much the same reasons that Kuhn advanced, i.e., that values and subjective judgements will always be influential). Theories, therefore, become little more than expressions of beliefs – a pick and mix collection of thinking that we choose because it resembles what we already believe to be the case. A good and extreme example of this lies in the diametrically opposed theories of the neo-liberalism and critical theory covered elsewhere in this book. Neither are theories in the sense that they can be 'proven' – they are metaphysical in that respect. One subscribes to one or the other (or neither) on the basis of whether they fit with values such as equality. Indeed, pragmatism itself is just such a theory that we believe or don't – it may fit our *weltanshauung* or worldview or may not. I discuss one particular application of this, disjointed incrementalism, below.

Following from the need for open and reflective discourses to develop and challenge established beliefs and morals, Dewey and Rorty explore the role of liberal democracy as a means to achieve this. It is here that advocates of pragmatism begin to diverge in their opinions, though, again, the finer detail of this is not of relevance to us. Dewey argues that pragmatics becomes an open-ended, contingent search for knowledge or truth. To achieve this he introduces two foundational truths of his own. First, that liberalism in its purest form, that is, concerned with the individual and freedom, is the best basis for a pragmatic society. Second, that a scientific approach or methodology is the best method of ensuring that liberalism remains relevant and is the most appropriate means of providing an open-ended and contingent search.

The two aspects of Dewey's pragmatism are obviously related; liberalism providing the political and societal framework best suited to pragmatism, while scientific method, with its emphasis on continual criticism and reflection, allows democracy and liberalism to evolve to meet changing needs and desires. Rorty places less emphasis on science in the pursuit of a pragmatic approach and more on liberalism and communication, arguing that there was, 'nothing more important than the preservation of liberal institutions' (quoted in Festenstein, 1997, p. 113). Rorty does develop his alternative idea of a methodology. Most disagreements between people will occur under what Rorty terms 'normal' discourse situations – where there is common agreement upon values such as tolerance, respect for difference, etc. Here, open communication and discourse will be enough to resolve differences. However, in situations that Rorty describes as 'abnormal' such an approach will not be sufficient. Abnormal situations are where deeply embedded worldviews confront each other. Discussion alone will not persuade either side to alter their position. Would pro- and anti-abortionists be able to come to some agreement on a mutually agreeable way forward? Would pro- and anti-development groups be likely to reach a middle way? In such situations, Rorty suggests philosophers (or in our case planners) take a more proactive position as mediator, provoking new views or different ways of describing a situation in a way to work through any impasse. Like the normal situation, abnormal discourse centres on discussion and conversation. Conversations must be 'kept going' so as to reach some kind of agreement and the potential for further agreement is to be maintained.

Whether or not any agreement between different worldviews is possible or not is, at the very least, open to question. What is more important to us is the role of the planner in such a process. Rorty describes this role as 'ironist'. An ironist (literally, one who uses irony or the use of words to express something other than and especially the opposite of the literal meaning) will speak and act in line with liberal philosophy (e.g., emphasizing individual and economic freedom, greater individual participation in government, and constitutional, political and administrative reforms designed to secure these objectives). The ironist planner will be committed to and act in a way that secures open and democratic government (through, for example, public participation). In private, however, the ironist planner has the potential and duty to rethink these concepts, secure in the knowledge that a liberal philosophy prevails. In some ways this role is similar to that advocated by the collaborative theorists in the need to be constantly critical of the status quo and aware of the potential dominatory uses of language and bureaucracy.

Rorty rethought his concept of the ironist following criticism from postmodern and feminist perspectives. Critics attacked the central and power-laden role given to professionals such as planners in initiating and championing change and challenging static and oppressive power structures. There were two problems according to the critics. First, professionals exist because they have specialized and expert knowledge. Opening up that role to include others is likely to challenge that, as well as the prestige and rewards that accompanying it (e.g., salaries, etc.). Is there any motivation on the part of professionals to challenge such forces of domination? This is not only a point related to pragmatism but can also be aimed at collaborative and postmodern theory and practice.

Second, professionals work in bureaucracies and even if individuals were minded to challenge existing structures they have to do so from a position within that structure, which may be resistant (both implicitly and explicitly). But any individual is also employed by that bureaucracy. Challenging it will require either the support of the organization or a brave person. Rorty's rethought approach involved replacing his concept of irony with the notion of prophecy: 'Prophecy is about thinking what is still unthinkable. By inventing new metaphors, languages and ways of thinking, the prophet entices society in a particular direction and makes possible what might not otherwise be' (Harrison, 1998, p. 10–11).

In a similar way to the ironist a prophet is charged with imaging and working towards better futures. The difference seems to be that prophets are under a moral obligation to do so. Thus a prophet is beginning to resemble Davidoff's advocate. What has not changed, however, is the embedding of the ideas and actions of a prophet within liberal principles and liberal democracy.

This provides a very basic outline of pragmatism and it will be obvious that there are some similarities and differences with post-modernism and collaborative planning. Like postmodernism, there is an emphasis on incommensurability, though pragmatists introduce foundational principles such as liberalism. Like collaborative planning, there is the emphasis on language, though pragmatists reject ideas of consensus and are more relativist in their acceptance of ideas and opinions. The pragmatist, in William James's view,

> turns his back resolutely and once and for all upon a lot of inveterate habits dear to professional philosophers. He turns away from abstraction and insufficiency, from verbal solutions, from bad *a priori* reasons, from fixed principles, closed systems, and pretended absolutes and origins. He turns towards concreteness and adequacy, towards facts, action and towards power. This means the empiricist temper regnant and the rationalist temper sincerely given up. It means the open air and possibilities of nature, as against dogma, artificiality, and the pretence of finality in truth. At the same time it does not stand for any special results. It is a method only. (Quoted in Muller, 1998, p. 296)

## Planning and pragmatism

What does such an approach mean for planning? Charles Hoch (1984, 1996, 2002) has been the foremost advocate and interpreter of pragmatic ideas and planning and follows Dewey's interpretation of pragmatism most closely. In this he emphasizes experience rather than theory as the best arbiter of truth and practicality. He also argues for practical answers – those that work – to real problems. Finally, such a practical approach should be achieved through socially shared and democratic means. Here is the link to a pluralistic society – one where competing ideas are tested and the most effective and popular is used. Such an approach is central to liberalism.

John Dewey imagined how liberalism might best facilitate pragmatism and practical democracy. In Hoch's words, such a society would be comprised of 'a cluster of communities held together by a diverse assortment of agreements, traditions and conventions, arrived at through democratic deliberation' (1996, p. 31). Hoch goes on to argue that such a perspective and the ideas of pragmatism have close conceptual ties with different theories of planning (Hoch, 1984). Again, it is worth emphasizing that Hoch's perspective is distinctively North American. His interpretation of pragmatic thinking for planning include Meyerson's 'middle-range planning', Lindblom's 'incrementalism', Davidoff's 'advocacy planning', Friedmann's 'transactive planning' and Grabow and Heskin's 'radical planning': 'Clearly there are many differences among these authors, but I think their reliance on pragmatic concepts outweighs those differences' (Hoch, 1984, p. 340). I discuss Lindblom's incrementalism in more detail below, though the other theories all emphasize liberalism, action and discussion.

Hoch does not uncritically develop philosophical pragmatism into an approach for planning. In his later work (1996) he fuses pragmatism with an acknowledgement of power relations through the work of Foucault (see Chapter 8 on postmodernism for more on Foucault). According to Hoch, Foucault demonstrates how institutions such as professions, which sought to provide scientific and objective knowledge, have actually formed new centres of power that limit freedom and direct choice. This occurs through the mediating role of professionals, taking individual struggles and turning them into a 'category' that represents them through professional discourse. Thus, planners analyze problems such as traffic congestion, evaluate options and choose and implement solutions. The individual has a marginal role in this and is categorized, anticipated and processed by a 'mediating layer' of professional groups.

> Under Foucault's scrutiny, the practice of professionals serves a perverse modernity that promises security as it ensnares individuals in the categories of need. Foucault's critique cuts to the very heart of any theoretical effort to justify planning as a privileged moral and scientific practice in the service of public interest. (Hoch, 1996, p. 35)

The way out of such a situation, according to Hoch, is in the philosophy of pragmatism. While accepting Foucault's critique of modern forms of power, Hoch rejects his ultimate conclusions that seem nihilistic. Instead, pragmatism provides a way forward based on 'shared inquiry and common purpose' (Hoch, 1996, p. 37). Like Dewey, Hoch sees this being achieved through individual communities coming together and sharing experiences and values, as well as developing trust. Here, Hoch does not only have in mind physical communities such as villages or towns, but also communities of interest such as single mothers or issue communities such as environmentalists. The problem is not solidarity and trust within communities but between them. Ignorance and prejudice as well as more mundane issues of power mean that there needs to be an explicit and deliberate stance by planners and others to overcome such impediments to justice in a democratic context.

It is to the work of Habermas that Hoch turns to provide such a stance. As I discuss in Chapter 9, Habermas stresses the need for intersubjective (discussion between individuals and groups) communication based on relations of trust, sincerity, comprehension and legitimacy. Using such tools and approaches, Habermas argues that the more pernicious forms of domination and power can be overcome. Planners obviously have a role in this. Although they benefit from being in a powerful position *vis-à-vis* individuals and groups through personal gain, they should resist the temptation to sit back and instead engage critically and actively with conventions and norms. This may require planners to become unpopular or cut themselves off from career prospects, after all, 'the sceptical and ironic artist or designer cannot make way for others without diminishing himself or herself' (Hoch, 1996, p. 40):

> Instead of relying on rational methods that require practitioners to seek greater political authority and more professional power in order to do good, planners might benefit more from a critical review of the limits to bureaucratic command and adversarial democracy. Planners might

> consider identifying with the powers of the weak, identifying with colleagues, neighbours, and citizens rather than with the protocols of professional expertise. (Hoch, 1996, p. 42)

John Forester (1989) has also combined pragmatism with the work of Habermas and his notions of ideal speech to form what he terms 'critical pragmatism'. For Forester, planning is a highly practical activity that is based upon solving problems and making things happen. But rather than a purely pragmatic approach, Forester, like Hoch and Healey, also recognizes that there are powerful forces at work that could mean planning practice would merely reproduce inequality. Thus, a normative dimension is added to pragmatic planning that argues for a more open, democratic approach that is concerned with opening up planning to a greater plurality of voices and opinions. As Forester puts it:

> When 'solving' problems depends in large part on the interests, perceptions, commitments, and understandings of others, how can planners best convey their ideas, show what is consequential, expose dangers, and open up fruitful opportunities for action? In planning practice, talk and argument matter. (1989, p. 5)

The pluralist perspective on power relations, a practical emphasis upon problem solving and the role of argument and communication provide the backdrop to planning in the USA generally. Here, there is a diversity of formal planning powers that, on the whole, is less explicit than in Europe and elsewhere. Consequently, there is a greater degree of and emphasis upon negotiation (Teitz, 1996a, 1996b). Given this confluence of theory or philosophy and practice, it is hardly surprising that much of the work on pragmatism originates from the USA and has certainly been championed there to a greater extent than elsewhere. For Forester (1989), planning is essentially a pragmatic activity that is structured and influenced by power. Planners need to be aware of the ways in which they can 'anticipate obstacles and respond practically, effectively, in ways that nurture rather than neglect – but hardly guarantee – a substantially democratic planning process' (1989, p. 5). Such planning is based on communication with planners acting as gatekeepers, who selectively draw attention to a variety of possibilities. Again, like the pragmatists, Forester sees this activity occurring within liberalism. Planners cannot challenge such a framework (though whether or not in a different world they could is not clear) because they are too busy 'putting out brushfires, dealing with "random" telephone calls, debating with other staff, juggling priorities, bargaining here and organizing there, trying to understand what in the world someone else (or some document) means' (1989, p. 15).

In work planners are aware of distortions and powerful interests and should seek to challenge them through communication or, more accurately, through adherence to Habermas's ideal-speech approach, in much the same way Hoch advocates above. In essence, Forester is arguing for more open and democratic processes but ones in which the planner plays an active role in exposing and challenging powerful interests. Here we see the link between Rorty's ironist and prophet and Forester's 'progressive planner'. The role and daily functions of such a progressive planner also meets the broad thrust of pragmatism in being grounded squarely in 'what works best' and the situation at hand.

One outcome of this approach could be relativism or an 'anything goes' attitude. If a planner is constantly adapting to specific circumstances, then is there a 'right' or 'wrong'? Should the planner have principles or values that guide action? While rejecting *a priori* theorizing, Forester also rejects the idea of relativism in practice:

> To say that all claims express interests does not mean that all claims are equally sincere or warranted or respectable. There is simply no reason to accept as equally deserving of public consideration a claim by the owner of a small business seeking a zoning variance and a claim by an avowed bigot seeking to send people of one race to another country, people of one gender to the kitchen, or people of one religion to the jails. (1989, p. 59)

The problem is how can one simultaneously be pragmatic and hold onto values and beliefs. Pragmatic philosophy does this by having its two foundational principles: liberalism as an arena within which debate and discussion take place and pluralism as a principle of competing ideas and positions. It is with these two concepts that pragmatism as an approach for planning must be understood. I look in more detail at some of the problems with this below.

There has also been a broad interpretation of pragmatism for planning that seeks to integrate some of the ideas of postmodernism (Harper and Stein, 1995). Two central themes that recur throughout that field are an emphasis upon difference and an acceptance of what is termed 'new times'. The first issue concerns an acceptance and encouragement of difference. This could be at an individual, political or institutional level. Planning and planners should not seek to stultify or conceal difference through procedures or ideals such as consensus but encourage a more active plurality of positions. This relates to the idea of new times – a significant shift in factors such as technology, capitalism and knowledge, which means that many of the concepts of modernity such as society and progress no longer have the significance they once did. There is now significant disagreement, for example, about what terms such as 'equality' mean.

Accepting such ideas necessarily involves challenging foundational concepts such as liberalism. It does not necessarily involve a rejection of them but it questions *a priori* thinking from a more fundamental perspective. Where Harper and Stein differ from some postmodern perspectives is in their rejection of the full implications of this. The implication of an extreme emphasis upon difference precludes *any* consensus and thereby does not challenge existing power relations. They too follow a distinctly pragmatic line in arguing for practical and incremental change but emphasize a more open and less nihilistic concern with difference. Nevertheless, their approach is still to be found within the boundaries of liberalism and liberal-democracy.

Given the practical nature of pragmatism, it is not surprising that a number of studies have emerged that look at the daily practices of planning (see Liggett, 1996; Watson, 1998). Jean Hillier (1995) has also looked at the ways in which planners work through her study of postgraduate planning practitioners. Students emphasized the 'practical' and 'common sense' elements of their work. This contrasts sharply with the more technical-based knowledge that professional institutes such as the RTPI and planning theories such as systems or rational planning emphasize. Students also confirmed that in evaluating options they were likely to discount some options and favour others on the basis of intuition or experience – in much the same way that pragmatists emphasize. A difference therefore emerges between Forester's (1989) championing of *a priori* principles, such as Habermas's ideal speech, Hillier's preference for a form of hermeneutics and Colman's (1993) emphasis upon more 'coal-face' learning.

Pragmatism involves a great deal of emphasis on rather vague concepts such as irony and critical theory without much explanation of what this means for planning. One approach that has almost become synonymous with a pragmatic understanding of and general approach to planning is found in the works of Charles Lindblom and his theme of incrementalism. It must be stressed that while there are similarities between pragmatism and incrementalism there are also important differences. Lindblom's work has different theoretical foundations to Dewey or Rorty's pragmatism and has been summed up by some as a description of the ways things happen with a normative preference for such an approach. Lindblom's earlier work is also rather naively pluralist and ignores inequality in power and its implications. Pragmatists such as Rorty are more aware of power inequality (particularly, like Lindblom, after it was pointed out to them), hence their emphasis upon a more critical stance. Where pragmatism and incrementalism do overlap, however, is in their focus upon action and implementation and their embedding with liberal democracy. As Faludi puts it, 'Planning theory is therefore well advised to study Lindblom's writing, especially his component review of behavioural studies of planning, whilst remaining circumspect about his prescriptions' (1973, p. 120).

Lindblom (1959) takes a pragmatic (in the ordinary sense of the word) or incremental approach to policy analysis and the normative description of how planners and others should approach policy questions. I deal with Lindblom's criticisms of the systems and rational approaches to planning in Chapter 3. Here, I want to focus more upon his alternative, usually labelled under the umbrella of incrementalism though the title masked significant developments in Lindblom's thoughts.

Central to Lindblom's approach, as I outlined in Chapter 3, is the argument that policy makers *cannot* and *do not* 'think big'. A further step is taken by Lindblom in also adding that they *should not* do so. The most important reason for this, as far as we are concerned, centres on agreement or consensus. Like pragmatists, he argues that within liberal-democratic societies bargaining and 'mutual adjustment' are democratic and open. It also leads to the situation where implementation of a particular policy is more likely because more people are 'on board':

> When bureaucrats from different programs and agencies have to come into agreement with each other, they will to some considerable extent be led to take account of a great many more angles on a problem than if left to administer their own narrow policy segment by themselves. (Lindblom and Woodhouse, 1993, p. 69)

Decision-making should proceed on the basis of choice and policies that are only marginally different from each other. There is no great goal or vision, as much as a focus on day-to-day issues and problems. The methods employed are based on trial and error – the intuition much discussed by pragmatists.

To help those involved, Lindblom (1977) advanced methods to help promote an incremental decision-making and focus and simplify complex problems:

- The limitation of analysis to a few familiar alternatives.
- Intertwining values and policy goals with empirical analysis of problems.
- Focusing on ills to be remedied rather than on goals to be sought.
- Trial and error learning.
- Analyzing a number of options and their consequences.
- Fragmenting of analytical work to many partisan participants in policy-making.

It is not a giant leap to see the link between Lindblom's emphasis on agreement, consensus and mutual adjustment and the recent developments in collaborative planning theory (see Chapter 9). Forester (1989) raises two themes early on in his seminal *Planning in the Face of Power*. The first is a question: 'In a world of poor information and limited time to work on problems, how are careful analyses of alternative futures possible?'. The second is a statement: 'In planning practice, talk and argument matter' (1989, p. 5). Both seem to go to the heart of Lindblom's project. Yet Forester and other collaborative planning theorists reject Lindblom's normative or prescriptive approach. The main reason relates to the lack of critical awareness and power blindness that such an approach entails. A further criticism accuses incrementalism for saying 'little about the improvement of planning practice, about what planners should be doing and how they might do it' (Forester, 1989, p. 32).

To be fair, Lindblom responded to such criticism and in his later work (1977) did include an acceptance of unequal power relations. Large companies and other powerful groups could and would set the agenda of policy-makers. His response to this was to place a greater emphasis upon analyzing policy. Such macro-thinking and associated techniques are meant to address the more short-term and power-blind directions (the 'disjointed' aspect of incrementalism) in order to give *some* direction. Lindblom is in danger of moving close to the systems and rational approaches here, though he emphasizes that such strategic thinking is limited by its own realization of incompleteness and possibility.

The work of Hoch, Forester, Lindblom and others significantly develops the central ideas of pragmatism for planning to the extent that it may seem to be a different animal altogether. What is worth remembering are the central tenets. Harrison (1998) has provided a useful summary of the characteristics of pragmatism in relation to planning. First, pragmatism can provide planners with an ironic perspective on themselves and their actions. It emphasizes critical mechanisms that can be used both as a reflection upon the role of planners and ways of describing and looking at situations anew. It sees planning as an evolving activity whose purpose will change over time. Second, planning does not seek to uncover reality but to serve a practical purpose in our understanding of it. The role of planning is to encourage, engage with and ultimately arbitrate between competing theories and perspectives using criteria such as 'How does this theory help us deal with the world as it is?'. This may give rise to approaches that are incremental or short term. Third, pragmatism is concerned with the practice of planning and this has led to a renewed interest in the micro-politics of planning practice. A consequence of this has been a turn away from abstract theorizing and a shift towards looking at the actual practice of planning – what planners do rather than what theories say they do or should do. Fourth, the pragmatic focus on choice and contingency rather than abstract foundationalism emphasizes ethical deliberation. While Forester advances some criteria against which to assess planning practice, and pragmatists such as Rorty claim that pragmatism is not value-relative, there is still undoubtedly a lack of an ethical dimension in pragmatic planning. This does not mean to say that pragmatism discourages ethical deliberation but it does not come out in the same way as some other approaches and say 'this is right or wrong'. It does not, however, go as far as postmodern thinking in this respect as it is embedded within liberalism, which does involve certain ethical dimensions such as freedom of speech, etc. Finally, Harrison identifies the emphasis on human action as opposed to the abstract thinking as found in idealism, realism, Marxism, etc. This allows one to look at the practical dimensions of such theories – what difference do they make to planning and planners?

## Discussion of pragmatism and planning

Forester presents planning as a potential non-zero-sum game – if unnecessary distortions are removed then he implies that everyone will be a winner as open communication will inevitably lead to agreement. A further issue, however, is that there is an uneasy relationship between Forester's liberal convictions and the pragmatic rejection of foundational thought on the one hand and the *a priori* Kantian ethical agenda and the critical understanding of power distortion in the other. For one thing, he wants to have his cake and eat it – a postmodern/pragmatist concern with recognizing difference and a modern desire for consensus, a pragmatic suspicion of prescriptive thinking and the grounded, though vague, ethical framework that rejects some claims (bigots) over others (small business owners). Now, as I set out in Chapter 7, this fusion of foundational and non-foundational thought is the common position of most postmodern thinking if it is seriously concerned with acting in the real world. However, the fusion detracts from his excellent exegesis of the undoubted communicative role of planners by advancing short-sighted and (ironically) uncritical claims. At the core of the problem is the question: 'What foundations?'. For example, 'distortion' is of central concern to Forester, but distortion from what? Whose standards? Rorty side-steps this issue to a degree by setting out his stall as being unashamedly western/North American liberal-democratic. By fusing pragmatism with critical theory Forester opens himself up to a critical analysis that Rorty avoids. On whose behalf is Forester speaking? Why should planners give up power? Forester's analysis presents us with a pragmatic approach to a largely pragmatic activity called planning – but in fusing his critical theory, however unsatisfactorily, he exposes some of the shortcomings of pragmatism itself.

While Hoch's analysis of the pragmatic foundations of American planning theory provide an unconvincing account, of more use is his criticism of both pragmatism and the basis of pragmatic planning theory. This can be summarized into three broad themes. First, Hoch considers that the pragmatic dependence on experience treats it as homogeneous and inadequate in the identification of problems. There is an inherent historicist and progressive assumption underlying Dewey's assumptions regarding the efficacy of social action and consequently the role of planners to tackle problems. This assumption, according to Hoch, provides no analysis of the problem beyond the boundaries imposed by the incremental and necessarily short-sighted limits of incremental action. 'Davidoff does not evaluate the specific injustices that require advocacy, Friedmann gives no agenda to guide transactive dialogue, and Lindblom provides neither size nor direction for any increment in particular' (Hoch, 1984, p. 341). Second, Hoch questions the assumption that the problems pragmatic enquiry seeks to tackle are founded in the obstruction of social learning and reflection. They assume that we share a natural predisposition to solve problems through instrumental enquiry and that this predisposition is both a value and a tool of human progress. Hoch considers that we cannot simply assume the significance of such learning, which may expose deep divisions within society based on gender, class or race for example. In other words, we cannot assume a single direction as an outcome of social learning nor should we expect common responses – irrationality or more deeply held desires, through the use and misuse of power, may distort the interpretation and process of social learning. Hoch's point seems to be more directed at some planning theories here rather than pragmatism itself, particularly in the light of the more relativistic basis of truth that was also a mainstay of Dewey and latterly Rorty's thought. However, his general point is that pragmatism is power blind and that there is a danger of it perpetuating rather than tackling social problems. This is a fair criticism until you realize that the whole liberal *weltanshauung* of pragmatism in Dewey's work accepts inequality of outcome but argues instead for equality of opportunity. As such, it is not power blind so much as power accepting. Hoch seems to be arguing for a different conception of pragmatism than the Dewey/Rorty variety that is more radical in its potential for change and would not really be pragmatism at all.

Finally, he criticizes Dewey's reliance on the role of professionals in initiating and championing greater public participation in order to challenge moribund and inhibiting social structures that stand in the way of individual freedom and development. He feels that Dewey's confidence in the ability of voluntary associations between different interests ignores the socio-historical influences upon the role and opportunities for professions to initiate change. Most professionals work for state bureaucracies that limit their role. Further, given the centralization of power and the vested interest of professionals, Hoch feels that it is unrealistic to expect professionals to urge more public involvement as, 'The practical development of plans, the implementation of regulations and the allocation of resources, while they require the use of problem-solving ability, are still guided more by the force of politics than by the force of argument' (Hoch, 1984, p. 342). The result, mainly due to the issue of power, is that pragmatism is more of a useful theoretical insight as opposed to a worthy normative position for Hoch.

## Conclusions

Pragmatism as a philosophy masquerades as 'anti-theory', but is actually deeply theoretical. In its translation into indigenous planning theory it has been subject to spatial mediation through different interpretations of what it is to be practical in the face of power inequality. Thus, the US approach, while critical of existing power relations, is deeply embedded within a liberal-democratic framework, while European interpretations have been more sensitive to existing institutional realities and the possibility of alternatives. Such differences have been part of the criticisms of the pragmatic approach.

Dewey has been criticized for providing the basis for 'technocracy', as scientific method invades the political and social realm. This is particularly so as Dewey's conception of liberalism involves an active rather than passive society. Rejecting negative conceptions of liberalism, he argues that to be fully reflexive people have to be given the means to participate fully in society. Avoiding *a priori* ideas of how this might be achieved, he instead argues from first principles that if liberalism is taken as the liberation of human capacities to achieve their full development then this may involve, for example, the redistribution of wealth to overcome the biggest obstacle to full participation through lack of resources. Such detailed policy prescriptions cannot be foundational within pragmatism – they need to be considered in the light of specific situations. This has led to the criticism of incremental conservatism, as well as the view that his interventionist society is basically another justification for socialism. He is aware of this latter charge and claims instead that he is aiming for a 'planning' rather than a 'planned' society. Here, again, we encounter some connections with the collaborative approach and its eschewal of *a priori* limits upon processes other than the ideal speech concerns of Habermas. And, like the communicative and collaborative school, there is little detailed prescription with which to assess how such a society would work or what it may look like.

Despite these criticisms, pragmatism has been part of a practical approach to real problems. Its eschewal of grand theorizing has also been the foundation of another school of planning theory: advocacy.

# 7 Planners as Advocates

## Introduction

Although this chapter is entitled 'Planners as Advocates', it covers more diverse and fundamental issues concerning planning. In planning theory, advocacy is normally associated with the work of Paul Davidoff (1930–84), who argued for a deeply personal and highly political view of planning and planners. Such a view is usually contrasted with the more apolitical, technical and bureaucratic perspective and approach of, for example, the systems and rational approaches (see Chapter 3). The division between these two worldviews represents a cleavage that reflected attitudes in society towards the role of the state and what it was attempting to do with the machinery it had established to control development. Thus, this chapter is also about some fundamental questions concerning what planning is and how to go about it. It also raises questions concerning who the planner is planning for – their employee (e.g., a local authority), a wider interest or a set of values upon which a professional layer of skills and values is added.

## The politics of planning

The systems and rational approaches to planning detailed in Chapter 3 saw it as a technical and not particularly democratic exercise. Planners were experts who could model and predict cities and regions and through the tools of planning control ensure that they worked efficiently and effectively. This was the instrumentally rational approach that was borne of the Enlightenment and modernity (see Chapter 8). It posited planners as professionals at the centre of the societal universe, pulling the levers of control. But, as I pointed out in Chapter 3, the actual result was far from apolitical. The consequences for those who were to be 'planned' were often highly political and personal, as a number of classic studies of planning in the 1960s and 1970s highlighted. It is worth reflecting on two such cases.

Norman Dennis (1972) was a graduate from a planning school and resident of an industrialized and working-class area of Sunderland called Millfield, located to the south of the river Wear in the north east of England. During the 1960s, the local council had allocated the area for clearance with the residents being re-housed. As Dennis puts it, the area was largely comprised of single-storey terraces built in the nineteenth century to house workers at the nearby factories. The condition of these houses varied. Some had evolved little from when they were originally built and lacked amenities that we would today regard as normal, such as inside toilets, washbasins, etc. However, the structural quality of the houses seemed to be largely adequate (despite the lack of a damp-proof course) and from the photographs in the book they look like attractive Victorian terraces.

Nevertheless, the local council were interested in securing money from central government for redevelopment. Millfield had a strong and united residents' association that was aggrieved by both the principle of clearance and the uncertainty hanging over the area. Implementation of the plan was a continually moving target and the area was understandably suffering from blight through such uncertainty. Residents who wanted to improve their homes were denied loans because of the possibility that the area would be cleared and redeveloped. As this went on for a number of years the overall state of the houses in the area deteriorated, thereby making the council's assessment of the quality of houses in the area self-fulfilling. A meeting with local officials pacified them when they were told to be 'patient' and 'wait for plans to emerge'. The new plan was announced some months later with (another) different schedule of works. Disquiet not only focused on the scheduling but also on the research that had been undertaken to provide the basis of those areas that were to be condemned. The definition of what the planning department regarded as 'unfit' seemed arbitrary and subjective. But it also became clear that a survey of facilities in houses in the area had been undertaken in a rather slapdash way. Information on the condition and facilities of some houses had been gathered from neighbours if the occupier was not in when the officials called. In many cases this information was, not surprisingly, inaccurate.

Such misunderstandings and factual inaccuracies might have been resolved if the council and its planners were willing to get involved in the area more. Although there were some meetings between planners and the residents association these were to announce plans or defend entrenched positions. Planners took no notes at any meetings and appeared to carry on with their plans regardless of the views of local people. One instance summed up the attitude of planners towards their role and that of the residents. At a local meeting, the chairman of the planning committee (also the local councillor) turned up and requested that the residents' association should in future address all correspondence to the planners rather than him. When the residents objected on the grounds that he was their elected representative he replied that he was only the chairman of the planning committee and that the committee followed the recommendations of planners. From that point on planners refused to acknowledge or answer any letter that was ~~not~~ sent to them rather than the elected representative of the area. At one point, a planner told a public meeting in Millfield that, 'In any normal organisation, any normal decent transaction goes through the officials. If you are dealing with an industrial firm, you don't write to the managing director. You go to the officials' (Dennis, 1972, p. 209). Apart from the interesting analogy between planning and an industry, the use of the word 'decent', as Dennis points out, implies the residents' association were indecent in its pursuit of representation and a voice. Writing letters to their elected representative, the planner continued, 'antagonises all of us. It antagonises all the staff that have to deal with this' (Dennis, 1972, p. 211). The outcome of this protracted series of proposals and procedures was that the area was not comprehensively cleared, though this had more to do with a lack of money to implement the plans rather than a lack of determination on behalf of the local planners.

The Millfield case demonstrates the use and misuse of rationality, as well as some darker questions concerning the attitudes, ethics and responsibilities of planners who were exposed as, at best, selectively using information and their position of power to force through unpopular proposals for an area of many thousands of people. While Dennis's account is compelling and believable, care needs to be taken. He is clearly sympathetic to the residents, being chairman of their association. He is also not unsympathetic to the use of systems and modelling in planning that the planners were seeking to employ – he thinks that they need improving to be more effective rather than dropping altogether. Nevertheless, as he states, the planners claimed that everything they proposed was based on inviolate technical foundations and impeccable factual data. The residents were simply acting 'irrationally' in the face of such information from trained professionals, who were acting in the 'public good'.

Jon Gower Davies (1972) provided a further damning study of the attitude of planners and the helplessness of communities in his study of Rye Hill in Newcastle. Rye Hill had some strong similarities and important differences with the nearby Millfield. Like Millfield, it was designated for 'improvement' by the council, though this was to be through compulsory purchase and refurbishment rather than clearance and rebuilding. Like Millfield, it was an area of solid Victorian properties, mostly owned by their occupiers. Like Millfield, the scheme was protracted and over the nine years when plans were made and remade the area suffered from considerable blight. The two main differences concern the disagreements within the community about what should happen (though they were united in their opposition the Council's scheme) and the refusal of the Minister for Planning to confirm the compulsory purchase order.

Davies' work achieves more of a balance between his case study and analysis of the wider implications, particularly of the context of planning at the time. His thesis concerns why planners took such a high-handed attitude towards communities. When the initial plan for Rye Hill was announced by the Chief Planning Officer in 1963, he commented that the plan was a bold one and 'many would be hurt by it'. He was lauded by the planning and architectural professions for his boldness, though throughout the city opposition was growing to the arrogance of such comprehensive planning. Davies argues that the planners managed to proceed in the face of such opposition through their self-belief. As one senior planner in the Newcastle Council Planning Department put it: 'You've got to have a touch of arrogance to be a planner – and the basic confidence to know that you're right even when you're wrong, and the present City Planning Officer is such a man' (Davies, 1972, p. 119). This evangelical zeal originated in the education of planners, which formed an ideology of self-righteousness that protected them against inevitable criticisms from an inherently conservative population. The Newcastle planners were proud of their reputation as being the most 'progressive' (arrogant?) in the country. They drew upon technical justifications to back up assertions, though Davies claims these were based on little more than whim in many cases. Bureaucratic evangelism may sound like a strong term (it formed the title of Davies' book), particularly from our perspective over 40 years on, but it is worth quoting again the Chief Planning Officer of Newcastle: 'Comprehensive social planning is unavoidable if we really believe in the love of human beings' (quoted in Davies, 1972, p. 121).

It is easy to look back at this period and reflect on how far things have developed in terms of participation. However, in 2000 Newcastle residents in the Walker and Scotswood areas of the city were battling with the city council over its plans. More than 40 years on, the same council was still pursuing redevelopment schemes, though this time they were proposing to demolish the housing that they had built to replace the Victorian terraces. The council has proposed a comprehensive redevelopment scheme that involves the demolition of 6,600 houses with no other options being examined. The leader of the Council commented that, 'The Council has got to have its own vision', while residents felt that it was not enough to be consulted over plans they feared were a *fait accompli* and demanded instead to be involved in decisions.

Other studies have demonstrated that this phenomenon of centralized, high-handed and arrogant planning is not restricted either to the UK or the 1960s. Bent Flyvbjerg's analysis of planning processes in the Danish city of Aalborg, for example, demonstrates a similarity in the separation between the 'planner and the planned', as I consider in Chapter 3. Both studies discussed above raise a number of important questions concerning the role of planners that I outlined at the beginning of the chapter. What does it mean to be a planning professional? Who are the clients of planning? To what extent can planning be separated from those who it will affect? Is it possible to have an objectively rational planning? The latter question was partly addressed in the discussion on rationality in Chapter 3, where it is clear that planners have no recourse to some objective, technical reality and that, consequently, planning was a highly political process. This was the view that Paul Davidoff and Thomas Reiner (1963) came to in the early 1960s – planning conflated both formal and substantive rationality. They presented issues and questions as all being in the realm of instrumental rationality. What is somewhat surprising is that this paper and a later one by Davidoff (1965) preceded the studies in Newcastle and Sunderland.

## Paul Davidoff and the planner as advocate

Urban problems were not and are not confined to the UK. During the 1960s many US cities were experiencing problems on a much greater scale than the poor housing found in Newcastle and Sunderland. Against a backdrop of large numbers of black Americans moving to cities and equally large numbers of whites fleeing to the suburbs, other powerful movements were also shaping society:

> Blacks and whites mobilised civil rights campaigns whose mass marches, boycotts and sit-ins were an awakening process. Students joined the movement and sparked campus-based protests against the escalating war in Vietnam. Local residents protested against the bulldozers of urban renewal and the routes of proposed expressways in the neighbourhoods, some of which erupted in rage against racism, poverty and widening disparities between Blacks and Whites. (Checkoway, 1994, p. 140)

Planners in the USA at the time were as wedded to a rational and technical perspective on planning as their UK counterparts. Davidoff entered the scene with an appeal for planning to become more than a technical exercise and instead embrace social justice. He started from a deeply pluralist position, underpinned by the idea that 'Appropriate planning action cannot be prescribed from a position of value neutrality, for prescriptions are based on desire functions' (1965, p. 331). In other words, like the analyses of formal rationality, we start from a position where values and facts cannot be separated. From this position, Davidoff goes on to argue that, because there is no such thing as value-neutrality, planners should actually be open about the values that have led them to choose a particular option or make a particular decision. But

Davidoff goes even further than this. Planners should not only be open about their values, they should also work for organizations with which their values coincide: 'Planners should be able to engage in the political process as advocates of the interests both of government and of such other groups, organisations, or individuals who are concerned with proposing policies for the future development of the community' (1965, p. 332). Davidoff claims that such a function for planners will enable citizens to play an active role in democracy. Planners would take the role of advocates in a courtroom who represent two opposing cases. They would argue their clients position whether the client is an individual, group or organization. Davidoff also raises another related dimension to his argument concerning the possibility of competing plans. At present, we usually have one plan for an area drawn up by the public authority. Under an advocacy approach there would be multiple plans prepared by different groups. Some of these plans would be in direct contradiction to the plan drawn up by the public authority. Rather than simply objecting to the 'official' municipal plan, groups could counter it with one of their own. The result would be a competition of ideas. This really opens up the idea of planning being a technocratic or instrumentally rational enterprise. If this were so then we should expect different planners preparing plans to come to the same plan in the end. Obviously, this is unrealistic. The role of publicly elected officials remains one of approving a plan, while the planners who are employed by that agency prepare one plan and have to compete with others to have theirs approved.

The advantages of such an approach, according to Davidoff (1965, pp. 332–3), are threefold. It would:

1. Serve to better inform the public of the alternative choices open to them.
2. Force councils to compete with other planning groups to win political support.
3. Force those who have been critical of council plans to prepare their own.

For Davidoff one main problem that will arise is how to choose between different and competing plans. Inherent in the advocacy approach is the idea of non-neutrality in assessing different plans –

we all have views and these colour any evaluation approach. The advocate planner would not only admit his or her values but also work in a way that exposed such values in other plans:

> In this way, as a critic of opposition plans, he would be performing a task similar to the legal technique of cross-examination. While painful to the planner whose bias is exposed (and no planner can be entirely free of bias) the net effect of confrontation between advocates of alternative plans would be more careful and precise research. (Davidoff, 1965, p. 333)

Davidoff gives few further clues as to how competing plans might be judged and it is left up to the reader to decide how this might occur.

Other dimensions of Davidoff's advocacy planning approach that are worth mentioning include the kind of organizations that would be likely to become involved. Davidoff highlights three: political parties, special interest groups and *ad hoc* associations. Political parties in an area should establish community plans based on their own values. Special interest groups, such as chambers of commerce, unions, etc., could also become involved in preparing their own community plans, though the often disparate nature of some of these groups might make it difficult. Finally, there are *ad hoc* groups that might be established in response to a particular issue, such as the proposed location of a supermarket or the demolition of an old building. Although Davidoff argues that it is at such a grass-roots level that advocacy planning is more likely to emerge, it is difficult to envisage how such groups might get involved in 'planning' as opposed to 'resisting'. While a particular group might have strong views on a single issue, the extent to which it has equally strong or agreed opinions on another unrelated matter is open to question.

According to Checkoway (1994), advocacy in American planning went beyond the theories of Davidoff to be implemented in various forms:

> Some advocacy planners worked with neighbourhood residents in opposition to federal programmes which threatened decline, and with community organisations which went 'from protest to programme' to develop services of their own. Others formed advocacy planning programmes and received funding for demonstration projects . . . Some city planning agencies assigned staff planners to prepare sub-area plans,

> organised sub-area planning councils and encouraged residents to participate in citywide planning. (1994, p. 141)

A number of questions arise in response to Davidoff's advocacy approach. He sees planners as 'seeking out' employers with whom he or she has a close affinity of values. How realistic this is must be doubted. There are few organizations that have a single worldview and most, such as employers' organizations or environmental bodies, involve a complex mixture of perspectives from the more radical to the more modest. It might, therefore, be simplistic to portray organizations in a homogeneous way that reflects a singular vision of the world. A related issue is: who will pay for advocacy planners? Ideally, Davidoff argues that government funding would be most appropriate, though in the short term specific foundations might support the work. More likely, as occurred in the UK, a form of advocacy planning would emerge through the operation of informal, voluntary organizations such as Planning Aid (see below).

A second problem alluded to by Davidoff and discussed above concerns how one might judge between competing plans (1965, p. 333). Although (as mentioned earlier) Davidoff does not come up with any convincing mechanism, it must be addressed as it goes to the heart of the advocacy approach. The lack of a mechanism to arbitrate and ultimately decide between different local plans is a significant drawback to Davidoff's arguments.

A third issue has been raised by Marris (1994) concerning the difference between resolving a conflict through legal advocacy and through democratic politics. While legal advocacy takes place in a court before a judge and jury who are responsible for reaching a decision that 'becomes the right answer to the set of issues raised in that particular conflict' (1994, p. 144), planning advocacy has no such equivalent. The difference would seem to be that legal judges recognize that there are competing versions of the truth, while planning authorities are driven by the idea that theirs is the only truth. Again, this comes back to the technical and instrumentally rational basis to planning that seemed to dominate the profession in the 1960s.

Another critique of the advocacy approach from a Marxist perspective has been advanced by Piven (1970). To what extent do planners who act on behalf of the poor merely provide a form of co-option that provides an illusion of influence? Piven argues that this illusion is all the more insidious because the planner actually believes it. Even if planners act on behalf of the poor or dispossessed, how likely is it that their alternative plan will succeed or that their lives will be changed for the better? Powerful economic forces are unlikely to yield to the force of better argument. Will exposing power be enough to challenge it? These questions are at the core of the critique of pluralism that formed the basis of Davidoff's world-view. I deal with pluralism in more detail below. First, it is worth dealing with an associated dimension to this issue: how did the situation arise where planners became advocates for themselves rather than 'the planned'? Davies (1972) argues it was part of a self-defence mechanism against doubt and inherent conservatism against change. There may be some truth in this but it does not explain how such an ideology, as Davies puts it, is maintained and reproduced through such mechanisms as institutions and professional bodies.

As I discussed in Chapter 2, town planning is a 'profession':

> During the last fifty years, the town planning profession has largely dominated matters of land use policy and practice in Britain. The Royal Town Planning Institute has established itself as the professional body with an exclusive, legitimate cognitive competence in these areas, and town planners have been successful in portraying themselves as the sole occupational group capable of pronouncing on what constitutes the 'best' pattern of land use, or the 'most appropriate' form of development for the built and natural environments. (Evans, 1993, p. 9)

The definition of a profession is, as Grant (1999) concludes, problematic and the idea of a professional status for planning has been attacked from a number of fronts. Reade (1987), for example, considers that planning has no endogenous body of theory and therefore cannot intellectually be a discipline or profession. For this discussion, the work of Bob Evans (1993, 1995; Evans and Rydin, 1997) is more apt as it focuses on the impacts of what it is for planning to be a profession. Evans (1993, p. 11) argues that professionalism rests upon a number of claims, principally:

- The claim to control a particular area of knowledge or expertise.
- The claim that problems the occupational group's members seek to solve are ultimately resolvable within the existing social and economic structures of society.

- The claim to altruism, that the occupation serves the public interest or common good.

This is the basis of many professions, such as law and medicine. There is a debate about whether planning actually meets these requirements but of more concern to us is their impact upon the practice of planning. Why should any discipline want to be a profession? What makes it want to meet the claims above? The main reasons are that being a professional or part of a profession is accompanied by social status, power to make decisions, greater financial rewards and employment security. The last two points arise because, by definition, not everyone can be a member of a profession – there are academic and other qualifications that mean the supply of a particular professional, such as a doctor or lawyer, is limited by the professional body itself. Who decides what is a profession? Here both Reade (1987) and Evans (1993) argue that there is a symbiotic relationship between the state and professions. Planning and the allocation of land must be seen to be fair and working in the public interest – it is not simply a straightforward bureaucratic exercise:

> Thus, the state enters into corporatist intermediation and grants to interest organisations such as professions, a high level of influence on policy matters in their respective areas. In exchange, the interest organisations are expected to participate in achieving policy goals which fit within predetermined parameters and limits. Crucially, this means delivering the compliance of organisation or profession members in the implementation of policy. (Evans, 1993, p. 12)

This idea of a 'bargain' between the state and the professions is not uncontroversial. However, it does make sense if one begins to put such an understanding upon the issues we have been discussing so far in this chapter. Figure 7.1 sets out the basic argument described above in graphical form.

## Pluralism

As Clavel (1994, p. 146) argues, 'Davidoff's proposal was that planners could, by providing services to underrepresented groups, contribute more to an inclusive pluralism.' Mazziotti (1982, p. 207)

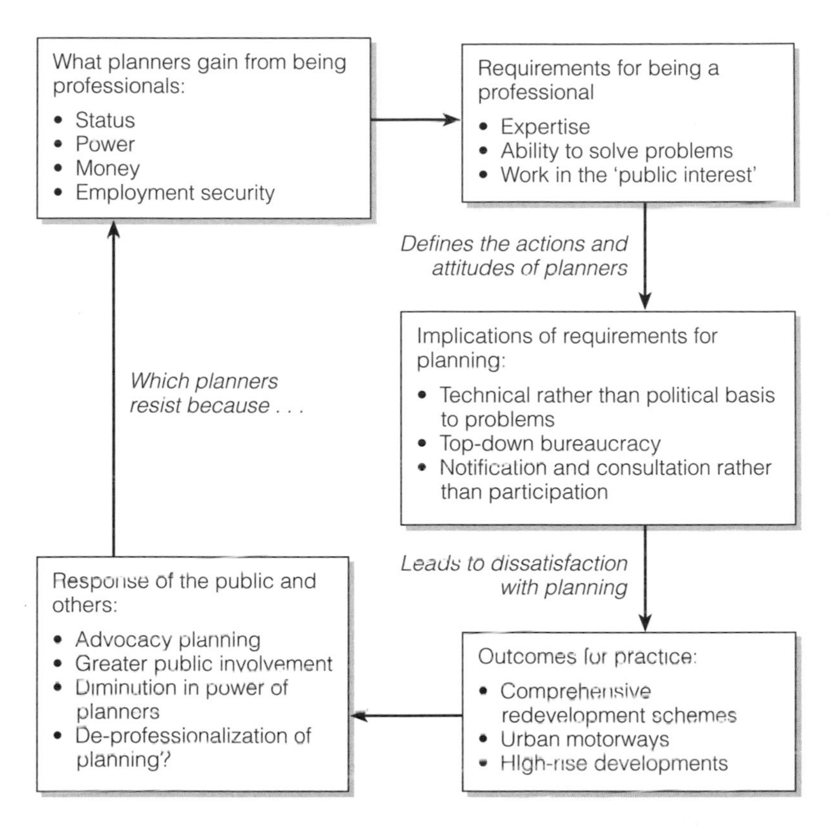


**Figure 7.1** The 'vicious circle' of planning as a profession

further claims that the assumption that is central to the concept of advocacy planning is that of pluralism. Notwithstanding the difficulties in defining what is meant by pluralism and whether it is a descriptive (what is) or normative (what ought to be) model of society and democracy, it is possible to tease out general tenets. According to Jordan (1990), the main characteristics of the pluralist model are:

- Power is fragmented and decentralized in society.
- There are dispersed inequalities in that all groups have access to some resources to make their case.
- That power dispersal in society is desirable.

- That such dispersal of power varies across policy sectors, meaning that political outcomes will themselves vary across these sectors.
- That the exercise of political power goes beyond elections and formal arenas such as councils.
- That in an ideal pluralist world the interaction of interests would provide a competition of ideas and legitimacy for any outcomes.
- That participants in the pluralist system will be bound to it by the uncertainty of the bargaining process.

We can see that a pluralist interpretation of society and politics involves a fractured polity of many competing interest groups with overlapping memberships and widely diffused power. Whereas some perspectives on society see power as being cumulative, for example, money passed through generations, pluralists see society as being comprised of non-cumulative inequality. Such a view admitted to inequality in power and access to decision-making, though argued that this was a more fluid situation than, for example, a political economy analysis. Equally, the possession of resources is only as important as the ability to use them: that, again, is unequally diffused.

Although the idea of a pluralist conception of society emerged in the USA during the 1960s, there have been various studies that sought to explore whether or not this model represented society in the UK. A study of Birmingham by Newton (1976) examined housing, education and race relations and found differing participation by groups depending upon the policy area. Thus, housing was characterized by more involvement than race relations. Newton therefore found a mixed picture on whether pluralism on the US model could be found in the UK – in some areas this was more so and others less so. This also extended to the inequality in access to resources that was also a characteristic of pluralist understandings and also varied in Newton's Birmingham study.

In another dimension to the concept of pluralism there have also been studies that have tried to link the evolution of urban areas with the extent of pluralism within policy-making. Crudely, the argument goes that as cities become larger and more sophisticated then policy-making evolves from an elitist model to a more pluralist model as interests diversify and it becomes more difficult to rule such an area in a homogenized way. Rather than a more open and diverse polity, there is a danger that increasing pluralism leads to ungovernability.

The environment of policy making and the character of urban problems determine the shape of urban policy. Policy outcomes are a product of highly fragmented and unstable problem and policy contexts. And it is precisely because urban policy makers must deal with so many different, fragmented problem and policy contexts that urban policy making as a whole is so fragmented, unstable and reactive (Yates, 1977, p. 85):

> This situation points away from 'planning' and towards chaos. But it also hints at a more aggressive and more fluid pluralism where the sheer number of groups means that competition to be heard and the ability to influence policy becomes more difficult. This concept of 'street fighting pluralism' is not universally accepted. Some more recent case studies have backed up the idea of a hyper-pluralism but have then argued that the interface between different interests has shifted from society as a whole to the 'corridors of power'. As political power becomes increasingly pluralistic so coalitions and other means of ensuring that chaos does not reign become necessary. So, far from there being a shift back to a more elitist form of governance, we are witnessing a more fragmented landscape that is adapting to the drawbacks of being so.

Pluralists have never argued that power in society was equally shared. In response to a number of critics who pointed to the more structural inequalities in society (see below), pluralists did begin to pay more attention to the inequalities of power within an increasingly pluralist political landscape. One area that did receive attention was the emergence of 'anti-regimes' or a particularly obstructive form of hyper-pluralism that seeks to promote one agenda over others, for example, economic development. The pro-economic development lobby is characterized by pluralism in its diversity and increasing fragmentation but those involved have enough in common to seek alliances with each other and local government. In the UK there has been a similar recognition that the growing diversity in and of politics has been accompanied by a resistance by certain powerful interests.

This was confirmed by the work of Healey, McNamara, Elson and Doak (1988) who found that certain rules within planning 'significantly favour some groups and interest claims' (1988, p. 219). But their study also paints a far more complicated pluralist landscape in planning than alluded to in the broader studies outlined above. While recognizing the plurality of interest groups within the sphere of planning (1988, p. 257), they nevertheless argue that the design of the UK planning system involves a mixture of processes (Table 7.1).

***Table 7.1*** **Policy processes in contemporary British public administration**

| | |
|---|---|
| Bureaucratic-legal | The determination of action in terms of formal procedural and legal rules |
| Techno-rational | The determination of actions in terms of the judgement of experts and scientific reasoning |
| Semi-judicial | The determination of actions through formal hearings of the arguments of conflicting interests, with an assessor balancing the relative merits of the arguments |
| Consultative | The determination of actions through negotiation and debate with, and among, concerned and affected groups; the forms of such consultation may include:<br>*Corporatist:* negotiation of a wide range of issues over a long period of time with specified representatives of particular groups;<br>*Bargaining:* negotiation with specific groups over a particular issue where mutual dependency between the group and the state is involved;<br>*Pluralist politics:* political debate among pressure groups, with politicians determining the balance and advantage in political terms;<br>*Open democratic debate:* 'rational' debate, where all affected parties discuss the advantages and disadvantages of particular courses of action and reach agreement without domination |
| Politico-rational | The determination of action by the judgement of politicians in the formal arenas of representative democracy |

*Source:* based on Healey *et al.*, 1988, p. 257.

The different forms of the policy process as set out in the left-hand column of Table 7.1 have different implications for the practice of pluralist politics. We can see how the different policy processes work in practice by comparing the kind of process we would encounter if we were submitting a planning application (techno-rational) or being involved in the preparation of a development plan (consultative). What does not come across so well in the work of Healey, McNamara, Elson and Doak is the way in which these processes may be embedded within each other and often be running simultaneously. For example, a planning application will involve some techno-rational process (e.g., the determination of facts and opinions by professional planners), some consultative (the involvement of interested parties) and politico-rational (the final decision by elected members of the council). Subsequent work by Brindley, Rydin and Stoker (1996) added a further dimension to this through the identification of different planning 'styles' in different parts of the country, which had changed over time. This temporal and spatial dimension to the processes of planning means that we cannot 'read off' the nature of pluralism in planning from theories and understandings taken from other policy processes and areas.

One important point that arises from the above discussion of pluralism is the distinction between pluralism as *analysis* and pluralism as a *normative position* (i.e., what ought to be). Davidoff drifts between the two, though it is clear that advocacy planning is underpinned by a clear normative pluralist framework.

Another clear message from the preceding discussion of pluralism is the dependence upon space, time and context in the existence of pluralism in both the analytical and normative forms. We cannot expect there to be a uniform pluralism spatially or sectorally, and neither can we expect that trying to encourage a more pluralist politics will lead to similar outcomes. Instead, we should expect different places to approach advocacy planning in different ways and with different results. As we shall see below, this is indeed the case.

## Advocacy in action? Planning Aid and equity planning

Although there has been less enthusiasm for advocacy planning as advanced by Davidoff in the UK compared with the USA, there are two important exceptions to this. The first involves Planning Aid. As Thomas (1992, p. 47) defines it, Planning Aid is 'the British term for the provision outside the orbit of the State of free advice on planning matters to those who cannot afford the services of planning consultants'. Thomas (1992) argues that Planning Aid and advocacy planning are actually quite far apart, though one would not necessarily expect that any British approach would be similar to Davidoff's model given the different social, institutional and political backgrounds between the UK and USA. What is clear is that the idea of Planning Aid began to be discussed in the early 1970s, around the same time that Davidoff's ideas began to become popular in the USA. The President of the Royal Town Planning Institute commented in 1971 that

> It is a curious and discreditable anomaly of British justice that a man can obtain free legal aid to defend himself in a court of law, yet a community or group threatened with extinction or disaster can get no assistance for its defence. It would do much to make the planning process more democratic and more sensitive to its effects if a free planning advice service could be made available to those in need. (Quoted in Thomas, 1996, p. 50)

Planners acting as advocates began to emerge in the early 1970s and the Royal Town Planning Institute decided to support branches in establishing Planning Aid services in the mid-1970s. In 1987 there were around 400 planners offering their services from a total of around 12,000 members of the RTPI.

The research undertaken by Thomas on Planning Aid Wales shows that many planners involved in Planning Aid did not have a burning commitment to the cause. Nearly as many became involved to widen their experience of planning as for altruistic purposes. Unlike the writings of Davidoff, some volunteers did not question the role of planning but merely wanted to correct misconceived ideas that planning was 'bad'. There were also different conceptions of the relationships between volunteers and the users of the service. Thomas (1992) identified three attitudes. The first was Planning Aid as assistance at a distance. Here, volunteers decide that their advice should consist of a clarification of terms or plans and form what could be seen as a technical advisory service. Another model that was followed was more of a consultancy role, where the Planning Aid volunteer undertook a more pro-active role including discussions with the local authority and the preparation of a case to the authority. This is more of an advocacy role in the legal sense, as, again, the volunteer does not have to agree with the position of the client, just represent him or her. Finally, there is Planning Aid as education. In the Welsh case this involved helping clients to increase their own abilities to engage with the planning system through assistance and advice, though leaving the actual work to others.

My experience of working for Planning Aid Scotland (PAS) partly backs up some of Thomas's findings. I dealt with individual cases concerning refusal of planning permission, advice to neighbours concerning objections and an educational role for community councils and others concerning how to get more involved in the planning process. Thus, Planning Aid Scotland seems to cut across some of the approaches described above and involve a more tailored service, depending upon the situation. Partly for geographical reasons it was not possible to visit most of the sites and people with whom I dealt. This meant that the vast majority of the work comes under Thomas's 'assistance at a distance' category. But there is also an important context provided by Planning Aid for Scotland that reinforces this and frames the work I undertook. With every case that arrived there was a guidance note that explained the role of PAS:

> Giving advice and guidance to clients on planning proposals is done for their benefit to enable them to make informed decisions or express informed views. PAS does not itself make representations on a particular proposal. Where a volunteer provides written advice or guidance to a client, it is possible that *this* may be seen by other parties and the terms need to be clearly stated.

In a recent case one of our volunteers gave a client written advice on a planning proposal. This was presented by the client to the local authority and, as a result, came to the attention of the developer. He, in turn, misinterpreted the written advice and took the view that Planning Aid for Scotland had lodged a written objection to his proposals.

This particular case has been looked into by the Management Committee of PAS and, as expected, the volunteer concerned had made it clear in *his* letter to the client that the advice given was for *his* benefit and was not an objection to the proposal by PAS.

In light of this case, the Management Committee has agreed that the good practice of highlighting to the clients that advice and guidance given does not constitute representations made by PAS should be adopted for all written correspondence. Accordingly, the following footnote should be added to all written advice and guidance.

The above advice and/or guidance is for the benefit of the Planning Aid for Scotland client only and does not constitute a letter of representation by Planning Aid for Scotland to any proposals (PAS, 2000):

> This obviously sets out the expected relationship between PAS and its clients in a way that would not be recognized as advocacy by Davidoff.

There are a number of crucial differences between advocacy planning as operated in the USA and Planning Aid in the UK, the most significant of which would be that institutionally Planning Aid involves local authority planners undertaking voluntary work in their own time. Until recently there was no significant financial backing from the state. Another crucial difference regards the motivation of Planning Aid volunteers who do not, on the whole, question the role of planning *per se* but see it as misunderstood or (at worst) a bureaucratic force that people need help through. The final difference concerns the kind of service that Planning Aid volunteers provide. There is little, if any, evidence that Planning Aid volunteers seek out clients whose values they sympathize with. The role of planners in Planning Aid is more 'arms length'.

Planning Aid is only one way that planners can act as advocates on behalf of individuals and groups within society. There are opportunities for planners working for the state to fight on behalf of others, even if it means that such a stance may put a person in conflict with their employer. The Royal Town Planning Institute's Code of Professional Conduct requires that planners:

- Shall act with competence, honesty and integrity.
- Shall fearlessly and impartially exercise their independent professional judgment to the best of their skill and understanding. (RTPI, 1994, p. 1)

In addition, 'Members shall not make or subscribe to any statements or reports which are contrary to their own bona fide professional opinions and shall not knowingly enter into any contract or agreement which requires them to do so' (RTPI, 1994, para. 3).

This sounds clear enough though it can lead to problems when a planner is employed by a public authority. For example, planners are employed by local authorities to represent the interests of that authority though those interests may conflict with his or her professional opinion, which includes matters such as values. Take this example, the principles of which will be familiar to many planners. A planner is allocated an application for a halfway house for ex-offenders trying to readjust to life outside prison. Local residents in this well-to-do village are appalled at such a prospect and are particularly concerned about the value of their properties being diminished. They petition the local authority to 'do something' about the proposal.

The planner dealing with the application visits the site, checks the policies in the development plan and concludes that there are no planning grounds for refusing this application. The highways, conservation and environmental health departments similarly have no objection. Nevertheless, councillors and senior planning officials are coming under pressure to refuse the proposal. Although the planning officer in charge can argue his ground with colleagues, it is the councillors who make the final decision. Although recommended for approval, they overturn this recommendation and refuse it, giving no planning reasons. It is then up to the planning officer to draw up reasons and fight the inevitable appeal.

At the appeal the planning officer reads out a statement she prepared on behalf of the council (none of whom attend) and then has to answer questions under cross-examination. In doing so she totally undermines the council's case and the appeal is upheld.

It could be argued that the planner had broken the RTPI Code of Professional Conduct when preparing the reasons for refusal and the council's case at appeal against her own professional judgement. But the problem is this: planners are employed as advocates for the council as well as being advocates of their own professional judgement. This is one area (an almost daily occurrence in planning) where there is a conflict between those two clients. Another point arises, however. In the end, the halfway house was approved. Would users have been best served if the planner had refused to become involved with the case after it had been refused or could she, feeling the way she did, act as an advocate for them *within* the council? Again, this is another very grey area involving many ethical and value judgements that planners encounter and deal with daily.

John Forester (1989) has examined in detail these kinds of ethical questions in his study of US planning and Norman Krumholz (with John Forester) (1990) has similarly looked at issues of planning for a purpose other than the organization within which a planner may find herself. As Krumholz and Forester put it:

> For the decade between late 1969 and 1979, the city of Cleveland was the site of a quiet but important experiment. What would happen if a group of professional planners, working for the city, devoted themselves to serving the needs of the poor even while the national mood, federal dollars, and local politics chased other priorities? (1990, p. xv)

Krumholz and his team set about planning in a radical way that sought to use various planning mechanisms to benefit the residents of the city. They aimed to move away from an apolitical stance to one that was politically sensitive to the decisions they were making to issues such as poverty, race and power. Their annual report set out their mission:

> City planning takes as its ultimate goal the challenge of promoting a more equitable allocation of society's benefits by helping to overcome obstacles to access and choice among those poorest and least powerful members of our society: and to accomplish this goal the commission functions as an agency for social and economic change. (Krumholz and Forester, 1990, p. 50)

They set about achieving a more equitable form of planning in various ways and through a classic advocacy approach:

> Our immediate objective was to transfer the power of planning professionals – our access to information, critical analytical skills, and institutional role – to a group of low income black citizens who had neither the resources nor the professional skills to deal with a complex redevelopment scheme. (Krumholz and Forester, 1990, p. 52)

They tried to improve housing subsidies for the poor, require developers to provide low-cost housing, improve public transport and recreational facilities. As Krumholz points out, through various case studies they had a mixed bag of success, though the positive impact they did have came without much political support and against the interests of many powerful forces within and outside the council. What power they had came down to using their discretion to lever open 'closed' topics (who decided what and in whose interest), as well as introducing new ideas.

Criticism came not only from others within the council but also from other planners around the USA. They were accused of being 'too ideological', which they countered with the claim that all planning is ideological and they were simply being more explicit and open. It was claimed that their approach lacked technical analysis, to which they argued that planning was as much political as technical. They also claimed that planning was not simply about land use planning but should draw upon other areas of public policy to achieve any objectives.

We should be wary of placing too much emphasis on the Cleveland approach, given the unique social, institutional and procedural context. Power in Cleveland resides far more with the mayor and councillors than in other places and, although there is a separation between the legislature and executive, there was a good deal of corruption:

> When I was appointed community development director in 1977, I spent the first two days of my tenure listening to various council members tell me the names of their relatives and friends, who were liberally sprinkled throughout my 270-person staff and whose jobs I 'had to protect' if I didn't want 'trouble' with the legislation I had before Council. (Krumholz and Forester, 1990, p. 10)

The relationship between councillors and officers was further complicated and open to abuse through various formal and informal relationships:

- Chairs of the committees control the agenda – they can bargain with officials about what is on the agenda.
- The council approved all expenditure above $3,500, giving it significant control over departmental spending and again opening up the possibility of bargaining.
- Ward councillors were given ultimate powers of zoning and planning permission in their area.

- There was a liberal use of law firms to lobby other members of the council.
- There were very strong links between businesses and developers and the work of the council.
- Officials and councillors seemed to be corrupt: 'It is common knowledge that zoning changes might be sold for cash or business favours.' (Krumholz and Forester, 1990, p. 14)

Thus, advocacy of a particular set of excluded interests takes on a rather more immediate and identifiable nature in such a context. It is far clearer who is gaining and who is losing in an arena where there is little interest in planning for a 'public good' (even if that public good is not uncontroversial itself, as Davidoff points out). Where there is blatant abuse of power the target for a committed radical such as Krumholz is far easier to identify than the more subtle 'hidden' inequities of planning 'in the public interest' (even if the two may be as difficult to counter in their own ways).

## Conclusions

Changes to planning since the 1960s have involved an opening up of planning to include more public participation and involvement. Advocacy planning as championed by Davidoff has been a powerful model but has had a mixed impact. It would be fair to say that planning is now more plural in its process than at any time in its past. Nevertheless, we still come up against the need to have 'one plan' (a problem that postmodern planning also encounters). It would also be fair to say that advocacy as Davidoff envisaged it has been more influential in the USA than in the UK:

> Davidoff's advocacy article formed the basis for empirical research, added a new 'model' to the field, and was widely cited in the planning literature. It stimulated serious debate about planning practice – including charges that advocacy planners were not always representative of their client communities, that they did not empower them to advocate for themselves that they diverted them from more powerful forms of social change, and that the advocacy planners lacked the power to implement their plans. (Checkoway, 1994, p. 141)

In the UK the advocacy approach has helped academics and practitioners think about the conflicts that they encounter on a daily basis. According to Marris (1994, p. 143), Davidoff's conception of the planner as advocate is perhaps the only way of reconciling professionalism and political engagement. For any planner working in practice there are a number of key issues raised by advocacy planning that are worth remembering:

- Planning is essentially a political activity, rife with value judgements.
- The simple notion that planners advise and politicians decide is a myth that has never reflected practical experience.
- A planner who undermines or embarrasses a powerful politician is skating on thin ice with the day warming rapidly.
- Neither planners nor politicians should decide issues based on their own pecuniary or non-pecuniary interests.
- Those who own the most property generally also have the most influence in the law and in planning decisions. (Krumholz, 2001, p. 96).

# 8 After Modernity

## Introduction

A central theme in contemporary theorizing around planning is fragmentation. Not only are the places in which people live and work characterized by diversity (what Sandercock has termed 'mongrel cities' [2003]), but also the ways in which planners and others understand and think about places and spaces has begun to reflect an underlying uneasiness with the ways in which planning and planners seek to unify such diversity into a 'plan'. In short, as the world has seemingly become more diverse and fractured along social, cultural and political lines so planning and planning theory has had to account for and reflect such multiplicity. Rather than providing a way forward, much current theory seeks to break down and critically engage with planning practices. Indeed, the nature of much contemporary theorizing eschews single, ubiquitous methods and understandings. One outcome is to reinforce Thompson's view that current planning theory is 'impenetrable' and 'unnecessarily obscure' (2000, p. 132).

The gap between theory and practice is growing and the issues that both are grappling with are becoming more complex. This is at a time when there is an increased necessity to better understand the contribution of each to the other. A common issue for both theory and practice concerns the notion that society and the form of planning it supports has moved beyond what has been termed modernity. Planning theory and practice is, broadly, searching for a new or 'postmodern' paradigm. In this chapter, I discuss what is meant by modernity and its 'posts'. In the next chapter, I explore a similarly motivated approach but one that is based upon a 'reformed modernity'.

**What are the modern and the postmodern?**

Current theorizing in planning takes a common point of departure from the modern or modernity. Modernism is closely linked to a period generally termed the Enlightenment. The Enlightenment is a complex mix of ideas, attitudes, sensibilities etc. that broadly emerged at the beginning of the eighteenth century and sought a 'Rational form of social organisation and rational modes of thought [which] promised liberation from the irrationalities of myth, religion, superstition, release from the arbitrary use of power as well as from the dark side of our human natures' (Harvey, 1990, p. 12). Sir Isaac Newton was one of the central figures of the Enlightenment. Scientists such as Newton were seen as being able to lift minds above the 'ignorance' of dogma and tradition in the world to a new and objective sphere. This was not only in the field of natural sciences. Enlightenment thinkers 'tried to apply the scientific style of thinking to the regions of the aesthetic, social and political theory' (Gay, 1969, p. 126).

One central aim of the Enlightenment was the idea of liberty through knowledge. The human condition could be improved through certain tenets or principles, including:

- Reason
- Empiricism
- Science
- Universalism
- Progress
- Individualism
- Tolerance
- Freedom
- Uniformity of human nature
- Secularism. (Hamilton, 1992, p. 21)

These factors provided the building blocks of modernity – a broad movement that has sought to advance such ideas and has led to certain distinct characteristics of society in what has become known as the 'modern era'. While many see modernity and its associated accoutrements, such as the state, capitalism, liberalism and democracy, as a positive shift in the direction of human development, there are those who are more willing to see a downside or negative dimension. For the supporters of modernity it has led to 'human emancipation from myth, superstition and enthralled enchantment to mysterious powers and forces of nature through the progressive operations of critical reason' (Docherty, 1993, p. 5). For those less enthralled, modernity has been the source of unbridled horror:

> the Holocaust was not the antithesis of modern civilisation and everything (or so we like to think) it stands for. We suspect (even if we refuse to admit it) that the Holocaust could merely have uncovered another face of the same modern society whose other, so familiar, face we so admire. And that the two faces are perfectly comfortably attached to the same body. (Bauman, 1989, p. 7)

A middle way is a more common stance.

> To be modern is to find ourselves in an environment that promises adventure, power, joy, growth, transformation of ourselves and the world – and, at the same time, that threatens to destroy everything we have, everything we know, everything we are. (Berman, 1982, p. 15)

Much planning theory, including the schools of thought already covered in this book, is widely regarded as being the product of modernity. The broad underpinnings of contemporary planning theory, on the other hand, are part of a long tradition of questioning the basis and impacts of modernity. How can a process concerned with broad ideas such as liberty, individualism etc. be seen as both creative and destructive? The answer lies in the dynamics of modernity. Its essential traits are of restlessness, innovation and constant progress. Essential to the idea of modernity is the belief that everything is destined to be speeded up, dissolved, displaced, transformed and/or reshaped (Hall, 1992a, p. 15). 'The only secure thing about modernity is insecurity, its penchant for totalising chaos' (Harvey, 1990, p. 11). The main difference between theorists who take a middle position recognizing the benefits and disbenefits of modernity comes down to where the balance lies: do the benefits outweigh the disbenefits?

One of the main criticisms of modernity has been the central role it ascribes to instrumental rationality (see Chapter 3). For critics such as Nietzsche the world had been reduced to one form of reasoning that excludes all others. Everything that could be is transformed into mathematical abstractions and everything that cannot is ignored or suppressed. The struggle to understand and control nature through instrumental rationality leads inevitably to the control of free will, the diminution of human emancipation, individual responsibility and initiative. Marx thought this was an even greater threat to mankind than class repression. Thus, the problem with modernity lay not in its theory but in its practice.

This dominance and the downsides of instrumental or scientific rationality are accepted even by those who are sympathetic to the 'project of modernity', as Habermas terms it. The supremacy of instrumental rationality was an unintended consequence of modernity that has crowded out other ways of thinking based on, for example, intuition or open, reasoned conversation. As I pointed out in Chapter 3, there are problems in separating facts and values in instrumental rationality. However, modernism has become, in Lyotard's famous phrase, a meta-narrative (over-arching explanation or framework that dominates others) that sees such questions concerning values or politics as merely details. Modernity is a juggernaut that destroys all before it (Giddens, 1990).

The modern view, based on instrumental rationality, is that there *are* absolute truths and it is possible to plan rationally for ideal social orders (Harvey, 1990). Nevertheless, there is broad agreement around the pernicious affects of such assumptions that have been translated into bureaucratic institutions and processes. The issue that current planning theory is grappling with is what to do about it. Four broad movements in planning theory have emerged from this: postmodern planning, post-structuralist planning, complexity and collaborative planning. In this chapter, I explore the first three broad movements and in the next chapter, I cover the fourth.

## Postmodern planning

Some theorists, such as Jürgen Habermas, argue that we should not give up upon the central ideas of modernity, but should instead attempt to finish the unfinished project of modernity through other forms of thinking and knowing. Others, on the other hand, argue that modernity cannot be finished or 'rescued'. Instead, we should move beyond it and accept that there is no such thing as absolute truth. This latter position corresponds broadly with postmodernism. However, it is difficult to ascribe a postmodern position or approach to planning theory both from a philosophical perspective (labelling something postmodern involves 'closure' and isn't very postmodern) and practical perspective (few planning theorists explicitly identify with a postmodern approach). Nevertheless, there are two postmodern schools of thought that stand out in planning theory. The first could be termed the 'postmodern as epoch' and the second the 'postmodern as social theory'. In practice, the latter usually builds upon the former.

It is widely accepted that planning is a product of modernity (see, for example, Healey, 1993a; Low, 1991, p. 234; Sandercock, 1998, p. 2) and that planning finds itself in a postmodern period (e.g., Filion, 1996). The implication is of a potential and real mismatch between planning as a modern project and the needs and demands of the postmodern or new times, which, according to the proponents of this theory, explains the lack of participation and democratic content, failed, resulting in unrealized results and expectations, urban decay and a host of other outcomes intended or not that characterize 'planning':

> Evidence of this seemed to be everywhere, from the disaster of high-rise towers for the poor to the dominance of economic criteria justifying road building and the functional categorisation of activity zones, which worked for large industrial companies and those working in them, but not for women (with their necessarily complex life-styles), the elderly, the disabled, and the many ethnic groups forced to discover ways of surviving on the edge of established economic practices. (Healey, 1993a, p. 235)

Building upon the 'new times' perspective, postmodern social theory has provided new ways of understanding the role of planning in society *vis-à-vis* societal control and power. Bent Flyvbjerg, for example, has demonstrated the ways in which supposedly open and democratic processes can and have been abused in ways similar to those outlined by postmodern thinkers. He takes a Foucauldian perspective on the role of power relations in planning through a detailed case study of planning practice and concludes that

> power does not limit itself to defining a specific kind of knowledge, conception, or discourse of reality. Rather, power defines physical, economic, ecological, and social reality itself. Power is more concerned

> with defining a specific reality than with understanding what reality is. This power seeks change, not knowledge. (1998, p. 36)

The thrust of these arguments is that planning is part of modernity and needs to change, to be more aware of power relations and more sensitive to local needs and demands. Such demands are pushing at an open door, as many changes to planning over the past decade or so have been towards a more open and democratic form of planning. If planning is changing, is it moving away from its modern basis and towards a more postmodern form and, if so, to what extent? According to Beauregard, planning finds itself suspended between modernity and postmodernity, with 'practitioners and theorists having few clues as to how to (re)establish themselves on solid ground' (1996, p. 227).

I have some difficulty with the crude idea of planning being a modern institution in a postmodern world. The reality is far more complex than that. Before I go on to explore why that is the case it is worth establishing the basis to 'planning as a modern enterprise in a postmodern world'. Chapter 3 outlined the systems and rational views of planning summed up by McLoughlin as

> Planning [that] seeks to regulate or control the activity of individuals and groups in such a way as to minimise the bad effects which may arise, and to promote better 'performance' of the physical environment in accordance with a set of broad aims and more specific objectives in the plan. (1969, p.59)

This is the idea of planning portrayed by the advocates of postmodern planning. Sandercock (1998) develops Beauregard's arguments further. She argues that the mismatch between modern institutions such as planning and fragmented and pluralistic times is crowding out the possibility and desirability of multi-ethnic, multi-racial diverse societies and cities. Current planning is anti-democratic, race- and gender-blind and culturally homogeneous:

> Modernist architects, planners, engineers – Faustian heroes, all – saw themselves as experts who could utilize the laws of development to provide societal guidance. The hubris of the city-building professions was their faith in the liberating potential of their technical knowledge and their corresponding belief in their ability to transcend the interests of capital, labour, and the state, and to arrive at an objective assessment of the 'public interest'. (1998, p. 4)

Sandercock goes on to identify five pillars of modernist planning wisdom:

1 Planning – meaning city and regional planning – is concerned with making public/political decisions more rational. The focus, therefore, is predominantly on advanced decision-making: on developing visions of the future; and on an instrumental rationality that carefully considers and evaluates options and alternatives.
2. Planning is most effective when it is comprehensive. Comprehensiveness is written into planning legislation and refers to multi-functional/multi-sectoral spatial plans as well as to the intersection of economic, social and environmental and physical planning. The planning function is therefore said to be integrative, coordinative and hierarchical.
3. Planning is both a science and an art, based on experience, but the emphasis is usually placed on the science. Planners' authority derives in large measure from a mastery of theory and methods in the social sciences. Planning knowledge and expertise are thus grounded in positive science, with its propensity for quantitative modelling and analysis.
4. Planning, as part of the modernization project, is a project of state-directed futures, with the state seen as possessing progressive, reformist tendencies, and as being separate from the economy.
5. Planning operates in 'the public interest' and planners' education privileges them in being able to identify what that interest is. Planners present a public image of neutrality, and planning policies, based on positivist science, are gender- and race-neutral. (Sandercock, 1998, p. 27)

These pillars need to be 'demolished', according to Sandercock, because of the recent processes of change that point to a more diverse composition of the urban and increasing demand for a more heterogeneous planning approach.

The problems with this view are threefold. First, it separates theory from practice. In theory planning could be described as modern but this is to ignore how planning is actually undertaken. To characterize planning as modern is to give it a homogeneous character, which, ironically, postmodernists supposedly seek to avoid. Claims that planning is approached as a technical and objective endeavour ignore the plethora of studies that point to its alternative, often messy and highly political basis. In a revealing examination of planning practice in the Danish town of Aalborg, Bent Flyvbjerg (1998) points to the duplicity, conflicting objectives, bargaining, abuse of power and *post hoc* rationalism that go under the name of planning practice. The second objection concerns the ways in which planning is portrayed as modernist by postmodernists. Interpreting planning from a postmodern perspective necessarily involves looking for certain characteristics and not others. As a consequence, the interpretation of planning as a modern enterprise is a 'straw man', whereas in reality the UK planning structure, for example, of a national legal framework and guidance allows wide interpretation by different levels of government and actors. Similar differences exist elsewhere, particularly in federal states. The result is often that you cannot assume or automatically 'read off' local responses and actions from policies and procedures operating at a different (often national) level (Allmendinger and Thomas, 1998). The practice of planning strongly suggests aspects of both modernism and postmodernism.

Moving on from analyzing planning as a modern enterprise in postmodern times, there have been attempts to develop postmodern forms of planning. Such attempts fall broadly into two categories. First are those that seek to critique planning from a postmodern perspective and in doing so provide a postmodern basis for planning largely by default. Second are those approaches that take a more direct route and seek to develop a framework for postmodern planning.

Critiques of planning from a postmodern perspective tend to draw upon the work of writers such as Foucault to deconstruct the 'hidden world' of power in planning (see, for example, Boyer, 1983). Another school has focused on what has been termed the 'darker side' of planning. Such views broadly follow the critics of modernity outlined earlier and their belief that the emancipatory dimensions of modernity have been subsumed into being tools of more nefarious forces. Yiftachel (1994, 1998, 2000), for example, has explored the ways in which planning can and does have an impact on this minimization of peripheral cultures 'by creating settlement patterns, dispersing or concentrating certain populations, placing communal, religious or ethnic facilities, housing and services in particular places, and governing the character and norms of urban public places' (1998, p. 11). Planning has the potential to oppress subordinate groups and is structurally devised to exert control and oppression. According to Yiftachel anti-progressive planning can take four forms:

1. *Territorial*: Plans and policies determine land use that can be used to control weaker groups and minorities in such deeply divided societies. This can be achieved through containment of minority settlements and allowing members of the majority group to settle there, thereby altering the cultural homogeneity of the area. Further, territorial segregation according to class, race and/or ethnicity can be achieved through land use policies that maintain distinctions and reinforce the status quo.
2. *Procedures*: Planning can directly affect power relations through its communicative nature. But its processes also affect the amount and level of participation and negotiation and thereby can be used for exclusion of groups or minorities, reinforcing or extending existing exclusion or repression.
3. *Socio-economic dimension*: This is a longer-term impact of the 'darker side' of planning which results in both positive and negative distributional changes. Yiftachel has in mind here the mainly monetary impacts of planning such as land price rises due to the granting of permission to develop or the development of a road, thereby improving accessibility. Planning can therefore be used as a form of 'socio-economic control and domination by helping to maintain and even widen socio-economic gaps through the location of development costs and benefits in accordance with the interests of dominant groups' (1998, p. 11).
4. *Culture*: Yiftachel claims that a core culture within a city or nation state is usually favoured over minority cultures, thereby forming another method of social and ethnic control.

A different stream of work takes a more direct route and begins to develop ideas of how a postmodern planning might actually look or work. There is no clear 'this is what postmodern planning should be', for the reasons I highlighted earlier. One instead finds hints or suggestions. Beauregard, for example, argues that planning in a postmodern form should involve key themes such as openness and fluidity: 'The texts of a postmodern planner, in fact, should be consciously fragmented and contingent, nonlinear, without aspiration to comprehensiveness, singularity or even compelling authority' (1996, p. 192).

Similarly, Soja (1997) highlights various dimensions that follow from the themes of the postmodern explored earlier:

> Such adaptation requires a much deeper and more disruptive critique than has yet occurred, especially if planning is to maintain the progressive project and emancipatory potential that have always been central to its purpose and development. For planning and planners to take advantage of the new possibilities and opportunities of postmodernity and to avoid its very powerful anti-progressive tendencies and enticing diversions into whimsy, planning theory and planning practice must engage in far-reaching deconstruction and reconstruction, perhaps a more far-reaching and wrenching conceptual restructuring than has ever occurred before. (1997, p. 238)

Within this concept of postmodern planning are warnings concerning the possible anti-progressive or less desirable elements of the postmodern, such as relativism. Notwithstanding such warnings Soja goes on to advance some more specific principles that would underpin a more postmodern planning. First, any new postmodern planning theory must build upon openness and flexibility and be 'suspicious of any attempt to formalise a single totalising way of knowing, no matter how progressive it may appear to be' (1997, p. 245). Second, such openness should be used as a basis for understanding *and encouraging* social reality, including fragmentation, multiplicity and difference. Here Soja appears to move towards endorsing a form of incrementalism and political fragmentation in practice (though it is difficult to gauge because the point is not developed sufficiently). Finally, the basis for Soja's approach is the critical writing of a host of postmodern theorists who provide a number of directions that postmodern planning theory might take, including an interest in the politics of the body, non-oppressive built environments and a new cultural politics of location, positionality, place, site and context (1997, p. 247).

Soja has stuck his neck out and thought about how a postmodern planning might work, and for this he should receive some credit. His approach takes a moderate postmodern line that seeks to avoid the more nihilistic and relativistic possibilities of postmodern thinking more associated with the likes of Baudrillard. Soja does, however, follow a less desirable aspect of postmodern thought through his need to enforce diversity much in the same way that Lyotard felt this necessary. The question that arises is: to what extent is Soja replacing modern over-arching narratives with postmodern ones? There is another issue about the level of generality Soja advances. To be fair, one cannot criticize Soja for being too prescriptive and then not prescriptive enough, though the interpretation of what phrases such as 'fragmentation, multiplicity and difference' (1997, p. 245) actually mean for planning is unclear.

The second attempt to develop a more prescriptive or detailed approach for a postmodern planning has been advanced by Sandercock's *Towards Cosmopolis* (1998) and her subsequent *Cosmopolis II: Mongrel Cities in the 21st Century* (2003). Her slant on the postmodern is through diversity and, specifically, ethnic and racial tolerance. For her, planning should work towards a more plural and diverse society. Currently, planning is based on modern principles and is socially exclusive, gender biased, racially intolerant and unifying the diverse voices of minorities. For planning to work towards a postmodern and pluralistic form, Sandercock identifies five principles that are 'The minimum foundations necessary to create a new order of urban civility out of the current new world disorder, and link these to debates about urban governance and planning' (1998, p. 183):

1. *Social justice*: The problem of current conceptions of social justice is that they are equated with market outcomes. Sandercock argues that a broader definition of injustice and/or inequality is required that is not limited to the material and/or economic realm. Gender studies and feminist critiques have provided an alternative approach that links injustice with oppression and domination. Oppression is particularly relevant in the forms of cultural imperialism and violence against increasing diversity in the new world disorder.
2. *The politics of difference*: Having identified the problem, the answer Sandercock proposes lies in an improved politics of

difference based on an inclusionary commitment through discussion. Such a discursive commitment would emphasize the positive aspects of difference. Concerns over group unity, and the focus of such on a proposal or immediate or local issues in such an 'identity politics', are raised and addressed by Sandercock. These groups, she claims, now participate in broader coalition politics to achieve more macro-level aims such as social justice. And the homogeneity question is not an issue, according to Sandercock, as in *realpolitik* such demarcation does not exist. A politics of difference requires 'big tent' politics, which includes such groups rather than excludes them.

3. *Citizenship*: Building on the inclusionary ethic, the next principle of a postmodern city concerns the question of citizenship. The outsider status of many citizens in increasingly fragmented societies requires a more fluid conception of citizenship that constantly reinterprets and refines what is meant by the term, rejecting homogenizing approaches that set out *a priori* what it is to be a citizen.
4. *The idea/l of community*: Building on the individually orientated concept of citizenship, Sandercock goes on to argue for a reformed conception of community. Communities have traditionally been associated with either territorial exclusion (we're in so you're out) or been so vague as to be almost meaningless. Instead, like in formulation of citizenship, there are communities of resistance that refuse homogeneity and argue instead for multiple communities based on the multiple interface of 'I'.
5. *From public interest to a civic culture*: Modernist planning is based on the vague and unified notion of the 'public interest' – how does this relate to a postmodern planning concerned with difference. Implicit in the notion of the public interest is a split between planner and planned – the technical expert working towards what are assumed to be commonly agreed goals. This assumes a high degree of uniformity and sameness within society, all of which has come unstuck with postmodern critiques. Consequently, Sandercock's unified public interest becomes a heterogeneous pubic interest. Avoiding the natural response to this that it would consequently lead to nihilism and inaction,

> Sandercock instead argues that it is not the fragmentation of politics that would pit groups or individuals against each other, but power and domination. Here she begins to raise the spectre of the collaborative approach by arguing for a more inclusionary and pluralistic politics ('decision-makers' are retained, though a veto power remains for 'important' aspects). The struggle is therefore *against* representation (though what it is for is not clear). The assumption is that allowing '"hidden" voices to speak will change existing processes and outcomes to the appeal to some overall concept of justice' (1998, p. 198). So, the demonized 'public interest' becomes a more pluralistic and open 'civic culture'. Then, reluctantly, Sandercock turns to the *realpolitik* that precludes 'togetherness in difference' (1998, p. 199) because of the economic rationality that divides society (though the link between the two is left for the reader to assume).

These principles have significant implications for the practice of any planning. Planners would be encouraged to take more eclectic approaches to processes such as plan-making, as well as the ideas and goals within them. Planning would also go well beyond our current understanding of its forms to embrace and encourage civil disobedience and strikes. As opposed to the instrumental rationality of modernity, there would be a rationality based on communication much as the collaborative school advocates. Such processes would seem to be only fit for the micro-level politics of planning, however, as there will need to be some more formal level that provides the framework and boundaries.

Sandercock's approach clearly embodies some elements of postmodern thought through its emphasis on diversity and difference. Unlike Soja's approach, it is wedded to a more practical level, though like Soja's approach it is not a postmodern planning *per se* but a mixture of modern and postmodern thought. The actual foundations of Sandercock's postmodern thinking are vague, however, which has provided the basis of criticisms from some quarters: 'the book frustratingly does not explain the nature of postmodern planning in which we presume that theory is either conspicuously absent or becomes intensely personal and wide ranging – reflecting each person's *Weltanshauung*' (Sorensen and

Auster, 1998, p. 4). There are two more criticisms of Sandercock's approach that are worth airing. The first is the extent to which it is based on a fictitious view of planning practice being akin to a modern enterprise. I have touched upon this earlier so will not repeat my arguments again. The second point comes down to what planning can actually achieve and its role in the ills of a racial and ethnic monoculture that Sandercock ascribes to it. This is a point that Sorensen and Auster raise too and both argue that income inequality and ethnic intolerance are best tackled through other more related mechanisms such as adjustments to tax regimes, public education and anti-discrimination laws.

These criticisms help highlight some of the problems with translating postmodern social theory into postmodern planning theory, an enterprise that is fraught with difficulty. In more recent times attention has switched from the more general postmodern understandings and approaches to two related and more focused understandings: post-structuralism and complexity.

## Post-structuralism and complexity

There can be confusion over the terms post-structuralism and postmodernism. However, there are important differences (as well as some overlaps). While postmodernism is concerned with wider shifts in contemporary society and the philosophy of science that move on from modernism, post-structuralism is more specifically concerned with a rejection of structuralism and the ways in which society is composed of much more diverse and dynamic forces. At its core post-structuralism rejects or questions the idea that there are structures (economic, social and linguistic) that shape society and our thoughts and actions. Political-economy approaches discussed in Chapter 4 posit the idea that the state and individuals, as well as laws and wider cultural manifestations, are the product of an underlying economic structure to society. Structural linguistics looks for structures that underpin any language system. Similarly, structuralists look for underlying forces and mechanisms that explain the apparent randomness and complexity of what we see and experience in everyday life. Post-structuralists, on the other hand, argue that society is not closed or linear, as in the structuralist interpretation, but much more open, dynamic and fluid.

Further, any attempts to try and establish causal mechanisms (structures) are historically and culturally situated. In other words, the ways in which we interpret the present cannot be objective or 'for all time'. Instead, we interpret a situation and provide a specific, individual view that is mediated through and influenced by wider social and cultural lenses. Structures are therefore not separate from actors or processes but are closely related and constituted. Consequently, post-structuralism has a concern with how knowledge is produced. Nigel Thrift (2004) has argued that under a post-structuralist perspective knowledge is indefinite (open and fluid) and contextualized, while theory is a practical though reflective means of advancement in the world. Post-structuralists therefore emphasize the ways in which some interpretations are 'closed down' so as to allow a dominant view to emerge (e.g., views that privilege male over female perspectives). On the other hand, there are movements to 'open up' some interpretations to allow other views to challenge more dominant ones.

Another theme of post-structuralism is the connectivity between the social and the spatial. Post-structuralists argue that spaces and places are open and engaged with other places and spaces. Further, space is constituted by diverse physical, biological, social and cultural processes, which also influence each other. What we see around us is a temporary stabilization of such processes. The question for the post-structuralist becomes: in whose interest did such stabilizations occur and what were the alternatives that did not emerge? The role of power, contestation and consensus in space-making become the focus. Any 'temporary stabilization' should not detract from the underlying understanding that space is always 'becoming' and therefore always likely to be unfinished (Massey, 2005).

Few approaches explicitly draw upon post-structuralism, though many embrace the notion that structures are themselves indistinguishable from the actors within them. Others also draw upon the way in which post-structuralism problematizes issues such as identity and argues that, rather than being fixed, identities are actually fluid and transformed through interpretation. Murdoch (2006) traces the lineage of a number of schools of planning thought to a post-structuralist perspective, including collaborative or communicative planning. I cover these two approaches separately in Chapter 9 because they are based upon and embrace the distinction between structure and agency and therefore are not post-structuralist *per se*. Where I do agree with Murdoch, however, is that collaborative and communicative approaches are participatory-based, focus upon relationships and processes and are underpinned by the multiple meanings that reflect different groups and individuals.

Ananya Roy (2005) explores the ways in which planning might produce the 'unplannable' in places where formal, 'planned' approaches are inappropriate or counterproductive. In an echo of earlier (e.g., Banham *et al.*, 1969), sometimes extreme libertarian (see, for example, Denman, 1980) perspectives, Roy argues that planning is an attempt to impose or restore order and, in doing so, brings land and property into the realm of market relations. 'Legitimated' land can be bought and sold, whereas informal developments can lie outside of market relations and play an important role in providing affordable property. Thus, planning should also consider that some objectives of planning can be achieved by 'non-planning' or, in Roy's categorization, regulatory exceptions. The example given concerns the way in which formalized planning might require land and development to meet certain standards (e.g., infrastructure provision, density, landscaping, etc.) that would make the land/development itself unaffordable. In the UK, a parallel might be the widely used exception to the normal restrictions on new development in the open countryside for agricultural workers. Because of the restrictions upon new supply, the value of existing homes in rural areas is often much higher than agricultural workers can afford. Exceptions can be made to allow new houses, which are then reserved in perpetuity for agricultural workers, thereby reducing the market value (and inviting widespread abuse of the system).

There is an important distinction between Roy's informal planning and the more ideologically driven libertarian approaches, however. Roy is arguing that formality and questions of land and property ownership can raise important issues that will have multiple and contested responses. In other words, the function of planning and the 'taken for granted' role of formalizing space and place are contestable.

In a similar vein, Holston (1995) claims that modernist planning seeks to plan without contradiction or conflict through presenting a homogeneous future. The question that Holston seeks to explore is how planning can better engage with and even encourage the variety of ways in which the 'social' derails and subverts state (planning) agendas. Of particular concern are those with multiple identities (e.g., business people with a concern for environmental issues) and those that exist at the edges of the state (e.g., the homeless). Such individuals constitute what Holston refers to as 'insurgent citizens', as they introduce new identities and practices, which disturb established histories. Planning should be based on the notion of a constant reinvention of the social and the present.

Such locally sensitive planning can have downsides, as Holston concedes. It can allow small groups to establish themselves as being somehow 'outside' of society, which can result in exclusion and intolerance, for example gated communities. As a result, planning needs to be both modern and postmodern or, in Holsten's words, encourage a complementary antagonism between these two engagements. How planning should achieve this is not entirely clear, though some methodological techniques and attitudes are suggested.

Like postmodernism, post-structuralism is an emerging approach to planning theory and has not yet enjoyed significant interest. As with much contemporary planning theory, questions still remain whether such approaches are post-stucturalist or simply sensitive to difference. Perhaps the panoply of theory for what are quite simple and straightforward developments of planning practice is not justified (I'm sure this is a point that many practitioners and students would agree with in relation to a lot of planning theory). For example, in the view of Harvey, the role of planning in a post-structuralist interpretation becomes one of 'carving out' permanences from the flow of processes that create spaces (1996). But how permanent is permanent? If space is always 'becoming' in Massey's phrase (2007), then many plans and strategies actually 'freeze' the flow of the social and the spatial. Planning can make the temporary become much more permanent. For example, many historic places have strict controls upon future development. As an approach, conservation allows the controlled evolution of such places, though at a much different pace to, say, edge of city commercial developments. The limit upon the size of new development in the City of London, in order to protect views to St Paul's Cathedral, has helped create demand for places such as London Docklands, where such limits are far less stringent. St Paul's

Cathedral was completed in 1708 and the City of London has restricted development that would affect views of it since 1938. It would be almost unthinkable that this policy would change in the near or even distant future. Similarly, the policy of a green belt around London that restricts new development was introduced in the 1930s and remains as popular as ever.

If the idea is for planning to create an oxymoronic 'temporary permanence', then planning begins to act as a structuring force upon spatial 'becoming'. If the emphasis is upon temporary, then less planning or, at least, a lighter regulatory touch would seem to be the model. Such approaches would allow for more temporary 'permanences'. So while post-structuralist approaches are part of the contemporary face of planning theory, they actually echo more traditional concerns with 'non-planning' (see Chapter 5): in the view of neo-liberals, the spontaneous order of society is preferable and more efficient than 'planned' places. Like post-structuralists (but for different reasons), they argue that we can never 'know' the full complexity of decisions.

What is clear is that post-structuralism poses a number of problems for planning practice, which is based upon future action and the necessity of agreement or fixity around a plan or strategy. Strategic plans can have timeframes of 15 years or more. But a more pertinent issue is that of planning doctrine (Alexander and Fauldi, 1996). Ideas in planning, such as the role of green belts, can and do have a powerful permanence outside of formal planning policy or plans. Planners and their knowledge and ideas, therefore, can act as structuring forces and create other permanences.

One final issue relates to the extent to which the concerns of post-structuralism are new. Sandercock, for example, claims that

> Contemporary cities are sites of struggles over space, which are really two kinds of struggle: one a struggle of life space against economic space, the other a struggle over belonging. Who belongs where, and with what citizenship rights, and with what citizenship rights, in the mongrel cities of the 21st century? (2003, p. 4)

It's difficult to argue with that, but to what extent is this a contemporary phenomenon? Was nineteenth-century New York a homogeneous place that didn't involve struggles over space and belonging? What contemporary planning theorists have excelled at is the 'rediscovery' of messiness and conflict. Arguably, this is nothing new. What are different are the responses of the state and planners to such messiness and these have varied through time.

## Complexity and post-structuralism

In Chapter 3 we looked at attempts to model places though reductionist approaches based upon systems analyses: cities were a form of system, much like biological systems, that could be broken down, understood and modelled. Planners embraced the notion that computers provided a way of 'testing' and predicting changes to 'the system' caused by a new development, for example. While the approach has largely been discredited for its failure to accurately account for and model the complexity of places systems, analysts did not simply die out to be replaced by more political and social perspectives. Instead, attention turned to how better to understand cities as complex places. This led, as I set out in Chapter 3, to cities and places being seen as 'open' rather than 'closed' places or systems.

This has, in turn, led some to explore how we can move forward (as planners) and 'carve out permanences' (e.g., create plans) in a postmodern world, underpinned by a post-structuralist sensibility. One way forward has been to link post-structuralism to a rethought systems approach – complexity. Complexity is based on an understanding of places being complex, open systems, which are nested spatially and relationally with other places at different scales, as well as with individuals, households, neighbourhoods etc. At the same time, urban systems are also linked to ecological systems. No system or scale is privileged as changes and dynamics in any part of the system can affect other parts. From this perspective, planning is a process of understanding and helping manage change, but it is not deterministic and nor are traditional structural influences such as the economy.

Cilliers (1998) identifies a number of links between post-structuralism and complexity:

1. Complex systems consist of a large number of elements. Post-structuralism is underpinned by the notion of multiplicity.

2. The elements in a complex system act dynamically. Actors within a post-structuralist understanding consider that the self is constituted by its relation to others.
3. There is a rich level of interaction. Post-structuralists emphasize the breakdown in distinctions between structure and agency and the historically contextualized understanding of structure.
4. Interactions are non-linear. Post-structuralism highlights the 'open' and asymmetrical nature of society – the same piece of information or cause may have different effects at different times.
5. Feedback and emergence. Complexity and complex adaptive systems are interdependent and co-exist, influence and are influenced by other systems.

Byrne sees the relationship between complexity and post-structuralism and post-modernism thus:

> I generally think of complexity in rather dialectical terms. If traditional 'positivist' science, which planning engaged with through its relationship with engineering, is a thesis, and 'postmodernist' and related relativisms, which dismiss 'real' understanding as a basis for action, constitute an antithesis, then complexity which allows for real understanding, i.e., agreed descriptions of context and potential, but delimits the range in time and space of that understanding, is a synthesis. (2003, pp. 173–4)

The distinction between the understanding and use of complexity in this chapter as opposed to Chapter 3 comes down to a difference between modelling and theory. This chapter is more concerned with the use of complexity as a way of understanding and conceptualizing spaces and places and, in that sense, there are strong connections with post-structuralist approaches. According to Byrne (2003), the link between planning and complexity is one that allows progress back into the narrative, bringing planning back from the postmodern abyss of indeterminacy. It is not inevitable that planning all our progress through complexity: there are multiple futures, and social actions can determine which of all possible futures becomes real.

So where does this overlap between complexity and post-structuralism take us and planning theory? The answer at the moment is 'not very far'. Cilliers (1998) links and Byrne's understanding both highlight the similar worldviews of post-structuralist thought and complexity, but neither provide much in the way of engagement with planning theory or practice. In Byrne's view planners and planning should follow traditional 'survey-analysis-plan' techniques, though embedded within participatory processes. Dialogue between 'the planner' and 'the planned' will give a better understanding of social realities as well as an iterative technique for pragmatic planning that accounts for multiple realities and possible futures (Figure 8.1).

In terms of how planning approaches survey, analysis and proposal, Byrne suggests methodological pluralism, combining quantitative and qualitative, ethnographic and historical, analytical and holistic as ways of understanding the multiple causality of complex systems and their relationship to other systems (2003, p. 176). What this process and approach rejects is probably as important as what it includes. Gone are the deterministic understandings and approaches, including technological determinism (e.g., cities and regions are being shaped by new technological change), to be replaced by a more modest and balanced understanding of the influences upon the future, including that of human agency through collective action and everyday practices. While this is mainstream post-structuralism, there are nods in the direction of important structural forces too. As Byrne notes, complex systems basically remain the same for long periods and then change quickly and significantly. In other words the *long durée* of places clearly implies that cities themselves are some form of structure or major influ-

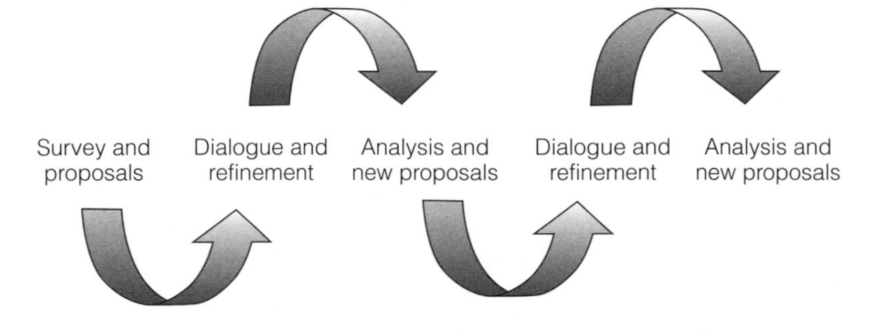


**Figure 8.1** Iterative and interactive process for complex systems planning

ence upon change. Batty develops this and tries to focus the attention of planners and others upon five distinct drivers of change in cities: randomness, historical accident, physical determinism, natural advantage and competitive advantage (2005, p. 21).

Here we begin to notice some of the differences between post-structuralism in theory and complexity. Structure or the significance of some drivers of change *are* clearly important in different futures. The question is what weight to put on them both as part of the process and in a realistic assessment of the likely impacts upon possible futures. Davy (2008) takes a slightly different approach in thinking of a post-structuralist planning. Rather than a concern with structures, he focuses instead on rationalities and the need to move the monorationality that currently dominates planning to polyrationality. Monorationality is any attempt to make stakeholders agree on a common future (see Chapter 9). Polyrationality, on the other hand, would work by explaining the outcome of places as being the product of four different rationalities. These four rationalities – hierarchy, individualism, community and fatalism – are groupings of distinct approaches to the social creation of space and as such each creates its own style of character of place. The trick, according to Davy is to allow or facilitate cities to be planned in ways that accommodate all four rationalities in order to better reflect places where people feel comfortable or happy. And, because each rationality and its place-product can be read as being desirable (city of the self) or undesirable (city of the other), there are eight broad possibilities (Table 8.1).

The possibility and desirability of producing a city of multiple faces and places is not limited to these eight categories because, as Davy points out, the interface or border of such different places is one where the juxtaposition of characteristics creates more, differ-

***Table 8.1*** **Eight cities**

| *Rationality* | *Cities of the self* | *Cities of the other* |
|---|---|---|
| Hierarchist | The well-ordered city | The despotic city |
| Individualist | The bold city | The careless city |
| Egalitarian | The sharing city | The excluding city |
| Fatalist | The relaxed city | The indifferent city |

*Source*: based on Davy, 2008, p. 308.

ent places. The underlying point of Davy's approach is that diversity, not unity, creates successful places. Some post-structuralists would accuse Davy of falling back into traditional modes of planning by his limit of rationalities and options, though the general point remains that his approach builds upon complexity and seeks difference in its future searching much in the same way that Holston and Roy do.

## Conclusions

Once one begins to look, it is not difficult to see the influences of post-structuralism in current understandings of planning:

> the 'places' of cities and urban areas cannot be understood as integrated unities with a singular driving dynamic, contained with clearly defined spatial boundaries. They are instead complex constructions created by the interaction of actors in multiple networks who invest in material projects and who give meaning to the quality of places. The webs of relations escape analytical attempts to 'bound them'. (Healey, 2007, p. 2)

The implications for planning as an activity are many. The notion of spatial planning captures some of the multi-sectoral, coordinating role of planning: planners and planning can legitimately be concerned with health, education and social issues, as well as the more traditional land use concerns. One problem with this 'planning as everything' approach is where to draw the sectoral 'boundaries'. Another is the need to deliver and act, particularly around issues such as climate change and housing affordability. While there is a difference between spatial planning as an approach to thinking and spatial plans as a product, the relationship between the two can be driven and influenced by legal requirements to produce plans to certain formats and in certain ways, as well as administrative boundary limitations.

Clearly, then, there is a yawning gap between the trajectory of post-structuralist thought on planning and the practical implications for planners on the ground. The webs and networks of relations between people and places do not easily, if at all, translate into planning practice. According to Healey (2007), existing governance landscapes also preclude such an approach. There are obvious practical difficulties that, at present, remain unbridgeable or, at least, it is difficult to conceive of how they might be bridged. The outcome might be that postmodern and post-structuralist approaches, like Marxist interpretations, are more suited for analysis.

Contemporary planning theory has been very good at 'opening up' processes and thinking (Rydin, 2007) and postmodern and post-structuralist approaches emphasize an 'epistemology of multiplicity' (Sandercock, 1998). In such understandings there is a breakdown between the 'planner and the planned'. Experiences are taken as knowledge and there is a relativist approach to validating different knowledges. In other words, all views, whatever their basis, are regarded as equal. The same is true of relational webs and networks. As Rydin (2007) rightly points out, planning action requires a parallel ability to 'close down' knowledge, inputs and 'voices' and provide criteria against which to judge different knowledges. Without this action becomes, at the very least, difficult. A useful example that Rydin advances to support the problems with relativist knowledge claims and planning concerns climate change (2008). Despite the weight of scientific evidence on the relationship between climate change and human activity, a relativist or social construction of knowledge approach can dismiss this as being simply one perspective. In other words, under this view there is no recourse to 'objective truth', just a host of different claims regardless of validity. How can planning and planners move forward in the vital task of addressing such issues if it cannot be proven that such a link exists? Clearly planning practice *is* addressing climate change and in doing so it is making absolutist claims. It is planning theory or, more accurately, some planning theories, that reject this.

One dimension of this, as Alexander (2008) points out, is to modify the broad notion that knowledge is socially produced:

> The 'social construction' model does not recognize any absolute truth-claims – it implies that there's no single observable reality out there – while 'engagement with material reality' must acknowledge that some absolute truth-claims may be valid (the presumption behind 'closing-down'), based as they are on a material reality that exists. (Alexander, 2008, p. 208)

The upshot of this is significant and it represents a departure from the whole postmodern/post-structuralist *oeuvre*: postmodern planning theory is built upon the notion that knowledge is socially constructed. Rydin attempts to refine and modify postmodern theory through a differentiation of different kinds of knowledge. But the fit is not comfortable. Rydin's hope to construct 'an alternative, still postmodern, planning theory' (2008, p. 212) that was based upon both socially constructed knowledge *and* absolute truth claims needs to recognize the fundamental challenge that the latter makes to postmodern positions.

The other main route that planning theory has taken following disenchantment and rejection of modernism is that of reformed or neo-modernism. The main approach or epistemology for planning in this approach is collaborative or communicative planning and it is to this that we now turn.

# 9 Collaborative Planning

## Introduction

Like postmodern approaches to planning theory, collaborative planning starts with the question: how can we 'make sense' of what is happening and plan for the future within a dynamic and increasingly complex society? When there is wholesale distrust of the political process, a fragmentation into single-issue politics and a plurality of positions, how can we come to agree on matters of concern? The problem for planners is that society is changing and changing quickly, while planning as a practice and as a collection of processes remains wedded to ideas and procedures from a different age. Central to these ideas is the debate over rationality. Despite attempts to improve public involvement and widen participation, planning processes remain dominated by instrumental rationality, born of the Enlightenment and modernity and typified by the systems or synoptic approach to planning of, among others, McLoughlin (1969) and Faludi (1973). This involves separating means from 'given' ends and systematically identifying, evaluating and choosing means in a technical and 'apolitical' way, as discussed in Chapter 1. The challenge to the systems approach has come from a variety of quarters, not least the political economy-inspired critiques of society and planning. But the normative poverty of this approach is still with us – how can planners work with disparate and diverse communities, reach agreement between them and formulate a 'plan'?

One approach that has gained increasing theoretical popularity is to see planning as a communicative or collaborative process. As Healey (1996, 1997) points out, there have been three main influences upon this perspective. First and most important is the work of Jürgen Habermas, who has sought to reconstruct the 'unfinished project of modernity'. Habermas has questioned the dominance of instrumental rationality in everyday life and sought instead to re-emphasize other ways of knowing and thinking. Second is the work by Michel Foucault (among others), who began to look behind language and meaning and its potentially dominatory nature in hiding existing power relations. Finally, there is the work of Anthony Giddens and the institutionalist school, which examines ways in which we interrelate through webs of social relations as well as ways in which we can co-exist in society. Of these different influences, the work of Habermas stands out as the backbone of the communicative approach and has heavily influenced the work of those concerned with planning as a communicative process (e.g., Forester, 1989, 1993; Healey, 1993a, 1994, 1995, 1997, 2003).

The background to Habermas's work is a critique of modernity. I outlined 'the modern' and modernity in Chapter 8. There, I set out the main difference between the postmodernists and the reforming or neo-modernists as being about whether modernism as social thought can be 'modified' or 'redefined' by recognizing tensions and criticisms, as Habermas has proposed, or whether it never had any legitimate basis in the first place and has been overtaken by events as postmodern and post-structuralist thinkers argue.

What the two schools agree about is that there are problems with aspects of modernism. As I discussed at the end of the previous chapter, modernists wish to hold on to some form of 'objective' knowledge though shift it away from scientific or instrumental rationality, while the postmodernists argue that there is no such thing as objective knowledge in any form, that all knowledge is relative and becoming more so as society becomes more fragmented or plural. Put in another way, McLennan (1992, p. 330) argues that the postmodern challenge involves questioning the following typical modern tenets:

1. The view that our knowledge of society, like society itself, is holistic, cumulative and broadly progressive in character.
3. That we can attain rational knowledge of society.
4. That such knowledge is universal and thus objective.
5. That sociological knowledge is both different from and superior to 'distorted' forms of thought, such as ideology, religion, common sense, superstition and prejudice.

6. That social scientific knowledge, once validated and acted upon, can lead to mutual liberation and social betterment among humanity generally.

Lyotard questions the whole Enlightenment basis of objectives and scientific knowledge; science has always been in conflict with narratives. Judged by the yardstick of science, the majority of these prove to be fables or myths. But to the extent that science does not restrict itself to stating useful regularities and seeks the truth, it is obliged to legitimate the rules of its own game. It then produces a discourse or legitimation with respect to its own status (1984, p. xxiii). In Lyotard's view, science has no more claim to objective knowledge than what he terms 'narratives' or stories. Instead, science is itself based on higher-level narratives or 'meta-narratives', which involve values and assumptions. McLennan (1992) explains this point further. Scientific progress, he argues, is often seen as a necessary and crucial part of the drive for industrial and commercial growth. However, Marxists, for example, would argue that science ultimately serves, or ought to serve, the liberation of humanity from exploitation.

Others would ascribe a different ultimate goal for science: 'many supposedly objective aspirations to science inevitably tend to be framed by some kind of metanarrative involving distinctly value laden notions of social progress and human emancipation' (McLennan, 1992, p. 332). This obviously questions the entire basis of the Enlightenment idea of objective knowledge, as scientists themselves have different views on what they are pursuing and why. As such, postmodernists argue that we should abandon the modernist search for 'truth' and instead embrace uncertainty and agnosticism. This is particularly so as the world becomes more pluralistic and fragmented with a variety of cultures, language, histories etc. How can modernists argue that knowledge can be objective – surely it depends on where you stand? And if this is the case then can there really be common 'rules'? According to Habermas (1984, 1987) and others the answer is yes. Unlike postmodernists, Habermas is more concerned with building upon modernism rather than abandoning it altogether. There is not one over-arching rationalism in modernism, as postmodernists claim, but three, based on science, morality and art. Although knowledge and access to these different rationales may have been hijacked by 'professionals', such as planners, the answer is to reclaim rationality from a narrow instrumental/scientific focus, which has dominated the non-'scientific' world, and rediscover what Habermas (1984) terms 'communicative rationality'. This involves breaking down the dominance of scientific objectivism and building instead a different kind of objectivity based on agreement between individuals reached through free and open discourse.

The problem has been that instrumental rationality has 'crowded out' other ways of thinking and knowing and distorted power relations in society. It is this development of modernism that is the basis for planning as a communicative process. But this approach has not been without its critics from the postmodernists. For Lyotard (1984), the pluralistic nature of the world is irreducible and the search for common links pointless and misleading. Habermas accepts the existence of a complex mix of cultures and discourses, though argues that there are ways in which people can 'make sense together'. It is possible for a proliferation of subcultures to take place precisely because the need for agreement as basic rules of social interaction is satisfied at even higher levels of abstraction. It is precisely because the world is getting more not less fragmented that it needs to be able to agree common 'rules' when communicating. Further, the relativist position of Lyotard (that everywhere and everyone is so different that we cannot ever achieve an 'objective' truth) is self-contradictory. As McLennan (1992, p. 339) puts it, 'to say that discursive values are always radically and necessarily unmatchable looks itself suspiciously like an absolute claim to validity, and this is something that the relativists hold to be impossible'. To some extent the reformed modernists and postmodernists seem to agree on two things. First, that society is complex and getting more so and, second, that scientific rationalism has dominated other ways of thinking and knowing and is not itself 'objective'. The disagreement is that Lyotard (1994) and Bauman (1989) believe that no form of rationality can exist and Habermas (1984, 1987) and others (e.g., Giddens, 1990) believe that it can through communicative rationality. This then is the debate between modernism and postmodernism in terms of social thought. It is here that we can leave postmodernism and explore the ideas of communicative rationality developed in the abstract by Habermas and in the practical for planning by Forester (1989, 1993) and Healey (1993a, 1994, 1995, 1997). But the arguments of the postmodernists provide a useful critique of the whole principle of communicative rationality which, when added to the more practical criticisms, helps us put it in perspective.

## Communicative rationality

To understand communicative rationality we must also know something about discourse. Hall (1992a) defines a discourse as a group of statements that provide a language for talking about (representing) a particular kind of knowledge about a topic. Foucault (1980) adds to this by claiming that discourse is about the production of knowledge through language, though discourse is itself produced by a practice – discursive practice – the practice of meaning. As such, language is related to a power struggle as it 'gets in the way of' deciding what is true and false (Hall, 1992a). For critical theorists like Habermas, the power behind language and discourse is derived from the capitalist mode of production. So, not only is discourse related to power it is also a way in which power is applied. Language is a way of maintaining or developing power relations. But it has the potential to expose such relations as well.

The problem, according to critics of modernity, is that the instrumentally or scientific rational way of thinking and approaching discourse has limited this potential. Scientific or instrumental rationalism, born of the Enlightenment, has been defined in terms of the capacity to devise, select and affect good means to clarified ends. Allied to this is the Enlightenment idea that rational choices concerning theories and beliefs about matters of fact, values and morals should be made through reference to a set of objective standards that are equally applicable to all individuals (Dryzek, 1990). The problems with this approach have been identified as:

1. Destroying the more congenial, spontaneous, egalitarian and intrinsically meaningful aspects of human association – an 'iron cage' around human existence, according to Weber.
2. Being anti-democratic through the concentration of political power, either by professions or bureaucracies.
3. Repressing individuals by repressing freedom and the potential for individuals to express themselves.

4. Being inadequate in representing complex social problems without disaggregating them into their constituent parts.
5. Making effective and appropriate policy analysis impossible.

As we have seen above, these criticisms have led to two approaches; the first to discard modernist modes of thought altogether (Lyotard, etc.), the second, to attempt to reclaim modernity back from instrumental rationality (Habermas, among others). There have been various approaches that have worked towards alternative forms of rationality, more or less based on Aristotle's ideas of 'practical reason', which involved persuasion, reflection upon values and free disclosure of ideas. Nevertheless, the main exponent of alternative forms of rationality was Jürgen Habermas.

Habermas presents us with the concepts of 'lifeworld' and 'system'. The lifeworld is a symbolic network in which subjects interact and, through shared practical knowledge, coordinate social action. As Healey and Hillier (1995) put it, it is the realm of personal relationships. The system, on the other hand, such as the capitalist economy or bureaucratic administration, operates through power and interest and forms the context within which the lifeworld operates. Habermas (1987) argues that the system dominates the lifeworld (though it was created from the rationalization of the lifeworld) and restricts the scope for communicative action. Communicative action (or rationality) has been in constant battle with instrumental rationality since the Enlightenment. But, as opposed to the roll-call of problems identified with instrumental rationality and objectivism identified by Dryzek above, communicative action allows people to 'develop, confirm and renew their memberships in social groups and their own identities' (Habermas, quoted in Healey and Hillier, 1995, p. 21). And, as opposed to the processes for reaching agreement that we experience on joint action at the moment (e.g., the planning process), which involves power, capital, compromise etc. (whether pluralist, corporatist, elitist or whatever), communicative rationality has the prospect of a completely different way of achieving joint action. This would involve the lifeworld reclaiming ground lost to the system.

However, as Dryzek (1990) and others have pointed out, communication is concerned in part with the coordination of actions, so communicative rationality cannot totally replace instrumental rationality; it can only restrict it to a subordinate role. Here we must distinguish between communicative *action* and communicative *rationality*. Communicative action is orientated towards intersubjective understanding, the coordination of action through discussion and the socialization of members of the community. Communicative rationality is the extent to which this action is characterized by the reflective understanding of competent actors (Dryzek, 1990). The battle between the lifeworld and the system involves institutions and processes that we encounter in the public realm every day – from battles over bypasses to spending on healthcare. Public opinion in such arenas actually seems to make little difference, as many who have dealt with a planning application will appreciate. People are then forced to 'play the game', that is, begin to exercise their influence in ways that will make their voices heard. This involves becoming 'part of the system' by such measures as lobbying or questioning the basis of instrumentally rational decisions. More often than not it also involves alienating and excluding people. Measures such as 'public participation' serve to maintain the legitimacy of the 'system', while concentrating power and decision-making in the hands of bureaucrats and politicians. But the potential for people to reach decisions through communicative action and 'reclaim' ground lost to instrumental rationality is still there.

To do this Habermas (1984) explores the assumptions we make when we communicate and convey knowledge from one person to another. We try to reach agreement on the basis of reciprocal understanding, shared knowledge, mutual trust and accord. Implicit are at least four claims that convey the validity of our communication, without which we would not claim to be communicating at all:

1. *Truth* of propositions about our external reality.
2. *Rightness* of our interpersonal relations with the other person.
3. *Truthfulness* about our internal subjective state.
4. *Comprehensibility* of our language. (Low, 1991)

Although we may fail to achieve these claims, communicative action requires us to attempt to achieve them through discourse that is characterized by:

1. Interaction free from domination (the exercise of power).
2. Interaction free from strategizing by the actors involved.
3. Interaction free from (self-) deception.
4. All actors being equally and fully capable of making and questioning arguments.
5. No restrictions on participation.
6. The only authority being that of a good argument. (Dryzek, 1990)

Any consensus reached under these conditions can be regarded as 'rational', but there are large questions regarding the extent to which agreement can be reached (what about self-interest, for example?). This has been a common criticism of Habermas. The way out, according to Habermas (1984) and Bernstein (1983), is to claim that communicative rationality provides only procedural criteria about how disputes and arguments might be resolved and about how principles might be constructed (Dryzek, 1990, p. 17). Further, a difference of views is acceptable, providing these views are reached in a communicatively rational way.

The theory of communicative action and rationality has been criticized as being too abstract (Low, 1991) and Habermas himself has been criticized for providing few indications of how such an approach could work in practice (Healey and Hillier, 1995). But some attempts have been made to translate highly abstract ideas into a practical approach, as detailed below.

## The practical application of communicative rationality

Not only has instrumental rationality and modernism dominated discourse but it has also dominated the institutions of liberal democracy; their form and their functions. But while critics of modernity have spent a great deal of time exposing its weaknesses they have spent far less time in proposing alternatives. Although some attempts have been made I shall focus here on one specific approach. Dryzek (1990) sets out how a communicatively rational approach to institutions could work* and compares it to the

* While Dryzek terms his approach 'discursive democracy' for the purpose of consistency, we shall retain the term 'communicative rationality'. Dryzek's term seems to be aimed at combining communicative rationality with communicative action.

Popperian ideal of 'open society', that is, a liberal democracy that works *within* instrumental rationality. In order to challenge Popper's model, Dryzek identifies six elements of the political organization and sets out to produce a communicatively rational alternative.

*Ideal speech*

Habermas's ideal speech situation (truth, rightness, truthfulness and comprehensibility) may not exist in liberal democratic society (where power and interests dominate) and neither, he claims, could it ever exist – ideal speech is and will always be violated in the 'real world'. But it does exist in daily communication between individuals (as opposed to communication between, say, two countries or institutions). In this sense it can be used to create consensus and expose existing power relations, including the dominance of instrumental rationality. It is this exposure role, its critical function, which is its main strength. The communicative rational world would seek to facilitate ideal speech through providing the necessary conditions for it – an authentic public sphere.

*An authentic public sphere*

Central to the practical use of communicative rationality and ideal speech is the 'public sphere' defined as:

> wherever two or more individuals . . . assemble to interrogate both their own interactions and the wider relations of social and political powers within which they are always and already imbedded. Through this autonomous association, members of public spheres consider what they are doing, settle how they will live together, and determine . . . how they might collectively act. (Keane, 1984, quoted in Dryzek, 1990, p. 37)

Such public spheres existed in the eighteenth century, though were eventually dominated by instrumental rationality and the existing power structures in society. Today it is difficult to envisage a public sphere in Habermas's sense because groups all around us are directed by 'normal' relations. For example, a residents' association, local council or parent–teacher association are all places where individuals come together, but they are guided in their actions, speech, discourse by a variety of traditions, norms, cultural baggage etc. – for example, the election of a chair, the taking of minutes, an agenda all serve to 'direct' any meeting. In Habermas's public sphere, the precepts of communicative rationality are followed. However, some more contemporary examples of a genuine public sphere are identified below. The public sphere could be created on the basis of two ideas: discourse and holistic experimentation.

### *Discourse and holistic experimentation*

The public sphere would require two facets. First, free and open communication in political life orientated towards reciprocal understanding, trust and an undistorted consensus. This would avoid goal-directed pursuits, which thrust imperatives on political interaction. At one (very limited) extreme this could take the form of a 'freedom of speech' ideal, much as in the USA, though this would appear not to guarantee ideal speech or freedom from domination. Alternatively, political practice could take the form of experimentation with the aim of improving the conditions of the 'subjects' of any experiment through reflection and consensus, that is, allowing people to create their own politics, processes etc. through experimental and free association. This is not an experiment in the normal sense of the word, but it is an experiment that would be carried out repeatedly by the participants in the public sphere to determine their own political practices.

### *Discursive designs*

As Dryzek freely admits, the field of institutional designs is where communicative rationality is at its weakest. There is recognition of the need for some kinds of institutions, which may even be based along instrumentally rational lines as action is still required (remember that communicative rationality never sought to displace instrumental rationality but to create a better balance more favourable to the former). But how can institutions be sensitive to the variety of needs of communicative rationality? With difficulty, would seem to be the answer. Institutions that need to allow political decisions to be reached without restriction upon participation seem to be the guiding principle.

Nevertheless, as Dryzek points out, communicative rationalists are at a disadvantage here. First, communicative rationalists are profoundly suspicious of the modern liberal state. Second, the idea of an organization tends to imply some sort of instrumental rationality and imposing processes and procedures; better to leave it to the individuals involved. But the 'design' process itself can be discursive. The best that seems to be possible is a set of criteria to be followed by participants when coming together, including the principle of no power except the power of better argument, no barriers to participation and no constitutions or rules (as these are up for negotiation too). But what about enforcing decisions or decision rules? The typical response is that consensus would be achieved and rule enforcement would not be necessary, but is this realistic? Can ideal speech ever be realized? Reasoned *dis*agreement through open discussion is more likely. According to Dryzek, individuals can then seek agreement on *what* is to be done while disagreeing on *why*. A communicatively rational social institution is therefore built on the convergence of expectations. Individuals should participate as citizens, not representatives, and membership is open to all. The institution is orientated towards the generation and coordination of actions for a particular problem context. Within a liberal democracy, such an institution would help expose existing power relations within the state.

### *Incipient designs*

Incipient designs refers to existing situations within liberal democracy where communicative action is possible. Examples include the mediation of civil, labour, international and environmental disputes (Wall, 1981). Such communicative practices (though they are not termed as such) have a number of characteristics. First, they resolve problems of interest to all parties. Second, the context is initially characterized by a degree of conflict. Third, a neutral third party facilitates the discussion. Fourth, discussion is prolonged, face-to-face and governed by 'rules' of reasoned discourse (lack of threats, disclosure of bargaining position, etc.). Fifth, the product of the process is a reasoned, action-orientated consensus that is purely voluntary. Finally, such exercises are fluid and transient, lasting no longer than the particular problem. Recent interest in alternative ways of solving problems seems to have emerged from the success of these mediations, but it appears that people have invented or reached these processes themselves without regard to existing structures or norms but equally in the absence of any idea of what communicative rationality is.

*New social movements*

To demonstrate its practical nature, Dryzek claims that communicative rationality (though not by name) is already practised in a number of organizations, including movements concerned with peace, ecology, opposition to nuclear power, feminism, civil rights and community authority. The internal politics of such organizations is generally structured on a freely discursive basis and can contribute to the establishment or revival of free discourse generally. They tend to be characterized by uncompromising demands because they are not allied to any part of the state. The problem arises when groups such as the 'greens' become more politicized and organize as a political party. They then are in danger of compromising free and open discourse by having to play by the system's rules. Dryzek claims that communicative rationality is fully capable of inspiring a realistic programme for political organization. However, can it ever be more than a specialized solution in limited, non-conflict-ridden circumstances?

The problem is that communicative rationality has not really been attempted on a large scale and remains at the margins of politics. Part of the problem is that communicative rationality is just one competing paradigm among many, arguing that theirs is the most appropriate model for the role of the state. Others (e.g., representative democracy, legal democracy, etc.) are all firmly located within instrumentally rational or 'modern' systems. Communicative rationality is not only fighting instrumental rationality but also its manifestation in liberal democracy – a system that involves a prescriptive model of man that is uniform, atomistic and in a rational pursuit of an arbitrary set of purely subjective preferences (Dryzek, 1990, p. 52). Other problems include the growing complexity of society and problems generally, which, according to Weber, will require more not less instrumental rationality. Criticism of communicative rationality can be levelled at the theory and the practice, the latter shedding light on the former. So before we examine some of the problems we will turn to how it has been looked at in terms of planning, both theory and practice.

**Planning as a communicative process**

Planning is thoroughly 'modern': problem solving and the resolution of conflict in a positive manner leading to a solution is, of course, precisely what 'planning' does, in the sense of purposive rationality (Low, 1991, p. 234). While the debate concerning rationality and planning has a long history, alternative approaches have been far less obvious than critique. In this vein there are two challenges to instrumental rationality that are of concern to us: the *critical* and the *normative.* The critical approach sets out to demonstrate that current planning theory merely serves to perpetuate the status quo through the undemocratic nature of instrumental rationality, while the normative approach seeks to develop alternatives to instrumental rationality for planners that work towards 'democratization'. Before embarking on an exploration of communicative alternatives (normative), we will first briefly address the critical views of instrumental rationality and planning. These should be read in conjunction with the critiques advanced in Chapter 3.

Although planning theorists have been aware of criticisms of instrumental rationality and planning since the early 1970s, following Friedmann's transactive approach (Friedmann, 1973), practice is still dominated by the concern to be seen as 'objective' or 'scientific': 'planning aspires to be a science, to follow the rules of scientific activity and to embrace all these principles that are held high by the scientific community' (Camhis, 1979, p. 8). The scientific aspiration is probably best summed up in Faludi's rational comprehensive or synoptic approach (see Chapter 3). Such views see planning as a special way of deciding and acting, which involves the application of scientific knowledge in order to solve problems and achieve goals of a social system (Camhis, 1979, p. 8). This rational comprehensive approach requires people to consider what they ought to do in the light of what it is they want to accomplish. It assumes that

> objectives can be identified and articulated, that the outcome of alternative strategies can be projected and their expected utilities assessed by some goal-related objective criteria and that the respective probability of occurrence of relevant conditions can be predicted on the basis of available information. (Alexander, 1986, p. 47)

Various stages in the process are followed, including identifying objectives and constraints, evaluating alternative solutions and choosing the 'best' alternative to achieve any objectives. According to Friedmann, planners claim that their advanced degrees in relevant disciplines and professional fields give them privileged access to scientific knowledge and technical know-how. They also claim that this knowledge is generally superior to knowledge gained in other ways (from practical experience, for example). In this respect they speak as the true heirs of the Enlightenment (Friedmann, 1989, p. 40). So what are the problems with instrumental rationality and planning? According to Darke (1985), it involves a distinction between means and ends. While some, such as Reade (1985), believe that rational methods can be used to identify means towards particular 'given' ends, others, such as Alexander (1986), distinguish between two kinds of rationality in planning: formal and substantive.

Planning has favoured formal rationality – the use of formal procedures such as those outlined above to achieve 'given' ends. Substantive rationality, on the other hand, includes values, ideals and morals about the ends themselves (Darke, 1985, pp. 18–19). Two problems arise if planning merely follows formal (means) rationality. First, bureaucracies can raise formal rationality above substantive. For example, speed of decision-making in planning is not strictly an 'end', but it can become so at the expense of other ends such as quality in decisions. Second, ends themselves are not clear. Goal-setting is closely allied to the identification of alternative means. Planners have been accused of presenting political issues as if they were matters of fact or in some way 'value-free' (Darke, 1985) and believing that formal rationality will automatically lead to appropriate policy content (Camhis, 1979). As Forester (1989, p. 16) puts it, planners are more than navigators who keep their ship on course: they are necessarily involved with formulating the course. So planners are involved in both formal and substantive rationality. But the big question according to Alexander is: whose goals, which goals, goals when? (1986, p. 55). The problem is that you cannot separate means from ends. As Simon put it 'if you allow me to determine the constraints, I don't care who selects the optimisation criterion' (quoted in Alexander, 1986, p. 55). This challenge to value-neutrality is considered by Friedmann (1987), who poses six questions of the instrumentally rational planning approach:

1. Knowledge from instrumentally rational approaches is based on past events but planners need to have knowledge covering future events. What assumptions must be made in order to claim that knowledge of events in the past is relevant to 'knowing' the future?
2. The hypotheses, theories and models through which all scientific knowledge is expressed are radical simplifications of the world. But planning in the 'real world' is more complicated. Does knowledge lose its 'objective' character when the assumptions under which it is claimed to be true are relaxed?
3. All scientific and technical knowledge is either theoretical or methodological. By what criterion do planners choose among competing theories? Is choosing one theory instead of another a political act?
4. What are the claims of other kinds of 'knowledge' and what grounds can scientific and technological knowledge claim superior to other kinds of knowledge, especially when its application yields different results?
5. All empirical knowledge (scientific and other kinds) is validated by talking about the evidence, The construction of knowledge must therefore be regarded as an intensely social process. Such processes based on communication are structured politically and theoretically The knowledge we have about these processes is based on 'knowledge of the world', knowledge that is facts, experiences, beliefs and visions. Consequently, all knowledge is created through a social process. On what grounds, therefore, can planners argue that their view of the world should prevail?
6. Personal or shared beliefs about the world are an important obstacle in obtaining objective knowledge. How can planners claim to have privileged access to objective knowledge? When the personal knowledge of actors clashes with the scientific knowledge of planners is there any reason to think that one or the other is inherently better and should therefore be followed?

According to Forester (1989), the answer to such questions revolves around what he terms 'distortion'. Although both rational and incremental planning are realities, in practice they do not capture the realities of planners daily tasks: 'When we look at the day to day work of putting out bushfires, dealing with "random" telephone calls, debating with other staff, juggling priorities, bargaining here and organising there, trying to understand what in the world someone else (or some document) means the ... means-end view quickly comes to be a tempting but inadequate reconstruction of what actually goes on' (1989, p. 15). So, not only is instrumentally rational planning objectionable in principle, it is also limited in practice, or 'bounded' as Simon (1957) puts it. As opposed to the 'perfect' conditions required for the rational comprehensive approach, planners face:

- Ambiguous and poorly defined problems.
- Incomplete information about alternatives.
- Incomplete information about the baseline, the background of the 'problem'.
- Incomplete information about the range and content of values.
- Incomplete information about the range and content of values, preferences and interests.
- Limited time, limited skills and limited resources. (Forester, 1989, p. 50)

In addition to theoretical and practical limits there are also structural limits to rationality. Power in society is not diffuse and the ability to invest and act are unequally distributed. Similarly, powerful social, political and economic structures will determine not only who shouts loudest but also who is listened to most. Such conditions are of as much importance in structuring the planners' agenda as ambiguous information or unclear objectives (Forester, 1989, p. 60). The results of practical and structural limits to rationality for the planners are considerable. Planners will 'satisfice' (lower expectations of success from optimal), use social and organizational networks, draw on allegiances of other bodies and actors and bargain and adjust aims (Forester, 1989, pp. 54–9). Yet planning still sees itself as a 'rational' enterprise.

The results of planning's fascination with instrumental rationality are clearly visible according to Healey (1993b, p. 235); from the disaster of the high-rise tower block to the dominance of economic criteria to justify road building. A number of alternative conceptions of planning have developed to address this situation including Friedmann's 'transactive' planning (1973) and Etzioni's 'mixed scanning' (1967) among others though the latter retains instrumental rationality at its core. Obviously, the one that we are concerned with here is the development of communicative rationality and, more specifically, communicative action. What does communicative rationality 'mean' for planning? Certain issues repeatedly emerge in the literature: equity, social justice, democracy and sustainability. Planning as a communicative process has definite ideas about what planning is, ideas that challenge professional 'neutrality' and the *raison d'etre* of many planners: it is about planners having an agenda. Its content is the dilemma faced by all those committed to planning as a democratic enterprise aimed at promoting social justice and environmental sustainability (Healey, 1993b, p. 232). '[T]echnical and practical organisational knowledge alone will not help planners come to grips with problems of equity, the concentration of accumulation of wealth and the perpetuation of widespread poverty and suffering' (Forester, 1989, p. 76). The main focus is on domination and distortion. Critical theorists like Habermas are concerned with the influence of capitalism upon language or how it distorts the truth and creates or perpetuates domination. The role of planners is to expose this domination through recognizing and avoiding distortions. But this is not a simple relationship. Planners tend to work for organizations and, as Forester (1989) concludes, organizations not only produce instrumental results, they also reproduce social and political relations through mechanisms such as information control, the use of networks or the 'framing' of problems. Because of distortions in communication, citizens are not only misled but also excluded from their democratic 'right'. Instead of finding citizens organizing politically and participating actively in the planning process, planners may find them depoliticized and quiescent, deferring to apparent status, title or expertise (Forester, 1989, p. 77). Planners can expect the organizations within which they work to perpetuate this situation. They therefore need to understand how this came about in order to tackle it and work with people to acknowledge different ways of experiencing, while seeking to 'make sense together' (Healey, 1993b, p. 236).

According to Forester (1989), planners already do far more than the prescriptive rational-comprehensive approach of Faludi or the descriptive disjointed incremental ideas of Lindblom (see Chapter

3). In the face of power or dominance they improvise, change objectives, respond to problems, adjust priorities and efforts, they are moral improvisers, they interpret mandates, obligations, promises and threats (1989, pp. 178–9). One of the most obvious outputs of these processes in planning is the plan itself. Plans are the result of various 'discourses' and how different ideas have come together through language to create a particular 'view' or plan. Healey (1993b) claims that there could be several competing discourses within a single plan – an example might be ideas from those wanting protection of the countryside competing with those pushing for greater economic growth in rural areas. How these 'discourses' are resolved and presented in the plan is at the heart of communicative rationality.

Looking at a number of development plans in the UK, Healey (1993b) explores the system of meaning within a plan, its conversations (discourses) and the participants (discourse communities). We therefore move from not only analyzing 'winners and losers', but also how the plan was arrived at, what it says and how it says it. Planners often see their role as balancing these discourses, but, as Healey points out, choices have to be made between different discourses – how these choices were made and on what basis is often not made clear in the plan. The communicative rational approach would argue that because such choices are not transparent they could be based on narrow instrumentally rational criteria and/or be distorted (implicitly and explicitly) by powerful forces in society (capital, political, etc.). The point is that we do not know because the bases of choices are not clear. How can planning avoid this? Healey (1993b) offers some simple solutions to the development plan situation above. What planners should do is acknowledge different arguments in the plan. This could involve being explicit about which option has been chosen and why (e.g., 'There are three arguments on this issue, A, B and C, we have chosen B and these are the reasons'). Plans should admit to differences, for example, why the plan cannot be expected to achieve certain objectives because they are outside its realm.

But this seems to limit debate to output, while communicative rationality is also concerned with process (in as far as the two can be separated). As Dryzek (1990) noted, the idea of systems and procedures are anathema to communicative rationalists, conjuring up visions of new forms of domination. All those involved in looking to the future should therefore also be involved in deciding the rules and processes to be followed. In doing this, constant critique of the rules and processes must be maintained to ensure that they avoid becoming dominating themselves. Forester (1989, 1993) develops Habermas's four criteria of ideal speech (comprehensibility, sincerity, legitimacy, accuracy) as a basis for communication and the need to pay attention to both content (what is being talked about) and context (when and in what situation it is being said) (Forester, 1989, pp. 145–6). He then goes on to develop an approach that planners could (not 'should' – wanting to avoid being prescriptive and dominatory) develop. Planners should think about how to:

- Cultivate community networks of liaisons and contacts.
- Listen carefully.
- Notify less organized interests in the planning process.
- Educate citizens and community organizations.
- Supply technical and political information.
- Ensure non-professionals have access to documents and information.
- Encourage community-based groups to press for full information on proposed projects.
- Develop skills to work with groups.
- Emphasize the importance of building their own power, even before negotiations begin.
- Encourage independent, community-based project reviews.
- Anticipate political/economic pressure.

These guidelines clearly bypass institutional aspects and, rather than bind institutional rationality by communicative rationality, achieve the reverse (and, as Low [1991] points out, resemble an old-style pluralist formula). Healey (1993b), in discussing the implications for what she terms spatial strategy formulation (or plan-making?), asks five questions of planning if it is to develop alternative systems and processes and tentatively suggests some answers:

1. *Where* is discussion to take place, in what forums and arenas; how are community members to get access to it? These are traditionally found in formal political, administrative, statu-

tory and legal systems. But the discretion within the UK system allows for opportunity to reflect upon processes but it also requires those in power or control to recognize this opportunity. The spatial and interest-based nature of communities need to be 'mapped' or identified and they then need to be invited to discuss the processes and kinds of access they require prior to any other work starting. In terms of the 'where', Bryson and Crosby (1992) identify three kinds of 'place': forums, where strategies concerning values are articulated; arenas, where policies are more precisely defined; and courts, where outstanding disputes are acknowledged.

2. In what *style* will discussions take place? What styles are most likely to be able to 'open out' discussions to enable the diversity of 'languages' among community members to find expression? In the current system this could be seen to correspond to the 'survey' stage in a plan. What is required is the 'opening out' of issues to see what they mean to different people to avoid reinforcing stereotypes, narrowing agendas and alienating people. Three aspects are important: style (who speaks when, what they say, the use of rooms etc.), language (the use of ideal speech, translations etc.) and 'call-up' (trying to balance discussion to avoid dominance of more vocal people).
3. How can the jumble of issues, arguments, claims for attention and ideas about what to do, which arises in discussion, be *sorted* out? A huge array of issues can be brought up. Conventionally, this is filtered by planners to a 'point' to make sense. This needs to be much 'richer' than at present – values and morals need to be explored by planners, whose role is to help others understand.
4. How can a strategy be created that becomes a *new discourse* about how spatial and environmental change in urban regions could be managed? There is a need to get others involved to argue on issues, the purpose of actions and the way the costs and benefits can be assessed, rather than depending upon planners 'expertise'. One example could be green belts, which seem to have become a dominant 'discourse' though it is not clear how. Healey recognizes this is the most dangerous aspect of the process; new discourses

need to be subjected to constant critique to avoid them becoming dominatory.

5. How can a political community get to *agree* on a strategy and maintain that argument over time, while continually subjecting it to critique? Disagreements are bound to occur and there needs to be a method of resolving this. What is important is that communicative rationality is used to agree on this method and on the critique.

Other suggestions of alternative systems for planning (e.g., Hoch, 1984; Albrecht and Lim, 1986) seem to follow similar routes – trying to achieve a fine balance between normative suggestions and not wanting to 'impose' a process or system that should be done by those involved. What we are left with, as Healey (1993b) lists, are hints of what planning could look like:

1. Planning should use other types of analysis techniques and presentational forms.
2. No common language can be attained between discourse communities. Planning should therefore focus on a search for achievable levels of mutual understanding.
3. Planning should facilitate respectful discussion within and between discursive communities.
4. It should involve the construction of arenas within which processes are formulated and conflicts identified.
5. All kinds of knowledge and rationality are allowed.
6. A reflective and critical capacity must be maintained by the use of 'ideal speech'.
7. All those with a stake are included (or not excluded, at least). Dilemmas need to be addressed 'interdiscursively'.
8. Interests are not fixed. People will alter interests through interaction and a process of mutual learning.
9. There is a potential to challenge existing power relations through critique and highlight oppression and dominatory forces.
10. The purpose is to help planners begin to proceed in mutually agreeable ways based on interdiscursive understanding.

The point is, nobody really knows what a communicative process or institution would look like for fear of dominating possible alternatives. Hoch (1984) talks of a 'radical pragmatism', where a planner recognizes the unequal distribution of power and seeks to work towards alternatives. Albrecht and Lim (1986) believe that planners should have a high degree of self-awareness, should not presume to 'know' more than others and should follow the ideal speech rules of Habermas.

In seeking to translate the ideas of Habermas, we have simply moved from the highly abstract to the abstract. As opposed to Dryzek's communicatively rational alternatives to Popper's 'open society', which bounds instrumental rationality within communicative rationality, the planning alternatives seem to do the opposite – retaining the instrumentally rational state structure and placing communicative rationality within it as a 'tool' or procedure. How can we use this approach? Two main uses seem to have been found so far. First is the analysis of current systems and procedures. Second, it has influenced some current processes, especially in relation to participation.

## Analyses of current practice

Analyses of planning have ably exposed the communicative nature of planning work (Lauria and Wagner, 2006). Two questions seem to be at the heart of these studies. In what ways are power relations embodied in the possession and use of knowledge? What kinds of communicative acts convey this knowledge? In her examination of development plans, Healey (1993b) attempts to expose the different discourses within the plan, as well as the processes behind them, and in doing so she claims to be able to judge the democratic content of the plan. Planners concern themselves with producing an agreed 'storyline' in the plan rather than how different storylines are produced and the criteria upon which some are chosen and not others.

This point also troubles Forester (1989) in his study of the micropolitics of daily decision-making. A notion of judgement that depends heavily upon procedures, tests or methods of justification obscures the prior work of problem perception and recognition and the crafting of action must be an inadequate one (1991, p. 200). Healey (1993b) claims that the existence of different discourses and their mediation by planners has the potential to mask powerful forces behind such decisions and exposes the myth of a common discourse behind the government's view that plans should be clear and understandable. Such daily decisions involving knowledge production and exchange are infused with ideological and political practices that protect the powerful and confuse the powerless (Healey, 1992, p. 9) – planners should be aware of this 'misinformation' (Forester, 1989).

In her study of a typical day in the life of a development control planner, Healey (1993b) identifies three situations in which this can occur: offering information, structuring the agenda and strategy development. In these three situations, images and language are used by the planner (and other professionals involved, such as architects or surveyors) that should not exclude people or 'close off' avenues of investigation – planners therefore exemplify the possibilities of ideal speech discussed earlier. Such ideal speech seems to have been lacking in a study of community participation by Healey and Hillier (1995). Using Habermas's conception of system and lifeworld, a 'tug of war' was identified between the planners and the community. The planners and the planning process were seen to fit the system through the use of rituals of consultation rather than participation and, in doing so, maintained the legitimacy of the system (1995, p. 22). The community, on the other hand, attempted and failed to participate in the process on their terms and were forced through the planners' routinized vocabularies to argue on a technical basis rather than communicating practical knowledge. By deconstructing the planning process and residents' roles, Healey and Hillier demonstrate how alienated and forced existing processes and outcomes are.

Although illuminating, these analyses need to be normative if practice is to change. Healey (1993b) claims that such studies will help advise plan writers and readers how to prepare and use plans skilfully and democratically – but what are the alternatives? Recognizing the power of government to impose administrative (and ideological?) discourses upon planning, Healey recommends that plan content and participation strategies are reviewed. Similar exhortations are made by Healey and Hillier (1995), who believe that planners have much to learn from practical knowledge. Forester (1989) comes forward with another list of lessons for planners as 'moral improvisers', which includes:

1. The need to learn about value – recognizing the imaginative and exploratory role as well as the justificatory role.
2. The need to exploit ambiguity – do not accept at face value what people say, explore and probe.
3. Deliberate about ends as well as means.
4. Practical judgement is reconstructive as well as justificatory – focus on how the problems were framed, perceived, recognized, rather than on justifying choice.
5. The need for public deliberation in the face of power – deliberation should be based on conversation in which people voice their concerns. Practical judgement comes to depend less on instrumental calculation and more on potential consent.
6. The need to bridge inclusiveness in participation and the perception and recognition of value – without the perception of value, participants can have little to say; without the inclusion of citizens, deliberation can have little legitimacy. Again, there are tensions between criticizing the existing situation and offering an alternative that does not end up as dominatory as the system or process it replaced.

## Conclusions

It would be wrong to ascribe a single position or coherent theory to communicative planning (Watson, 2008). Nevertheless, despite the different emphases and nuances there are strong commonalities. Communicative planning is an attempt to find a way forward for planning, to justify its existence and provide a normative basis, which it has lacked since the rational-comprehensive approaches of the 1970s. As such it should be welcomed. But is it the right way forward? To accept communicative planning you must accept its foundations of planning as a redistributive activity, of planners as more than apolitical arbiters between different interests and, most importantly, of planning as a participative process. These are definite political stances that involve a radical break with the concept of planners held by the profession, their employers, the public and society. It also questions the whole basis of a 'planning profession' – how can you have a profession (whose *raison d'être* is the application of expert knowledge) if you argue that there is no such thing as expert knowledge, only different opinions to be brought together? These are questions that have not been fully explored by those advancing this view and, as Rydin (2007, 2008) has highlighted, are not fully addressed by collaborative planning theory.

Some of the implications are also anathema to planners. Take one example; 'Planners *do not decide* ultimate questions of policy. Planners *give advice* to elected councillors then the councillors make the decisions' (Greed, 1996, p. 21, author's emphasis). The apolitical role of the planner appears to remain as firmly embedded in the professional psyche as instrumental rationality as a process and representative democracy as a means of decision-making. The point is that the full implications of this approach are not evident in the literature for two reasons. The first is the paradox that runs throughout communicative planning. To paraphrase Healey, it is future-pointing, not future-defining. It holds out the prospect of change but draws back from prescribing it because change cannot be prescribed under communicative planning. As such it is difficult to point to it as an alternative because it remains at an abstract level. Second, because of its *a priori* assumptions of what planning is, you must accept a definite stance of what planning is about. If you do not agree with the basis of planning as a democratic process, then don't bother. Consequently, it has lacked a critique – something that the theory itself recommends upon planning. Perhaps the most important aspect of planning as a communicative process, its basis upon participative forms of democracy, is taken as read by its proponents without acknowledging a host of practical and theoretical problems associated with this. Pateman (1970) has claimed that participative democracy, where there is direct participation of people in the regulation of key institutions of society and experimentation with political forms fosters human development, enhances a sense of political efficacy, reduces a sense of estrangement from power centres, nurtures a concern for collective problems and contributes to a formation of a knowledgeable citizenry capable of taking a more active interest in government (Held, 1987, pp. 258–9).

However, Held (1987) agrees with Weber and Schumpeter that it is unlikely that the average citizen will ever be interested in the all the decisions made at national level, as (s)he would be nearer to home. Further, many of the key institutions of liberal democracy – competitive parties, political representatives, periodic elections – will be unavoidable elements of a participatory society. Direct participation and control over immediate locales, complemented by party and interest-group competition in government affairs, can most realistically advance the principle of participatory democracy (Held, 1987, p. 260). The communicative theorists give few indications of how representative democracy will be combined with participative democracy and consequently it is difficult for planners and others to envisage how communicative rationality can ever be more than an abstract theory.

Another perspective upon this comes from the critique of modernism by the postmodernists, including Lyotard and Bauman covered earlier. Although the postmodernists would agree with the communicative rationalists that planners cannot claim that they have more objective knowledge than anybody else, proponents such as Healey and Forester attempt to achieve agreement through consensus. What if, as the relativists argue, agreement reached through this process is as flawed and dominatory, as through traditional instrumental rationalism? The view of Held, above, would suggest that in practical terms a participative process is as likely to be hijacked by cliques and those with the time and power as representative democracy. Communicative rationality could simply be another way of legitimizing existing power relations. Lyotard's answer is to embrace agnosticism and uncertainty (though this does not take us forward if we still need to look ahead), which has resonance with some neo-liberal theorists. Such practical problems would seem to dog this theory. Although exploration of the practical aspects is being undertaken (see Flyvbjerg, 1998; Sager, 1994; Bryan and Crosby, 1992; Innes, 1992) there remains a distinct feeling that this will never be more than an interesting perspective upon planning. Low (1991) takes this further. Under what conditions does undistorted communication become possible? It becomes possible in the *absence* of domination, repression and ideology. These conditions generally do not exist in any interaction between state planners and the people they have dealings with; those who feel the effect of their policies. Domination is part of the operational rules of society in which planners are enmeshed (Low, 1991, p. 256). Alexander asks another pertinent question of collaborative planning. As he sees it, 'The result may be a fine plan, but will this plan actually be implemented?' (Alexander, 2001, p. 313). This has less to do with the plan itself being impractical and more to do with the role of the planner in 'getting things done'.

# 10 Conclusions

## Introduction

I have included seven schools of what I termed indigenous planning theory in this book that represent distinct but related 'clusters' of ideas. The relationships between these different sets of theories can be analyzed in a number of ways. I have chosen to draw upon post-positivist ideas concerning socially embedded and contingent foundations to theory and an emphasis on the idea of time and space, in particular, as being significant in understanding the origin, use and evolution of theory. While I think that this understanding has a number of advantages and fits in with the zeitgeist of planning theory and social theory generally (see Dear, 2000; Flyvbjerg, 2001), it does have a number of drawbacks. There are three issues that are worthy of mention. The first is the lack of an awareness of cross-cutting themes that are pertinent and significant in each of the schools. The second drawback is the lack of discussion of the ways in which different kinds of theory that do not belong to any particular school (i.e., what I have termed exogenous, framing and social theory) are used by planners. Finally, there is the over-simplistic representation of theory driven by the typology I have employed. I discuss these three issues in more detail below.

One of the main problems of this approach is that in drawing together collections of theories it misses a number of recurrent themes, theories and ideas. One theme that I have tried to emphasize is that of relativism, particularly in the collaborative, postmodern and pragmatic approaches. Pluralism or hyper-pluralism (Yates, 1977), which characterizes urban politics, can lead to an indeterminate, almost chaotic or helpless position from which to decide upon action – everyone seems to have a legitimate and different viewpoint. This is not helped in some circumstances by theories that seem to exacerbate the very real nature of 'too much choice' by arguing that not only is this an inherent characteristic of life, but also that we should seek to make it more so. Extreme forms of postmodern planning theory take this line, leading many critics to argue that it should be equated with nihilism (Eagleton, 1996). Planners operate against this backdrop of hyper-pluralism and have to consider the ways in which a plethora of different perspectives have to be reconciled against the need to act. Consequently, the issue of relativism is highly relevant and worth considering in more detail.

Each school of theory mentioned above addresses relativism from a different perspective (which is one of the main reasons why they are distinct from each other). Thus, a defining characteristic of collaborative planning is its recognition of difference and the reconciliation of this with the need to reach consensus and act. As I pointed out in Chapter 9, the collaborative school does this by holding onto some form of objective knowledge, though it embeds it within a more communicative understanding and approach to planning. In its more extreme guise, postmodern planning theory rejects this and the idea that knowledge, like society, is holistic, cumulative and broadly progressive. There is a recognition of relativism in both approaches, though both deal with it in different ways.

Many have argued against the postmodern form of relativism because they equate it with an 'anything goes' attitude. Nevertheless, as Giddens (1990) has pointed out, modernity itself is founded upon both certainty and uncertainty – the 'juggernaut' of modernity brought with it uncertainty and chaos through its penchant for constant revolution. In practice, therefore, postmodern relativism perhaps means that little is lost as we deal with issues such as uncertainty, disagreement and multiple choices for action on a daily basis (Kumar, 1995). What the postmodern actually does is highlight these issues and helps us understand why they arise. The collaborative school's response to relativism is to acknowledge it and argue that incommensurable views can be reconciled through open discussion. In this perspective, relativism disappears as a practical issue in the face of interpersonal communication. The cross-cutting nature of these questions means that a more holistic perspective is difficult in the approach taken in this book.

From this brief discussion it should be clear that there is at least one important issue and a number of related questions that both unites and divides some schools of theory. There are many others. Cross-cutting questions that are pertinent are partly raised in individual chapters and some, such as the debate on structure and agency and the broader shifts in social theory generally towards post positivism, are touched upon in Chapters 1 and 2.

The second drawback to the 'schools' approach includes the lack of attention paid to the ways in which what I have termed framing theory, exogenous theory and social theory (see Figure 3.1) are used by planners to reflect upon planning separate from a particular school of planning theory. Regime theory is a good illustration of this.

Regime theory came to the attention of planners and others from the mid-1980s onwards and developed from pluralist (see Chapter 7) and elitist models of democracy and behaviour. Again, time and space are significant factors in this theory. *Temporally*, it is no coincidence that it emerged in the mid-1980s, given its emphasis on the shift in urban areas towards a coalition of public and private forces cooperating to maximize inward investment in a global economy. This was a time when neo-liberal ideas were emphasizing a reduced state and greater partnership and direct provision of services with and by the private sector. *Spatially*, the interpretation and implications of this theory vary due to the differing institutional and political contexts in individual states. However, it was in the USA and UK that such ideas emerged as a way to understand the prevailing market orthodoxy.

Regime theory seeks to account for the changing context of local government and the growth in alliances and cooperation between public and private interests in meeting the challenge of global economic competition. Against a backdrop of pressures for increased local control, central financial constraints and the growth of quasi-government bodies attention has focused upon varieties of local 'governance' rather than government. Regime theory examines the ways in which such complex arrangements for local governance emerge, are reproduced and impact upon urban life. As capital and investment decisions are largely privately directed, pubic authorities have to enter into coalitions or alliances and cooperate to meet wider societal objectives. Unlike more mainstream Marxist perspectives, regime theorists argue that the local state has a significant influence upon privately owned capital. However, there is an increasingly complex set of relations between the public and private, particularly as the boundary between the two is becoming more blurred. Against such a backdrop, regime theory explores how different centres of power combine to benefit each other. This involves compromise and cooperation and the establishment of 'regimes'. Such regimes are underpinned not by more traditional relations of power and authority (such as the power to grant or withhold planning permission) but through the establishment of relations based on trust, solidarity, loyalty and mutual support.

One can immediately see how such a perspective has relevance for planning. The formal and informal mechanisms of planning control make it a pivotal actor in any such regime. Is planning compliant in regimes? What are the implications for concepts such as the 'public good' and professional impartiality? Regime theory draws upon and develops a number of theoretical 'schools', such as pluralism, but does not belong to a 'school' of planning theory (i.e., indigenous planning theory as I defined in Chapter 2).

Instead, it provides an understanding of contemporary planning practice and even alerts planners and others to the characteristics of urban governance that they might encounter. It does not represent an approach to planning in the same way that the systems or collaborative approaches do. Neither is there a planning interpretation of regime theory. I could have included more on regime theory as a backdrop for advocacy planning in Chapter 7, but it 'isolates' it rather than using it (and other understandings such as regulation theory) as a backdrop to understanding the context and subject of planning. The general point is that there are other areas of theory more or less related to planning that exist outside the schools approach taken in this book.

A related drawback of the approach in this book relates to the categorization of planning theory itself. The typology I developed in Chapter 2 is simplistic, though this is inevitable with any categorization of what is a complex subject area. One dimension that is underplayed in the typology, though less so in the individual chapters, is that of planning practice. The post-positivist perspective on the relation between theory and practice was set out in Chapter 1. Briefly, I argued there that planners picked theories to suit their needs in a political game tied up with power relations and particularly 'who gets what'. I also raised the possibility that certain theories were more popular than others because of their implications for individuals such as planners, who hold powerful positions.

Unlike the 'theory–practice gap' of Alexander and others, practice in the post-positivist perspective is conflated with theory. This helps explain why, for example, there has been little interest from planners in bridging the 'gap' between theory and practice. What this approach underplays is why planners should choose some theories that run counter to their own interests. Further, although this approach allows for planners to use their discretion in interpreting theories as they see fit, it does not provide much information or indicate the ways in which using theories may lead, through feedback, to the theories themselves adapting or changing as a result. Such feedback undoubtedly exists, but is difficult to identify or quantify. At a broad level, theories are 'refined' through a number of mechanisms of which the exposure to empirical testing is one, while peer group review is another.

A final theme that is significant is whether or not a typology is possible or desirable under a post-positivist understanding. If post-positivism is anything, it is about the possibility of as many different theories as there are interpretations – a scenario where there are more answers than questions. How can we justify a typology under such circumstances? Partly, this comes down to the difference between epistemology and ontology.

Epistemology is the studying of ideas and how they relate to each other. The different schools identified under my typology represent different sets of ideas – all have different ways of explaining the world. However, when we move onto more fundamental questions of what such understandings of the world assume – whether, for example, there are absolute truths or facts – then we move into the world of ontology. Post-positivism's ontology is that there are no absolutes. Consequently, a post-positivist typology casts more positivist theories, with their fundamentally different ontologies based on absolutes, in a critical and less than sympathetic light. The post-positivist perspective on the incommensurability of ideas and the essentially subjective nature of the world immediately jars with the positivist basis of systems or rational theory. The driving force of my typology is one that rejects the hegemony of any one theory, that is, it is deliberately and openly relativist. In addressing the question of the possibility of a post-positivist typology, the answer is yes – but with provisos regarding the implication of positivist approaches above. Turning to desirability then, if anything, there is more need for a map of ideas from the (relativist) perspective of post-positivism.

I have included some of the drawbacks to the 'schools' approach adopted in this book to highlight what I consider to be issues worthy of attention, but that does not detract from the advantages of the approach. I now want to turn to some of those advantages, develop them further and briefly explore possible implications for an understanding of planning theory.

## Tracking back: the influences upon planning theory

The broad thrust of an emphasis upon time and space is to question the idea of ahistorical and aspatial theory. In other words, it questions the idea that theories are somehow separate and independent of the influences of wider societal forces that are themselves related to contingent and particular relations created in space. This opens up the possibility that planning can be practised and thought about in different ways in different places and at different times. The perspective that theory is temporally and spatially, as well as socially, contingent carries with it the presumption that we cannot decide which theory is right or wrong. However, as Dear (2000, p. 42) points out, 'we may be able to identify the particular circumstances under which a theory best applies'.

The complex relationship between theories, society, time and space denies an easy analysis. But it is worth highlighting that at different times different theories have been more or less popular in academia and practice – systems and rational theories in the 1960s, Marxist in the 1970s, New Right in the 1980s, collaborative, pragmatic and postmodern in the 1990s. I have avoided putting a 'timeline' upon the different schools of theory, as I have rejected the linear approach to theoretical development (though see Yiftachel, 1989, and Taylor, 1998, for examples of these). Such perspectives tend to emphasize a development of theories much along the lines of positivist perspectives on scientific theory, for example, Einstein built upon Newton's theories, etc. In the social sciences, such understandings (while attractive and simple) break down. There is no simple linear development of theory but a more complex situation. Planning theories exist side-by-side with varying degrees of overlap. Thus, pragmatism, postmodern and collaborative schools have significant overlaps as well as differences. Further, the interpretation of such theories cannot be assumed to be uniform across space. At a broad level (and I will go into more detail below), the specificities of a particular place will naturally influence the ways in which planning theory is interpreted and used. A consequence of this is that we should expect to find different theories influencing practice in different ways in different places.

There is evidence of the emergence of different planning 'styles' within the same country (Brindley, Rydin and Stoker, 1996). The reasons for this seem to be complex but two stand out. The first is the inherent flexibility of planning practice in organizing itself and determining priorities locally. This arises in both federal and unitary states. Unitary systems, such as the UK or France, direct broad change centrally, though leave the implementation and interpretation to professionals and locally elected authorities. Federal systems, such as the USA or Australia, tend to formalize flexibility and difference and allow states the ability to approach planning laws and processes in their own way, though within an overall constitution. The second reason comes from the various social, political and economic differences that such localities exhibit and the ways in which such local manifestations provide a 'filter' through which such implementation and interpretation is viewed.

Brindley, Rydin and Stoker (1996) identify six styles of planning practice in the UK that have evolved (Table 10.1). The typology in Table 10.1 highlights the relative importance of economic performance to the form of planning through the far left-hand column. However, the response to these economic situations – broadly categorized as market-critical and market-led – is more politically motivated. The links to the different theories of planning and space become more apparent. In a buoyant area, where there is a good deal of market demand, the typology identifies two broad responses. A traditional regulative approach that places the expert planner at the centre of any form of land use control buttressed by the rational and systems theories of planning (Brindley, Rydin and Stoker, 1996, p. 14). Planners here seek to

***Table 10.1*** **A typology of planning styles**

| *Perceived nature of urban problems* | *Attitude to market processes* | |
|---|---|---|
| | *Market-critical: redressing imbalances and inequalities created by the market* | *Market-led: correcting inefficiencies while supporting market processes* |
| Buoyant area: minor problems and buoyant market | Regulative planning | Trend planning |
| Marginal area: pockets of urban problems and potential market interest | Popular planning | Leverage planning |
| Derelict areas: comprehensive urban problems and depressed market | Public investment planning | Private management planning |

*Source*: based on Brindley, Rydin and Stoker, 1996, p. 9.

make decisions in the interests of society as a whole, balancing public and private needs. In the same broadly buoyant environment, the other approach Brindley, Rydin and Stoker identify is 'trend planning', where both theories and practice seek to facilitate market-led development through, for example, attempting to allocate adequate areas of land in a market-determined area, while reducing red tape and lengthy decision-making. This approach is clearly aligned with the New Right or neo-liberal school of theory.

The other four styles of planning identified in Table 10.1 similarly demonstrate a link between theory and space. What Brindley, Rydin and Stoker do not investigate (mainly because this was not the focus of their work) are the reasons why a particular area has approached planning in a particular way.

What are the factors that differentiate society and government and where did such distinction derive from? One area of theory that has sought to address social, political and economic differentiation is broadly termed 'locality theory'. According to this perspective, the starting point in any search of the origin of distinctiveness is uneven economic spatial development, that is, areas developed economically at different rates. Some areas with access to natural resources such as minerals, rivers, etc. will have been more profitable than others at different times and therefore will attract more economic activity. Such an uneven spatial economic development leads in turn to an uneven social and political development as new rounds of investment interact with existing physical and cultural/social patterns:

> The practices of civil society are constituted contingently, in the context of nature, of each other and of world capitalism. For example, gender divisions of labour in simple gatherer-hunter societies . . . owe much to the cultural interpretation and organisation of labour . . . The same principle holds in capitalist societies, except that now the uneven development of capitalism overlaps natural unevenness. (Duncan and Goodwin, 1988, p. xx)

Lawson and Warde (1987) trace examples of the locally specific connections between social relations in the process of production, the domestic sphere and urban politics. Savage's account of weaving in Preston from the late nineteenth century to the interwar period, for example, illustrates the ways in which patriarchal structures in the domestic sphere extended to and were associated with patriarchy in the workplace. His evidence shows that in prewar Preston's weaving sheds it was unusual for (male) heads of households whose daughters or wives were employed as weavers to agree variations in working conditions (e.g., time off) directly with their (male) overseer, who – in the weaving shed – acted as a kind of surrogate head of household, regulating morals as well as quality of work. However, in the early twentieth century, though patriarchal relations remained, the role of the overseer in sustaining them was undermined by changes in both the forms of ownership of mills (joint stock companies with specialist managers becoming more usual), and state-sponsored changes in the labour market – namely the introduction of National Insurance – which reduced the scope for discretion in recruitment on which overseer power rested in large measure. The example demonstrates some of the links between the spheres of production and also the intertwining of local conditions, changes in the management of capitalist enterprise and state policies implemented uniformly throughout the country.

In a related piece of research, Mark-Lawson and Warde (1985) explore the implications of gender relations in the workplace for urban politics, comparing Preston with neighbouring towns of Lancaster and Nelson. The comparisons between Preston and Nelson, both cotton towns, are especially interesting. They are persuasive in arguing that the general segregation in Preston's labour market (whereby, weaving was largely a female occupation supervised by men, with men also employed in other industries to which women were not recruited) is central to understanding the low priority attached by the local Labour Party to welfare issues. The Preston Labour Party's links to trade unions, from which women were excluded by patriarchal attitudes and power, isolated women from it and also insulated the party from the influence of women activists. In Nelson, on the other hand, employment opportunities were not restricted to cotton, with the result that substantial numbers of men worked alongside women as weavers, both subject to the supervision of (male) overseers and managers. This experience of equality of conditions and lack of segregation in the labour market underpinned women's involvement in both trade unions and labour politics, with a correspondingly greater prominence attached to welfare issues than in Preston.

The link between spatially variant social and economic development and theory is not unproblematic. As Bagguley *et al.* (1990, p. 185) suggest, there is no direct correlation between economic restructuring and political action. Nevertheless, such events will shape attitudes and political action and previous events set the agenda for change, shaping the issues that will be pursued, the groups involved and the resources available to them. Local government has become a reflection of and focus for these forces. Duncan and Goodwin (1988, p. 114) have explored the role of local government against the backdrop of such historical influences:

> Because social relations are unevenly developed there is, on the one hand, a need for different policies in different places and, on the other hand, local state institutions to formulate and implement these variable policies. Local state institutions are rooted in the heterogeneity of local state relations, where central states have difficulty in dealing with this differentiation. But . . . this development of local states is a double edged sword – for locally constituted groups can then use these institutions to further their own interests, perhaps even in opposition to centrally dominant interests.

*Table 10.2* **Unpicking epistemologies of planning theory**

| | *PURPOSE* *What is the focus of planner decisions?* | *ROLE* *What is the role of the planner in making decisions?* | *ORIENTATION* *To what extent is planning oriented to the future?* | *FUTURE* *What does a planner know about the future?* | *PUBLIC INT* *Is there one?* |
|---|---|---|---|---|---|
| Systems theory/ Rational comprehensive | Control; scientific and objective | Planner-centric expert | Positivist; instrumental rationality | Can be predicted | Output: maximum utility |
| Critical theory | Accumulation, distribution, and the role of the state | Puppet of market | Means/ends | Market-driven | Capitalism |
| Neo-liberal | A combination of a market-oriented competitive state (liberalism) and an authoritarian strong state (conservatism) | Minimal; provide conditions for the continuation of the market mechanism | Via the market mechanism | Can foresee barriers to market functions | The market |
| Pragmatism | 'Getting things done' | Act on ideas or beliefs that make sense and help others to act | Spontaneous order | The outcome of using an idea | Impossible to aggregate |
| Advocacy | Solutions to address power inequalities | Advocate | Outcome of competing ideas | A variety of futures | Pluralism |
| Postmodern | Focus on and release 'difference' | Narrator | Focus on day to day | Rejects objective knowledge | No great vision; fragmented and atomistic |
| Collaborative | Break down scientific objectivism; agreement through free and open discourse | Introduce other (non-instrumental rationality) ways of thinking and knowing | Pluralistic | Difference | No meta-narrative; lifeworld |

*Source*: the author thanks David J. Connell for this contribution.

As Bagguley *et al.* (1990, p. 185) put it:

> The local state then becomes both a means by which central government deals with the problematic effects of uneven development and mode of representation of interest groups potentially opposed to the centre. From the potentially contradictory nexus comes the dynamics of local policy variation.

This discussion on localities helps explain why different areas vary politically, socially and culturally, even where state apparatus, that is, local government, is superficially similar. It also helps explain why theories differ spatially in terms of content, interpretation and development – the workers and their representatives in Preston and Nelson would be likely to interpret theories or class consciousness in different ways. What it does not do is provide us with any criteria as to how to develop theories for places. Under the post-positivist approach, there are no agreed criteria to evaluate and develop theories that best fit particular circumstances. As Michael Dear argues, in deciding between theories:

> Different criteria may be appropriate in different circumstances. We may, for instance, prefer a theory because it specifies the causal connections among a set of variables; because it has the capacity for prediction and empirical verifiability; because it possesses a strong internal consistency; or because of its elegance and parsimony. The very existence of a smorgasbord of evaluative criteria is testimony to the lack of general consensus, the elusive nature of truth. (2000, p. 42)

The onus, therefore, is on interpretation and persuasion:

> Analysts/advocates [of theories] should expect to specify and defend criteria through which their claims of privilege are sought; and they should anticipate that such claims may then be systematically analysed, and counter positions advanced. The development of such a mode of comparative discourse is, unsurprisingly, one of the most difficult tasks in philosophy and theory – both technically and politically. (Dear, 2000, p. 43)

The implications of this vary depending on your standpoint. One view is that it is a good thing that there are no absolutes to judge against ideas and theories that will (more likely than not) vary in time and space. Alternatively, a more pessimistic view would be that we should spend less time 'opening up' and celebrating difference and more time thinking about how to communicate between different paradigms. The current field of planning theory is mainly characterized by different attitudes towards these two views.

In arguing that there are drawbacks to any approach and understanding of planning theory, including the one taken in this book it is worth stressing that some common analysis is possible based around common questions of the activity of planning (see Table 10.2).

## Conclusions and the future

What of the future? Following from the general premise of this book, the future must be seen as unknowable and deeply subjective – we should be wary of the inductivist basis to prediction and keep in mind 'Hulme's puzzle' (see Chapter 1), that is, how can we predict the future based on the past? The evidence and hopes of the Enlightenment have been shown to be over-optimistic at the very least. But the future is also bound up in hope and expectations. While being wary of prediction, we can nevertheless work towards a future – an activity which, after all, is the basis of planning. What I intend to do here is speculate on how current schools of theory may develop, particularly with regards to the two positions outlined above, that is, whether to keep 'opening up' and searching for difference or to seek ways of trying to reconcile it. There is also a component of how I would like to see them develop in this speculation, based upon the strengths and weaknesses of various schools of theory. In what follows I identify three scenarios for future theoretical development in planning theory.

Scenario one posits the further development of the broad postmodern school of theory. As I argued in Chapter 8, the postmodern *oeuvre* rejects holistic analyses of society and emphasizes a discursive basis to reality:

> Thus, different social theories should be viewed merely as conflicting narratives or as incommensurable perspectives rather than as portrayals of external social realities that can be judged and evaluated on the basis of research and discussion employing inter-subjective standards and procedures for determining valid knowledge. (Antonio and Kellner, 1991, p. 129)

Some extreme postmodern theorists, such as Jean Baudrillard, further claim that people are confused and apathetic, mindlessly consuming mass-produced images. What ability and desire people have to think about the future is going to be severely limited.

If postmodern theory is to develop beyond analysis to help inform future planning, then it needs to be able to address issues that are undoubtedly more than local and individual. What does postmodern social theory have to say about globalization and its effects, for example? Postmodern analyses also have little to say about alternatives to the status quo. There are some hints at how postmodern alternatives to the status quo might work, for example, Lyotard's pagan politics or Baudrillard's idea of symbolic exchange (see Allmendinger, 2001, pp. 193–5, for more on this), but all are half-hearted attempts to escape from the constraints imposed by their own theory:

> As many feminist inspired critiques of postmodern theory have argued, many of the extreme approaches fail to tackle the practical problems of politics as well as ignoring modern emancipatory themes such as liberty and fraternity that are necessary to challenge the mainstays of repression. (Allmendinger, 2001, p. 196)

The problems with a postmodern basis to planning are many, particularly its seemingly endless celebration of difference. Postmodern planning, even in a less extreme manifestation, is more akin to fragmented and atomistic neo-liberalism than it is to a holistic and coordinated understanding of society. Even those who have attempted to think about a 'postmodern planning' admit it is a strange fit, if not an oxymoron. Consequently, it is unlikely that postmodern theory, if it is to remain postmodern in the sense used by its main proponents, is capable of moving beyond an insightful critique.

This is not to deny its usefulness as a critique; even as a powerful insight the postmodern is of definite use and worthy of further development. Postmodern analyses have been enlightening and productive in exposing the rigid and power-laden aspects of a modern institution such as planning. The kinds of questions that postmodern social theorists such as Foucault sought to address are typical of those that would benefit planning. In Best and Kellner's view, the elements of postmodern social theory that are worthy of retention include:

- Detailed historical genealogies of the institutions and discourses of modernity and the ways in which these normalize and discipline subjects.
- Micro-analyses of the colonization of desire in capitalism and the production of potentially fascist subjects.
- Theorization of the mass media, information systems and technology as new forms of control that radically change the nature of politics, subjectivity and everyday life.
- Emphasis on the importance of micro-politics, new social movements and new strategies of social transformation.
- Critiques of flawed philosophical components of modernity;
- New syntheses of feminist and postmodern theories. (1991 pp. 262–3)

If we are prepared to move away from some of the more extreme versions of postmodern social theory, then there is hope that it could be developed into a theoretical basis for planning. In another book (Allmendinger, 2001), I have sought to develop postmodern themes into a postmodern theory and practice of planning. To foreshorten a long debate in the book, the following is a list of principles upon which a postmodern planning could be built:

1. Narratives (written and oral 'stories' or descriptions such as plans) are always open to redescription and different analyses. Another way of saying this is that plans and other guiding documents are only one way of looking at the world.
2. As a consequence, a postmodern planning should be based on an underlying assumption that all processes and procedures are not 'closed', that is, there is no 'best' plan for every situation. Any decisions that are made, particularly concerning a 'closed' decision such as a plan, are taken on the understanding that it is a temporary alignment of interests only.
3. To maintain openness throughout any process all options and views need to be maintained up until the point of decision or closure. In other words, planners have to ensure that they maintain an open process that does not railroad differing perspectives and ideas.
4. To avoid merely the appearance of openness, procedural and systematic checks have to be in place that ensure constant reflection. This relates to the more formal point 3

above. Such checks could include regular forums for alternative perspectives, votes, etc.

5. Procedures need to be open to change. A fluid framework of rules (which are themselves open to challenge and change) should ensure that processes and procedures are modified or altered regularly as necessary. There are, therefore, no preconceived ideas about how planning should be approached or if there should be any planning at all. Processes such as how to approach planning need to be invented and agreed anew.
6. A suite of explicit rights that encourage a radical and challenging attitude on behalf of citizens will be required to engender an attitude to challenge and allow procedures and processes to be legally and legitimately challenged.
7. Part of the aim for mechanisms to create a radical form of democracy must include a stronger link between voter and representative. This may sound a bit pious and vague but traditional forms of representative democracy are breaking down in the face of demands for greater accountability from the electorate.
8. Existing relations of power need to be both exposed and challenged. This can be achieved by both maintaining constant reflective mechanisms and making decision-makers and other actors more accountable and processes more transparent.
9. Planners should take a more active and creative role in the sustenance and encouragement of fluid structures and processes (Allmendinger, 2001, pp. 225–6). This places a grave responsibility on planners to think about their existing roles and how they might reinforce existing power relations

These principles involve taking postmodern thought and adding some foundational elements. In the eyes of some, this would not be postmodern at all. Nevertheless, if we were to accept a less extreme form of postmodernism as a basis for a more realistic way forward (see Laclau and Mouffe, 1985, for another attempt at this), then postmodern planning theory could usefully be used and further developed.

Scenario two posits the development of more neo-modern fields of theory, such as the collaborative or communicative schools. Neo-modern theories that follow the Habermasian understandings touch upon many of the concerns of postmodern thought, such as difference, power and domination, but still actively seek a modernist solution of a single voice linked to progress and absolute ideals such as emancipation. This is the antithesis of the fragmented and nihilistic implications of the extreme postmodern approach. It differs from the less extreme approach of postmodernism outlined above mainly in its ontology – the postmodern approach would still argue that foundational truths do not exist while the collaborative approach maintains that they do. Further development of this school of theory needs to address a number of critical issues that I discussed in Chapter 9. In addition, collaborative theorists also need to engage more with the growing criticism of its theoretical foundations and practical consequences.

The first area of criticism that requires a development of collaborative theory is the gap between the rather naive perspective on the motivation and professionalism of planners and a more realistic/cynical view: 'planning authorities and planners often act regressively exerting domination and causing inequalities in what has been termed the dark side of planning' (Yiftachel and Huxley, 2000, p. 910). One implication of this is, naturally, to recognize that planners and planning can have a malignant as well as beneficial impact. But equally as important is what this recognition says about how planning should be theorized. The collaborative approach is what could be termed ethnographic, that is, it approaches planning through direct observation and often includes participant observation. The danger is that those observing can become 'too involved' with those being observed, often missing the 'big picture'. This requires, 'a critical distance, that is, the positioning of the researcher outside the internal discourse of planning, free from a-priori faith in the profession's supporting ideological apparatus' (Yiftachel and Huxley, 2000, p. 910). The second area of criticism that needs to be addressed by the collaborative school regards the lack of acknowledgement in collaborative theory to the role of the state and planning as part of a wider process of spatial production, including wealth, inequality, power and regulation. Planning cannot be studied or theorized in isolation from such wider processes and influences. Focusing on the day-to-day operation of planners and the language they use misses out significant forces and influences upon planning and that planning contributes to.

Ultimately, like postmodernism, the collaborative school is caught in a trap of its own making. It needs to overcome some of its aspects that define it, for example, its reliance on open and inclusive discourse challenging existing power relations and leading to consensus. This is perhaps why much of the work on collaborative planning is concerned with analyzing existing practice and highlighting shortfalls rather than proposing alternatives. Nevertheless, the 'collaborative turn' could address these issues by developing aspects of its approach. Specifically, it would be beneficial if the collaborative school added some elements of postmodern thinking/theory relating to the role of difference and consensus, as well as a more holistic perspective on the role of planning as only a part of how towns and cities come to be the way they are.

The final scenario relates to a 'middle way' between the two extremes of neo- and postmodern schools. A number of different writers are developing alternatives to the extremes of neo- and postmodern theory that seek to build on the best aspects of both. Best and Kellner (1991), for example, seek to develop what they term a reconstructed critical social theory that combines modern concerns such as democracy and equality with the micro-political focus of postmodern social theory. While the micro-level theories of postmodernism provide a powerful tool in uncovering the intricacies of power and domination, they miss out on *the* structuring force in society – capitalism. Like Jameson, Best and Kellner see the postmodern as a manifestation of capitalism that cannot be separated from it by simply ignoring it.

While capital accumulation is the driving logic in society, account needs to be made of other dimensions that are more or less related to such macro-level understandings, such as gender and race:

> Without such macrotheories that attempt to cognitively map the new forms of social development and the relationship between spheres like the economy, culture, education, and politics, we are condemned to live among the fragments without clear indications of what impact new technologies and social developments are having on various domains of our social life. (Best and Kellner, 1991, p. 301)

Thus, Best and Kellner embed postmodern critique within a materialist framework that acknowledges the intricacies of domination and its wider basis. Another attempt to overcome the dualism of neo- and postmodern social theory has come under the broad label of critical realism. Critical realism challenges the postmodern and post-positivist view that reality is ultimately 'unknowable' and that all we can hope to do is better describe it. As critical realists point out, however, 'Given that we have scientific theories, and that on the whole they seem to work remarkably well as an explanation of the world, what must the world be like in order for science to be possible?' (Outhwaite, 1987, p. 18). If we cannot ever grasp reality, how come scientific theories based on a knowable reality work? Thus, critical realism takes an ontological point of departure from postmodern social theory, that is, it is not relativist, believing instead in ultimate foundations to truth and reality. A second major departure concerns the roles of individuals. Postmodern thinking downplays the role of structures, while critical realism introduces structures. This contrasts with the postmodern portrayal of actors as passive dupes and instead portrays them as active and reflective and able to determine their future.

The balance between structure and agency (see Chapter 1) favours structure in the critical realist conception. This would seem to align it less with postmodern social theory than the neo-modern collaborative school. There are significant overlaps between aspects of critical realism and postmodern thought, however. Critical realists are wary of totalizing and reductionist approaches such as Marxism, which reflects the common distrust of foundational and absolute truths.

Like critical social theory, the critical realist approach provides a middle way between the post- and neo-modern opposites of collaborative and postmodern planning. This is not to say that the two approaches outlined above are the only alternatives, nor that they do not have critics themselves. However, they do provide interesting and potentially fruitful bases for future developments in planning theory outside the collaborative and postmodern schools.

Options other than those outlined above exist, of course. One area that seems to be gaining increased attention from academics and practitioners is systems theory. Work on retail impact assessment, environmental impact assessment and strategic environmental assessment emphasize an instrumentally rational and systematic approach. There are, however, differences between such new approaches and the 'classic' systems and rational understandings outlined in Chapter 3. Significantly, these approaches are embedded within more open and accountable understandings of the role and purpose of planning and are not ends in themselves.

# Bibliography


Albrecht, U. and Lim, G.-C. (1989) 'State and Society: Some Reflections on Theory and Theory-building', *Environment and Planning C: Government and Policy*, 7(4) 475–82.

Alexander, E. (1986) *Approaches to Planning: Introducing Current Planning Theories, Concepts and Issues* (Philadelphia: Gordon & Breach Science Publishers).

Alexander, E. (1997) 'A Mile or a Millimetre? Measuring the "Planning Theory–Practice Gap."', *Environment and Planning B, Planning and Design*, 24, pp. 3–6.

Alexander, E. R. (2001) 'The Planner-Prince: Interdependence, Rationalities and Post-communicative Practice', *Planning Theory and Practice*, 2(3), pp. 311–24.

Alexander, E. (2003) 'Response to "Why do Planning Theory?"', *Planning Theory* 2(3), pp. 179–82.

Alexander, E. R. (2008) 'The Role of Knowledge in Planning', *Planning Theory*, 7(2), pp. 207–10.

Alexander, E. R. and Faludi, A. (1996) 'Planning Doctrine: Its Uses and Implications', *Planning Theory*, 16, pp. 11–61.

Allmendinger, P. (1997) *Thatcherism and Planning: The Case of Simplified Planning Zones* (Aldershot: Avebury).

Allmendinger, P. (1998) 'Planning Practice and the Postmodern Debate', *International Planning Studies*, 3(2), pp. 227–48.

Allmendinger, P. (2001) *Planning in Postmodern Times* (London: Routledge).

Allmendinger, P. (2004) 'Palliative or Cure? Reflections on the Practice and Future of Planning Aid', *Planning Theory and Practice*, 5(2), pp. 269–71.

Allmendinger, P. and Tewdwr-Jones, M. (1997) 'A Mile or a Millimetre? Measuring the "Planning Theory–Practice Gap. A Response to Alexander."', *Environment and Planning B*, 24, p. 6.

Allmendinger, P. and Thomas, H. (eds) (1998) *Urban Planning and the British New Right* (London: Routledge).

Amin, A. (ed.) (1994) *Post-Fordism: A Reader* (London: Blackwell).

Antonio, R. and Kellner, D. (1991) 'Modernity and Critical Social Theory: The Limits of the Postmodern Critique', in D. Dickens and A. Fontana (eds) *Postmodern Social Theory*, University of Chicago Press, Chicago

Arrow, K. (1951) *Social Choice and Individual Values* (New York: John Wiley).

Aughey, A. (1984) 'Elements of Thatcherism', conference paper, University of Southampton, 3–5 April.

Banham, R., Barker, P., Hall, P. and Price, C. (1969) 'Non-Plan: An Experiment in Freedom', *New Society*, 20 March..

Batty, M. (1982) 'The Quest for the Qualitative: New Directions in Planning Theory and Analysis', *Urban Policy and Research*, 1, 15–23.

Bagguley, P., Mark-Lawson, J., Shapiro, D., Urry, J., Walby, S. and Warde, A. (1990) *Restructuring, Place, Class and Gender* (London: Sage).

Barker, K. (2006) *Barker Review of Land Use Planning Interim Report – Analysis*, HM Treasury, London

Barnes, B. and Bloor, D. (1982) 'Rationality, Relativism and the Sociology of Knowledge', in M. Hollis,and S. Lukes (eds), *Rationality and Relativism* (Oxford: Oxford University Press).

Batty, M. (1982) 'On Systems Theory and Analysis in Urban Planning', in M. Batty and B. G. Hutchinson (eds), *Systems Analysis in Urban Policy-Making and Planning* (New York: Plenum Press), 423–47.

Batty, M. (2005) *Cities and Complexity – Understanding Cities and Cellular Automata, Agent-Based Models, and Fractals* (London: MIT Press).

Bauman, Z. (1989) *Modernity and the Holocaust* (Oxford: Polity).

Beauregard, R. (1996) 'Between Modernity and Postmodernity: The Ambiguous Position of US Planning', in S. Campbell and S. Fainstein (eds), *Readings in Planning Theory* (Oxford: Blackwell).

Beesley, A. (1986) 'The New Right, Social Order and Civil Liberties', in R. Levitas (ed.), *The Ideology of the New Right* (Cambridge: Polity).

Bell, D. (1973) *The Coming of Post-Industrial Society* (New York: Basic Books).

Berman, M. (1982) *All That is Solid Melts into Air* (London: Verso).

Bernstein, R. (ed.) (1983) *Habermas and Modernity* (Cambridge, MA: MIT Press).

Best, S. and Kellner, D. (1991) *Postmodern Theory* (London: Macmillan).

Bhaskar, R. (1979) *The Possibility of Naturalism* (Hemel Hemstead: Harvester).

Bhaskar, R. (1998) 'Societies', in M. Archer, R. Bhaskar, A. Collier, T. Lawsonand A. Norrie, *Critical Realism: Essential Readings* (London: Routledge).

Boddy, M. (1982) 'Planning, Landownership and the State', in C. Paris (ed.), *Critical Readings in Planning Theory* (Oxford: Pergamon).

Boddy, M. (1983) 'Local Economic and Employment Strategies', in M. Boddy and C. Fudge (eds), *Local Socialism?* (London: Macmillan).

Bohman, J. (1991) *New Philosophy of Social Science: Problems of Indeterminacy* (Cambridge: Polity).

Boyack, S. (1997) 'Fruits of Modernity', *Town and Country Planning,* November, p. 308.

Boyer, C. (1983) *Dreaming the Rational City* (Boston, MA: MIT Press).

Bracewell-Milnes, B. (1974) *Is Capital Taxation Fair?* (The Sydney Press, Sydney).

Braudel, F. (1984) *The Perspective of the World* (New York: HarperCollins).

Breheny, M. and Hooper, A. (1985) *Rationality in Planning: Critical Essays on the Role of Rationality in Urban and Regional Planning* (London: Pion).

Brindley, T., Rydin, Y. and Stoker, G. (1996) *Remaking Planning: The Politics of Urban Change in the Thatcher Years* (London: Unwin Hyman).

Brown, A., McCrone, D. and Paterson, L. (1998) *Politics and Society in Scotland* (London: Macmillan).

Bryson, J. and Crosby, B. (1992) *Leadership for the Common Good: Tackling Public Problems in a Shared-Power World* (San Francisco: Jossey Bass).

Buchanan, J. M. (1975) *The Limits of Liberty* (Chicago: Chicago University Press).

Bulpitt, J. (1986) 'The Thatcher Statecraft', *Political Studies, vol. 3.*

Byrne, D. (1998) *Complexity Theory and the Social Sciences* (London: Routledge).

Camhis, M. (1979) *Planning Theory and Philosophy* (London: Tavistock).

Campaign to Protect Rural England (2006) *Policy Based Evidence Making: The Policy Exchange's War Against Planning* (London: CPRE).

Campbell, S. and Fainstein, S. (1996) *Readings in Planning Theory* (Oxford: Blackwell).

Castells, M. (1977) 'Towards a Political Urban Sociology', in M. Harloe (ed.), *Captive Cities* (London: John Wiley).

Casti J. L. (1994) *Searching for Certainty: What Scientists Can Know About the Future* (London: Abacus).

Chadwick, G. (1971) *A Systems View of Planning: Towards a Theory of the Urban and Regional Planning Process* (Oxford: Pergamon).

Chalmers, A. F. (1994) *What is This Thing Called Science?* (Milton Keynes: Open University Press).

Checkoway, B. (1994) 'Paul Davidoff and Advocacy Planning in Retrospect', *American Planning Association Journal,* Spring, pp. 139–43.

Cherry, G. (1988) *Cities and Plans: The Shaping of Urban Britain in the Nineteenth and Twentieth Centuries* (London: Edward Arnold).

Cilliers, P. (1998) *Complexity and Postmodernism* (London: Routledge).

Cladera, J. and Burns, M. (2000) 'The Liberalization of the Land Market in Spain: The 1998 Reform of Urban Planning Legislation', *European Planning Studies,* 8(5), pp. 547–64.

Clavel, P. (1994) 'The Evolution of Advocacy Planning', *American Planning Association Journal*, Spring, pp. 146–9.

Cloke, P., Philo, C. and Sadler, D. (1991) *Approaching Human Geography. An Introduction to Contemporary Theoretical Debates* (London: Paul Chapman).

Cohen, R. B. (1981) 'The New International Division of Labour, Multinational Corporations and Urban Hierarchy', in M. Dear and A. Scott, *Urbanisation and Urban Planning in Capitalist Society* (London: Methuen).

Colman, J. (1993) 'Planning Education in the 1990s', *Australian Planner*, 31, 2: 19-23

Cooke, P. (1983) *Theories of Planning and Spatial Development* (London: Hutchinson).

Couvalis, G. (1997) *The Philosophy of Science: Science and Objectivity* (London: Sage).

Cullingworth, B. and Nadin, V. (1994) *Town and Country Planning in the UK* (London: Routledge).

Darke, R. (1985) 'Rationality, Planning and the State', in M. Breheny and A. Hooper, *Rationality in Planning: Critical Essays on the Role of Rationality in Urban and Regional Planning* (London: Pion).

Davidoff, P. (1965) 'Advocacy and Pluralism in Planning', *AIP Journal*, November, pp. 331–8. See also S. Campbell and S. Fainstein (1996) *Readings in Planning Theory* (Oxford: Blackwell), pp. 305–22.

Davidoff, P. and Reiner, T.A., (1962) 'A Choice Theory of Planning', reprinted in A. Faludi (1973) *A Reader in Planning Theory*, 11-39 (Oxford: Pergamon Press).

Davies, J. G. (1972) *The Evangelistic Bureaucrat* (London: Tavistock).

Davy, B. (2008) 'Plan it without a Condom!', *Planning Theory*, 7(3) 301–17.

Dear, M. (2000) *The Postmodern Urban Condition* (Oxford: Blackwell).

Dear, M. and Scott, A. (1981) *Urbanisation and Urban Planning in Capitalist Society* (London: Methuen).

Denman, D.R. (1980), *Land in a Free Society* (London: Centre for Policy Studies).

Dennis, N. (1972) *Public Participation and Planners' Blight* (London: Faber & Faber).

Docherty, T. (1993) *Postmodernism: A Reader* (Hemel Hemstead: Harvester Wheatsheaf).

Downs, A. (1957) *An Economic Theory of Democracy* (New York: Harper & Row).

Dryzek, J. (1990) *Discursive Democracy. Politics, Policy and Political Science* (Cambridge: Cambridge University Press).

Duncan, S. and Goodwin, M. (1988) *The Local State and Uneven Development* (London: Polity).

Eagleton, T. (1996) *The Illusions of Postmodernism* (London: Blackwell).

Eccleshall, R. (1994) 'Conservatism', in R. Eccleshall, V. Geoghegan, R. Jay, M. Kenny, I. MacKenzie and R. Wilford, *Political Ideologies: An Introduction* (2nd edn) (London: Routledge).

Edgar, E. (1983) 'Bitter Harvest', *New Socialist,* September/October.

Etzioni, A. (1967) 'Mixed Scanning: A "Third" Approach to Decision Making', *Public Administration Review,* 27, pp. 385–92.

Evans, A. and Hartwich, O. (2006) *Better Homes, Greener Cities* (London: Policy Exchange).

Evans, B. (1993) 'Why We No Longer Need a Town Planning Profession', *Planning Practice and Research,* 8(1), pp. 9–15.

Evans, B. (1995) *Experts and Environmental Planning* (Aldershot: Averbury).

Evans, B. (1997) 'Town Planning to Environmental Planning', in A. Blowers and B. Evans (eds), *Town Planning into the 21st Century* (London: Routledge).

Evans, B. and Rydin, Y. (1997) 'Planning, Professionalism and Sustainability', in A. Blowers and B. Evans (eds), *Town Planning into the 21st Century* (London: Routledge).

Faludi, A. (1973) *Planning Theory* (Oxford: Pergamon).

Faludi, A. (1982) 'Towards a Combined Paradigm of Planning Theory? A Rejoiner', in C. Paris (ed.), *Critical Readings in Planning Theory* (Oxford: Pergamon).

Faludi, A. (1987) *A Decision-Centred View of Environmental Planning* (Oxford: Pergamon).

Festenstein, M. (1997) *Pragmatism and Political Theory* (Cambridge: Polity).

Feyerabend, P. (1961) *Knowledge without Foundations* (Oberlin: Oberlin College).

Feyerabend, P. (1978) *Science in a Free Society* (London: New Left Books).

Feyerabend, P. (1981) *Realism, Rationalism and Scientific Method, Philosophical Papers, Volume 1* (Cambridge: Cambridge University Press).

Feyerabend, P. (1988) *Against Method* (2nd edn) (London: Verso).

Filion, P. (1996) 'Metropolitan Planning Objectives and Implementation Constraints: Planning in a Post-Fordist and Postmodern Age', *Environment and Planning A,* 28, pp. 1637–60.

Fischer, F. and Forester, J. (eds) (1993) *The Argumentative Turn in Policy Analysis and Planning* (London: University College London).

Fischler, R. (2000) 'Communicative Planning Theory: A Foucauldian Assessment', *Journal of Planning Education and Research,* 19, pp. 358–68.

Flyvbjerg, B. (1998) *Rationality and Power: Democracy in Practice* (Chicago: University of Chicago Press).

Flyvbjerg, B. (2001) *Making Social Science Matter: Why Social Inquiry Fails and How it Can Succeed Again* (Cambridge: Cambridge University Press).

Fogelsong, R. (1986) *Planning and the Capitalist City* (Princeton, NJ: Princeton University Press).

Forester, J. (1989) *Planning in the Face of Power* (London: University of California Press).

Forester, J. (1993) *Critical Theory, Public Policy and Planning Practice: Towards a Critical Pragmatism* (Albany: State University of New York).

Forester, J. (1997) *Learning from Practice: Democratic Deliberations and the Promise of Planning Practice* (College Park, MD: University of Maryland).

Forester, J. (1999) *The Deliberative Practitioner: Encouraging Participatory Planning Processes* (Cambridge: MIT Press).

Foster, J. and Woolfson, C. (1986) *The Politics of the UCS Work-In: Class Alliances and the Right to Work* (London: Lawrence & Wishart).

Foucault, M. (1980) *The History of Sexuality* (New York: Vintage Books).

Friedmann, J. (1973) *Retracking America: A Theory of Transactive Planning* (New York: Doubleday and Anchor Books).

Friedmann, J. (1987) *Planning in the Public Domain: From Knowledge to Action* (Princeton, NJ: Princeton University Press).

Fukuyama, F. (1989) 'The End of History', *The National Interest*, 16, Summer, pp. 3–18.

Gamble, A. (1984) 'This Lady's Not for Turning: Thatcherism Mk III', *Marxism Today*, July.

Gamble, A. (1988) *The Free Economy and the Strong State* (London: Macmillan).

Gamble, A., Marsh, D. and Tant, T. (eds) (1999) *Marxism and Social Science* (London: Macmillan).

Gay, P. (1969) *The Enlightenment: An Interpretation. Vol 1: The Rise of Modern Paganism* (London: Wildwood House).

Geertz, C. (1983) *Local Knowledge. Further Essays in Interpretive Anthropology* (New York: Basic Books).

Gellner, E. (1983) *Nations and Nationalism* (Oxford: Blackwell).

Gibson, T. (1995), 'The Real Planning for Real', *Town Planning Review*, 64, 7 July.

Giddens, A. (1976) *New Rules of Sociological Method* (London: Hutchinson).

Giddens, A. (1984) *The Constitution of Society* (Cambridge: Polity).

Giddens, A. (1990) *The Consequences of Modernity* (Cambridge: Polity).

Glass, R. (1959) 'The Evaluation of Planning: Some Sociological Considerations', *International Social Science Journal*, 11, pp. 393–409.

Gleeson, B. and Low, N. (2000) 'Revaluing Planning: Rolling Back Neo-Liberalism in Australia', *Progress in Planning*, 53, pp. 83–164.

Grant, J. (1994) 'On Some Public Uses of Planning Theory', *Town Planning Review*, 65(1), pp. 59–76.

Grant, M. (1999) 'Planning As a Learned Profession', available from the Royal Town Planning Institute, 26 Portland Place, London.

Gray, J. (1993) *Beyond the New Right: Markets, Government and the Common Environment* (London: Routledge).

Greed, C. (1996) *Implementing Town Planning* (Harlow: Longman).
Griffiths, R. (1986) 'Planning in Retreat? – Town Planning and the Market in the 1980s', *Planning Practice and Research*, 1.
Habermas, J. (1984) *The Theory of Communicative Action, Vol. 1: Reason and the Rationalisation of Society* (Cambridge: Polity).
Habermas, J. (1987) *The Philosophical Discourse of Modernity* (Cambridge: Polity).
Hague, C. (1990) 'Scotland: Back to the Future for Planning', in J. Montgomery and A. Thornley (eds), *Radical Planning Initiatives: New Directions for Urban Planning in the 1990s* (Aldershot: Gower).
Hall, P. (1988) *Cities of Tomorrow* (Oxford: Basil Blackwell).
Hall, P. (1998) *Cities in Civilisation* (London: Weidenfeld & Nicolson).
Hall, P., Gracey, H., Drewett, R. and Thomas, R. (1973) *The Containment of Urban England* (London: Allen and Unwin).
Hall, S. (1992a) Introduction, in S. Hall and B. Gieben, *Formations of Modernity* (Milton Keynes: Open University Press).
Hall, S. (1992b) 'The Question of Cultural Identity', in S. Hall, D. Held and T. McGrew (eds), *Modernity and its Futures* (Cambridge: Polity).
Hall, S., Held, D. and McGrew, T. (1992) *Modernity and its Futures* (Cambridge: Polity).
Hamilton, P. (1992) 'The Enlightenment and the Birth of Social Science', in S. Hall and B. Gieben, *Formations of Modernity* (Milton Keynes: Open University Press).
Harper, T. L. and Stein, S. M. (1995) 'Out of the Postmodern Abyss: Preserving the Rationale for Liberal Planning', *Journal of Planning Education and Research*, 14, pp. 233–44.
Harrison, P. (1998) 'From Irony to Prophecy: A Pragmatist's Perspective on Planning', paper presented to the 'Once Upon a Planners Day' Conference, University of Pretoria, 22–3 January.
Harvey, D. (1973) *Social Justice and the City* (London: Verso).
Harvey, D. (1985) *The Urbanization of Capital* (Baltimore, MD: Johns Hopkins University Press).
Harvey, D. (1989) *The Urban Experience* (London: Blackwell).
Harvey, D. (1990) *The Condition of Postmodernity* (London: Blackwell).
Harvey, D. (1996) *Justice, Nature and the Geography of Difference* (Oxford: Blackwell).
Hay, C. (1995) 'Structure and Agency: Holding the Whip Hand', in D. Marsh and G. Stoker (eds), *Theory and Methods in Political Science* (London: Macmillan).
Hay, C. (1999) 'Marxism and the State', in A. Gamble, D. Marsh and T. Tant (eds), *Marxism and Social Science* (London: Macmillan).
Hayek, F. (1944) *The Road to Serfdom* (London: Routledge & Kegan Paul).
Hayton, K. (1996) 'Planning Policy in Scotland', in M. Tewdwr-Jones (ed.),

*British Planning Policy in Transition: Planning in the 1990s* (London: University College London).

Hayton, K. (1997), *Town and Country Planning*, July/August.

Healey, P. (1991) 'Debates in Planning Thought', in H. Thomas and P. Healey, *Dilemmas of Planning Practice: Ethics, Legitimacy and the Validation of Knowledge* (Aldershot: Avebury).

Healey, P. (1992) 'A Planner's Day: Knowledge and Action in Communicative Practice', *Journal of the American Planning Association*, 58(1).

Healey, P. (1993a) 'The Communicative Work of Development Plans', *Environment and Planning B: Planning and Design*, 20, pp. 83–104.

Healey, P. (1993b) 'Planning Through Debate: The Communicative Turn in Planning Theory', in F. Fischer and J. Forester (eds), *The Argumentative Turn in Policy Analysis and Planning* (London: University College London).

Healey, P. (1996) 'The Communicative Turn in Planning Theory and Its Implications for Spatial Strategy Formulation', *Environment and Planning B: Planning and Design*, 23, pp. 217–34.

Healey, P. (1997) *Collaborative Planning: Shaping Places in Fragmented Societies* (London: Macmillan).

Healey, P. (2003) 'Collaborative Planning in Perspective', *Planning Theory*, 2(2), pp. 101–23.

Healey, P. (2007) *Urban Complexity and Spatial Strategies: Towards a Relational Planning for our Times* London: Routledge).

Healey, P. and Hillier, J. (1995) 'Community Mobilisation in Swan Valley: Claims, Discourses and Rituals in Local Planning', Working Paper No. 49, Dept and Town and Country Planning, University of Newcastle.

Healey, P., McDougall, G. and Thomas, M. (eds) (1982) *Planning Theory: Prospects for the 1980s* (Oxford: Pergamon).

Healey, P., McNamara, P., Elson, M. and Doak, A. (1988) *Land Use Planning and the Mediation of Urban Change: The British Planning System in Practice* (Cambridge: Cambridge University Press).

Held, D. (1987) *Models of Democracy* (Cambridge: Polity).

Hillier, J. (1995) 'The Unwritten Law of Planning Theory: Common Sense', *Journal of Planning Education and Research*, 14(2), pp. 292–6.

Hillier, J. (2002) *Shadows of Power: An Allegory of Prudence in Land Use Planning* (London: Routledge).

Hillier, J. and Healey, P. (2008) *Critical Essays in Planning Theory. Volume 1, Foundations of the Planning Enterprise* (Andover: Ashgate).

Hirst, P. (1989) *After Thatcher* (London: Collins).

Hoch, C. (1984) 'Doing Good and Being Right – the Pragmatic Connection in Planning Theory', *American Planning Association Journal*, 4(1), pp. 335–45.

Hoch, C. (1995) *What Planners Do?* (Chicago: Planners Press).
Hoch, C. (1996) 'A Pragmatic Inquiry About Planning and Power', in J. Seymour, L. Mandelbaum and R. Burchell, *Explorations in Planning Theory* (New Brunswick, NJ: Center for Urban Policy Research).
Hoch, C. (1997) 'Planning Theorists Taking an Interpretive Turn Need not Travel on the Political Economy Highway', *Planning Theory*, 17, pp. 13–64.
Hoch, C. (2002) 'Evaluating Plans Pragmatically', *Planning Theory*, 1(1), pp. 53–75.
Holston, J. (1995) 'Spaces of Insurgent Citizenship', *Planning Theory*, 13: 35–52.
Howe, E. (1994) *Acting on Ethics in City Planning* (New Brunswick, NJ: Center for Urban Policy Research).
Hutton, W. (1995) *The State We're In* (London: Jonathon Cape).
Innes, J. (1992) 'Group Processes and the Social Construction of Growth Management: The Case of Florida, Vermont and New Jersey', *Journal of the American Planning Association*, 58, pp. 275–8.
Jackson, P. (1992) 'Economic Policy', in D. Marsh and R. A. W. Rhodes (eds), *Implementing Thatcherite Policy: Audit of an Era* (Buckingham: Open University Press).
Jacobs, J. (1961) *The Death and Life of Great American Cities* (London: Penguin).
Jessop, B. (1990) 'Regulation Theories in Retrospect and Prospect', *Economy and Society*, 19, p. 153–216.
Johnson, C. (1991) *The Economy Under Mrs Thatcher 1979–1990* (London: Penguin).
Jones, R. (1982) *Town and Country Chaos* (London: Adam Smith Institute).
Jordan, G. (1990) 'The Pluralism of Pluralism: An Anti-Theory?', *Political Studies*, 38(2), pp. 286–301.
Judge, D., Stoker, G. and Wolman, H. (eds) (1995) *Theories of Urban Politics* (London: Sage).
Kavanagh, D. (1987) *Thatcherism and British Politics* (Oxford: Oxford University Press).
Kellner, D. (1989) *Jean Baudrillard: From Marxism to Postmodernism and Beyond* (Cambridge: Polity).
Kerr, P. and Marsh, D. (1999) 'Explaining Thatcherism: Towards a Multidimensional Approach', in D. Marsh, J. Buller, C. Hay, J. Johnston, P. Kerr, S. McAnulla and M. Watson, *Postwar British Politics in Perspective* (Cambridge: Polity).
King, D. S. (1987) *The New Right: Politics, Markets and Citizenship* (London: Macmillan).
Klosterman, R. E. (1985), 'Arguments for and Against Planning', *Town Planning Review*, 56, p. 1.

Kristol, I. (1978) *Two Cheers for Capitalism* (New York: Basic Books).

Kristol, I. (1996) 'America's "Exceptional Conservatism"', in K. Minogue (ed.), *Conservative Realism: New Essays in Conservatism* (London: HarperCollins).

Krumholz, N. (2001) 'Planners and Politicians: A Commentary Based on Experience from the United States', *Planning Theory and Practice*, 2(1), pp. 96–100.

Krumholz, N. and Forester, J. (1990) *Making Equity Planning Work: Leadership in the Public Sector* (Philadelphia: Temple University Press).

Kuhn, T. (1970) *The Structure of Scientific Revolutions* (2nd edn) (Chicago: University of Chicago Press).

Kumar, K. (1995) *From Post-Industrial to Post-Modern Society. New Theories of the Contemporary World* (Oxford: Blackwell).

Laclau, E. and Mouffe, C. (1985) *Hegemony and Socialist Strategy: Towards a Radical Democratic Politics* (London: Verso Books).

Lai, L. W. C. (1999) 'Hayek and Town Planning: A Note on Hayek's Views Towards Town Planning in The Constitution of Liberty', *Environment and Planning A*, 31, pp. 1567–82.

Lauria, M. and Wagner, J. (2006) 'What Can We Learn from Empirical Studies of Planning Theory? A Comparative Case Analysis of Extant Literature', *Journal of Planning Education and Research*, 25(4), pp. 361–81.

Law-Yone, H. (2007) 'Another Planning Theory? Rewriting the Meta-Narrative', *Planning Theory*, 6(3), pp. 315–26.

Lawrence, D. H. (1998) *Lady Chatterley's Lover* (London: Penguin).

Lee, D. B. (1973) 'Requiem for Large Scale Models', *Journal of the American Institute of Planners*, 39, 163–78.

Levitas, R. (ed.) (1986) *The Ideology of the New Right* (Cambridge: Polity).

Liggett, H. (1996) 'Examining the Planning Practice Conscious(ness)', in S. Mandelbaum, L. Mazza and R. Burchell, *Explorations in Planning Theory* (New Brunswick, NJ: Rutgers University).

Lindblom, C. E. (1959) 'The Science of Muddling Through', *Public Administration*, Spring.

Lindblom, C. E. (1977) *Politics and Markets: The World's Political-Economic Systems* (New York: Basic Books).

Lindblom, C. E. and Woodhouse, E. J. (1993) *The Policy Making Process* (3rd edn) (Englewood Cliffs, NJ: Prentice Hall).

Lloyd, M. G. (1999) 'Response to Scottish Office Consultation Document, Land Use Planning Under a Scottish Parliament', in Scottish Executive, 1999.

Longino, H. (1990) *Science as Social Knowledge* (Princeton, NJ: Princeton University Press).

Low, N. (1991) *Planning, Politics and the State: Political Foundations of Planning Thought* (London: Unwin Hyman).

Lyddon, D. (1980) 'Scottish Planning in Practice. Influences and Comparisons', *The Planner,* May, pp. 66–7.

Lyotard, J.-F. (1983) 'Answering the Question: What is Postmodernism?', in I. Hassan and S. Hassan (eds), *Innovation/Renovation: New Perspectives on the Humanities* (Madison: University of Wisconsin Press).

Lyotard, J.-F. (1984) *The Postmodern Condition: A Report on Knowledge* (Minneapolis: University of Minnesota Press).

Marx, Karl (1971) Preface to *A Contribution to the Critique of Political Economy,* tr. S. W. Ryanzanskaya, ed. M. Dobb. (London: Lawrence & Wishart).

Macdonald, R. and Thomas, H. (eds) (1997) *Nationality and Planning in Scotland and Wales* (Cardiff: University of Wales Press).

MacLaren, A. A. (ed.) (1976) *Social Class in Scotland* (Edinburgh: John Donald).

Mandelbaum, S., Mazza, L. and Burchell, R. (eds) (1996) *Explorations in Planning Theory* (New Brunswick, NJ: Rutgers, Center for Urban Policy Research).

Mark, K. (1971) *A Contribution to the Critique of Political Economy* (London: Lawrence & Wishart).

Mark-Lawson, J. and Warde, A. (1987) 'Industrial Restructuring and the Transformation of a Local Political Environment: A Case Study of Lancaster', Lancaster Regionalism Group Working Paper No. 33, University of Lancaster.

Marris, P. (1994) 'Advocacy Planning as a Bridge Between the Professional and the Political', *APA Journal,* Spring, pp. 143–6.

Marsh, D. and Rhodes, R. (1992) 'Policy Networks in British Government: A Critique of Existing Approaches', in Marsh, D. and Rhodes, R. (eds), *Policy Networks in British Government* (Oxford: Clarendon Press).

Marx, K. and Engels, F. (1985) *The Communist Manifesto* (London: Penguin).

Massey, D. (2005) *For Space* (London: Sage).

Massey, D. (2007) *World City* (Cambridge: Polity Press).

Mazziotti, D. F. (1982) 'The Underlying Assumptions of Advocacy Planning: Pluralism and Reform', in C. Paris (ed.), *Critical Readings in Planning Theory* (Oxford: Pergamon).

McConnell, S. (1981) *Theories for Planning* (London: Heinemann).

McCrone, D. (1992) *Understanding Scotland – The Sociology of a Stateless Nation*(London: Routledge).

McLennan, G. (1992) 'The Enlightenment Project Revisited', in S. Hall, D. Held and T. McGrew (eds), *Modernity and its Futures* (Cambridge: Polity).

McLoughlin, B. (1969) *Urban and Regional Planning: A Systems Approach* (London: Faber and Faber).

McNay, L. (1994) *Foucault: A Critical Introduction* (Cambridge: Polity).
McPherson, A. F. and Raab, C. (1988) *Governing Education: A Sociology Policy since 1945* (Edinburgh: Edinburgh University Press).
Meyerson, M. M. and Banfield, E. C. (1955) *Politics, Planning and the Public Interest: The Case of Public Housing in Chicago* (New York: Free Press).
Moore Milroy, B. (1991) 'Into Postmodern Weightlessness', *Journal of Planning Education and Research*, 10(3), pp. 181–7.
Mounce, H. O. (1997) *The Two Pragmatisms: From Peirce to Rorty* (London: Routledge).
Muller, J. (1998) 'Paradigms and Planning Practice', *International Planning Studies*, 3(3), pp. 287–302.
Murdoch, J. (2006) *Post-Structuralist Geography: A Guide to Relational Space* (London: Sage).
Newton, K. (1976) *Second City Politics: Democratic Processes and Decision Making in Birmingham* (Oxford: Oxford University Press).
Norton, P. and Aughey, A. (1981), *Conservatives and Conservatism* (London: Temple Smith).
Oranje, M. (1996), 'Modernising South Africa and Its Forgotten People Under Postmodern Conditions', paper presented to the University of Newcastle 50th Anniversary Conference, 25– 27 October.
Outhwaite, W. (1987) *New Philosophies of Social Science: Realism, Hermeneutics and Critical Theory* (London: Macmillan).
Painter, J. (1995) *Politics, Geography and 'Political Geography'* (London: Arnold).
Paris, C. (ed.) (1982) *Critical Readings in Planning Theory* (Oxford: Pergamon).
Pateman, C. (1970) *Participation and Democratic Theory* (Cambridge: Cambridge University Press).
Paterson, L. (1998) 'Scottish Home Rule: Radical Break or Pragmatic Adjustment?', in H. Elcock and M. Keating, *Remaking the Union: Devolution and British Politics in the 1990s* (London: Frank Cass).
Pearce, B. J., Curry, N. and Goodchild, R. N. (1978) 'Land, Planning and the Market', Cambridge University Department of Land Economy, Paper 9.
Pennance, F. (1974) 'Planning, Land Supply and Demand', in A. Walters *et al.*, *Government and the Land* (London: Institute of Economic Affairs).
Pennington, M. (2000) *Planning and the Political Market* (London: Athlone Press).
Pickvance, C. (1982) 'Physical Planning and Market Forces in Urban Development', in C. Paris (ed.) *Critical Readings in Planning Theory* (Oxford: Pergamon).
Piven, F. F. (1970) 'Whom Does the Advocacy Planner Serve?', *Social Policy*, 1(1), pp. 32–5.

Planning Aid for Scotland (PAS) (2000) 'Guidance Note for All Volunteers Undertaking Casework', Planning Aid for Scotland, Edinburgh.

Ploger, J. (2004) 'Strife: Urban Planning and Agonism', *Planning Theory*, 3, pp. 71–92.

Popper, K. (1966) *The Open Society and its Enemies*, Vol. 2 (5th edn) (London: Routledge).

Popper, K. (1970) *Objective Knowledge* (Oxford: Oxford University Press).

Popper, K. (1980) *The Logic of Scientific Discovery* (10th edn) (London: Hutchinson).

Poster, M. (1998) 'Postmodern Virtualities', in Berger. A.A (ed.) *The Postmodern Presence: Readings on Postmodernism in American Culture and Society* (Walnut Creek, CA: Altamira Press).

Poulton, M. C. (1991) 'The Case for a Positive Theory of Planning. Part 1: What is Wrong with Planning Theory?', *Environment and Planning B: Planning and Design*, 18, pp. 225–32.

Ratcliffe, J. (1974) *An Introduction to Town and Country Planning* (London: Hutchinson).

Reade, E. (1985) 'An Analysis of the Use and Concept of Rationality in the Literature of Planning', in M. Breheny and A. Hooper, *Rationality in Planning: Critical Essays on the Role of Rationality in Urban and Regional Planning* (London: Pion).

Reade, E. J. (1987) *British Town and Country Planning* (Milton Keynes: Open University Press).

Richardson, T. (1996), 'Foucauldian Discourse: Power and Truth in Urban and Regional Policy Making', *European Planning Studies*, 4(3), pp. 279–92.

Riddell, P. (1983) *The Thatcher Government* (Oxford: Martin Robinson).

Rittel, H. J. W. and Webber, M. M. (1973) 'Dilemmas of a General Theory of Planning', *Policy Sciences*, 4, pp. 1555–9.

Rosenfeld, Michel (1998) 'Pragmatism, Pluralism and Legal Interpretation: Posner and Rorty's Justice without Metaphysics Meets Hate Speech', in M. Dickstein (ed.), *The Revival of Pragmatism: New Essays on Social Thought, Law and Culture* (Durham and London: Duke University Press).

Rowan-Robinson, J. (1997) 'The Organisation and Effectiveness of the Scottish Planning System', in R. Macdonald and H. Thomas (eds), *Nationality and Planning in Scotland and Wales* (Cardiff: University of Wales Press).

Roy, A. (2005) 'Urban Informality: Towards an Epistemology of Planning', *Journal of the American Planning Association*, 70: 133–41.

Royal Town Planning Institute (1994) *Code of Professional Conduct* (London: RTPI).

Royal Town Planning Institute (1996) *Planning Schools' Handbook* (London: RTPI).

Rutherford, M. (1983) 'Review of Politics Under Thatcherism', ed. Stuart Hall and Martin Jaques, *Marxism Today*, July.

Rydin, Y. (2007) 'Re-Examining the Role of Planning Knowledge within Planning Theory', *Planning Theory*, 6(1), pp. 52–68.

Rydin, Y. (2008) 'Planning' Response to E.R. Alexander's Comment On `The Role of Knowledge In Planning', *Planning Theory*, 7(2): 211–12.

Sager, T. (1994) *Communicative Planning Theory* (Aldershot: Avebury).

Sandercock, L. (1998) *Towards Cosmopolis* (Chichester: John Wiley).

Sandercock, L. (2003) *Cosmopolis II: Mongrel Cities of the 21st Century* (London: Continuum).

Savage, S. and Robins, L. (1990) *Public Policy Under Thatcher* (London: Macmillan).

Scott, A. J. and Roweis, S. T. (1977) 'Urban Planning Theory in Practice: A Reappraisal', *Environment and Planning A*, 9, pp. 1097–119.

Simons, H. W. (1994) *After Postmodernism: Reconstructing Ideology Critique* (London: Sage).

Soja, E. (1997) 'Planning in/for Postmodernity', in G. Benko and U. Strohmayer (eds), *Space and Social Theory, in Interpreting Modernity and Postmodernity* (Oxford: Blackwell).

Soloman, R. C. (1997) *Introducing Philosophy* (6th edn) (Fort Worth, TX: Harcourt Brace).

Sorenson, A. D. (1982) 'Planning Comes of Age: A Liberal Perspective', *The Planner*, November/December.

Sorenson, A. D. and Day, R. A. (1981) 'Libertarian Planning', *Town Planning Review*, 52.

Sorensen, T. and Auster, M. (1998) 'Theory and Practice in Planning: Further Apart Than Ever?', paper presented to the Eighth International Planning History Conference, University of New South Wales, 15–18 July.

Steen, A. (1981) *New Life for Old Cities* (London: Aims of Industry).

Stephenson, R. (2000) 'Technically Speaking: Planning Theory and the Role of Information in Making Planning Policy', *Planning Theory and Practice*, 1(1), pp. 95–110.

Stranz, W. (1990) 'Community Action', *Town and Country Planning*, 59(1).

Taylor, N. (1980) 'Planning Theory and the Philosophy of Planning', *Urban Studies*, 17, pp. 159–68.

Taylor, N. (1998) *Urban Planning Theory Since 1945* (London: Sage).

Teitz, M. (1996a) 'American Planning in the 1990s: Evolution, Debate and Challenge', *Urban Studies*, 33(4–5), pp. 649–72.

Teitz, M. (1996b) 'American Planning in the 1990s: Part II, The Dilemma of the Cities', *Urban Studies*, 34 (5–6), pp. 775–96.

Tewdwr-Jones, M. and Lloyd, M.G. (1997) 'Unfinished Business', *Town and Country Planning*, November, pp. 302–4.

Tewdwr-Jones, M. and Thomas, H. (1995) 'Beacons Planners Get Real in Rural Plan Consultation', *Planning*, 3 February, p. 1104.
Thomas, H. (1992) 'Volunteers' Involvement in Planning Aid: Evidence from South Wales', *Town Planning Review*, 63(1), pp. 47–62.
Thomas, M. J. (1982) 'The Procedural Planning Theory of A. Faludi', in C. Paris (ed.), *Critical Readings in Planning Theory* (Oxford: Pergamon).
Thompson, R. (2000) 'Re-defining Planning: The Roles of Theory and Practice', *Planning Theory and Practice*, 1(1), pp. 126–33.
Thornley, A. (1993) *Urban Planning Under Thatcherism. The Challenge of the Market* (2nd edn) (London: Routledge).
Thrift, N. (2004) 'Movement–Space: The Changing Domain of Thinking Resulting from the Development of New Kinds of Spatial Awareness', *Economy and Society*, 33, 4: 582-604
Tullock, G. (1978) *The Vote Motive* (2nd edn) (London: Institute of Economic Affairs).
Underwood, J. (1980) *Town Planners in Search of a Role* (Bristol: University of Bristol, School for Advanced Urban Studies).
Van Dijk, T. A. (ed.) (1997) *Discourse as Structure and Process* (London: Sage).
Waldrop M. M. (1992) *Complexity: The Emerging Science at the Edge of Chaos* (New York: Simon & Schuster).
Walters, A. *et al.* (1974) *Government and the Land* (London: Institute of Economic Affairs).
Warde, A. (1985) 'Spatial Change, Politics and the Division of Labour', in D. Gregory and J. Urry (eds), *Social Relations and Spatial Structures* (London: Macmillan).
Watson, V. (1998) 'The "Practice Movement" As An Approach to Developing Planning Theory – Origins, Debates and Potentials', paper presented to the Once Upon A Planner's Day Conference, Department of Town and Regional Planning, University of Pretoria, South Africa, January.
Watson, V. (2008) 'Down to Earth: Linking Planning Theory and Practice in the "Metropole" and Beyond', *International Planning Studies*, 13(3), pp. 223–37.
Webber, M. M. (1983) 'The Myth of Rationality: Development Planning Reconsidered', *Environment and Planning B: Planning and Design*, 10, pp. 89–99.
Webster, F. (1995) *Theories of the Information Society* (London: Routledge).
Weinberg, S. (1996) *The New York Review of Books*, 43(13), pp. 11–15.
West, W. A. (1974) *Town Planning Controls – Success or Failure?* (London: Institute of Economic Affairs).
Wildavsky, A. (1973) 'If Planning is Everything, Maybe it's Nothing', *Policy Sciences*, 4, pp. 127–53.

Wilson, A. G. (2000) *Complex Spatial Systems: The Modelling Foundations of Urban and Regional Analysis* (London: Prentice Hall).

Yates, D. (1977) *The Ungovernable City: The Politics of Urban Problems and Policy Making* (Cambridge, MA: MIT Press).

Yiftachel, O. (1989) 'Towards a New Typology of Urban Planning Theories', *Environment and Planning B: Planning and Design*, 16, pp. 23–39.

Yiftachel, O. (1994) 'The Dark Side of Modernism: Planning as Control of an Ethnic Minority', in S. Watson and K. Gibson (eds), *Postmodern Cities and Spaces* (Oxford: Blackwell).

Yiftachel, O. (1998) 'Planning and Social Control: Exploring the Dark Side', *Journal of Planning Literature*, 12(4), pp. 395–406.

Yiftachel, O. (2000) 'Social Control, Urban Planning and the Ethno-Class Relations: Mizahi Jews in Israel's "Development Towns"', *International Journal of Urban and Regional Research*, 20(2), pp. 418–38.

Yiftachel, O. and Huxley, M. (2000) 'Debating Dominance and Relevance: Notes on the "Communicative Turn" in Planning Theory', *International Journal of Urban and Regional Research*, 24(4), pp. 907–13.

# Index

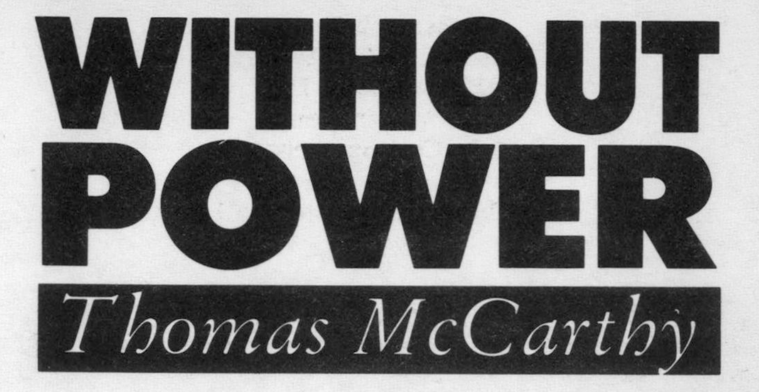

D0230296

POOLBEG

*All characters and events in this novel are entirely fictitious and bear no relation to any real person or actual happening. Any resemblance to real characters or to actual happenings is entirely accidental.*

*Had de Valera eaten Parnell's heart*
*No loose-lipped demagogue had won the day,*
*No civil rancour torn the land apart.*

WB Yeats

*To Denis FitzGerald,*
*Our beloved Geraldine*

# PART I

# THE CHAIRMAN'S EYES

# ONE

It was on the last Sunday in February, a week before the shock defeat of the government, that they buried the Unionist author, Mrs Cameron. Snow was falling lightly. The first flakes came around mid-morning, sending a flutter of nerves across the Southern Unionist world. The usually brave Unionists of Mrs Cameron's circle wouldn't venture alone into the uncertain snowy byways. Instead, they called out the local hackney-drivers and part-time chauffeurs. Most hackney-men were supporters of the Party and had been out since early morning ferrying candidates from village to village. Elections are good for the transport trade, so the dissolution of the nineteenth Dáil during the winter recess had come like a second Christmas to the bus-owners and hackney-men of the country. Ned Kenny, weary owner of twelve buses and Chairman of the local Party, had driven the Winslows to Mrs Cameron's funeral in his own well-polished Mercedes. His strong and heavy face was reflected in the car-mirror as he looked at his rich clients—with a sense of relief now, because they had spent over an hour in the churchyard.

"Sure's cold, Ned. Sure as hell it's cold." Mr

Winslow settled into his seat. His navy coat was peppered with melting snow. "Just like Connecticut."

"It's the dampness," his wife insisted. "It's not nearly as cold as New England, but this Irish dampness chills one to the bones."

"Let's go, Ned!"

"Terrible weather for an election." Ned spoke. He could see that Mrs Winslow's face was blue from the cold, and from the agitation of the north-east wind that had swept through the winter graveyard.

"Will it not damage your Party?"asked Mr Winslow.

"A disaster. It will be a disaster for us. On top of everything else, the fall-out from the Arms Trial, the lost ministers. Then Fine Gael and Labour with their bloody 'Statement of Intent.'"

"Yes, I think they caught you on the hop. Still, you've been in power for ten years."

"Sixteen. Sixteen years." Ned seemed amazed by his own information. Mr Winslow responded with what seemed to be an equal degree of amazement. He said that sixteen years was a veritable dynasty, that no American administration could hope to survive that long. Then he mentioned the thorny subject of the Party's *volte face* on the domestic rates issue. Ned was silent on that one.

Mrs Winslow coughed. "He adores European politics," she said suddenly. Her face was becoming less blue. Ned shifted slightly in his driving seat. He

had felt a sudden jab of pain in his stomach. Ned didn't know it, but he was already suffering from the disease that would kill him.

"This is one of the most bitter and difficult election campaigns I've taken part in," he confided.

"Why do you say that?"

"We've been fighting among ourselves, as well as against the opposition parties. Since the Arms Trial in '70 and the resignation of all those ministers things haven't been the same. I don't think the Party will ever be united again."

"They say Lynch is weak."

"So they say." Ned wouldn't condemn the Party leader, even to two Americans who had no vote. While they talked they crossed over the county boundary. They were now motoring through Ned's home constituency—new and more familiar faces and names were hanging from the snow-drenched placards. The cardboard backs flapped in the breeze; they were perishing in the wet snow. "God, but it's foul weather. We'll lose a load of seats!"

"But the weather is irrelevant, surely?" Mrs Winslow spoke again.

"Ma'am, if people are in a bad mood they'll blame the government for everything. People always punish a government. Most of us criticised the timing of this bloody election. Even Senator Glenville—you know him; he's Deputy Glenville's son—he spoke out

against this election."

"Too bad. I hate to see your government falling."

"I suppose we got our warning—four years ago the Labour Party said that the Seventies would be a socialist decade."

The snowfall thickened as they drove away. The narrow tree-lined roads became like wind tunnels, lifting snow off the ground and dumping it against the twin cones of the headlights. It was already twilight. "Will I go by Castletownroche?The old mill and bridge should look great in the snow." Ned spoke enthusiastically.

"No, no, we won't delay. Mrs Winslow's legs are beginning to make trouble. Anyway, it'll soon be dark." Her husband was worried. Ned could see that they had drawn closer. Mr Winslow was rubbing his wife's cold hands. His cheeks had become flushed from the heat of the car. He undid the top buttons of his coat, revealing a crumpled blue scarf. A strand of silver hair fell across his forehead. There was a long pause before he spoke again. The rhythmic sound of the windscreen wipers and the rattle of the loose blow-heater filled the warm car.

"I suppose Mrs Cameron—I mean Elizabeth Bowen—was very English," Mr Winslow said.

"One leg in Ireland, like all the Anglo-Irish," his wife replied.

"Her politics were British. Didn't she work for the

Englishman—what was his name? The Minister for Information, Brendan Bracken; didn't she report to him during the War?"

"They say her family were good landlords, Ned."

"Is that so? I wouldn't know anything about the family—they're not in our constituency. Farahy is in Cork, you see. Not my constituency at all."

"I suppose you think there were no good landlords, Ned?" Mrs Winslow spoke jovially.

Ned didn't reply.

"I think I'll have a cigar. Nothing like a cigar." There was the sound of a match being struck. "Damn!" Mr Winslow burned the tip of his finger.

His wife laughed. "Those cigars are far too strong," she said.

He was unmoved. "Try one, dear."

"Have you read any of Elizabeth Bowen's novels, Ned?" Mr Winslow cocked his cigar in the air, balancing the ash, while he waited for a reply.

"No interest in books, I'm afraid. Driving buses and politics, they're the things I'm interested in."

"Dear God, how I hate politics," Mrs Winslow sighed.

"A man doesn't need to read. People can be quite civilised without books," her husband continued. "Too many books can drive people crazy. Look at America—when I was young America was a happy and settled place. Then in the Sixties everybody

started reading books. The Kennedys are to blame for most of this, this literary craze. They forced everybody to go to school, even in the South. People became tense from all that reading...You've been lucky here in Ireland, Ned."

The snow continued to fall while they travelled and talked. They soon exhausted the possibilities of politics.

Silence. The Winslows seemed to grow tired easily. Ned wondered if they were worried about his concentration. In the twilight snow was as dangerous as fog. Before long they reached the village where Ned had promised to meet the Senator and his girlfriend, Julie Phelan. "I hope you don't mind, Mr Winslow, but I have to stop here to collect some election material from Senator Glenville. He's waiting for me in the pub." Ned spoke sheepishly. "I know you hired me for the whole afternoon. So if you don't want me to stop I'll go straight on. No problem. No doubt about it."

The Winslows didn't respond immediately. Ned saw them exchanging glances. "We'll go too, Ned," Mrs Winslow said.

Ned tried to dissuade her. He knew how filthy the pub would seem to Americans. "It's a dirty place...They only stock Irish whiskey."

"Irish *Scotch* is fine," Mrs Winslow said.

"A'right, ma'am," Ned smiled.

"Ned! Ned! The dogs!" Mr Winslow shouted, coughing the words, cigar smoke catching in his breath. "The dogs!"

It was too late. Ned overcame the urge to swerve to avoid two sheepdogs that had run across his path. He came to a halt slowly, solidly. He feared the snow. The smaller of the two sheepdogs was crushed by the rear wheel. It howled pathetically, high-pitched ear-piercing screams that upset Mrs Winslow. Ned got out of the car. The injured dog, a pup of four or five months, was bleeding from the ears and nose. Blood spotted the snow. The older returned to the footpath, wagging its tail nervously as if it expected to be scolded.

"The poor fucker's done for." Ned stood over it. "I'd say its back is broken."

"We'll have to get it to a vet. We must get it a pain-killing injection. Oh...how horrible, horrible. The poor thing."

"Ned will call a vet." Mr Winslow put his arm around his distressed wife.

"Will ye go into the pub. Get yerselves a hot whiskey." Ned pointed to the pub. Already people were coming out the doors. Other dogs barked. A scene. Ned was embarrassed. A postman came out of the sub-post-office and patted the older dog. "I'll deal with this," Ned insisted. "Don't worry."

"The poor dog. We must get pain-killers," Mrs

Winslow repeated.

"Don't worry."

Ned went back to the Mercedes and opened the boot. He returned with the steel handle of the jack.

"What's this, Ned? What are you doing?"

"Look away, dear." Her husband pulled her away.

Ned knelt down beside the injured sheep dog. It began to snap wildly, its teeth bared, still squealing in pain. Ned drew a deep breath and slammed the steel handle down on the pup's head. It lay back, stunned. Ned walloped it again as if it were a live salmon. He crushed its skull. Congealed blood oozed from its muzzle. "He's dead, the poor little bastard," Ned said. The other dog left the footpath and came over to sniff the carcass. It was the mother.

"I killed your pup." Ned addressed the farmer who had come out of the pub. "It was your one, wasn't it?"

"Thank God it was Mick, not Paddy. Paddy's the mother. You'll come in for a drink?" the farmer said. "You must have got a fright."

"I'm worried about the Americans. I was driving those two Americans from Farahy. They're very soft."

"We'll buy them a drink. I told my son to bring the dogs into the pub but he left them outside in the snow. The pup didn't have much sense—you know the old saying 'The old dog for the hard road, the pup for the boreen.' There's no damage done to your

car?"

"None."

"Mick is dead," the farmer addressed his son when they entered the pub. The Winslows were standing by the bar, unsure of themselves. The Senator and Julie didn't move from their warm perch by a huge turf fire. Rough sods spat and hissed at them.

"Mick was a useless hoor," the son replied, unmoved. He sounded like an old man.

"You could at least have brought them inside," his father insisted.

"We should have drowned Mick when he was born. He was too excitable to be a good shep."

"I'll make those decisions," the father said, angrily. "Let those decisions to your father, boy, I'm still in charge."

"There's a terrible fodder shortage...a pound a bloody bale." The son addressed the Winslows.

"'Tis terrible all right," the father agreed. "What'll you have, sir? And your wife?" He looked at Mrs Winslow.

"Ned, could I have a word with you?" Mrs Winslow took Ned's arm and led him towards the exit. When she reached the door she said, "We must go back to the car, my cheque-book's in my bag. I must give the poor farmer something for the dead dog. I feel I must..."

"What, pay a farmer!" Ned spoke as quietly as he

could, but he couldn't conceal his outrage. "Pay a farmer, for what?"

"His poor dog."

"Keep your cheque-book in the car where it's safe, ma'am. Open a cheque-book near a farmer and you could lose hundreds..."

"But the man was so courteous about it. He even bought drinks..."

"Farmers are rolling in money. The banks have been throwing money at them since we decided to join the EEC. They've bled the country dry, now they'll bleed Europe dry..."

"We must give him something. I insist."

"Forget about the cheque-book. I'll pay for the drinks."

When they went back inside they found the others already grouped around the fire, drinking and chatting. Julie and the Senator had surfaced from the haze of turf smoke and were now laughing and talking. Mr Winslow got up from his seat and his wife sat down without comment. Her husband's kindness was natural, not requiring comment or praise. Mr Winslow placed his overcoat over his wife's knees—she had delicate legs, the extreme heat of the fire would irritate them. "I don't think you know Julie Phelan," Ned introduced the two women. They shook hands.

"Mick Keating's my name," the farmer introduced

himself. "And me son there's Mick Óg."

"Wasn't the poor little pup called Mick also?" Mrs Winslow responded.

"It's a family name. Ever since the Land League days we've all been Mick Ógs or Paddies."

"Even the dogs?"

"Yes."

"I feel I must compensate you for the lost dog."

"Whatever you want to give, ma'am. It's up to yourself. He might have been a great dog, it's true."

"Did you get the canvassing material, Gerald?" Ned wanted to put an end to the dog exchange.

"Party headquarters sent only black and white stuff," the Senator replied. He pulled a large brown box from under his seat. "I told Morrissey you'd be disgusted. I said you'd probably ring him. He said there's no money. The local organisation should print some of their own material." The Senator looked at Julie nervously. She said nothing.

"Bloody madnes!" Ned said. He then appealed to Julie. "Don't you think so? Don't you think it's lunacy to expect us to print our own stuff?"

"I do. We owe money to two local printers already. Word will go out that the Party's got money trouble."

"Would twenty-five pounds be enough for the poor dog?" Mrs Winslow spoke again.

"I'll put pressure on Morrissey." Ned stood up

because a second round of drinks was coming from the bar. It wasn't clear who was paying for them. "I'll pay for these," he shouted. As he stretched to get the drinks he felt a sudden jab of pain. He rubbed his middle vigorously to ease the discomfort.

"Are you alright? Have you seen the doctor. What did he say?" The Senator looked worried.

"I saw him. I saw him...I'm fine."

"If you think that's fair, ma'am, if you think that's enough," the farmer said.

"Fifty pounds so," Mrs Winslow replied. She felt embarrassed. She thought she had hurt his feelings.

"Fifty pounds so? You wouldn't pay fifty pounds for a bloody greyhound!" Ned handed a second drink to Mr Winslow. "Five pounds is more than enough."

"It's not easy. To lose a dog in the middle of winter." The farmer did his best.

"Ah, rubbish."

"The poor dog," Mrs Winslow repeated. "I will write the cheque now." Ned's annoyance had no effect on her.

"It's bad weather, isn't it? Unusually bleak for Ireland." Her husband attempted some light conversation. It wasn't easy being caught between a dead dog and an election. Julie agreed with him. The others were drinking.

"Tisn't just sour weather," Ned spoke sourly. "It's the mood of the country. The whole country's gone

sour. And we only in the EEC for four weeks."

Mrs Winslow turned to Ned. "Could you fetch my bag from your car?" Ned did what he was asked, but reluctantly.

When he returned Julie was talking. "Ah I love the snow. You can't help loving the snow." She sounded cheerful. "Ye get lovely snowfalls in America, don't ye?" She looked at Mrs Winslow.

"We do, yes. Blue snow. I always imagine that our Connecticut snow is blue, quite wonderful." She tore the cheque from her book and handed it to the farmer.

Ned glared at her. He moved back suddenly and buttoned his coat. "We should go, Mr Winslow. The day's not getting any younger." Mr Winslow removed his coat from his wife's knees and she rose laboriously. The heat of the fire had stiffened her legs.

"That was nice. Such a lovely fire." She turned to Julie and shook her hand. "It was nice to meet you." She and her husband and Ned left the pub. The farmer and his son waved goodbye enthusiastically. Ned held the door for Mrs Winslow.

When they had gone the Senator stood up and made ready to go.

"Do we have to go? It's so cosy here." Julie touched his sleeve. He looked at her, his dark eyes reflecting the orange glow of the draughty turf fire. His winter coat made him look overweight, and his

lack of height exaggerated the middle-age spread.

"No, we should go," he said. "We should move while the roads are still open."

"What's the hurry?"

"Julie, there's an election on."

At the southern end of the constituency, "Condolences" Dineen was having a sandwich in his car with Michael Phelan. They had been canvassing along the high road in the Comeragh Mountains, but turned back, towards Dungarvan, when the snowfall thickened. Condolences was still flushed from an encounter with a woman who attacked him over the Offences against the State (Amendment) Bill, and the fifth amendment to the Constitution which removed the special position of the Catholic Church. She said that the old Volunteers would turn in their graves, that Lynch was a disgrace and that the Party was a pale version of its former self. "That woman, she really gave me the pip," he turned to Mick Phelan. "After all the Party's done for them over the years. That woman wouldn't have a county council cottage today if it wasn't for the Party."

"Ah, she's just mixed up. A lot of people were mixed up by Blaney and Boland."

"I blame Paudge Brennan; he's always been sniping at the leader." Condolences finished his sandwich and attempted to wipe his mouth with the cellophane

wrapping. He sighed deeply and unscrewed the top of his flask to pour more tea. "Sometimes, Mick, sometimes I worry about people. They have no memory, their minds are destroyed with television. People don't realise what the Party went through in the nineteenth Dáil. We lost three great ministers, justice, finance, agriculture, all because of the misfortunate fuckin' country, the North..."

"Four, we lost four ministers. Didn't the local government minister resign too?"

"That's true, Boland resigned. A lovely man, Mick. I shook his hand in 1966 during the Silver Jubilee. Do y'know, he was with Dev when England handed over the ports, he was."

"He was? He's been around that long?"

"That's what I mean, Mick, when I say that people don't realise what the Party has gone through. The Taoiseach has earned his place in heaven, even if he is a Corkman."

Mick drained the last drop of tea from Condolences' flask. They watched the snow falling lightly, the flakes settling on the still windscreen wipers. It reminded Mick of early summer, the way the flakes settled like petals of flowering cherry in gullies and hollows. Mick was a gardener at the local convent. All the sandwiches were eaten. Theirs was a low-budget campaign, the last such campaign fought in Ireland.

"Will we go home?" Mick asked tentatively. A yellow Land-Rover passed by, moving quickly. "That's Cochrane, the dentist, he must be rushing to Dungarvan for a free supper. All the Coalition men are getting a free supper."

"Well, they've published their Statement of Intent, that's as good as a Coalition. Condolences, what does a man like Humphrey Cochrane, a rich dentist, what does a man like that want in politics. That man has everything, he's even got a salmon licence..."

"A hobby," Condolences said. "With them people it's a kind of hobby. They don't need politics like we do. If you're a dentist you don't need protection, you can be sure of that."

"And your children wouldn't need protection. Priests and nuns would be falling over backwards to give your child a job."

"That's the way," sighed Condolences. "We can't change the way we're made. If we come from poor families we come from poor families and that's that..." Just then a powerful hand rapped at Mick Phelan's window.

"Jesus," he exclaimed, "who's that?" He couldn't see the face of the hooded figure in the snow outside. Other figures, sinister, uniformed, surrounded the car.

"Open your window, Mick. Ask him what he wants," Condolences barked.

"I will not! You open your own window." Another uniformed figure tapped at Condolences' window. Both Mick and Condolences thought they heard the second man say, "Ye're under arrest."

"We got a puncture near Toor West," the uniformed man said when Condolences eventually opened his window. "About a mile up the road. The bus skidded, we're in a ditch. And we're supposed to be in Dungarvan at six for the competition."

"What competition?" Condolences pulled up his collar. A cold draught blew in the open window.

"The brass competition," the man explained. "We're the Padre Pio Brass and Reed Band. We have to get to Dungarvan."

Condolences jumped out of his car and stood in the snow. "Was it one of Ned Kenny's buses?" he asked.

"Kenny, yes it was." The bandsmen stood in the snow without moving, dishevelled, like a defeated rifle company.

Condolences pitied them. "I know Mr Kenny personally. He's at a funeral in Co Cork today. But if I phone his depot they might send out another bus."

"That'd be too late," the bandleader said sadly. "If we kept on walking we'd be in Dungarvan before six. But our instruments, we couldn't carry them in the snow. They'd be ruined."

Condolences had a brain-wave. "Listen, why—by the way, what's your name?"

"Collins," the man replied. "Michael Collins."

Mick Phelan laughed. "You're having us on."

"I'm not."

"Are your any relation of Tom Collins, the storekeeper at Buckley's Engineering?" Condolences wanted to place the man within his social milieu.

"The very same family. He's my brother."

"Ah sha, isn't it a small world!" Condolences was delighted. "I know Tom well, he's been in the Party for years. Listen, why don't ye keep walking. The snow is getting lighter. You'll be in Dungarvan in half an hour. Mick Phelan and myself will see to the instruments. Has the driver stayed with the bus?"

"He has. He has," several bandsmen replied at once. Then they started to shuffle along the road in single file.

"I know a man with a van," Condolences explained. "He only lives about ten minutes from here... Come to think of it, he owns a half-ton trailer as well. We could hook it up to my car."

Mick Phelan was watching the uniformed bandsmen moving away in the dusk. "They remind me of a film I saw in the Desmond Cinema years ago. It was all about Napoleon. You know what they remind me of, Condolences? They remind me of the retreat from Moscow. Look at the poor bastards. All for the sake of music."

"Mick, you're too well educated for this world." They drove away into the dusk in search of the man with the van. Condolences was determined to unite the Padre Pio Brass and Reed Band with their instruments.

"What'll we do if the man isn't at home?"

"Doocey? Ah, if he's not there I'll just take the trailer. It's always left in the drive of his house. He won't mind."

"You're a hard man, Condolences—and generous. I never noticed that generous streak in you before. A mighty generous streak."

Condolences laughed. A ribald laugh. "Look at it this way," he explained, "there are twenty-two men in that band, twenty-two votes in one fell swoop. If they'll have a good word for me they'll have a good word for the Party. And they have wives, remember, some of them even have children who can vote. That's what I call a decent bit of canvassing. Twenty-two votes, and rising."

## TWO

"Does that car use diesel, Ned?" Dr Forrestal startled the Chairman. "Your car, is it diesel?"

"What? Yes, yes. Yes, it is."

Ned had been looking at the old photographs hanging above the fireplace in the surgery. There was a portrait, brown with age, of a young woman in a graduation gown—the doctor's sister. There were three large photographs of racing fours on the Blackwater. One of the oarsmen was probably Dr Forrestal's father, who had been a world-class sculler.

"I was looking at the new diesel, the Volkswagen. They're very neat. With my mileage I need something more than neatness, though...How's your good wife? One can be very depressed after a flu like that."

"She's fine now."

"And your own stomach?"

"More pains. I've been getting really sharp pains around here...here." Ned traced a line across his lower stomach.

"You'll need new glasses too." The doctor removed Ned's glasses and stared into his face. "You've been tiring your eyes. Too many late nights in smoky rooms..."

"But my stomach, what did they find?"

"It wasn't benign. I can't understand why they let you out."

"Cancer?"

"I just can't understand why they let you out."

"'Tis cancer then. I created such an auld stink they had to let me home."

"I'm sorry."

"Yerra, don't be sorry. It's not your fault."

"It's more in the bladder than the stomach. It shows itself as stomach pain in your case. If they got a knife to it now you could have a bag. You could go on for years." The doctor looked at Ned intently, standing back as if surveying a painting or studying a horse. "I just can't understand why they let you out...criminal."

"Bags, my arse. Nobody's going to start carving me."

"What about Rebecca, doesn't she have a say? Doesn't she deserve some time? An artificial bladder could give you a lot of time." The doctor cleared his papers from one of his leather chairs and sat down. He was annoyed.

"I suppose I'd see one more election."

"Is that all you can think about? Rebecca deserves better."

Ned rubbed his eyes to get rid of the sudden irritation. He looked at the doctor confidently, even brazenly. "She wouldn't like to see me withering

away slowly."

"Ask her."

"I won't. I'm certain she wouldn't want to see me dying with a bag, like a bloody kangaroo. Jesus!"

"Ask her."

"No."

"It's Rebecca's life too. She's a lovely woman."

"She is." Ned took his glasses back. "But I'd like to get those new glasses. The sooner the better..."

"You're not worried about your eyes?"

"My mother was blind. Blindness is the worst thing of all. I'd prefer to be dead than blind."

"You'll be both, the way you're carrying on."

"I have the prescription for your pain-killers somewhere." There was a silence between them while he fumbled through manila folders and upset a tray of dark brown bottles. He reached above the bookcase for a box of files, but he couldn't make it. "Could you reach those, Ned, I'm a bit on the short side." Ned stood up and rescued the pile from their perch.

"Sorry, that stretching must be painful."

"Not at all, it's just an effort because I'm so fat—on top of everything else."

The doctor put the prescription in a tiny brown envelope. When he placed his hands on Ned's shoulders he said, "I'll let you out. It's the least I can do."

"For God's sake, don't be so sad. It's not your

fault."

"You'll have to go back to the hospital soon—if not for surgery, at least for some treatment." The doctor opened the door and walked with Ned as far as the pavement. They shook hands. "You're wrong about having one election left. You're forgetting the presidential one..."

"Will I live to see it? That's the big question. Will I live to see it?"

"It's your decision." Dr Forrestal punched him on the shoulder. Ned climbed into his car and drove away. He thought about Rebecca, how she would react to the terrible news of his illness. She probably already knew something—she was a regular visitor at Dr Forrestal's. Premature death was such a daft and unreal thing. Pointless. Ned couldn't quite grasp the seriousness of his ailment; he had spent a lifetime resisting the effects of bad news. Then his thoughts turned to the Senator—who would look after him? Who would protect his interests?

When he reached the junction at the centre of the village he had to brake suddenly. There was a black cat lying down in the middle of the road. *For luck,* Ned said to himself, and he laughed at the thought of good luck. He could see himself laughing in the mirror.

# THREE

"How could it take ye by surprise? Didn't the Party fix the date of the election? It's the other bloody parties that should have been surprised!"

"'Twas kept hush-hush until the last minute. What do I know, I'm only a director of elections..."

"Listen, black and white canvassing material is useless at this stage. People will think we're broke."

"We *are* broke."

"Those dull posters look miserable after all the snow. I think they're a liability, Paddy." (Ned decided to switch to first-name familiarity.) "Paddy, we haven't a penny to spare down here. We owe the local printers a lot of money. If we look for more credit the word will get out that ye've abandoned us...We need that colour material, and soon. Soon! The word isn't good."

"The word is bad all over. We don't look good."

"Winter is shit..."

"You said it. It is...I'll tell you what, I'll get someone here to skim off a few hundred canvassing cards, posters and things, from the city consignments. Not more than a thousand bits in all...Would that help?"

"Anything—"

"That bad?"

"It is. Paddy, there are some funny things happening in the Party...The regional stores have given us nothing. They've done nothing for our electoral area—and this constituency is supposed to deliver an extra seat! How the hell can we deliver on anything if the regional offices are dead set against us."

"Do you want to put in an official complaint?"

"Later, maybe," Ned continued, "I don't want to get anyone into trouble. But things are not working as they should. The response from some quarters is hopeless, even hostile. There are some people in the party who want us to sink this time round."

"That's an extraordinary statement."

"It's useless at this stage...They have their own favourites, they're not backing the full panel. Those who haven't been strong on Ulster are getting no support. There's been too much talk about guns, bags of guns."

"Ah that's only whiskey talk. The old fellows love to go on about guns and what they'd do to the Unionists...It's only talk. You're being too sensitive about this. That in itself is not good for the party. You must understand the strength of feeling in the country."

"It's not talk. I'm not worried about the old fools, it's people talking to the youngsters that worries me."

There was a long pause. Then Morrissey said "Did ye get the receipt for the annual collection?"

"We got that receipt!" Ned had to shout into the phone because Morrissey was drifting away on a sea of static.

"We'll send the extra material right away...Don't worry about the other thing. All talk, talk..."

"No, I don't think it's just talk. Half the people in our constituency are bulling for Haughey. They'd love to see Lynch with egg on his face."

Morrissey was silent. After a long pause he shouted down the line, "The Arms Trial is over Ned, it's in the past. Nothing can be gained from dragging Haughey through the dirt. He's taken his punishment. Don't blame him for the antics of his supporters."

"People should support the present leader. The organisation has always come first. We have to talk about Haughey if his people are pulling against our campaign. If we lose this election he could come back."

"Don't be an alarmist, Ned. Charlie's finished, he's finished with the Party."

"Well, if he comes back we'll be run by wild men from the border counties, mad men from Cavan and Monaghan and Donegal."

Morrissey laughed. "You're a gas man, Ned. The things you imagine! The Haughey thing is all talk. Believe me."

"Wild men, I tell you."

# FOUR

On the Wednesday before the election Ned chaired the final meeting organised by the electoral area committee. It was the most important local gathering of the campaign. Officers and delegates from every village attended, bringing with them lists of voters who needed transport as well as lists of personation and transport volunteers. Each willing car-owner would be matched with a list of isolated or invalided Party supporters. A team of Party officers would be appointed to accompany each candidate on a final walkabout of every town and village. Armed with the various registers of electors they would fine-comb their lists to see if they had missed out on any possible stray voter or isolated sympathiser. This was the most feverish night of the campaign. Everyone present loved the atmosphere; they were bound together by that sense of being part of a winning team.

The room in the hotel filled very quickly. There was only one female delegate, the red-haired widow of James Curley, a councillor from Mooncoin.

"You're a brave woman," Ned said to her as she took her seat. "After your recent grief an' all. You're

in rough company." Ned couldn't recall her first name.

"I'm better off out and about. If I stay inside I'll die from sadness. The house is so quiet."

"Well, you're a great woman."

The young Senator had noticed Mrs Curley too. He called to her from a table at the side of the hall. "Will you help me with these registers, Mrs Curley?"

She left her seat and went over. The Senator handed her a pencil with which she began to tick off names. Ned watched her. It occurred to him that she might make a good councillor. She had a lot going for her—no children, a young widow, her husband's name, lovely hair and an open friendly face.

Just as Ned was making a mental note to talk to Morrissey about Mrs Curley, a delegate from Ballyduff burst through the doorway, balancing two trays of porter on the palms of his hands. He worked as a butler in one of the big Unionist houses in East Waterford. He was showing off. There was a roar of concern, then a greater roar of greeting when he announced that the first round of drinks was on the house. The Senator, embarrassed by his tiny glass of lemonade, ordered a pint of Cidona. The word pint was a magical, totemic word in the male world of the Party, so that heads nodded in approval.

The delegates worked together for nearly four hours in that committee room. The smoke-filled air

thickened and hurt their throats. The alcohol helped them to relax, yet gave them energy. Cigarette butts littered the floor like dried-up slugs. One could almost touch the sense of shared pride when Ned finally pinned the large map of the constituency, covered with names and numbers, to the wall. The map displayed the name of every personation officer and every transport volunteer and outlined the final canvassing area of each man on the panel of candidates (in the last two days of any campaign no candidate was allowed into the central territory of another Party man).

The meeting was just coming to an end when Condolences Dineen gathered himself off his seat and stood to attention. Condolences was a small man, but he had that strange ability to create an aura of dignity around his rotund frame.

"Well, Condolences?"

"The list of condolences," Condolences announced.

"Ah, for Jasus sake. Don't bother about them tonight. It'll be too late for the papers anyway." One delegate saw the prospect of a final pint ebbing away.

"Well you may say it—*for Jesus' sake*. But also for the sake of our beloved Party. The local papers will be on sale at four o'clock on polling day. That's five hours of reading time before the polls close. It would be stupid to forego the possibility of losing even one vote just because some delegates are more interested

in porter than the Party." He threw a patronising glance at the small caucus of serious drinkers who had assembled near the door.

"Ah, blast it. Read away so..."

Condolences drew himself up to his full height and addressed the assembled crowd. "The Party members offered their sympathy to the Murphy, Maguire, Allen and Phelan families on their recent bereavements. They offered particular sympathy also to Dean Nesbitt-Hall on the death of his wife, Victoria..."

"A great flower-woman. Jasus, she was a great flower-woman," the butler from East Waterford interjected.

"May Mary the Mother of God watch over their souls."

"Amen," someone said, and the serious drinking caucus continued their exit—the proprietor in the next room, had just shouted "Time please."

"Hold it! Hold it...one minute's silence!"

The delegates stood to attention awkwardly. It was a thirsty silence. They watched the merciless hand of the clock moving towards closing-time, and they cursed Condolences for that vote-catching farce which had given him his nickname. For over twenty years he had scoured the newspapers for news of local deaths, his telephone had become the clearing-centre for all the grief of the constituency. He offered the Party's name at the list of mourners at every

funeral. He had been indefatigable and pedantic in the Party's interest, and had mislaid at least thirty umbrellas while following lonely coffins in the name of politics.

Over two minutes elapsed before he allowed the delegates to move away. "They're mad at me now, just because I try to do something for the Party...I make the effort, I make the effort." He spoke loudly as he walked across the room to join Ned. Condolences had the moral confidence of someone who felt certain that earthly reward awaited him.

"I'm always making the effort. And did Condolences every look for a county council nomination, a health board seat, even a justice of the peace? Some thanks? No, Condolences did not—and they're still mad at me."

"The're not, Condolences," the Chairman replied. "But surely you won't be able to get that sympathy vote into the papers in time?"

"I'll drive to Waterford before midnight. I'll get it into the offices myself."

"You're a great man. The roads are dangerous."

"I am."

"I don't think the Senator is very happy," Ned confided.

"What's wrong with him, for God's sake," Condolences pulled no punches. "Hasn't he got everything. He's on the panel for the election. He might even get the third seat if we can spread the

votes. I don't know what's wrong with him. If I was his father I'd give him a good shaking. Wake him up, d'ya know. That young fella has everything."

"He thinks the Party didn't give him enough exposure during the campaign. We only allowed him to speak on a few occasions. But we allowed the sitting deputies to speak on every platform."

"He's not much of a speaker; anyway we have to protect the sitting deputies. Look at him now," Condolences nodded in the direction of the Senator. "Look at him, in a corner with the widow when he should be out in the bar winding up the delegates. Jesus Christ, spare my patience..."

"You're too hard on him."

"I'm not. People with no fight in them shouldn't be in politics. They depress everyone, including the voters."

"You're a hard man, Condolences."

"The Party must come first."

Ned looked across at the Senator. Drinkless, tired-looking, he was listening intently to Mrs Curley. "You know, Condolences, I think he'll take that extra Dáil seat for the Party. He's a lad with great quality."

"He won't, and I'll tell you something else. He'll be lucky to hold onto the Senate seat. He was supported by the teachers because of his late father's interest in education. But he hasn't done much for the teachers. I know that for a fact."

"He's been good about attending the Senate. His record is good."

"He hasn't cultivated the teachers' organisations."

"God, you're dead set against him, Condolences." Ned sat down, as if making ready for a long conversation. But Condolences had no intention of sitting down; he was determined to deliver the sympathy vote to the newspapers before midnight. "I'm not against him. I'd be glad to work for him if I could see some effort coming from himself. Some spark of ambition..."

"He's just very quiet."

"Ah Jasus. The electorate isn't a woman." Condolences turned and began to walk away. "I must go."

On the day after the election they arrived at the counting-centre in good spirits. Brandishing their official passes they pushed through the crowds of onlookers and made themselves at home inside the dilapidated building. But less than three hours later, after the first ballot boxes had been opened, and after they had checked their tallies with the opposition tally-men, the bad news began to filter through. The Party had anticipated a loss of first preference votes because of the foul weather, but they hadn't foreseen the way the third and fourth preference votes would transfer between the two opposition parties. The electorate had not only *not* voted for the Party in

greater numbers, but had pitched the vital secondary preferences in favour of the opposition. As lunchtime drew near, the tally-men of the opposition loosened their ties and became talkative—they shouted at each other nervously, compared figures and raised their eyebrows in disbelief.

The Senator, who was standing beside the Chairman in silence, had accumulated a good first preference vote, more than four thousand. Ned knew it wasn't enough to guarantee him a seat, but it was enough to fight off any challenge for a Party nomination as a candidate in the future. The older Party men, many of whom were veterans of election counts, were becoming uneasy in their seats. Now and again after they had formed an opinion on a group of ballot-boxes, they would leave their seats and move to another table. They were upset by those first inklings of defeat. When the count was adjourned for lunch no councillor or candidate would leave the centre.

"None of them will go down to lunch," the Senator said. "Will I order sandwiches and tea from the hotel?"

"Do," the Chairman replied. "Get them to send up soup as well...and make sure they send napkins."

"Trouble is we've no authority from the committee to buy sandwiches."

"If we have authority to buy eighteen lunches we surely have authority to buy a few sandwiches.

Nobody wants lunch." Ned spoke abruptly. The Senator turned and walked away, like a spurned pup.

When he came back again, Julie was with him. Ned thought that she looked radiant—grainy-skinned, thick-haired, brown-eyed; a firm healthy look that was unusual in a red-haired person.

"When are ye two going to get married. My God, ye're wasting the best years," Ned blurted it out.

"I have the paper napkins, Gerald said you wanted them." Julie looked at Ned, cutting him off. But she smiled broadly. She knew that Ned enjoyed her looks, and she was well able to flirt.

"We shouldn't be eating here at all, I suppose," Ned admitted, "but nobody would leave."

"Why not?" Julie sat down and scrutinised his face.

"Well, everybody's worried about the transfer of preferences. It's the preferences that are added to the candidates total until someone reaches the quota. Unfortunately a lot of our own voters have given third or fourth preference to the opposition. At the end of the day it could mean the loss of one seat. Surely, you understand proportional representation?"

"No."

"Do you understand it, Paddy?" Ned turned to a Party tallyman.

"Not completely," the Party man admitted.

"Nobody understands it," Julie said.

"I don't believe ye," Ned shook his head. A dozen

Party men, including the Senator, had assembled at the table. Many of them still held their indelible pencils and wads of thumb-marked paper. Condolences Dineen was among them. As he sat down to eat his sandwich he said, "I'm saying nothing."

"Say nothing so," the Chairman suggested. "Say nothing, we're all depressed."

"One thing I will say," Condolences couldn't keep his mouth shut. "One thing I will say, it doesn't look good."

"You said you'd say nothing." Julie turned towards him, brushing back her hair from her face. "Say nothing then. Please."

"It doesn't look good," Condolences insisted.

They ate in silence after that. It would be a long day. They were still nibbling cheap biscuits and drinking cold tea when the returning officer and his officials came back into the room. Condolences was still busy with his sandwich. When a garda sergeant and two gardaí left the far corner where they had been guarding unsealed boxes, Condolences shouted "Clear the decks!" Pieces of meat and bread spewed from his mouth.

"We will," replied Julie. A small piece of meat had attached itself to her hair. The Senator fished it out.

By seven o'clock that evening the Party had won its two expected seats. The first preference vote had fallen significantly, as the tally-men had feared; by

three or four per cent. An unusually large number of the Senator's transfers had crossed over to the Labour Party candidate who was based in Gerald's own electoral area. At that stage, by watching the TV monitors, listening to radio reports from other centres and phoning Party HQ they got the impression of a small but fatal drift in the Party's fortunes.

"No point in staying here any longer," Ned suggested. "There's no point in staying here any longer—that fourth seat is gone to the Labour man."

"Oh. Do you think so?" asked the Senator, stupidly.

"Where else could it go, for God's sake," Ned replied sharply. And just in case the Senator would feel reprimanded he added, "You did very well. It was a great showing for the first time out. A great showing."

"A good show," Condolences admitted.

"The Party was depending on me to take that final seat. In the last few days they put a lot of effort into it. Even Morrissey came up with the goods."

The Chairman agreed. "But there was a lot of inertia. You complained about that yourself. We really got no help from the bigger constituency people. Do you know what I mean?"

"I do."

He didn't.

The Chairman didn't believe that he knew. The Senator's antennae weren't sensitive enough; he still couldn't gauge the depth of feeling in sections of the party. He was weak on the North.

# FIVE

The loss of that third seat, the one that should have come to the Party through the Senator's transfers, was a catastrophe for the organisation. Towards the end of the campaign the Party had realised its importance, and had worked harder to help the constituency team: the deputy leader of the Party visited the four main towns in the region, a major commitment during a snap election. Almost every child in the Senator's electoral area wore a Party button, whether its parents were Party supporters or not. In the last two days of the campaign the winter countryside had been transformed into a fairground of partisan colours and smiling Party faces. But the tide of public opinion had flowed against the Party from the beginning of the campaign. Nothing could stem that flow.

In the early hours of Saturday morning the Party leader conceded defeat. As they listened to the leader speaking, Ned and the Senator accepted that they had been banished into a bleak period without power. Condolences was less willing to admit defeat. "They'll never be able to keep a coalition together.

We'll be back next month."

"We always say that," the Chairman said.

"Coalitions never work. How can big ranchers and trade union officials pull together. They'll be at each other's throats before the next budget." The Senator spoke. "If only...if only I'd won that third shaggin' seat. I'll never get that chance again."

"Well. That's that. We'll have to pull up our socks before the next election." The Chairman rose from his chair. "I'm off to bed. I'll see ye out..."

"No need," Julie replied. "It's cold out there."

"Cold, cold," Condolences sighed.

"There's nothing more to be said." The Chairman took Julie's hand.

"Nobody can find fault with you, Ned. You were a great committee chairman," said Julie.

Ned looked at her, a weary late-night look. "Now you can say that. Our vote is down. The transfers went badly."

"No use going over it now," the Senator shouted from his driving seat. "Come on, we'll all get a good rest."

They left then, and Ned returned to the house. When he reached the bedroom he found Rebecca asleep. There was a deathly quietness in her slumber—no agitation of blankets, no heaviness of breath. He slipped in beside her and switched off the bedside lamp. But he couldn't sleep. He pumped his pillow and sat up in the semi-darkness. He thought he

heard a mouse scratching away in the corner of the bedroom, but it was the sound of hail against the window-glass.

As he sat up in bed the images of that final nomination convention crowded into his mind. He remembered the night that he and the Senator, Condolences, Julie and the Senator's cheeky young nephew, Eamon, had arrived together at the convention hall. Ned had won official status for Julie and Eamon by convening a parish committee meeting the previous night. So they arrived with a block of votes—Ned was certain they'd pick up between five and eight further votes which would see the Senator elected to the panel of four candidates. Each candidate was given five minutes to address the convention. There were eight candidates—the Senator was fourth on the list after Allingham, Conory and Dwyer, all of whom were from the eastern, more urban part of the constituency. The first three candidates spoke about the desperate situation in Ulster, the plight of the Catholics and the fundamental duty of the Party to speak out on behalf of the Ulster Catholics. The candidates did make passing references to the economic situation and the scandal of over seventy thousand unemployed. But it was clear that they were all really interested in Ulster. Theirs was the first generation in the party to see Catholic ghettos burning, victims of police terror interviewed, British soldiers wandering along Irish streets.. Relentless

television newsreels had traumatised the Party faithful and led to a resurgence of fundamental Republican feeling.

When the Senator's turn to speak came he seemed very agitated and nervous. "You may think it presumptuous of me," he announced gravely, "to stand before you without the ancient credentials of the previous speakers. I'm afraid my father never saw the inside of a prison, but when he was a deputy he lived for his constituency. I feel that I can promise you my father's credentials, the credentials of excellence and tolerance..."

"What about Ulster. What's your view of Ulster?" a delegate shouted.

"Be quiet, he has only five minutes," Ned replied.

"I'm as much a Republican as you'll ever be!" The Senator's face had grown crimson with anger.

"Bullshit. Your big dictionary words won't protect a fellow Irishman from the RUC!"

The Senator didn't reply to this provocative remark, but continued his little speech. He made a brief reference to the youthfulness of the electorate, and explained that the Party should field even *more* young candidates.

After the interval, when the votes had been cast and counted, the Senator won his place on the panel. He got seven votes, just enough to win. He had been placed ahead of Conory and Allingham. There were jeers from Conory's corner; but silence from

Allingham. "I've made an enemy there," the Senator whispered to Julie.

"Yes, you watch. You'll have to watch your back."

"Allingham really wanted that seat," Ned admitted.

Usually those who are defeated in a fight for nomination to the panel of candidates rise to congratulate the winners. But now there was silence; not a word of support was offered. All of those images—words of anger, bitter votes, the frosty Christmas weather—all passed through Ned's mind on the morning of the Party's defeat. While he sat up in bed a chink of morning light came between the heavy curtains. The yellow light struck the large mirror and illuminated part of the room. Rebecca turned in her sleep, turning away from the area of light. Ned covered her exposed shoulder and slid a little further under the blankets. But she woke. "Go to sleep," she said. "You'll drive yourself mad with that election."

He eased himself against her warm body, just to reassure her. "Have ye lost?" she asked, sleepily.

"Looks like it," he muttered.

"Ah well, somebody won. Somebody won. That's the main thing."

Ned wanted to say something after that, but sleep was more important.

# SIX

Ned decided to skip mass and stay in bed. He didn't want to face the jubilant Coalition supporters who would want to shake his hand in mock commiseration. It was easier to face mortal sin than political humiliation. Anyway, the pains in his stomach had returned. He took some pain-killers; they left him in a state of semi-consciousness. But the pain still seeped through like a strong dye. He was hovering in that state when the phone rang. He let it ring. Silence. Then it started to ring again—whoever it was just wouldn't give up.

"Are you alright?" It was the Senator.

"I was half-asleep."

"Are you okay? Are you sick?"

"I'm sick now, so I am."

"Is Rebecca away?"

"She's gone to her sister's place. She couldn't stick my company. I told her to go over to her sister's for a bit of a chat."

"Conory and Allingham have called an extraordinary general meeting. They want the county executive to ask for your resignation as chairman of the electoral committee. They're trying to finish us

off..."

"Who?" The painkillers made Ned feel very relaxed. He tried to calm the Senator. "They need the Secretary's signature to call an EGM. He's on our side."

"He's not. They have his signature."

"We should meet about this. I wouldn't worry too much."

Just then there was a knock at the door. Ned shouted to the visitor to hold on, then he said to the Senator, "Someone's here. Call up here on Wednesday." He put down the phone before the Senator could reply.

"Well?"

"Hello, Mr Kenny, how'ya doin'?" It was Eamon, the Senator's nephew. He looked like an underfed Cistercian in his dirty cowled duffle-coat. "I was just passin'. I went to early Mass. Are you all right?"

"Your uncle sent you."

"Well...he was worried that you weren't answering the phone. He phoned my father."

"Why didn't your father call over. I haven't seen him around."

"You know Da...he's a lazy bastard. He was stuck in a book, something about English politics."

"Your father loves English politics."

"He does. He says it's the key to our troubles."

"Come in, come in." The Chairman closed the door and led Eamon into the sitting-room. "Your

uncle's worried."

"Ah, he is, he is. He thinks he'll be blamed for the Party not getting a third seat."

"He shouldn't worry..."

"If you ask me, I think he's a fuckin' clown. Da says he was born worried." Eamon took off his duffle-coat and flung it on a chair. "I wouldn't mind a cup of tea. Do you know how to make it?"

"I suppose I should have gone to Mass. There would have been a lot of canvassing after that Mass. Conory and Allingham didn't waste much time, did they?"

"No."

"How are you getting on at school?"

"Fine. My father says the uncle is a fool, that he's not fit for politics. Will he ever be a deputy?"

"Are you doing the Leaving Certificate this year?"

"Would you be able to persuade my uncle to get out of politics? It's become very sinister. Even the SDLP are being shot at now."

"Did you say you'd like a cup of tea?"

"Great. I did."

Ned got up again. He was groggy and unsure of his step. "I'll get you that cup of tea."

"Are you drinkin'? Are you a drunkard?"

"Jesus Christ, I'm not. Leave me alone. I'll get you your tea."

"There's someone at the door."

"What. Someone else? I didn't hear the bell."

"She didn't ring. I'll get it."

"Good man. I'll get the tea."

Ned heard giggling from the hallway. He didn't see Eamon putting his small red hand on Jennifer's breast.

"Ah Jennifer!" Ned was surprised to see Condolences' daughter and surprised by her mature look, the ear-rings, a touch of mascara, lipstick.

"She'll be seventeen next week," Eamon announced proudly.

"Great. I'll have to find some cake. Where does she keep the cake?"

"You're a lovely man," Jennifer said emotionally.

"Popular in defeat."

"Ah no. You're lovely. It's a pity you're old."

"Why is it a pity?" Ned asked.

"Well, if you're old you'll die."

Ned didn't know where to look; whether to laugh or cry. While he was cutting the cake Jennifer pushed Eamon's hand away from her tightly-closed thighs. Ned was too stunned with tiredness to notice what was going on.

# SEVEN

"You know, I think these new glasses have brought myself and Rebecca even closer. It's true...don't laugh. I can see her more clearly running around the house." Ned was on the phone when Rebecca came scurrying into the kitchen. She was carrying his shirt in on one hand, dripping wet, and in the other hand something small, crinkled and damp.

"Look at this! Look, look!" she said, "The only photograph of me when I was young."

"You're still young. For God's sake...hold on a minute," Ned shouted into the phone.

"You big fool. Why can't you carry a photo of me in your wallet, like any decent husband, instead of in your breast pocket. Look what's happened to it in the wash." She handed him the pathetic crinkled image. The photograph had been taken at a hurling match in Thurles in 1953. She was wearing the blue sash of Waterford on her blouse and a white and blue cap. Four months before their marriage.

"We'll iron it. We'll see if that'll help."

Ned put down the phone and they moved to the ironing board in the corner. "There," he said as he

ironed nervously, "it's coming together now."

"And there's no copy of that anywhere. You've ruined it."

"I'll be careful about it in future," Ned replied.

Rebecca didn't respond. She didn't believe that he could be careful. "There was a lot of talk about the Party after Mass," she said, changing the subject abruptly. "They say that the constituency is going to split between those who support the Taoiseach—I mean Jack Lynch—and those who support Haughey. You should have gone to Mass. Just to be seen."

"I wasn't feeling well."

"I know."

"Did they say anything about Allingham or Conory."

"They did. Especially Allingham. But the two of them are stirring things up since Friday. Allingham has been saying that the Party could have won a third seat if ye had made stronger speeches about Ulster. He's blaming you and the Senator..."

"And how would our extra seat have helped the people of Ulster?"

"Allingham says that the stronger the Party is the better chance we have of winning Ulster. Can we win Ulster?"

"Ulster isn't a prize, Rebecca. There are people there who want nothing to do with us. It's not like a prize in a raffle."

"The black Protestants?"

"Any kind of Protestant, black, white, green or blue. We'll have to do a lot of work on them first."

"Shit, the phone!" Ned remembered that he'd not finished on the phone. When he took it up again he could only hear the beep-beep of a hung-up line. "Shit!"

"Who was it?"

"Just the Senator. He knows Allingham is on the war-path. He's worried about his place on the Party panel."

Later that day Ned phoned the county secretary of the organisation. The man's wife insisted that he wasn't home but Ned could hear a clinking of tea-cups and the rowdy chorus of male conversation.

The next day Ned went back into hospital for further treatment. He went there more to please Dr Forrestal than for any other reason. That day in hospital was as long as a lifetime, a lifetime of floating around in a room of white lights and polished steel. He guessed that he was there for fourteen hours. He was annoyed that he had been offered nothing to eat, not even a biscuit. That was all that worried him. The monotony of the hours was broken only now and again by the sound of a patient being sick, or the sound of a radio coming from the hospital kitchen whenever a nurse or assistant opened the door.

"Mr Kenny," a young nurse or doctor would say. The next question was inevitable. "How long have

you been waiting?" Then they would disappear as efficiently as they had entered, with nothing achieved.

"All my life. All me life I've been waiting," the Chairman said to one beautiful nurse with a high white forehead and dark braided hair.

"Didn't you know that you were asleep?" she asked.

"I was *not*," Ned retorted. "I've been lying here on my back for hours."

"You've been asleep for seven of those," the nurse replied cockily. "Are you all right?"

"I'm fed up with being asked that question. If I was all right I wouldn't be here."

"Well, aren't we annoyed!"

"We are."

"You can't go home until tomorrow."

"I have a man collecting me tonight. He should be here at ten."

"You'll have to see a doctor so. And sign some papers."

"Did ye work on me while I was asleep?"

"We did," she smiled. "Aren't we great?"

"Amazing. It's a miracle what can be done."

"It's the one thing you can depend on, science, Mr Kenny."

Yet again Ned noticed how pretty she was. He needed his glasses so that he could have a closer look.

Dr Forrestal warned him about the long bouts of melancholia that would develop as a result of the

drugs. Ned wasn't a melancholy sort of person—indeed he had always been short-tempered with depressed people. Now, however, the bouts of melancholy that struck him were more intense and real than anything he could have imagined. One morning, for instance, Rebecca said, "You're looking at me in a very peculiar way."

"I'm sorry, love. Something came over me. I just noticed how fine the shoulder-strap on your night-dress is, and how good you look. It's sad, girl."

"You're as soft as butter."

Ned knew he was going to be sad for the whole day after that. Another time—a few days previously—he had been sitting by the fire listening to a radio programme of Irish music broadcast to emigrants in England, when Rebecca's cat leaped onto his lap. As she purred and trembled with happiness he was overcome by another bout of melancholy. He knew it was a chemical melancholy caused by drugs, but each time he was caught unawares.

In his depressive mood he nearly always thought about the Party. The shock of electoral defeat might unhinge its logic, driving it towards a split. Ned knew there had never been so much resentment before—so much bile and frustrated ambition. That night he rose from his fireside chair and paced the gravel drive in front of the house. While he walked up and down

the drive he recited the rosary:

*Hail Mary, full of grace,*
*The Lord is with thee.*
*Blessed art thou amongst women,*
*And blessed is the fruit of thy womb, Jesus...*

# EIGHT

Ned's melancholia of the previous day had lifted. He walked out of the house like a man who had made it through dense and oppressive jungle. He spent the day repairing Rebecca's greenhouse and checking the shrubs for frost damage. He was pleased when he discovered that the camellia buds were still intact and unbrowned. He had inspected, too, the hedge-like shoots of the azara and the thickly budded branches of the mezureum—their time hadn't come yet. That was something to look forward to. He was happy, or, at least as happy as any other cancer sufferer.

While he worked in the greenhouse his black labrador bitch—called Helen because she was a gift from a Mrs Troy—drank some water from a rusted tray. The standing water was warm from the heater and probably poisonous. She lay down and curled lazily around the heater.

"Get up, Helen. Get up, you lazy old bitch of a dog!" He feared that she'd catch fire. Helen moved, but in doing so she knocked over a seed-tray near the heater. The glass cover of the seed-tray fell to the ground and shattered; it was followed by a hard-

covered book that had been holding the glass in place. The book fell into the tray of foetid water.

"Shit! Come on, out!" Ned flung the greenhouse door open and Helen bolted. "Clear off, brr... Bold dog." Ned bent over stiffly to retrieve the drowning book. Its covers were already swollen with dampness. He looked at the book briefly, sadly. It was *To Katanga and Back* by Conor Cruise O'Brien, a library book borrowed by Rebecca and forgotten; the date-stamp said "10 Nov 1972."

"Damn, that's what the notices were about before Christmas." Ned shook the book violently. But it was now beyond recall. Ned looked at the author's name again. "Bloody Coalition propaganda," he muttered. He carried the book with him into the orchard behind the garden. He wanted to check the winter grease-bands.

"Hello, Ned."

The gate of the little orchard opened. The Senator had entered, crushing the gnarled and frost-hardened mud on the path. His head was buried in a massive grey scarf so that his words seemed to come from the mouth of a nearby ventriloquist. Behind him was Condolences, sauntering at a safe distance like Sancho Panza.

"Hello, Ned."

"Were you readin' out in the orchard. A quare place for a quiet read."

"Don't be smart."

"Is that an apple book? Are you studying apples?" Condolences bumped against the Senator.

"Steady on, Condolences."

"Sorry."

"Why did ye come this way?"

"Rebecca said you were up here. What's the book?"

"A library book."

"I never knew you were a man for the books."

"I'm not. It's Rebecca's."

"It looks fairly shagged."

"It is. She left it in the greenhouse. It's a book by the Cruiser O'Brien, the Labour man."

"More Coalition rubbish. Don't know why we do be spending good county council money on libraries." Condolences was serious. Books always made him defensive.

"Oh shut up, Condolences," the Senator replied. "We have to have public libraries."

"And what about the unemployed? There's nearly seventy thousand unemployed. We could start some roadworks, get men working."

"Yerra..."

"That book is ruined anyway," Ned admitted. "Rebecca'll have to pay for it."

"Good riddance to it!" Condolences walked past the Chairman and headed for the kitchen. His mouth was already open because he could smell Rebecca's fresh scones. The smell of baking had been

drifting through the orchard for hours. "She's a great woman, that wife of yours," muttered Condolences.

"Have you read it?" the Senator asked Ned. "The book, have you read it?"

"No, no. It's Rebecca's. She must have been pottering in the greenhouse and forgotten it."

"But she's not interested in politics?"

"Ah no, not at all. She ordered a book about a nun in the Congo, a Belgian nun. What was it called...oh, *A Nun's Story*. Remember the film? 'Twas in the cinema in Cappoquin. The library couldn't get it, so they offered the Cruise O'Brien book. I suppose she was disgusted when she discovered it wasn't a religious book. You know Rebecca, she can't sleep until she reads a few pages of religion."

"I didn't know that." The Senator eyed the book with interest.

"Well, you know now. Women are a funny lot..."

"They say it's well written."

"It's well baptised now!" Ned laughed. He held the swollen book aloft, dripping.

Through the laughter they could hear Rebecca calling. Condolences had talked her into an early tea.

"It's bad news from Ulster, isn't it?" The Senator took the dripping book from Ned. "Eleven Protestants returned as English MPs. They'll probably do a deal with Heath. They want the old Stormont back. That's the end of the Council of Ireland."

"I think they'll do a deal with Wilson. Wilson's

a shifty bastard. He has no feel for Ireland either."

"It must be bad for an Englishman to have any feeling for Ireland," the Senator said, tentatively.

"Why shouldn't they have feeling? They caused the problem, didn't they? They spoilt the country, didn't they?"

"The Provos would gut us too if they got the chance. They attacked Austin Currie, and didn't they shoot Mr Duffy's wife?"

"Come on, we'll go in," Ned said. "Don't mention Ulster to Condolences."

But before they reached the kitchen-yard they were waylaid by Condolences, cup in hand. They interrupted a conversation he seemed to be having with a bare and woody hedge. "I was just saying, there's nothing like a hot drink on a cold afternoon. It's as good as working for the Land Commission." He held out his cup.

"Did Rebecca throw you out?" asked Ned. He put his arm around Condolences. "Come on, we'll try to get you past the bouncer."

# NINE

But Condolences stood his ground. He had opinions to offer and the others couldn't go inside until they gave him a hearing. "It's like this, we fought a casual election. Everybody knows that. We were slow to put up our posters, we were slow in booking good advertising space locally and we were slow in organising transport. If ye don't know them things it's because ye're out of touch...And the blame has to be put at the door of the electoral committee Chairman." Condolences was in a mood for blunt talking. "Say what ye like, do what ye like, Ned. At this point in time you're fucked."

"Ah it's never that bad," the Senator interrupted him.

"Think what ye like," Condolences repeated. "It would be better if you never turned up at this meeting. Conory and Allingham have been phoning and driving all over the place in the last two days. Stay away, Ned. Meself and the Senator will defend you. Go off sick..."

"I'm sick as it is," Ned said desperately. "Sick as a dog."

"Well then, you're saved."

"We just can't give in. We can't give in like that...I want to make sure that the Senator isn't pulled off the panel of Dáil candidates. We should concentrate on the councillors."

"Conory and Allingham, they're councillors. You can be sure that they've been working on the Party men in the county."

"We've every right to go after the councillors too," Ned insisted.

"Quigley's sick."

"Is is genuine?"

"Ah, it's true...he had the doctor."

"That leaves three...I suppose we can forget about canvassing Conory and Allingham." Ned just managed the joke. The other two laughed.

Condolences threw the dregs from his cup into the hedge and put the saucer into his coat pocket. He played with the delicate cup, dropping it from hand to hand with an indifference that alarmed Ned. "There are two delegates from each electoral area," Condolences went on. "That makes twelve. Conory, Allingham and Quigley are out, that leaves nine. And three of those are councillors, that leaves six. I think we should go after the lot of them. Phone them until they're blue in the face."

"We should concentrate on the councillors," Ned repeated. "We've only a few days."

The Senator didn't agree with that. He said that they couldn't be sure that the other delegates would

follow the councillors. Everything had been changed by the Party's defeat. Now many delegates would see *themselves* as potential candidates. His poor showing was a good opportunity for someone else to jockey for a position on the panel.

"After all, Ned, I became a candidate because Ryan had done so poorly in the last election."

"We'll go inside while we're still able to see where we're going," Ned suggested. The light was fading. They walked towards the house in the semi-darkness.

The kettle was boiling on the hob when they went in. Rebecca removed a clean tea-towel from the table, revealing a large plate of buttered scones. "How's Julie?" she asked, before the Senator had the chance to sit down. "And how are all her German friends?"

"She's fine, fine. I don't know anything about the Germans, though. They're all managers, very reserved."

"I suppose they can't speak English," Ned suggested.

"At least they speak their own native tongue," Condolences grumbled, patriotically.

"How have you been, Rebecca?" The Senator studied her. He thought that she looked thinner—there were dark rings around her eyes. Ned's illness had exhausted her. Ned himself had the look of an old man, a grey-skinned old pensioner. Condolences, in contrast, looked ruddier and livelier than ever.

"When are you going to make a decent woman

out of her?" Rebecca wasn't going to let him off the hook.

"She's decent enough as it is..." the Senator said weakly.

"She'd make a great wife, a great home-maker like her mother."

"Died in March 1967," Condolences said. "Used to vote at Mullana school."

"She's so neat and so strong," Rebecca went on. "I'll tell you one thing, Gerald, and I won't tell you again—if you let that girl slip away you're a fool." Then she got up from the table, looking very serious. The Senator thought she was going to strike him. But she merely lifted the empty bread-plate and took it away.

"A man has to make up his own mind. Marriage is a serious thing," Ned said.

"Jesus, if women had to wait until men made up their minds there'd be no marriages in this country."

"They're a sound family, no doubt about it," Condolences insisted. *Sound* and *staunch* were Condolences' words of highest praise. The words implied a Republican background and a steady voting-pattern. No higher praise.

"She's too involved with that German factory now," the Senator defended himself. "She even takes technical stuff home to translate."

"A wonderful girl." Rebecca stared at him.

"Well, it's a man's decision, I must say that." Ned

rose slowly from his chair. “Let’s go into the sitting-room. We should decide who’ll phone who...”

Condolences made a bolt for the kitchen door. As he did so the Senator noticed the bulge in his pocket.

“The saucer,” he said. “Condolences!”

# PART II

# EXIT OF A SENATOR

# TEN

They were driving to the electoral area committee meeting; Julie sat in the back seat with Eamon. She was silent, at ease. They all approached the meeting with confidence because of what Condolences had unearthed by checking the registers of electors kept by the Party's personation officers for Hallgrove and Toorlyra. Condolences had discovered that less than half the Party's supporters had come out to vote in the election. This was the fault of Conory and Allingham; they were councillors for those areas. "They were too busy canvassing in our area to bus the people to the booths in their own districts," Condolences roared. The registers of electors handed into the Party HQ contained damning evidence against those two councillors.

"Somebody should put a gun to the head of that bastard Conory," said Ned, uncharacteristically violent.

"Now, that's no thing to say. This is politics now, there's no need for any kind of bad feelings." The Senator turned to Eamon again. "Our friend Conory is in for a shock tonight..."

"Wasn't Condolences very clever to notice the

registers of electors?'

"The registers are always checked. That way we do know who votes and who doesn't vote. Some people never vote. We don't have to waste energy canvassing people who never bother to vote," Ned explained.

When they reached the venue they saw that most of the other delegates' cars were already parked outside. "Uncle, you're always late for meetings. That can't be a good thing for your politics," Eamon said sternly. The others laughed. Julie poked the Senator in the back.

The Senator parked his car and as they walked towards the door he noticed that Allingham was in their midst. Despite Allingham's presence, or perhaps because of it, Ned decided to be friendly: "Hello, men. Clear night, thank God. How'ya Morrissey? Mr Allingham, how are you?" He nodded.

His friendliness pricked their consciences and led to a release of rumbling acknowledgements.

"Friendly folk," young Eamon said.

"Oh, very nice," Julie responded. The two of them shouldered each other like football players and giggled.

"Right, we'll have a jar." Ned, who was carrying a red minute-book of the Party's electoral committee, as well as the registers of electors, took control in his characteristic fashion. Eamon asked Ned to buy a glass of porter for him. When it was eventually placed on the table the youth fondled it with the

practised delight of a veteran drinker. The Senator noticed this and was shocked; Eamon was starting young at everything. After about ten minutes Morrissey came into the lounge to announce that their meeting should begin. None of them moved until Ned himself gave the signal.

They seated themselves along a huge formica-topped table. Most of the delegates had rows of drinks assembled in front of them, stout and chasers. The harsh overhead lighting caught the full and half-filled glasses, and bounced about, so that each Party man sat beside his own personal kaleidoscope of alcoholic light.

Ned was on his feet instantly. "This meeting is premature and pointless."

"It hasn't begun yet," Allingham said.

"Order, now, gentlemen." The County Secretary used his tone of extreme boredom. It was his way of deflating potential arguments. "This will be an important meetin'. Let's keep it important. We're here to discuss results, and to find the right men for the right job. Let's keep it important."

"Where's the agenda for this extraordinary meeting?" Ned asked. "I never received an agenda, and I'm supposed to be the Chairman! The Senator here didn't receive one either. You can't have a proper meeting without an agenda." He looked at the Secretary. "You should know that."

"It's here." The Secretary pushed a typewritten

sheet of paper across the table. Ned went over it in silence, then looked at the Senator before speaking. "As Chairman of the committee I should have been consulted. I don't think that this meeting is legal. Agendas are supposed to be signed by the Secretary *and* the Chairman."

"Not if more than half the committee feel that the meeting is necessary. In such cases one or other of the signatures will do. Now the Secretary has signed the agenda. That's sufficient, isn't it?" Allingham looked at the Secretary, who nodded in agreement.

"In that case I want to register my strongest protest at the timing of this meeting. Right in the middle of winterish weather. The roads outside are freezing already, and some delegates have come over fifty miles. It shows a contempt for their welfare, if nothing else...There will be plenty of time to discuss the election results when the weather improves."

"Spring will be too late," Conory said. "We may be fighting another election by that time. The Coalition will probably collapse in the next few weeks."

Ned became angry. He began to read the agenda in a mocking tone. "Item four: A review of the Party panel of candidates. Well, well." He rooted around in his pocket for his tobacco pouch. He held their attention while he stoked and fused his pipe... "Those four items are merely sub-sections of one single item. They hardly constitute a full agenda.

Quite apart from the fact that this committee has no jurisdiction over the panel of candidates. That's a matter for a full convention. This agenda boils down to one thing—your nervousness over the last election."

"We're all in politics to win elections," Conory stated. "Or, at least, that's what I'm in politics for. Maybe you're not in it for that reason. Last week's performance may tell us something about that." He smiled boldly. Some of the delegates laughed, nervous laughs.

The Senator couldn't take this. He shouted at Conory that a review of the previous week's débâcle might be instructive; maybe it would teach them something about Conory's nature. Ned looked at the Senator in despair. He didn't want any outbursts from him, or any behaviour that would damage his image. If there had to be outbursts, Ned wanted to be responsible for them.

"If you could hand me that minute-book, Mr Chairman. You are acting as Chairman, Ned?" The Secretary spoke. That return to formality helped to quench the developing tension. Ned, as Chairman, read out the items for discussion yet again. "They are all about the same thing," he repeated, "so I suggest that we wander around the four items...and consider them dealt with when we've exhausted ourselves."

"Certainly," Morrissey, the Director of Elections, marked his approval.

"Fine by me," Conory nodded in agreement.

"I believe it was yourself that felt compelled to call the meeting, Mr Allingham. Will you tell us the reasons for this?" asked Ned.

"Sure, certainly." Allingham rose to his feet and as he did so, drew a white index-card from his pocket. While ironing the crumpled card with his fingers, he said that there were many painful things that had to be said. "Now is the right time for criticism, before things hot up again. The Coalition won't last. Let us not wait until another election is called before setting up a new election committee."

"It's not our function to set up a new electoral committee," the Senator interrupted him.

"There are two things we can do," Allingham suggested. "We can select a new panel of candidates to be presented to the constituency council, or to a full convention. And we can choose new officers; cut out the dying wood."

"Choose away, I'm not afraid," Morrissey said guiltily.

"I thought we were here to discuss the election results!" Ned remarked. He sat forward in his chair so that he could stare aggressively at the Toorlyra councillor.

But Allingham replied that everything was connected. Many of the delegates felt that the election had been botched by the present officers, that those officers responsible should step down and

present themselves for re-election. He also insisted that all the candidates should resign from the panel and submit themselves to an internal Party vote. That re-vote, Allingham concluded, should include all those candidates who failed to get on to the panel before the election.

"That's stupid. How can we be sure which candidates want to present themselves for a new panel? At least three people who expressed interest before the election are missing tonight. How can we know what they want?" The Senator spoke confidently.

"Councillor Allingham and I have been speaking to them about this," Conory spoke. "They all want to go forward again."

"It's just your word," Julie said.

"The word of a Councillor," Conory reminded her.

"Are we agreed that the officers and candidates should resign?" Councillor Leonard, an old man, sprang to his feet in a sudden burst of energy.

"We are not," the Senator said loudly.

"We should vote on it then," Conory insisted. He seemed pleased.

"Here we are...talking about fundamental changes in the constituency organisation and we haven't even discussed the bloody election results!" Ned came back into the discussion.

"We need fundamental changes," said Conory.

"We lost a vital seat for the Party. It was lost because of a faulty transfer of votes. The panel as chosen didn't stand up to the election. We must have coherence."

"Ye must get rid of me, is that it?" the Senator shouted, like a schoolboy.

"I have nothing against you personally, Senator. Many many's the time I canvassed for your father... But your transfers lost us the third seat. Everyone knows that."

"You may be too young to blend in, just yet," Allingham said in a soft, fatherly way. "Being young, you talk like a member of the Labour Party. People get confused, they don't know what we really stand for."

"We don't stand for more trouble in Ulster, if that's what you mean," the Senator said angrily.

"What's that supposed to mean? That's slanderous."

"Take it any way you like."

"I want to know what you're talking about. You're making insinuations."

"I don't want to reopen all of last year's arguments," the Senator said.

"Well then, don't," Allingham said. "The plain truth is that your vote ruined the Party."

"Your own organisation left much to be desired. In both Hallgrove and Toorlyra," the Senator went on.

"A savage thing to say!" Councillor Conory jumped to his feet and glared at the Senator. "Councillor Allingham will support me in this view: the Party vote held up very well. It was nearly average."

Allingham asserted that the Senator's was a scurrilous allegation, that every Party man had done his best on the day. As always. But Ned would have none of this. The time had come to beat them with the wooden spoon. Ned asked Allingham to explain the registers of electors marked by the personation officers in Toorlyra and Hallgrove; to explain why over fifty per cent of the party faithful never showed at the booths. He wanted to know if any Party workers had called to their homes. He wanted to know why their homes weren't checked in the afternoon of polling-day. "Look at Toorlyra, Mr Allingham, your own area. Whole families never turned out to vote. Look, the Sweeneys, with three votes in the house, the Colberts with four votes...and I could go on. There are Whelans, O'Callaghans, Uniackes. All firm Party families who never voted. What the hell were ye doing on that day?"

"They were canvassing inside *my* area on polling-day, too busy to look after the Party's interests in their own area," the Senator said.

"Not true, not true." A frightened look came over Allingham's face. He knew that he was cornered, a nightmare. "Not true," he repeated while searching for a plausible explanation. But the Senator wouldn't

let go: "Both Julie and Eamon saw you in my area. They *saw* you!"

"We were checking on canvassing material, that was it," Allingham said at last. "Or, no. We were short of registers of electors. Yes, we were short of copies for our personation people."

"Registers are my department," Morrissey said. "If you were short of registers you should have contacted me. Nobody in the other districts would have copies of registers for your district."

"Show them to me," Allingham said briskly. "I don't believe this."

While the other delegates sat in silence, the two councillors studied the registers. None of the others wanted to get involved in the developing sting. It looked like a public humiliation. Everyone present was afraid to earn the enmity of the eventual losers. The silence seemed to home in on the two councillors like a prosecutor; a merciless accuser amplifying their flaws. Some of the delegates supped at their flat pints; one or two breathed sighs in an effort to contain the tension.

"The personation lads mustn't have ticked off all the people who voted. That's what I think," Conory said at last. It was a daft, lame excuse.

Ned inhaled heavily, to demonstrate his contempt for the explanation. "All the registers are initialled by the personation officers and the local chairmen. You'll see your own initials on some of them." Then

he turned to some of the other delegates. "Does anyone have any comment, observations?"

"Give us a look at the registers," Councillor Leonard said. He studied them in a pained myopic way. Allingham left his seat to walk around the table to talk to Conory. The two delegates who flanked Conory joined in the discussion.

"Discussion through the Chair, please," the Senator said.

Allingham returned to his seat. Then he spoke. "Mr Chairman, fellow delegates, Councillor Conory and I really are deeply disappointed by the Party's performance in our own areas. We share the Chairman's concern—but we feel that unfair conclusions are being drawn from the markings on the registers. I have always pursued my political business with complete honesty."

"Sure," Ned murmured.

Allingham then suggested that the committee should drop the idea of replacing the election officers until after the next election. But the committee had a responsibility to do something to answer the criticisms of the Party followers within the constituency. Some gesture must be made. The best gesture would be the resignation of the present panel of candidates, and a re-vote before the night was over. It would be something to show the Party faithful, a sign of concern at committee level.

"It was a poor performance, all right," old Leonard

shouted. He had finished reading the registers.

"We're all agreed on that," Conory turned to Leonard. "Listen to Councillor Allingham, will you!"

Allingham resumed his speech. He connected the disquiet of the Party faithful with the troubles in Ulster; and the troubles in Ulster with the loss of the election. He said that there wasn't enough "strong talk" coming from the leadership at regional or national level. The Senator wanted to interrupt him then, but he let the moment pass. He was surprised that Ned didn't interrupt the speech and he wondered if Ned was too tired. Finally, the Senator did speak.

"I've no objection to the committee taking a re-vote here and now. I've no objection to this at all."

"It's too irregular. It's a matter for a convention," Ned said.

"It would be an inspiring move," Conory commended the Senator.

"A show of hands would be quicker," Allingham suggested.

"There's no need for this," Ned explained. "The list of candidates must stand. Remember it includes two sitting deputies. Neither of them are here tonight. This whole idea is daft."

"No, Ned. Let us have a vote. Let's see what all the other delegates really think. I'm not afraid of this." The Senator spoke confidently. Ned shook his head angrily.

"A show of hands on who wants a ballot!" Conory

shouted. Even before Ned or the Secretary had voiced their approval, most of the delegates raised their hands in support of an instant ballot.

"Let me make this clear so," Ned spoke again. He went through the list of previous candidates and mentioned the names of the two sitting deputies. They were returned automatically. The delegates were asked to write two names on blank sheets of paper to complete the four-man panel. While he explained the details of voting, he could see Julie flicking through the pages of the Party's rule book. She was hoping to find there something to halt Conory's filibuster. There were only four pens in the committee-room and this slowed down the voting. Eventually, all the papers were marked and handed back to the Secretary.

There was a general exodus from the room. Knowing that there would be a delay, the delegates decided to replenish their glasses. Julie, Eamon and the Secretary stayed behind to count the ballot papers. When Ned and the Senator returned to the room they saw that Julie was upset. Eamon frowned when the Senator caught his eye; his frown was enough. Julie was checking the papers over and over again. She wouldn't meet the Senator's look.

"Gentlemen, are we all back in the room?" the Secretary addressed the delegates. "According to these papers the two candidates to join the panel with the sitting deputies are Councillors Quigley and

Allingham."

There was a burst of applause. Allingham heaved forward with delight and said: "Sorry, Senator, but it's only a matter of time. Your time will come, I'm sure of it." Victory, its sweetness, had made him momentarily generous.

"This new panel—for it is a new panel—will have to be ratified by the constituency council. It isn't over yet," the Chairman said.

"That's only a formality," Conory insisted. He was jubilant because of Allingham's victory.

"I'm afraid it isn't only a formality," Ned replied angrily. "This committee is only an electoral committee—not a bloody constituency convention. You can't change a panel of candidates without a convention."

"The sitting deputies are not against this."

"How do you know?" Julie challenged him.

"We've spoken—I spoke to them today. They said they'd agree with any new panel formed tonight."

"They haven't said that in public, or you haven't got it in writing," the Chairman said. "This whole question of a panel will have to go back to the convention."

"It won't. It won't, and that's that. The Party has had enough trouble since the Arms Trial. It'll accept our decision here. The General Secretary doesn't want trouble.

"We'll see," Ned insisted. "We'll have to see...I've

never known anything as strange as this."

The Senator didn't know what to say. At least they didn't have the power to take his Senate seat away—but the Senate was a useless place, unless it was a stepping stone to the Dáil. He had hoped to be a Dáil deputy like his father. Now this humiliation of losing his place on the panel of candidates.

"The Party will have to return to its Republican principles," Allingham said suddenly. "Since the Arms Trial this country has become an accomplice with the British in crucifying Ulster. It'll have to stop."

"Good man," Conory said.

The other delegates were silent. Then Ned spoke up. "Our job is to follow the Party's line on Ulster. We should try to put the Arms Trial behind us. Forget it, forget that whole bad episode."

"We won't forget it!" Allingham said. "Why should we forget the betrayal of the Party's Republican instincts. Our instinct must always be to help the Nationalist people of Ulster. We've forgotten them for fifty years."

"Here, here," Conory said.

"This isn't the place for grand speeches, this is the electoral committee. There are no newspapermen here." Ned tried to deflate the victorious Allingham. Just then Allingham turned towards the Senator and stretched out his hand. At first Gerald hesitated to shake it, to offer congratulations, but Julie kicked

him on the shin and he accepted the councillor's handshake. Julie winked at the Senator, a huge conspiratorial wink, a lover's gesture in a time of despair. The Senator felt a desperate need to leave the room. "We should get away soon," he said to the Chairman and Julie. The other delegates wanted to get away too.

The meeting soon broke up after that. The delegates left the place quickly, not wanting to hang around—there had been too much bad feeling.

"You'd better put tonight out of your head," Ned addressed young Eamon in a friendly avuncular way. "You were supposed to see us skinning Allingham and Conory. Instead you saw the bloody mess we made of things. Don't let it disappoint you. Next time round you'll see us all in fighting form."

"I wish Condolences had been there," Julie said.

"His wife is sick again," Ned explained. "The whole thing was my fault anyway...I should have insisted on a vote of censure on Conory and Allingham on the bad turn-out in their neck of the woods."

"Morrissey should have put a stop to it all, he should have spoken more; after all, he's the Director of Elections," the Senator complained. "I suppose he was keeping an eye on his own position as Director of Elections."

"He was," the Chairman agreed. "He's a cute boyo. But he's important to us. We mustn't antagonise

the man."

Then the Senator said that he should have spoken to Morrissey before they left the meeting.

"Plenty of time," Ned suggested. "Despite the fact that he always looks after himself first, he likes you."

"Dad'll be disappointed," Eamon said.

"Why, sure he has no interest in politics?" The Senator sounded annoyed.

"Well, it was Grandad Glenville's seat you were trying to win back. That would matter to Dad."

There was silence after that.

The Senator dropped Ned at his house. They had nothing more to say to each other, their political failure was too new. After Eamon left the car, the Senator was alone with Julie for the first time that night. The silence of the car renewed his sense of embarrassment, allowing the pain of it all to come to the surface. "You'll get back," Julie said quickly, stepping into the breach. She wanted to cry, but she didn't want to be sentimental. "You'll get back in time, I know." She placed her arm around his shoulder and squeezed his neck as they drove along.

"I have a half-day tomorrow. Will you collect me at the factory?" The Senator said that he would. He was feeling angry with himself. He knew that he had allowed something of value to slip out of his reach too easily. In losing his place on the panel of candidates he had lost a piece of property, part of the family's estate. He had no right to lose it.

"I'd love to meet you tomorrow," he said, and then: "Julie, you're the one thing I have left."

It was then she decided to cry. "Am I your last straw then? The bottom of the barrel for you?"

"That's not what I meant."

"Gerald, I wish you'd tell me what you mean."

"I usually feel strong when you're near." When he spoke she looked at him with intensity and expectation. He continued, "Is that wrong? Is it wrong to borrow strength from you? You're the person I've leaned on ever since my father died, since they persuaded me to go for the Seanad."

"They should have allowed you to go forward at the by-election after your father died. That would have been the logical thing to do. Instead of pushing you sideways into the Seanad. There was some dirty work going on. Those Senate sub-panels are such a waste of energy. How many phone calls did we make the last time? Was it six hundred? Over eight hundred voters scattered all over the bloody country."

"That's not important now."

"It is important." Her tears went quickly. She forgot herself as the Senate election came to her. It was hard to escape from strategic thinking. She was thinking of all the work that had to be done to get elected. One had to canvass so many councillors.

"It's not important. I'll get my nomination to the same panel. Cultural and educational. I was talking to Senator Fox and Deputy MacGahon. I have the

four nominations."

"What about canvassing? Have you organised the letters, have you made a list for phoning?"

"Listen, Julie, don't worry about it."

"I wish you wouldn't sulk like a boy," she said. There was bitterness and resignation in her voice.

# ELEVEN

Julie was hugging the white telephone when the Senator walked in. She motioned to him to sit down, and to stay quiet. *"Irre ich mich nicht...Da mag wahr sein,"* she said, grimacing. The Senator got the impression that her caller was agitated.

*"Man muss das nicht tun,"* she replied sternly, then paused. She smiled at her distant caller. *"Danke, Herr Sabais."* Laughter then. *"Es regnet,"* she admitted, knowing that to her German caller Ireland and rain were synonymous.

*"Ja. Trotz des schlecten Wetters..."* She held the phone between her shoulder and chin, glancing at the Senator while she tidied her desk. *"Danke. Sie mussen sich breiten. Danke."* She put down the phone.

"Friendly German," the Senator commented.

"Extremely. He's worried about the weather. He's due back at the end of the month, but he wants to bring his car through England to carry all his fishing gear. Profits and salmon," she laughed, "and he catches them with equal skill. He's trying to buy a house five miles up river. Well, his company wants to buy it. Their executives could use it for fishing."

"A clever fellow."

"And why not?" she said. "He works hard. When he's back in Germany I spend half my time trying to contact him. His secretary in Hamburg had to go away for a rest cure last year. That's how hard he works." She took a bunch of keys from a drawer, then began to tie her hair back with a green scarf that had been hanging across the back of a chair. "We're ready to go."

"Don't you have to clock-out or something?"

"They still trust me."

"Let me kiss you now." He reached out to catch her arm, to halt her busy trot.

"It's OK. You should have kissed me when you came in," she dismissed his effort.

"Ah Julie...don't pull away from me like that."

"I'm still at work."

"I can see I'm in the dog-house anyway."

They decided to drive through the oak woods by the river and to stop at a tourists' viewing place four miles away. Julie twiddled the knobs of the car-radio to find a station with a clear signal. It would be easier than talk. He could see that the effort was beginning to frustrate her, but she wouldn't give up. "Leave it," he said. "There's something wrong with the aerial."

"I thought cold weather was good for reception. You told me that."

"Cold clear weather, not muggy weather."

"Oh."

When they reached the lay-by opposite the great

mansion of an old Anglo-Irish family she told him to stop. They pulled over onto the gravel. Through the thin mist they could see the Big House standing on its mammoth plinth of sheer rock. They saw a light in one of the windows, a desolate yellow glow quivering in the river mist like phosphorescent bog-light. "A warm light," the Senator said suddenly. "It's lovely to see a light still burning in an old place like that."

"I thought you were a Republican," Julie said.

"I am. But it isn't good to see the life going out of anything. There were kind landlords too, you know. Especially around here."

"True."

"And so much of the countryside is dying. The Big Houses were part of that old stability. You know. We've nothing to put in their place. Nothing to give that much employment."

"For God's sake, it's not all that bad," she pleaded. She placed her hand over his on the gear-stick.

"A lot of things will change, Julie. We weren't prepared for EEC membership. In another ten years, by 1983, say, there could be over a hundred thousand people unemployed."

"Never, that would never happen. There'd be a revolution! But you must accept change. The only thing that will never change is the Ulster problem. But everything else will change. Are you afraid of change?" she asked sternly. "It's terrible if you are."

"Why?"

"At your age you should be thinking of change. We should all be thinking of change. Throw out the rotten things, start anew." She turned her head away and looked through the windscreen. In turning she caused her scarf to come unstuck on the head-rest. Her scarf loosened and fell away across her shoulders. "Shit," she exclaimed. "When I listen to you sometimes I think there's no future for us. We're destroying each other's enthusiasm for things." She pulled the loosened scarf from her shoulders and began to roll it into a ball. "You'll get your nomination back, if that's what depresses you."

"It's not that."

"What then?"

"It's us. We've grown apart," he admitted. "I can feel a hostility between us."

She looked at him then, intensely. "What good is friendship at our age? I'm nearly thirty. What good is friendship? We need to be getting somewhere... that's what I think."

"I was sure I'd be a deputy by now," the Senator replied. "I feel less worthy of you. You know, now that I've lost the nomination, done so badly. It was presumptuous of me to think I'd be a deputy."

"It was," she said. Becoming interested, she raised herself on the seat. "But that has nothing to do with us. Nothing. You won't be more worthy—or less worthy—because you're a deputy. That's silly." She

paused and drew breath. "You know, Gerald, what we should do is get married. At least we'd keep each other warm." She laughed, a nervous laugh. "There, I've said it now."

"Them Germans have made you very impatient," he said.

"Fuck you. Fuck you too," she said angrily. "I'm going for a walk." She left the car and walked quickly toward a bank of reeds where a bitumen-covered fishing boat was moored. The Senator followed her.

"Look, I'm sorry. I'm just a bit low in spirits, that's all."

"So are we all," she said, humiliated.

"I'm sorry."

She kicked the black stern of the board, causing it to rock and make sucking noises in the reeds. "I'm leaving here anyway," she said. "Nothing changes, despite all the hype about our joining the EEC, all that rubbish about change. For a woman Ireland means marriage or loneliness—that's how I feel, Gerald."

The Senator took her hand and she allowed him to take it without resistance. "I don't know what I should say. I hate to see you becoming bitter. But what's the point in becoming bitter, and why should you go away when you have your family here?"

She struck the stern of the boat again, making it rock more violently. Dead bracken and freshly cut alder branches that were part of a primitive

camouflage fell away from the gunwales and flopped into the water. The Senator asked her to come back to the car. "You go back if you're too cold," she said. "I want to stay here for a while. Go back to the car, Gerald." She pulled farther away from him.

"You'll ruin your shoes. You're just upset."

"Don't worry about me, please. I don't need pity, not now, I'm not that far gone. Not your pity, for Christ's sake." A cold, a bitterly cold wind blew off the river reeds, catching her red hair. She took her scarf from her pocket and with it battened down her wayward strands.

"Julie," the Senator spoke softly, "come back to the car now. This breeze is deadly."

She turned around and walked towards him. She gripped his hand tightly while they walked to the car. "We'll go for a drink" the Senator said. "You'd like a drink."

"No, take me home. I can never enjoy drink when you don't drink."

"I even deprive you of that," he replied, trying to sound sorry for himself. He switched on the radio when they were back inside the car. The only clear station he could get was broadcasting a political programme, an interview with the widow of a former minister. She claimed that she had been left penniless because her husband hadn't served enough time in government to qualify for a pension.

"Keep your eye on the road," Julie said. "I'll try

to find a bit of music."

"There you have it," the Senator said. "Another man who didn't make a penny from politics. I often wonder why good educated people like him get involved with politics. People never see how much politicians sacrifice, how much their lives are constrained...When people look at me they probably think I got my teaching job because my father was a deputy. Sometimes I wonder why I even bother to fight for a Dáil seat—to represent thirty thousand envious and stupid bastards..."

"Ah, give over, Gerald. You want to be a deputy for your own sake first. What the electorate wants is a secondary thing. Don't be stupid."

# TWELVE

The morale of the Party soared when the date of the presidential election was announced. Party nerves were steadied and minds were focused in an easy and confident way. The leadership wanted the presidential campaign to be taken seriously. During the previous elections many Party workers had stated openly that the presidency was a meaningless institution. But not now. There would be no cynicism now that the Party was in opposition. The leadership wanted a huge, spectacular campaign that would sink the government candidate.

One of the major stunts of the campaign would be a canvassing bus-tour of the provinces. The Party candidate would be installed into a custom-built election bus, along with the big names of the front bench. It was anticipated that the bus would be followed by a gaggle of newspaper reporters as well as television crews. Letters and mimeographs from Party HQ emphasised the importance of the television crew. They were an unknown quantity in the publicity equation. It was thought that they would be foreigners or Dubliners, people whose political outlook couldn't be clearly identified. Because the party couldn't be

sure of their point of view it was felt that the local organisations could stifle any potential hostility by providing them with good pictures. Scenes of enthusiastic crowds, local bands (preferably brass bands), buntings festooning the streets, all these things would keep the television people happy.

The fact that enmity was suspended for the duration of the campaign didn't diminish the local rivalry between parishes on the itinerary. The excellence of the reception and the degree of colour and enthusiasm provided by each village, would be compared and contrasted by the national Party men travelling with the candidate. Each reception, it was felt, would be a reflection of the local politicians' stature and organisational skills. Ned and the Senator were determined to put on a spectacular show. For that reason they called a general meeting of the Party faithful in their parish. The meeting was held in Gwynn's pub, the most select and respectable drinking-place that could be booked. Over twenty people turned up, including Condolences (who still had no deaths to report), Ned, young Eamon and even Julie. She arrived at the last minute, her hair trimmed and her manner subdued. She glanced at the Senator when she came in, then greeted the rest of the company without a trace of emotion.

"Good to see you, girl. Good girl." Ned shook her hand and squeezed it in a fatherly way. "You're looking great."

"A picture," Condolences said. "You're just like a picture."

"Get lost, Condolences," she replied, embarrassed. The Senator glanced at her. The weeks had changed her, made her more lovely, but self-conscious. He didn't want to botch her return.

"We'd nearly given up on you. You disappeared for weeks."

"You made a big effort to find me...How did the last sitting of the Seanad go?"

"Oh, the usual fuss about the Claudia affair and a few jibes at the silence of the Party in the reassembled Dáil. At least we got through all the stages of the Broadcasting Bill. I've missed you badly. That's the God's honest truth." Then, when he noticed that the others were listening—hanging on his very words—he complimented her on her hair.

"A style. Do you like it? What do you think?"

"It's lovely, Julie. It really suits you."

"I'm glad." Then she turned to Eamon. "How's school?"

"Great!" he replied. "I'm still doing electrical experiments...I'm trying to put together something for the Young Scientists' Exhibition in Dublin."

"The happy genius of the Party." She put her arms around him and embarrassed him with a kiss. She admired him despite his youthfulness—she admired the Glenville brightness, the zest for life that his uncle should have had. "You happy genius you," she

repeated.

Ned coughed, and Mrs Hyde, the butcher's wife, shuffled uncomfortably in her plastic seat. Then the Senator decided to open the meeting formally by reading one of the many memos sent by the Party headquarters. The memo set the tone for the meeting.

"A band is very important," Ned said suddenly. "Councillor Allingham has booked a very famous brass band from Waterford. And county council workers have been labouring away in and around Toorlyra for the past few weeks. No doubt they'll be back there just before the presidential cavalcade...We must have a band."

"Where's the money going to come from?" Condolences asked. "Is Allingham taking money from the annual collection funds?"

"You can't do that kind of thing," Mrs Hyde said roughly. "It doesn't matter anyway. At least the man has ideas."

"It won't cost that much," the Senator explained. "We don't have to hire a very famous band. That would be a bad idea; people would think that the Party was rolling in money."

Ned agreed. He said that there was no reason why the local party should get into debt just to outdo Allingham and his miserable village. Mrs Hyde then suggested that the Senator could provide the Party with a crowd by letting the children out of school when the bus arrived. The Senator explained that

that might create problems. If the presidential bus arrived in the village too early he couldn't give the children half-a-day off just to cheer. That would cause protests from the Coalition parents. He thought that he could give the children no more than an hour off. But he would have them shepherded into the camera's eye.

The worst thing that could happen, Ned suggested, was that the bus wouldn't visit the area until the schools had broken up for the summer holidays. If that happened there would be no crowd at all.

The Senator was sure that this wouldn't happen. The Party would be clever enough to send the bus to tour the rural areas before the schools closed. Schools were too valuable as focal points—for parents as well as pupils—for the Party to ignore their timetables. Mrs Hyde said that she would feel much happier if they had dates for the bus-tour. They couldn't even book a band until they knew the precise date.

"Don't worry, Mrs Hyde, they'll let us know soon enough. Just soon enough to put our nerves on edge. They think we'll work better that way," Julie said. Ned smiled, knowing that she was right. The Party's usual procedure was to send advance notice of an event without giving precise data like time and date. In this way the local members were keyed up and emotionally ready, while nothing was given away to the opposition parties. Nothing could be kept secret

in the countryside, especially in politics.

Between drinks and interruptions, it was decided that Ned would take charge of the local publicity for the candidate's visit. Ned's publicity methods were simple; he would drive up and down the village and out into the countryside on the morning of the fateful day, broadcasting through a loud-hailer.

Condolences was put in charge of crowd control. It would be his job to guide the presidential bus to the platform, and to discourage children from leaping under its wheels. He would also have to lead the crowd into applause. The Senator himself would welcome the Party candidate onto the platform. He would be expected to link him in some way to the locality. Mrs Hyde was put in charge of hiring a band.

"We need someone to drive out towards Toorlyra to give us advance warning. Would you do that, Julie?" Ned asked.

"I will, glad to help." She spoke quietly, without a breath of confidence. The Senator felt that she was like a person in shock, someone who had suffered a recent bereavement.

"Can I get you a drink?"

"No," she said.

The meeting was wound up a few minutes later. Ned and the Senator left the room to discuss the financing of the band. As usual, more was accomplished outside the meeting than within the confines of the agenda. Ned had already approached

a local garage-owner, a confidential supporter of the Party, to solicit money for the band. The man was delighted to help, and wanted to cover the cost of a reception for the candidate as well. Ned wouldn't allow him to do this; there was no point in killing a local golden goose. Mrs Hyde, who wasn't yet completely in their confidence, would be told that the national HQ had paid for the band. There were other matters—such as a bill still outstanding from a local electrician as well as two bills from the local printer—which would have to be settled privately as well.

When they finished their discussion, the Senator turned around to ask Julie if she needed a lift home. But she had slipped away.

It was four weeks later, on the second Friday in June, that the Party's election-bus arrived. All that morning the Senator was on edge. Before coming to school he phoned Party HQ but got no reply; then he phoned Morrissey to check that everything was organised. But Morrissey too was missing. Everyone was on the road.

He tried not to glance at his speech again, but couldn't resist the temptation. The pupils were fidgety and agitated in class, perfectly mimicking their teacher.

"Sir? Sir, can I go to the loo?" Young Hourican stood up, beads of sweat visible across his forehead. He had a glandular problem.

"The toilet, is it?" the Senator asked.

"Oh, the toilet, Sir," he said cheekily.

"I hope you *can*, Hourican, but you may."

"Can I go so?"

"You may! You may!" The Senator shouted. Heads bowed low over copybooks. The pupils feared his growing hostility; but even he was too preoccupied to proceed with a confrontation. Hourican slammed the door triumphantly on his way out. Silence. The metallic sound of Ned's voice through the loud-hailer could be heard, coming from the distant ring-road. Then the sound of Hourican's studs on the hard tiles of the school hallway. The Senator looked at his speech of welcome. *Ladies and Gentlemen, Canon* (would the Protestant Canon be there? The Party's candidate was a Protestant; a smart move, that). *It gives me great pleasure to welcome our future President.* Cheers (if Condolences does his work). How would he connect the candidate to the locality? He could find nothing in his background to suggest that he'd been through this part of the country. But he had been a good minister for health. *Every healthy child here today, and every happy parent, will have already met this wonderful man.* Perplexed silence. *Met him through his policies. Because our candidate was responsible for many of the free medical services that we enjoy today.* Then he would throw in a few statistics; numbers of children in medical care, the increased numbers of medical card holders. The emphasis would be on

children; a perfectly warm, innocuous subject upon which to peg a welcome. The Senator would conclude by introducing the Party's national Director of Elections. If Condolences did his job properly, the Party candidate would mount the rostrum to band-playing and the applause of the assembled schoolchildren.

At two-thirty the children were released from school. Miss Maloney, who had no politics, escorted the pupils to the village square, where a small crowd had already gathered. Condolences had marshalled them into a tight circle while the brass band played. It was difficult to hear the tune above the racket being made by the drummers, who seemed to form an independent and surly caucus within the group. In the background—much more determined and forceful than the sounds from the band was Ned's proclamation.

"THE FUTURE PRESIDENT IS COMING! HE WILL BE ARRIVING IN TEN MINUTES. THIS IS YOUR GOLDEN OPPORTUNITY. COME OUT NOW AND GREET THE FUTURE PRESIDENT OF IRELAND!"

His voice became more electric and deafening as he approached the platform. The Senator parked his car discreetly, away from the vengeful stone-throwing of his pupils. Clutching his little speech he raced towards the rostrum. As he mounted the platform he noticed Julie's car approaching rapidly along the river road. She was flashing her headlights. That was

the signal.

"Get them to play a march!" the Senator shouted at Condolences, who was facing the crowd. Condolences beckoned to the band-major and the whole company exploded into a rousing march tempo. "Christ preserve me," the Senator said. It was a short prayer, the zenith of tension, because he could just see the multi-coloured election bus bearing down on them from under the dark green canopy of roadside trees.

"Tell them to clap for the President!" he shouted to Condolences.

"Relax, Gerald," came the reply. "It's too early yet! We'd be out of breath by the time our man reached us."

"Everybody sing then!" The Senator waved at the crowd of schoolchildren, and the sea of Party mothers.

"What'll we sing? We can't sing a bloody march!" One mother shouted angrily.

"Sing anything!"

With that, the children broke into a song, a dainty, virginal ditty. It was a catastrophe—the band, which, after all, was getting paid to play, decided to play their own march even more loudly. The nun-like sweetness of the children's song skated across the surface of the march.

"Will ye SHUT UP!" Condolences shouted. Somebody had switched on the public address system prematurely. His ugly roar was probably the first

greeting that the presidential candidate heard. The Senator went scarlet with embarrassment. The children, seeing this, burst into laughter. The election bus pulled into the funnel of tarmac that had been marked off with lime by the local athletics club. The Senator took the microphone in his hand. "Now let's all clap. Our candidate is stepping down. Just applause. Band, please."

The band, which had been cut off by Condolences' scream, began to play a gentle piece of music. The children started to applaud and their applause dragged the adults into the vortex of enthusiasm. The candidate and his satellite stepped onto a carpet of superficial enthusiasm.

"Glenville, Gerald, Sir," the Senator took the candidate's hand as he mounted the platform. The man was smaller than the Senator imagined, very small for a Protestant. He had a small, luminous face. His father had been murdered by a Free State firing-squad, but he had never invoked that tragedy in order to further his political career. That refusal to be vengeful gave his life an almost Anglican integrity. Like the best statesmen, the man was obsessed with forgiveness, and this gave him a sacred, slightly eccentric, aura within the Party. The man's presence in the Party meant a great deal to the Senator. Gerald held his hand for as long as possible, hoping that some of his belief in the future would pass through his skin.

"Senator...Our man on the job. How nice to see you." His voice was out of the ordinary, very Anglo-Irish. The Senator knew that this worried many people in the Party. There was a rumour that the Director of Elections had instructed him not to speak for more than four minutes. In order to overcome the market resistance to his aristocratic voice, it was felt that it would be better if his words were reported rather than heard. The Party also dampened his Protestant effect by surrounding him with local speakers—for example the Senator was to introduce him now, and Councillors Hayes and Colbert, guttural mountain men, would conclude the proceedings with their few words.

When the candidate started to speak photographers from the national papers climbed onto the platform. The Senator felt that the poor man was being mauled by their flashlights. Strands of hair fell across his face, beads of exhaustion ran along the furrows of his genuinely happy smile.

"Clap for the President! Clap for the President!" the Senator heard Condolences shouting. A tide of childish roars rose up to engulf and petrify the Party's gentleman. It was obvious that he was made uncomfortable by Condolences' wild, happy, childlike yelping. While the candidate spoke, the Senator looked around at the crowd that had gathered; he saw that, apart from the strangers who had come on the election bus, there were no more than fifty adults

present.

"Were you nervous?" Julie was leaping onto the platform behind him. "Take my hand, please." She stretched out her hand and he pulled her up to him. The Senator was pleased. It was the first time in months that she had spoken to him in a friendly, girlish way.

"I wasn't a bit nervous," he shouted. "I wish you could always see me doing so well."

"My goodness, aren't we cocky," she said. He didn't hear her. "Mr Childers is a saint," she roared into his ear.

"He's like John XXIII, a true saint," the Senator agreed. "He isn't made for this world at all."

# THIRTEEN

One of the limousines that followed the presidential election bus was laden with hundreds of colourful, poster-sized photographs of the Party candidate. In a sudden burst of enthusiasm, Councillor Hayes asked for two hundred copies of the poster to be distributed by the local Party. "I got these for ye," he said to the Senator. "I knew ye were having trouble with canvassing materials during the last campaign."

The Senator gasped under the weight of the package. "Thanks," he replied, but before he could say more, Hayes had fled toward the nearest keg of lager. The Senator knew that he'd have to account for these expensive laminated posters; their possession implied real commitment.

And that was why a small group of Party officers, the Senator, Ned Kenny, Condolences and the young carpenter Moynihan, were touring the hill-country in the north of the constituency on the Saturday before the election. Julie, who didn't have a licence to drive the minibus, was at the wheel. She had insisted on driving in order to escape the company of young Moynihan in the back seat, who was very

emotional and tended to burst into tears if beaten in an argument. But they were all in a happy frame of mind, happy in the knowledge that they would beat the Coalition candidate.

As they motored along Julie noticed the beautiful June afternoon. The rough mountain land, cleared woodland, long stretches of peat bog where many of their ancestors had been born, all took on the pale green hue of early summer. Although an afternoon mist was gathering in the distance, the hills and heatherland were as clear as the spring water that flowed along the natural gullies in the roads.

"Just three more by-roads left," the young carpenter said. He held a little red notebook in his hand; it contained all the names of the roads they had covered, and the names of all the poster-points still outstanding. The carpenter was thorough.

"The Coalition fellows will be furious when they see all our new posters. The countryside is dazzled with the face of our man." Condolences spoke, then hesitantly..."We should have put some posters along the railings of the Abbey."

"We haven't even been there yet," Julie said.

"Where are we so?"

"Outside Oldcastle. At the constituency border," Moynihan said.

Ned shifted in his seat to uncover his pouch of tobacco. "We all deserve a pint and a sandwich. What do ye think, men?"

"Great idea!" Condolences whooped.

"Shut up, Condolences," the young carpenter said. "We have a lot of work to do yet. There's a mist gathering on the high ground. That could roll down onto the roads very quickly. I think we should keep going."

"Stop worrying, child," Condolences replied.

Julie suggested that they keep driving until they reached the crest of the hill country. There was a pub in that place called The Mountain Mire.

"Jesus, who are they?" she asked, spotting two boys on the side of the road.

"They're the nutty O'Haras," explained Condolences. "Angie O'Hara's boys. They're as mad as hatters. People say they should be put away."

"We should pick them up. They'll be run over on this road, or get caught in the mists," Ned spoke.

Julie pulled the minibus to a halt and the side door was slid open. The two youths were jumping up and down with delight. They pointed at the photographs of the Party candidate which decorated the exterior of the bus. They jumped wildly, pointing and shouting.

"Come in now!" Condolences shouted, catching one of them by the scruff of the neck and dragging him into the van. "Take it easy Condolences," the Senator said, annoyed.

"Uh Egg! Uh Egg!" they shouted at the Senator, pointing. "Uh Egg! Uh Egg!" they continued to cry

excitedly, breaking into laughter, clapping and shouting.

"What's wrong with them?" the Senator asked. "What the hell are they saying?"

"They know we're electioneering." Condolences waved to them and smiled while he explained. "They have election fever like the rest of us. Why shouldn't they? Aren't they Angie O'Hara's sons?"

"Uh Egg!" they roared.

"What are they saying, Ned?" the young carpenter asked nervously. He was about to cry; if someone didn't explain soon they would have three incoherent idiots in the minibus.

"Up Dev—of course!" Condolences explained indignantly. "Up de Valera! Isn't that right, boys?" he addressed the subnormal youths, raising his fist in a victory salute. The boys jumped and screamed with delight. They had been understood.

"Can you quieten them down," Ned appealed to Condolences.

"Good lads," Condolences said soothingly. "That's enough now." His words worked upon them like magic. They relaxed and became quiet. They put their arm around each other and smiled benignly on the assembled company. And because it was a Party minibus the assembled company embodied all that was good and holy in the eyes of the O'Hara boys. It was their mother's influence: she had talked her memory into their memories until the Party became

a magic healing influence. Having a ride in a Party bus was better than a ride on a magic carpet.

"Are ye going to have a sandwich with us?" Condolences asked. "I'd say ye're no strangers to a pint." But Julie suggested that they were too young to go into a pub. The people in The Mountain Mire were very touchy because they were always being raided by the Gardaí.

"These lads are well over eighteen. Haven't I registered them both?" Condolences said casually.

The Senator was amazed by this. The youths seemed barely capable of clothing themselves. "You've what?"

"Uh Egg!" One of them, the brighter one, waved at the Senator.

"Their mother wanted them registered," explained Condolences. "She wanted them to vote for the Party. They're not insane, you know, they're only subnormal. They're good Party people, as you can see..."

"But that's all they seem to know," the Senator protested.

"For God's sake, what more do they need to know? Hasn't the Party given them everything they want, free schools, free transport, free shoes, free everything? They're not a bit confused. Look at how happy they are."

"I suppose you're right," the Senator conceded.

"We're here!" Julie shouted as the van screeched

to a halt on the loose gravel. They all looked at the unique slogan of the pub: "The Mountain Mire; have a hot whiskey in the dampest place in Ireland." They went inside. The Senator ordered six pints, seven sandwiches and a pot of tea. The barman's jaw dropped in disgust. He disappeared from the bar, with a tea-towel hanging from his shoulder.

"That shook him," the Senator winked at the O'Hara boys. They smiled back; the anticipation of a pint was something they had experienced before. "We'll be here until nightfall," the carpenter complained.

"Stop whinging," Condolences said. "Don't we deserve an hour off? Have you a train to catch or somethin'?" Young Moynihan didn't reply. Condolences talked to Julie. He wondered aloud if the new owners of the pub were supporters of the Party, of if they were for "the other crowd." The young carpenter suggested that one could never be sure. They'd find out soon enough, he said, when the national collection day came round. The Senator watched from the bar while they relaxed into discussion. He could hear every word they spoke from his perch. He watched them happily, happy in the knowledge that they were getting the only two rewards that the powerless get from politics—a feeling of cameraderie and a sense of delighted conspiracy.

"Four votes, then." Moynihan pointed to the bar.

The proprietor and his tiny wife and two beautiful, black-haired young women appeared from the side hatch, carrying four plates and three raffia baskets. The two silent daughters were stunning, like twin versions of Sophia Loren in her prime; and their beauty was made even more effective, more mysterious, because it had emerged from an unpromising, squalid kitchen. But the pints of beer were even slower in the making, and when they did arrive there was a subdued but definite scramble to claim the one pulled by the landlord himself.

Nearly an hour passed. They ate unhurriedly, wondering if the two beautiful daughters would reappear. Suddenly the interior glass door of the bar was opened. It was an usual event in the lonely glen; too early in the day for a crowd. "Shit," a man said when he saw Ned and the Senator. It was a Coalition worker, Ned recognised him. The man turned quickly, saying, "We'll go into the lounge." But he was pushed inside by his companions. Ned also knew the companions. The Senator knew one of them, a trade-union official. Socialists.

"Ah hello, Ned," the leading man spoke. "How's the tummy, I hear that you've been having trouble." They moved on to the bar. They all had whiskeys, without water, as if to overcome their shock at stumbling into a hornets' nest of the Party. There was silence after that. The Senator watched his own companions finishing their second drinks, less

comfortably. He said that they should go.

"Good day now, gentlemen," Ned addressed the Coalition drinkers breezily as they went out the door. He loved the parting shot.

But they stayed much longer than they'd planned. The atmosphere of the pub held them in their seats. Conversation. Even young Moynihan relaxed and began to tease the O'Hara twins. By the time they got up to go the evening had begun to close in. "We let the light slip away, I think," Condolences said.

"Well, what did I tell ye?" the young carpenter replied. From the look on his face the Senator thought that he had a lot more to say, but was too afraid. They moved quickly along the narrow roads, scattering pools of brown water and grey crows, and weaving between scores of sheep dozing by the roadside with their hindquarters on the warm asphalt. Once in a while they would reach a wall or tree trunk that might support a poster. Then Julie would reverse, cursing quietly because the others blocked her view. Two of them would leap from the van, armed with poster and glue, to deposit an image of the future President. "That'll keep it warm," one of them would wisecrack, leaping back into the van, happier to be inside from the cooling and enclosing mist. Julie switched on the headlights. She was growing nervous.

"There are no more high walls along these roads, anyway. We may as well head for home," the young

carpenter suggested. "We've only ten posters left."

"What about the shepherd's hut, it's not too far from here." Condolences was determined that they should finish the job. The Senator said that there was no point putting a poster there; the hut was fifty yards off the road. No motorist would see it. But Condolences was adamant. He wanted to splash four posters together. He insisted that a splash of colour on a grey wall would attract attention. When they reached the hut, young Moynihan, Condolences and the Senator left the van and walked along the narrow muddy track. The carpenter said that it was irresponsible to plaster four political posters on what was really a private residence. "It's only used during the sheep-shearing," Condolences replied, "it's only half a home." Moynihan pouted sulkily, even as he spread paste on the mist dampened wall. He was on the verge of tears. The Senator tried not to laugh.

"Are you alright, lad?" Condolences asked. He didn't want the young carpenter to return home upset. His mother would be furious, and Condolences was afraid of her.

"I'm fine, fine."

"Then why are you pouting?"

"My pout is intellectual and tactical rather than ethical," young Moynihan replied. Like a threatened kitten, he drew himself up to his full height. Condolences was stunned by his reply. He was sure that Moynihan had insulted him. The two didn't

speak again until they opened the side door of the minibus.

"Only one man will see those posters," laughed Ned after they had all climbed aboard.

"Well, one vote is one vote."

"Except that the man can't read a word."

"He'll remember the image, won't he? Isn't that the true value of outdoor advertising? The image?" the young carpenter asked.

"He'll remember it all right," Julie said. "But he may think that our candidate is wanted for murdering his wife, or for growing ragwort. Sssh! Shush!" She suddenly raised her arm. They all stopped laughing, thinking that she had seen the shepherd, Ruark, bearing down on them with his iron-capped staff.

"Do ye notice those lights behind us? They've been behind us for a long time. I'm certain that they were following us even before we went into The Mountain Mire."

"Jesus, Mary and Joseph. Ghosts. This part of the mountain has a very bad reputation. My mother says that terrible things happened up here during the Troubles," young Moynihan whinged.

"Rubbish," Ned replied. "Have you ever heard of ghosts that needed headlights?"

"It could be something more disgusting than ghosts," Julie said. "I think we should drive back along the road to check on some of our posters."

"Shit. Nobody could be that low."

"You're thinking what I'm thinking." Ned spoke to the Senator. "We should drive back a few miles and see."

They turned and drove back to a wall that they had just posted. The mist had become so thick that they had to leave the van to check the wall. When the Senator saw what had been done he became furious. The Party posters had been torn from the wall and trampled into the ground. The Senator felt that a group of Coalition vandals might have been on the road all day, tearing down Party posters. Julie said that she had noticed a yellow Volkswagen following them earlier on. She thought at first that it must be a tourist, trailing along slowly.

Then Condolences said that he saw the same parked car near the pub when they were leaving. "Coalition bastards!" he shouted, outraged. The young carpenter burst into tears. Even the subnormal O'Hara boys were drawn into the abyss of disappointment and wasted effort; they wailed inconsolably in the rear seat. "Here's my hankie, lad," Condolences said gently, handing young Moynihan a square of blue linen that reeked of tobacco.

"We'll never be able to check the damage. The mist is too thick. A whole vital Saturday wasted."

Because of the new atmosphere of disappointment, Julie's confidence melted away. "I can't see a thing," she moaned. "Not a thing. O God...these roads are

very dangerous. There's a terrible cliff on our left-hand side." They all strained forward to see through the mist. But even with dipped headlights they could see hardly anything. Suddenly aware of the danger, they became as one eye, one ear—most of them had experience of these mountains, and they knew that one also drove by ear in fog, listening to the sounds of the wheels on the grit of the roadside. If one failed to hear an even, crunching sound, it meant that the wheels had begun to drift into the grass margin, the danger area. Beyond the grass margin there might be a sheer drop of fifty to eighty feet into a pool of deep murky water. The mist swirled around the beam of the headlights and nullified their value. That endless cone of mist and the sound of the windscreen wipers harvesting the wet beads from the glass, made them feel a peculiar coldness. It was as if the cold ghosts of the mountain's memory had taken over, and were now directing the progress of their minibus.

"I'm afraid." The young carpenter spoke again.

"Lights behind," Condolences said.

"It's the Coalitionites. Cowards as usual; they're following our rear lights as a guide."

"So that we'll go over the cliff first," the Senator said.

"Thanks," Julie muttered, annoyed.

"The dirty cowards, they're gliding home safely on our backs!" Condolences thumped his seat in anger. His excitement broke Julie's concentration. In

a split second the front and rear left wheels of the minibus skidded off the road. There was a scream, young Moynihan screaming, then several loud screams from the O'Hara boys in the rear. At first they thought that the bus would spin onto its back, but it remained upright as it fell. It rolled down the steep incline of shale and loose earth, eventually bouncing over peat banks and furze bushes until it hit bog-water. It was like falling onto a thick foam mattress that lay on a hard floor—the initial impact was soft, a crushing of glass, lights, then a hard thud as the body of the vehicle made contact with the hard-packed clay. The Party members were showered with crystals of glass from the shattered rear window; it felt like a hail of sand on the backs of their heads.

"Are you all right, Julie! Julie! Julie!...Julie!" from the Senator.

There was a muffled, stunned reply. "OK. My legs are a bit stiff."

"Young Moynihan's grand," Condolences said. "As for myself I could do with a further medicinal pint. Are ye all right?" he shouted to the O'Hara boys.

"Uh Egg," came the loud duet.

"They're fine, thank God," Ned said.

"They're unnatural creatures, like putty," the young carpenter observed.

"The Coalition hacks copped it too," Condolences went on, delighted. "I saw their lights dying out as

we came to a halt. They must be nearby."

"Leave them there to die," Julie suggested.

After a few minutes they scrambled through the shattered windows of the bus. They expected to drop into a pool of standing bogwater. But instead, they got a pleasant sensuous shock. They had landed on a huge undulating bed of wool. "Christ, we've dropped into a flock of sheep. The poor sheep," the carpenter said. The two O'Hara brothers shouted with delight.

"Whose sheep are they?" Ned asked.

"I'd say they belong to the Englishwoman who lives in the castle, the woman who's an actress," said Julie.

"The Party should write an apology to her as soon as possible," Condolences suggested. "Hasn't she got a vote in the local elections?"

"First of all we'll have to get out of this bloody place." The Senator pushed through a group of stunned, curious sheep. They all made their way through the woolly assembly and set out in search of the Coalition men. They found them nearby, as Condolences had guessed, standing around their spiked Volkswagen; drenched, shocked and silent. The Party men's first impulse was to beat the living daylights out of the vandals. But the sight of these three adults out of their depth, deep in Party bogland, soon created a peace-line of sympathy. Ned could see that one of them, Jim Cochrane, had a very bad gash

on his forehead. The impact of metal on Party territory had exacted its own punishment.

Cochrane found his voice. "We're...we're OK. But I think I'll never the same again. Ever again." Ned tried to reassure him. "Shush now, it was only a bad tumble. You'll be as right as rain tomorrow."

"I've heard about accidents like this. People die of exposure up on these mountains. We'll never get out of here alive," Jackie Power, a local trade union official, cried.

"Easy to know who has money in the bank; afraid to die and leave it all the taxman. Is that it?" the Senator teased him.

But Power was bereft. "It's no laughing matter," he said.

"The sheep are moving!" young Moynihan shouted. "They're starting to climb, look! We should follow them to safer ground."

"Maybe the bog itself is moving," a Coalition man said nervously.

Frightened by the disembodied voices, the sheep pushed more hurriedly up the steep incline. One could hear the squelching of mud, the crash when stones were dislodged, a rumble of hooves as the more frightened animals made wild attempts to reach the dry altitude. "Follow the sheep!" Ned ordered, and everyone took off in pursuit. After about ten minutes of scrambling and slipping, all of them reached the safer margin of the roadside. The

sheep stood around the roadway, as if they expected a vote of thanks or some small honorarium.

"What do they want?" asked the carpenter, becoming frightened yet again.

"Companionship," Ned quipped. The others stood around and brushed themselves. They all wondered what the next move should be. It was very likely that, by now, the non-arrival of the O'Hara boys to wherever they had been going would be noted. It was also likely that their family and the Gardaí would be searching the mountain roads with fog-lamps and whistles. The best thing to do would be to follow the sheep as they moved along the roadway. At least that way they would be unlucky to wander off the road in the fog. The sheep were already moving.

"Follow them," the Senator said quietly.

"Sensible words," Cochrane noted. Without further discussion they all moved along. By now all their jackets and light summer shirts had become saturated with sweat, bogwater or mist. Their limbs had become weary with shock and from the terrifying scramble onto the road. Fear had also drained their reserves. They brushed their hands over the fleece of the sheep to dry them and get some comfort. How many sheep had their vehicles killed? It was curious that they had heard no sharp cries of pain, nothing but the mutter and bleat of disturbance. The young carpenter walked beside the Senator. Julie was walking just behind them. The Senator could hear her breathing. He

wasn't very worried about her because she was wearing a mackintosh and she was very fit. Cochrane moved up front beside the carpenter.

Young Moynihan, finding himself beside a member of the government party, grew in confidence and decided to be friendly. "Mr Cochrane," he began, "Mr Cochrane, do you think that the EEC will be bad for Ireland?"

The Coalition man was silent for a while. When he did reply he spoke slowly, deliberately, like a drunk man. "This country will never get rid of some of its old-fashioned notions. Never, despite the EEC and all of the modern world. Take your own Party for example..."

Condolences, who had been listening, couldn't stand this. "Chrissake, men!" he shouted from among the undulating ranks of wool. "Will ye shut up talking about politics. Ye'll frighten the sheep."

Cochrane turned round to look at him. "Ah, Condolences, are you happy there among your own?" he said.

Then a cold hand slipped into the Senator's. It was Julie. She had come to join him in the front line, where he was putting all his trust into the native integrity of the sheep.

# FOURTEEN

Following the sheep, they made progress slowly through the dense fog. The young carpenter bawled out now and again as the idea of death in the mountains crossed his mind. The O'Hara boys, on the other hand, tried to challenge the darkness with cries of "Uh Egg! Uh Egg!"

After about two hours they were met by the strong fog-lights of two rescue vehicles. One was a police-car with a garda and the local sergeant, the other a Land-Rover carrying slightly drunk farmers who had attached themselves to the police search.

"Ten of us here, not counting the sheep!" Condolences shouted.

"You'll have to explain this," the sergeant said. He was a small man, and looked even smaller as he walked within the arc of the lights. "I hope you haven't abandoned your vehicles. Abandoning your vehicles is a dangerous business. Especially on narrow roads. Especially in fog."

"Come now, Sergeant," Mr Cochrane moved to greet the Law. "Am I the kind of person who abandons a vehicle? One doesn't abandon one's property."

The sergeant took a step backwards when he heard this. "Ah, Mr Cochrane, I didn't recognise you at once. Did ye have a crash or what?"

The young carpenter couldn't contain his excitement at being rescued. He burst into tears again and blurted out that they had gone right over a cliff, that they had driven right over it, and that he had lost his little red notebook with all the names and maps and addresses...

"Take it easy now, lad. We'll find all those things when the fog clears," the sergeant was happy to reassure him. They all stood to attention then while the rescuers turned their vehicles around on the narrow road. None of them would risk going over the edge a second time. Then all ten of them piled in, four into the police car and six into the Land-Rover. "We've never had two cars going off the road on the same day," the garda said. "We'll have to take statements from everyone."

"Not today," the Senator groaned, "we're too exhausted. We've all had a bad fright. We might have been killed..."

"That's exactly why we need statements," explained the garda. "By the way, who was driving?"

"Ju..."

"Ned was!" The Senator interrupted young Moynihan before he got Julie into trouble with the Gardaí.

"You have a licence to drive a minibus?" the

young garda addressed Ned. He was new to the district.

"Since before you were born," the Chairman replied sourly. The young garda was put in his place and Julie was covered.

When they arrived at the barracks they were met by Mrs O'Hara, who was holding flasks of tea and sandwiches for her boys. Julie's father was there too, looking old and frightened. Cochrane's wife stood at the door, wrapped in an expensive fur coat. "Dear, I thought you might be cold," she spoke to her husband, ignoring everyone else. "I brought your little Astrakhan collar, we should never have detached it from your jacket." She also handed him a small silver flask.

"Brandy," he said, "you're a delightful woman."

"Look at that for service," Condolences complained. "Where's my missus, I ask you? Where is she? I could be dead for all she cares."

"She's probably worried sick, at home by the phone," Julie said. Then the lesser mortals settled down to a cup of tea from the bottomless samovar of the Garda barracks.

The sergeant asked casually how the accident had occurred. He wasn't even remotely interested in the possibility of a dangerous driving charge. What fascinated him was the close proximity of the rival party groups on the same lonely mountain. "There must be a powerful population of voters in them

hills," he joked. "A population of adults that's well-hidden from the police."

They responded to his sarcasm with savage stares, making him regret his indiscretion. "We were pasting up new posters of our presidential candidate," Ned explained. "That's what we were doing. I don't know what Mr Cochrane's group was doing. Maybe he'd like to explain to us."

Cochrane wasn't a bit unnerved by Ned's challenge. The brandy had steadied his nerves. He said that his party and the Labour men had heard rumours that vandals were interfering with Coalition placards. They had gone into the hills to investigate. This was why they had stayed so close to the opposition vehicle; they suspected Ned's group were the vandals. He seemed to convince the Sergeant, so brazen was his dishonesty. Both Ned and the Senator laughed into his face.

But Cochrane came back even more boldly: "I'm surprised at you, Senator, a professional man, a teacher, not like some of the yahoos in your party. I'm surprised that you should laugh at so serious a business as the destruction of election material."

"Hypocrite and scoundrel!" Condolences shouted.

But Cochrane remained silent. It was his wife who spoke. "My husband hates to hurt people's feelings," she explained, staring at the Sergeant. "It is so difficult, nowadays, to be direct. One doesn't wish to imply that one's neighbours are vandals." The

Party men knew that they couldn't prove that the Coalition men had been vandalising their posters. But they could prove that they had tailed the Party's minibus in order to get out of the fog. They could say that without fear of contradiction.

And they did say it. For the few remaining days of the presidential campaign they told everyone about the cowardice of the Coalition men. How they had ridden upon the Party's efforts to get out of the mountain, how they had pushed the Party bus (well, almost) over the cliff. Those voters who refused to accept their malice at least accepted their cowardice. It was a dishonourable thing to stay close to a leading vehicle during fog: that was a strict code of the mountains. One kept far away from another car, not out of any concern for safety, but to show that one had found one's way home. Anything else was cowardice.

Four days later the Party's candidate won the presidential election. Once more the Party bathed in the sweet waters of victory. It was an excuse for everyone to feel excited again, to let off steam, to recollect once more the Party's triumphant capabilities. After the election the celebrations lasted two days. On the second night there was a get-together at Ned's house. The Senator was pleased to see Julie there; further proof that she had come back into circulation. Her father was with her. The Senator noticed that the white top she wore accentuated her

lovely tan, while it quenched the redness of her hair. They exchanged glances and meagre signs from the moment she entered the house. She was seated firmly beside her father and Rebecca, who jostled her while they exchanged jokes and rumours. For most of the night the Senator sat on a sofa with his nephew, Eamon, and Jennifer Dineen. Mrs Dineen was hovering somewhere in the background. The Senator couldn't see her, but he could feel the menace of her gaze whenever the two youngsters touched each other. He regretted that Eamon was using so much of his energy, his teenage concentration, on this Dineen girl. It was a romance that also worried the boy's father; they both feared that he might abandon his intellectual work for the mere dissipations of happiness.

"I can feel my blasted mother somewhere. She's just behind us, isn't she?" Jennifer turned to the Senator.

"Wh...what...Oh, she is...yes."

"Will you look around for us, just to see where she is exactly?"

"You won't get out of here without being noticed," he warned her. "If that's what you're thinking of."

Jennifer giggled, saying that her mother was a cruel bitch.

"Don't be stupid," he said, teacherly.

"You're an old prude too. For an Irish politician, you're fierce conservative about lust. Up in Dublin

they're always hopping off each other." She was annoyed, a tough, brazen little thing. "We'll escape, just you wait."

The Senator decided to stand up, to leave them to the mercies of her prowling mother. He made his way to the kitchen. He found refuge and an electric kettle in the corner. He had to search most of the presses before he found the teapot. Julie came in while he poured the boiling water. "Back on the tea. You must be bored."

"Something to keep me going. Rebecca seems to be in good form."

"Don't talk. My ears are still ringing. For the first time in weeks she's able to forget Ned's illness...You were babysitting, I could see."

"I always end up holding the babies," he joked. "That's what I get for not drinking. People think that I'm bursting with virtue." Then he added, "You look lovely. That white blouse makes you glow with health."

"It's not a blouse," she explained, "it's a top." She was surprised by the suddenness of his compliment. It wasn't even patronising like most male compliments, but sincere, vulnerable, an expression of feeling. "I've been going to the beach every day. Because of the good weather I start work early and finish early."

"Would you like if the two of us went there, on a picnic?" he asked quickly. "Maybe next weekend

or the one following. Or tomorrow. It would be nice to talk to you without the fear of interruption...Here, have a cup while it's hot." He poured the tea.

"That would be nice," she replied. "Next weekend, maybe. Wait'll I see."

"Christ, don't wait and see. You won't go then."

"OK. How about next Saturday?" She was about to burn her lips when he said, "There's no milk."

"Oh, my lips are bad enough."

"Your lips are perfect." He wanted to tell her how nervous he was about talking to her. How mean he must appear after the long silence of spring. He thought about his nephew and Jennifer outside in the sitting-room, how new they were to love, and how strong.

He felt ashamed of his own feelings, and his almost adolescent inability to handle love. In some ways his nephew was more mature. Julie sipped her tea while he thought like this.

Then Ned walked into the kitchen, looking frail. More than frail, the Senator thought; Ned's face was blue. "Good to see you two at it again," he laughed. Then, when he saw how they stared at him, he said, "I know I look weak. It's the drugs and the treatment. It knocks the stuffing out of me. Come on outside and sit down. Bring your tea!"

When they returned to the sitting-room they saw that Mrs Dineen had sat down between Jennifer and Eamon. The two teenagers looked bored and tired,

while Mrs Dineen seemed happy and animated. The Senator couldn't resist the temptation. "Enjoying ourselves, are we?" he asked.

"Very much, Senator," Mrs Dineen replied. "My two companions here are as quiet as mice. They're very shy you know. In my time youngsters were full of talk." She put her arm around Jennifer while Eamon looked on, disgusted. Ned found a wicker chair by the window and flopped into it. Neither Julie nor the Senator could find a vacant seat, so they leaned against the window-sill. Ned had very little to say. He was obsessed by his illness. The Senator felt that that was the sign of a beaten man.

Scorching sunlight. That Saturday was a beautiful summer's day. The beach where they picnicked rose steeply from the sea towards a copse of old and decrepit oak trees. They walked along until they found a patch that was almost deserted. A pile of dead wood, thinnings of oak that had been barked and bleached by the sea, provided a wind-screen and privacy. The Senator could see a child playing over a hundred yards away, following a beach ball into the water. The child rescued it from the crest of a wave and fell backwards, screaming, triumphant. Julie's skirt fluttered in the cross-wind. "I'm getting out of these." She unzipped herself and her skirt dropped to the ground, revealing the bottom of a mauve swim-suit. "Stop looking disgusted. I know

this is a terrible colour."

"Suits your hair."

"It does not." She folded her skirt neatly and stuffed it into her cane shopping-basket before undoing her blouse. "You can unbutton me if you want." She was on her knees. She straightened her back and threw back her hair, saying that the breeze was lovely. Her erectness emphasised the fullness of her breasts, which thrilled the Senator. He undid her, almost tearing a button away. "I'm off for a swim," she said. "Last in is an ass." She bolted towards the waves.

The Senator stripped quickly. But Julie was already bouncing in the waves by the time he reached the water, laughing and kicking. He remembered that she was always confident in water. He was less sure of the sea, but he ran, then paddled, then ploughed through the waves to reach her. "Lovely. Listen, if you want to swim around a bit I'll get the food out."

"Ah, stay." She splashed the water into his face. She was happy because, here in the water, almost naked, they could be familiar and friends.

"Right!" He pushed her backwards into the water, making her gasp. She swallowed some brine. "Thug!" she gasped. He swam away and she followed.

"Gerald"

"What?" Standing up to their elbows in water, barely standing, they embraced. The Senator thought that she was impressed to feel him hardened, aroused,

against her. His left hand was below her buttocks: he was pressing them with his arms, which made her seek his tongue hungrily.

"You're a hard ol' politician all the same," she joked, breaking away, swimming towards the food. He followed her. They had brought enough sandwiches to feed a battalion.

"I haven't been to Mass since before Easter," she said. "I think I've lost all my religion."

"What makes you say that?"

"Being with you now. It's the first time that we've really been alone—and happy—in months. Since we had our falling out. I know you won't believe this but I haven't been to Mass since you lost the nomination for the Dáil. Most of those votes were promised to you, the nomination was yours by right. Anyway, I've been too full of bitterness to face the Church. That's all. I just can't believe in God's fairness."

"You shouldn't take things to heart like that, Julie. Nothing is worth that."

"You're worth that. You're worth that much to me," she said openly. She trusted the moment. She sank back into the rug, overturning a flask of coffee. "Shit." Again he told her not to be worried about politics. The loss of the nomination was just a temporary setback. He was certain that no new candidate would gain the seat for the Party. And after the next election there would have to be another

completely open convention—Allingham and his cronies couldn't overturn that rule. He felt sure that he could get back, even if he lost the Senate seat in the meantime, which was very likely. He had done very little work on behalf of his vocational panel; anyway it had been his Party connections that had won him the seat on the educational panel. When he had finished his little speech Julie was silent and serious looking. Doubt was written all over her face. She always felt that he had an irresponsible degree of optimism. Presumption was what she called it.

"I think we should get married. Seriously," she said out of the blue.

The Senator didn't want that solution. "I don't want your love to be a consolation prize. That's hopeless, do you understand? I feel I won't be ready for us to get married until I win a blasted election." He smiled at her, as if he expected her complete acceptance; then he kissed her on the forehead. "Let's go for another swim."

"Don't dismiss me like that, Gerald. We should get married. I know we should."

"Will you wait—please wait for one more campaign. I have this feeling; it may be stupid... irrational...but it's my fear; that I'll lose my ambition if I get married now. I'll become domesticated, too happy, like my brother, Eamon's father."

"Maybe it's simpler than that, maybe you just don't love me." Her beautiful hair rose and fell in the

sea breeze. She got up from her rug and began to tidy the lunch things. He was silent.

"It always ends this way between us," she continued. "Us fighting over marriage...us never finishing what we should say..."

"Well, I'm going for another dip," he said casually; as if he hadn't been listening to her.

"Do what you like, Gerald."

The Senator paddled along the water's edge for a few minutes, kicking at the waves and glancing back in the hope that she would follow him. But she remained on the rug, tidying. He bent to pick up a small shell from the water. Julie collected shells; he knew that the sight of them usually made her happy. As he crouched in the water he saw his own reflection, constantly breaking up. "I will be a deputy," he said to himself. "I must, must do it on my own." While he poured the sea-water from the shell he was filled with the premonition that he wouldn't get through. It was then he left the water. "Here are some shells, pink ones," he said to Julie. "If you put them to your ear they might tell you their life stories."

"Christ. I hope they're happy ones. For a change."

"Ah, come on, Julie. It's not the end of everything. I just feel that the timing isn't right." He dropped the shells into her outstretched palm. One slipped and fell between her thighs. "Listen, I'll phone you about it—about us—tomorrow. Is that fair?"

"I don't mind." When she stood up the shell fell

away. He picked it up. "You mean you don't give a damn," he said.

"I meant, if you really want to talk." She began to walk towards the car. "Will you take the rug?" she added. The sun was still very hot. The best part of the summer's day still stretched before them as they walked away.

# FIFTEEN

The Senator found Ned sitting up in bed, propped by pillows. Ned was dozing, his face twitching in the harsh white light of the room. The neon striplight made a low buzzing noise, like a fly trapped in a jar. Before Ned became conscious of his presence, the Senator sat on the wicker chair beside a green dilapidated locker.

"Gerald! Senator! Hello." Ned raised his hand in greeting. The Senator shook it firmly. "I'm worried about those reports."

"What reports?" the Senator asked. Then he remembered the two small paragraphs in a national newspaper about disturbances in the local Party. The newspaper's stringer in the country was being fed information about discontent by either Allingham or Conory. One of the items had reported criticism of the Party's "backtracking" on its Republican principles. Ned felt that it was Allingham's work; the item had his particular flavour.

"Don't be worried about them. Nobody takes any notice of newspapers."

"People read papers, especially local items. It's amazing how quickly people are scandalised by

mentions of their own districts. People are beginning to feel that there's a split in the local organisation."

"To hell with what people feel. We must carry on regardless."

A young nurse entered the room and, ignoring the Senator, asked Ned how he felt. The Chairman said that he was fine. "You're sure?" she asked again. He was sure. Then she left the room, without acknowledging the Senator's presence.

"Come here, Gerald." Ned tapped the blanket as a signal for the Senator to move closer. When the Senator sat on the bed Ned talked more freely. "I'm worried about the newspaper items from an internal point of view. Listen, I don't give a shit if the Coalition people are laughing at us. Let them laugh. But if the national executive—our own people—in Dublin take these things seriously we'll lose our good standing in the Party. Three times since the fucking Arms' Trial in 1970 we've been told to clean up our constituency. We've been told to freeze out the Republicans. How many times have we been told that, how many? People like Conory and Allingham have a vested interest in embarrassing the Party over Ulster. As far as the national HQ is concerned you and me, and the other moderates, are seen as the real hope of the Party. But, Gerald, only as long as we can keep the lid on the Republicans."

"You shouldn't worry about this, Ned." The Senator looked at Ned intently. "How are you feeling?

How are you?"

"Forget about me. I won't see another election."

"They'll stop the thing from spreading. You'll see."

But Ned wasn't interested in his illness. He felt that he had already lost that argument. "I wonder who's writing for the newspapers?"

"Palmer comes from a Labour background. He's the reporter responsible, I'd say."

Ned grabbed the Senator's coat-sleeve. "Get my tobacco in the locker, will you. And fill the pipe. Pack it well." He pointed to the pipe propped up against an unopened Lucozade bottle. The Senator filled it with tobacco flakes, packed it, then lit it while pulling weakly at its stem. Ned took it and puffed a few times before speaking again. "Keep a copy of the news-items. You might find a way to link it with Allingham in the future. You must become sharp. I'm not doing well."

"You'll see us all to the grave yet," the Senator replied stupidly.

"You must develop a cutting edge." Then, "Julie was here."

"Oh?"

"Yes, indeed. My God, but she looks well. She was worried over the rumours about the creamery. She thinks it will be the first casualty of the EEC. Have you heard anything about it closing down?"

The Senator admitted he knew about it. It was

more than a rumour. As a result of EEC rationalisation all the workers would lose their jobs, even Condolences.

"We went into the EEC in order to get more jobs."

"I must admit I always had my doubts about its value."

"Julie's a big European fan, anyway," Ned continued. "She's decided to apply for one of those administrative jobs advertised in the *Examiner*. She could be moving to Brussels."

The Senator was shocked by this. Julie had said nothing to him; nothing definite. He revealed his anxiety. "Did she actually say that to you? Seriously?"

"Oh, she did. Those could be very good jobs. She could double her present salary. Wasn't she made for a job like that? And she might be able to buy a husband with all that money. She won't have to wait around for some delinquent Irishman." He gave the Senator's arm a blow with his fist.

"What about her father? I'd say she's only pretending."

"Pretending my arse," Ned replied. "Look at those lovely photographs a friend of hers sent over." He pointed to a long white envelope. "When I told her you were coming to see me she said she'd leave them so you could have a look. I told her you might like to see where she was going to live."

The Senator took the envelopes and studied the photographs. He recognised Helen Doocey in some

of them. She used to attend Party meetings with her uncle when she was going to school. The city of Brussels was older than he had imagined. "Was it Helen Doocey that told her about the job?"

"The jobs were advertised in all the papers. But I'm sure Helen is pushing her to make the move. Weren't you in college with her?"

"No. That was her sister. Eileen. A wild woman."

"They're a wild family. Julie won't be lonely anyway." Ned looked pleased. The Senator studied the photographs again. The streets of Brussels looked very clean, German rather than Belgian. Julie would like that. She loved neatness. He could feel Ned's eyes searching his face for signs of emotion.

"She'll never leave her family, her home-place."

"She's not afraid of change," Ned insisted. "Begod, she's not."

"She's serious so."

"She's serious alright," Ned repeated. "She was always a serious girl. No messing around." Then he began to laugh. He laughed until he began to cough; a combination of weakness and pipe smoke. The Senator was amazed by this fit of good humour. "I'm sorry for laughing, Gerald. I'm sorry, boy. But you have to admit—you deserved a good kick up the arse from Julie...Well? Admit it."

# PART III

# A WINTER OF COALITION

# SIXTEEN

"The Coalition women have taken over everything. It'd make you sick. Where were they for the last sixteen years when the going was tough?" Mrs Dineen vented her anger in Rebecca's presence.

"It's true, they've devoured the local committees. There are even two Coalition wives on the pensions board."

"Now that their husbands are government deputies and councillors there'll be no stopping them. You know they have even taken over our religion."

"What do you mean?" Rebecca was puzzled.

"Those charismatics. They've become leading lights in the charismatic movement." Coming from Mrs Dineen's lips the information sounded sinister. Rebecca said that when she first heard of the charismatic movement she thought it was a new dance-craze, like the samba or hucklebuck. "Bless your innocence, Rebecca," Mrs Dineen replied. "It's a rich woman's Legion of Mary. It has nothing to do with religion, you have to know all about the Bible. The poor women of our Party are not welcome."

Yet, the two women decided to attend a mass rally

in Dungarvan. Rebecca was intimidated by the atmosphere, but Mrs Dineen persuaded her to stay—even after a woman jumped at them shouting "Hallelujah! I'm saved!" in an American accent. Rebecca knew that the woman was only a shopkeeper's wife from Hallgrove.

"I just don't believe the Holy Spirit is American. America wasn't there when Jesus was around," Rebecca shouted.

"Oh, it was, it was," Mrs Dineen replied emphatically. "America was full of Redskins then. The Holy Spirit was everywhere." She gripped Rebecca's arm. "Don't go away yet. The place is full of rich women!" The two of them were pushed and jostled by the enthusiastic crowd.

One woman noticed that Mrs Dineen still gripped Rebecca so she pushed towards them, throwing her arms outward. "Oh, sister, share your experience. Share it!" She hugged Rebecca, but in doing so scratched Rebecca's face with a massive sharp diamond that hung from her ear. Rebecca's face bled, but the woman didn't notice this. "If you're having an experience, share it," she repeated. Then another woman moved towards them.

"Hello, hello, are we having a happening here?" A young curate with a dirty beard who was (Mrs Dineen knew) a Labour Party supporter, approached them hungrily.

"We're having nothing; you'll get no happening

here," Mrs Dineen replied boldly. "Mrs Kenny's face is scratched and bleeding."

"Oh!" He turned away then towards a promising group of young women who had gathered around a Franciscan with a guitar. The sound of numerous badly-tuned guitars wafted across the hall. Rebecca thought that it all sounded vulnerable, yet new as the Party's defeat. Her face was very sore, but there was no consolation here.

"I don't see anyone from our own Party here," Mrs Dineen complained. "Not one person. These are all big shots."

"God bless them, they need some kind of religion." Rebecca rubbed her hand along the line of the facial pain. "Jesus, I'm still bleeding. That woman was carrying half a South African mine on her ear."

"The poor aren't wanted here."

"The poor were never any good for religion. They can't afford to give the priests a good time. That's what I think."

"But the priest with the dirty face; he was a Labour Party man."

"They're not the poor," Rebecca said wistfully. "They're just educated people." She turned around and made her way through the side exit of the hall. Mrs Dineen followed. When they stepped outside into the open air they breathed deeply, and shook themselves violently, like animals leaving a river.

"There were no secrets to be given away there

today," Mrs Dineen said.

"What do you mean?"

"I mean some people often tell terrible secrets as a result of the Holy Spirit. Mrs Connolly of Toorlyra, for instance. Did you not hear about her? She told everyone that she was pregnant even before she married. And pregnant by another man, not her fiancé. She went to England to get rid of it. Isn't that disgusting? She has some neck to appear in public after that."

"Isn't the Holy Spirit amazing?" Rebecca answered, shocked. She knew Mrs Connolly well.

"Everyone was talking about it after last month's charismatic meeting."

"I'm not going back there, ever." Rebecca climbed into her Volkswagen. Before starting the engine she gave her wounded face a final dab of spit and hankie.

The Coalition wives spread their energies into other activities. One of the pet projects of that autumn was a scheme to bring twenty Catholic and twenty Protestant children from the "troubled" areas of Ulster and house them locally for a few weeks. It was felt that the children would be won over from sectarianism by the generous tolerant atmosphere of the charismatic South. Armed with the confidence of their husband's political victories, the Coalition women felt all-powerful at this stage. When the project was first suggested at a public meeting there were grumbles from the Party—not because the Party

was excluded from membership of the steering committee, but because it had some real contact with the situation. The Party knew about the strength of hopeless feelings in the North, their degree of integrity.

"Stupid, bringing them children here. They'll go back to the same old thing." Ned was sitting in one of his minibuses, awaiting the arrival of the Irish Army convoy that had brought the visitors from the Ulster border. He hadn't wanted to be part of the daft project; yet he didn't wish to be seen as someone uncaring and unchristian. If the Party pulled out of this it would have handed the others a significant moral victory.

Condolences was sitting in the front seat beside him. "I wonder if they've seen tractors before? Aren't they all townies?"

"Sure they have. Won't they see tractors on the way from Belfast? A lot of them probably have aunts and uncles on farms."

"I suppose you're right."

Ned's was the only minibus parked at the town square. But there were many tractors and Land-Rovers. Twenty farming families had agreed to take the children: one Protestant and one Catholic child would be housed in each home. Ned's minibus was the luggage transporter. After an hour a small convoy of trucks arrived. The children scrambled out into the cool autumnal twilight, subdued and suspicious

like bonded slaves. "God help them," muttered Ned. He opened the side door of the bus to begin taking the luggage. Carrying the cases was Condolences' job because Ned was too frail now. The children were lined along the footpath and told to call out their names. Their host families had already chosen their guests, so an apologetic, awkward farmer would step out to claim his charge. Mounting the tractors and Land-Rovers, they disappeared into the semi-darkness.

For most of the two weeks after that, it seemed that the Northern children had disappeared completely: the South had opened and absorbed them. Each family guarded its own children jealously. Sometimes a strange pair of children would be seen at the local creamery, or at the post office. People used to play guessing games, trying to guess which was the Protestant and which the Catholic child. Some farmer's wives compounded this game by dressing their refugees in the same jumpers and pants or skirts, like twins. The game was unending, because most people were too polite to ask a child the burning question. Those who were brave or heartless enough to ask were usually greeted with the same mean and poisonous reply: "Fuck Off!"

The Senator, back in his class-room after the summer holidays, noticed a gradual unease; there was a trivialisation, even an abandonment, of the Republican past. His night-time work with the

teachers' union and his continuing role as a senator, brought him into contact with many classrooms throughout the country. He noticed the removal of all the poster photographs of the heroes of the 1916 Rising. It was Mrs Hussey, the junior teacher, who seemed most interested in this. She offered her own explanation one afternoon while the Senator was rooting in his desk for an important letter he had received from the secretary of the Vocational Teachers' Union. "It's like this," Mrs Hussey explained, "we're all so in love with the future, the future in Europe, that our past embarrasses us. We're all trying to get the peat-smoke out of our brains. We live in a world of central heating now..."

"It must be deeper than that." The Senator looked up at her. She was still tanned after a healthy summer on her husband's farm. She seemed a perfect image of the healthy young middle-class mother. He guessed that her origins lay in a Fine Gael family. "It has to be deeper than that," he continued. It has a lot to do with the cult of this new Coalition, especially that Conor Cruise O'Brien fellow. Who the hell is he? What does he want? He's been rewriting history at a fierce rate since he became a minister."

"Well, the IRA have something to do with it. They've made us ashamed of ourselves with their bombs. It's got even worse since the British published their white paper. We don't like talking about the past now because that's where the IRA came from."

"You're thinking of the old IRA," the Senator replied. "The old IRA always answered to the Dáil; it was the army of the Dáil like the present Irish Army. The IRA don't come from our past, they come from Ulster's past. The attacks on the Catholic ghettos made the Provos. And fifty years of Stormont barbarism."

"It's a dirty word now, Republicanism. No use explaining it to people today. They won't listen. It's just a dirty word."

"We shouldn't allow it to become a dirty word."

"Do we have a choice? It is a dirty word. It's just not a part of modern Ireland."

"We shouldn't just give up our past like that. Would you see a Frenchman giving up his past, his heroes of the Resistance. No, you wouldn't. We shouldn't allow the IRA to take over our past." He found the letter. It had got stuck between the pages of Dineen's *Dictionary*.

"To hell with the past, that's what people say." Mrs Hussey was adamant.

"Ah well, some of us can't learn this new trick of forgetfulness," the Senator said softly. "They can take all our portraits of Pearse and Connolly from the classrooms but our children still live in the state these great men created. We live in the thing they created. No West Briton will ever be able to deny the distinctiveness of our politics." He pointed to a bundle of Oireachtas envelopes, printed matter from

the Seanad, letters from Party deputies, all brown envelopes with the distinctive central black harp. "That's what we are," he said. "That's why they died."

"I never thought you were such a rebel. Everybody thinks of you as a moderate," Mrs Hussey said, disappointed.

"I'm attached to the men of 1916. That has nothing to do with the Provos. The Coalition people are trying to make out that the love we have for Pearse and Connolly makes us Provos. I think that's grotesque, it's treasonable..."

"Treason?" Mrs Hussey repeated with alarm. "That's too big a question for me." She looked at her watch, then at the clock on the wall. "God, I must go. The babysitter will be wondering what's happened to me. Tomás is at the mart in Fermoy today and Declan has a bad chest."

"It was nice to talk to you like this," the Senator said. "We don't often get a chance."

"Well, you're always flying off on Senate business".

Meanwhile, the war wounds of the Ulster children were soon forgotten. Political discussions were ruled out, even on the farms where they were housed. When a child ventured to speak about a particular horror its audacity was quenched with a bowl of ice-cream or a long walk to inspect the fat and shivering yearlings. Ulster was far away. It had become an

abstraction, like God. No Southern host wanted to suffer that embarrassment. Like a child trying to tell someone about an incestuous rape, the Ulster child offered its experience to uninterested adult ears.

Autumn turned sour one night in the second week of this visit. It was the night of the local Anglican Thanksgiving, an important event. At that time of year the richest farmers who were part of the Anglican Communion swarmed into their little church. Tractors, Land-Rovers, even a few Mercedes, were parked along the side-streets near the church. The happiness of the singing Protestants radiated across the town, encompassing the Catholics too with a sense of autumnal achievement. Catholic children leaned against the heavy iron gates to listen to the foot pumped organ and the exotic Englishness of the hymns.

"Oh Jesus! Come 'ere quickly! The place will blow up!" The autumnal peace was shattered by cries of alarm. Fifty yards away from the church there was a sudden blaze of unnatural light. In the centre of this—scorched and peeling like a victim of the Inquisition—was a huge Massey-Ferguson tractor. There was a smell of burning rubber and vaporised diesel. Children were running around the doomed tractor, singing, shouting and clapping. In the smoke and the intermittent, blazing darkness it was difficult to see who the children were. But they were happy. There was a small explosion, a loud cheer. Flames

had licked the feed valves and they blew up. The explosion scattered the more timid village children. The tougher ones, all speaking in Ulster accents, moved closer. They were the Catholic ones, waiting for their Protestant companions to come from the service.

The hooter of the village fire-station was put into action by a concerned citizen. It bawled and wailed in the evening air like an air-raid siren. People ran out onto the street; the sight of the fire service going into action was something that couldn't be missed. The villagers weren't disappointed: from pubs and nuptial beds, from love-nests in motor cars and boats on the river, the part-time firemen bore down on the station. With a flourish of bells and red paint, the tender screeched down Main Street and came to a halt. But by the time they had worked up enough pressure for the hoses the tractor was a smouldering shell. When the water did hit it, it spat and steamed angrily, causing all the children—local and Northern alike—to cheer with a delicious, terrified delight.

"Who owns them blasted children?" a fireman shouted.

"Who owns that tractor is more important."

"It's Commodore Falvey's," a village child volunteered. He's in the chapel with the others. It's the Thanksgiving."

"He'll have fuck-all thanks to give when he sees this," the Fire Captain said angrily. "He'll have a kick

in the arse ready for you lot."

"It was the strangers, the ones from Ulster."

"Round 'em up," a fireman said. But the Ulster children scattered, most of them bolting towards the safety of unlit side-streets. The firemen and several village children gave chase. Two of the Ulster boys raced into a grotto that was built against the high wall of the Catholic church. They were trapped there.

"Come on out," a fireman shouted as he walked into the enveloping darkness. One child came out from behind the statue of St Bernadette, the other began to climb down from the alcove that housed the Blessed Virgin. "Ha! Ye ran into a trap there!" the fireman shouted, pleased.

"I'm Commodore Falvey," a horrified and wan Commodore Falvey addressed the crowd of youngsters. "This is most disappointing after we have all shown you our hospitality." He recognised one of the boys. "I'm deeply disappointed in you, Brendan McIneeny. What will poor Mrs Vandler say?"

Young McIneeny burst into tears, bitter tears. The night stood still, waiting for his explanation. "We were lonesome down here. We were all lonesome, so we wanted to burn something." Commodore Falvey's face became very sad and he put on a kind of burial -at-sea expression. As if to ease his sorrow, the youngster added, "We really meant to burn something small. We meant to burn only the front wheel."

# SEVENTEEN

The visiting children were sent back to Ulster. Hundreds of local people came into town to see them off, to make sure. As for the children themselves—they were delighted to be returning home to a more alert and colourful province. The burning of Commodore Falvey's tractor had been their only unstifled cry. When the civil defence trucks set off the children screamed and cheered with delight.

Not long after the visitors left town other tensions reappeared at a local and regional level within the Party. These tensions developed between the older members of the organisation who were angry with England because of Ulster and the younger ones who were angry with the IRA over the bombing campaign. The older ones had become less pacifist because they were pragmatists. They knew that a mere condemnation of violence would result in the Party being swallowed up in the "law and order" image of the Coalition.

In order to reconcile these different points of view, at least publicly, the Party organised a Grand Youth Weekend in Dublin. In a conference carefully orchestrated by the elders it was hoped that the Party

youth would emerge with a renewed sense of acceptable Republicanism, a sort of green rinse. The fact that there was no youth wing within the organisation didn't deter the officials in Dublin The Party produced its own youth wing within a few days for the purposes of the weekend. This was done quite simply by drawing up lists of sons, daughters, nephews, nieces, of Party deputies, senators and councillors. The more cooperative of these young people were organised into sub-committees for each electoral area. These sub-committees then appointed delegates to the youth weekend. A youth wing, young delegates and a youth conference—all were produced out of the Party hat within the space of two weeks. It was all part of the abiding miracle of the Party.

Eamon and Jennifer were among those "volunteered" as delegates for the conference. "The weekend will cost twenty pounds," Condolences explained. "The Party will pay twelve pounds; you're supposed to pay eight. But don't worry about that, you won't be out of pocket. We might even find a few quid in expenses for pocket-money."

Eamon was delighted. But he had sensed his uncle's growing disappointment with politics. He had shared his uncle's defeat at the hands of the pseudo-Republicans, Conory and Allingham. That defeat had bitten deeply. And his father, the son of a dead deputy, had retreated from politics altogether;

into a cocoon of book-collecting and dreaming. Eamon's delight had little to do with politics. What the weekend offered was an escape into a two-day love-nest with Jennifer.

"Julie is coming too. She wants to do some shopping in Dublin," Condolences said to Jennifer. "I told her that you'd go shopping with her on the Saturday evening. Will you do that?"

"Grand, Da. I will." She blew her nose.

"I'll be a fraternal delegate," Condolences explained. He loved the word "fraternal." He wondered if it was an American word.

Condolences was given the job of driving all the delegates from the area to Dublin. It was a long boring journey. A niece of Allingham's and a daughter of Conory's yapped endlessly about hairstyles and food. The two sons of Deputy Ryan discussed football and rowing between dirty jokes. Their breaths smelled strongly of Guinness, and Condolences had to stop twice, in Cahir and Portlaoise, so that the two sons of the Party could relieve themselves. Eamon and Jennifer sat quietly in the third row of the bus; they held hands intermittently or allowed their thighs to seek out secretive pleasures. They hid their affection from the Ryan boys and from the greater danger area of Condolences. But the Party had given their love the gift of a large hotel.

When they arrived the Senator was in the foyer to greet them. He introduced them to the General

Secretary, who was instantly buttonholed by Condolences about the rumours of higher unemployment. The horrified young Secretary was explaining to Condolences that the Party was in opposition, when a scuffle broke out in the foyer. A group of Communist students from Trinity College had tried to storm the Party meeting, and starting shouting abuse at the party delegates. "Capitalist creeps! Gutter-snipes! Bourgeois Lackeys!" One brave young Communist shouted, "Mother-fuckers! Freedom for Zimbabwe!" That was the last straw. A group of Party youths rushed at him and smashed his face with their fists. The youth fell to the ground, dropping his neatly-printed poster, moaning. A girl with red hair screamed at them to stop. But this had no effect. Eamon could see Tony Phelan, an inter-county footballer and Party councillor, kicking the young Communist in the chest. At that point the General Secretary, a dark, dapper young man, decided to intervene.

"Ah lads, no more of this agitation. he's had enough." He lifted the Communist from the ground. "The Party agrees with the UN position on Zimbabwe," he said cheerily. The injured Trinity man brushed himself ceremoniously, picked up his red and yellow placard, then threw a long contemptuous look at the Party youths.

"Good day," he said in a distinguished, bourgeois accent and, as he exited through the glass-panelled

door, "Vermin!" he spat into the foyer and joined his amazed Jacobin friends.

"There's manners for you," Condolences said.

"He's from Trinity—as daft as his politics," the General Secretary explained.

"We should have burned that place down while we had the opportunity," one of the delegates remarked.

"You're sharing a room with me," the Senator turned to Eamon. "Get your key at the desk. Number 232. There's a seminar in half-an-hour. On patriotism." Rather than taking the lift, which would have been a new experience, Eamon bounded up the stairs with his battered leather bag. He was back in the foyer within ten minutes.

"That room's grand, isn't it? I took the bed near the window," he said.

The seminar on patriotism was addressed by a successful airline executive who had been born in a slum district of Dublin. He was totally uninspiring because he reduced everything to the payment of taxes and a willingness to work overtime without bonuses. But the question-and-answer session that followed was more lively. Gradually the young delegates' questions drifted towards the Ulster crisis. One youngster with a Dublin accent wanted to know the difference between the Party, which was proud to be Republican, and the IRA which was, after all, a Republican army. The young man wanted to know

the essential political difference between the two organisations. The airline executive was at a loss. Eamon, feeling embarrassed for the man, decided to stand up and speak. He walked towards the rostrum and stood behind a copse of microphones. *I'd better be careful of what I say. They're recording this.* He had learned the first lesson of politics. Intervene but say nothing.

"The Party is the constitutional expression of Republicanism, the legal inheritor of the spirit of the 1916 Rising. It believes in the ballot-box and not the gun. The Party is constitutional, not wayward and out of control: that's the fundamental difference."

His legs felt weak. He wondered where the words had come from. There was polite applause. But he saw that the airline executive was applauding effusively. The man was relieved, saved. Instead of returning to his seat, he walked to the door at the back of the hall. The other delegates thought that this was a dramatic intensification of his point of view, so the applause grew louder.

"You were marvellous. You're just the kind of person we need in the party." The General Secretary shook his hand.

"Very good." The Senator was pleased with him too. "It's a great debut. Wait till I tell your father about this. He'll be really pleased. Politics is in the blood, it's really in the blood."

"Dad won't give a shit," Eamon said. He was

wondering what had happened to Condolences. Whether he suspected something.

"He will. Your father will be impressed. Go for a rest now. You've been doing a lot of travelling. But be back in half an hour. I've arranged for a photo to be taken for the Party journal."

The General Secretary gave him a patronising pat on the head. "One of our future leaders."

"Where's Condolences?"

"Looking for Jennifer, I think," the Senator said. "She's supposed to go into town with Julie."

"Ah!There he is now. Any sign of her, Condolences?"

"None. No sight of the little bitch. She's as slippery as a greyhound. Her mother will kill me if she does anything wrong. I'll be blamed."

"Go on up and have a rest before the photographer comes. Wash your face too, it's very sweaty." The Senator thumped Eamon on the shoulder.

"If you see that daughter of mine tell her I'm looking for her," Condolences shouted after him.

"I will."

When he reached his bedroom he knocked. There was no reply. He knocked again. "It's me, Eamon."

She opened the door.

"I was worried sick," she said. "I thought my father would find out that I'd taken the key from the desk. Come in quickly!"

When he closed the door they embraced. "I got

them too," she said. "Eilis Phelan met me in Switzers. She had them from her sister-in-law in England. Wasn't I well organised?"

"Can I see them?"

"She gave me two in case one breaks."

"If one of them breaks that'll be the end of us." It was the first time he had seen a condom. Suddenly, he was scared. At that moment he was more conscious of possessing the condoms than of Jennifer's near nakedness. He should have noticed that her clothes, skirt, blouse, pants, bra, were scattered over the Senator's bed. She was wearing the top of his pyjamas. It was the possession of condoms rather than the promise of sex that carried him outside the law. He was deliberately breaking the law for the first time in his life. His father would be ashamed, saddened. He tried to banish his father's sad face from his mind.

"Do I look good?" She swung around playfully, the unbuttoned pyjamas billowing.

"My God, are all your clothes off?"

"Everything. Can't you see for yourself?"

"I just can't believe this. It's too good. It's a feast."

She came to him then and hugged him aggressively, causing them both to lose their balance. They kissed deeply for a long time, and he felt himself becoming tough. Stronger than the law. She withdrew her tongue to pepper his face with short, playful kisses.

"Let me take my clothes off."

While he struggled out of his clothes she discarded her pyjama top. Then they were completely naked, facing each other. They seemed to recoil in surprise. The total exposure was new even to Jennifer. But that strangeness didn't last long. They lay on the bed together, clinging tightly. He wondered how they should start.

"Would you say I've small breasts?"

"I have nothing to compare them with. I haven't seen many breasts in my time."

He touched them, then slid down along the bed to try them with his tongue. His touching her breasts made her shiver. He wasn't sure whether it was from disgust or desire. She wasn't sure either.

"Will you put that on. I want to put you inside me," she said quietly, not quite sure. "You're very big."

He rolled the condom onto himself awkwardly. She was more relaxed when he turned again to face her. He noticed the long patches of redness on her face and neck where they had kissed. She guided him inwards, and he was amazed at the space she had made for him. She had such a small frame. "Don't go all the way up. It might burst."

She was nervous when he began to grow familiar. Sensing her fear, his own shyness fell away. He thought he'd explode.

"I think I'll explode."

"Yerra, you won't."

The phone rang. They let it ring. They lay together, frozen, lost in the antarctic of the bed-linen. The savage belling of the phone made Eamon feel that someone had been watching. The voyeuristic Party, the adult world.

"You should answer it, love." Her voice was gentle, womanly. It was the first time that he had ever been called love. It was amazing. He withdrew from the sweet, glutinous world. Nothing like this would ever happen again in his life. Her body sucked him as he withdrew. But the phone rang jealously.

"What?"

It was the General Secretary. The Party's photographer was waiting in the foyer. Would he hurry on down quickly, like a good lad. Photographers cost money. By the way, had he seen Jennifer Dineen? Her father was going round the bend.

"I'll be down right away."

Jennifer reached out with her long thin arm. She pinched his buttock. "Do you like me still?" He turned around and sat on the bed. His head was on fire with new things to say. How could he tell her what it felt like?

"I love you, Jennifer."

"Don't be going overboard. We're too young for that heavy stuff."

He didn't argue. But he felt that he had been through the world, that something clairvoyant had flowed through them. He dressed with insane urgency.

His toes got stuck in his underpants and he fell to the floor. Jennifer laughed. "Sssh. Shush! someone might hear!" She left the bed then and started to dress. She had arranged to meet Julie outside the GPO. Julie would say that she'd been with her all afternoon, that they had met outside the hotel. That they had got lost. Julie deserved better things.

"Julie deserves better things," she said.

"My uncle's a fool. Either that or he's queer. Julie is a real smasher."

"Better looking than me?"

"No way!" When he left the room he couldn't wait for the lift. He bounced down the stairs, bumping into the delegates from Toorlyra, and almost knocking over a former minister who had just said *In girum imus nocte* to a group of beautiful air-hostesses. When he reached the green pool of the foyer he saw the photographer, waiting patiently with a pint of Guinness in his hand.

"I'm Eamon Glenville. Are you supposed to take my photo?"

"Well now, laddo," the photographer had a Dublin accent and a Dubliner's patronising attitude to provincials, "you look burned out! Your face is as red as a beetroot. What have you been doing?"

"My yoga," Eamon replied.

"These Southern delegates are a weird lot," the man said as he searched for a safe perch for his unfinished pint. He seemed very worried about it.

"Listen, I'll hold it for you. I'm a non-drinker."

"Are you certain?"

"Honest to God," he lied.

"Another queer Irishman," the fat man laughed. "Hold it low and I'll take your head."

While the man played about with his lights and lenses Eamon thought of Jennifer. By now she would have escaped through the side door of the hotel. He imagined her bolting along the quays toward O'Connell Street, like an escaped mink. He felt that he loved her. There was no other word. He wanted to protect her. It never occurred to him that she might need some protection from their affair. Even if she were always wild, if she lived to be a wild old woman, he would cherish her with his precise, scientific eye.

"Smile," the man said.

# EIGHTEEN

Two weeks later there was a meeting of the constituency committee to discuss expenses arising out of the youth weekend. Eamon thought there might be some trouble because the Senator had asked him to attend. The Chairman, looking thin and even more frail after his recent stay in hospital, was nominally in charge of the proceedings. But he was too weak to prevent mischief from Allingham or Conory. At the start of the meeting, Condolences did his usual trick for the local papers. A minute's silence was observed after the names were read out; the Party would make the most of their memory.

"Thank you, Condolences," the Chairman said. "We need to just run through the list of expenses here and pass them as approved. The expenses concerned are the Party's contribution to the delegates' hotel bills and the Party's honorarium to Condolences for his services as a driver...That was twenty pounds, I think. Is that right Condolences?"

Condolences nodded impatiently. He didn't like to have real cold figures quoted in public. Especially when two representatives of the local press were present. Who the hell had asked them to a meeting

that discussed finance?

"I think that's an outrageous figure for a driving job." Allingham raised his voice in anger, which caused Condolences' face to turn scarlet. "After all, the Party paid for Mr Dineen's stay in Dublin, and the Party also paid for his petrol. It was the Chairman's minibus and he didn't ask us for any money. Money doesn't grow on trees, you know. Especially now that we're in opposition."

"I don't need the money," Ned explained.

"Must we really discuss this?" the Senator intervened

"Yes. We must," Conory interjected. "We must... And what about the payments to the hotel?"

"They're all in order." The Chairman spoke.

"They are not," Conory continued. "For example, and this is only one example, why has the Party paid for the full amount of Eamon Glenville's expenses? Every young person was supposed to pay a proportion, to demonstrate their good faith. That weekend wasn't meant to be a holiday."

"It certainly wasn't," the Senator replied. "Young Eamon made a great impression during one of the seminars. His photograph will be in the Party journal."

"That's all very well, but we can't allow certain people privileges. Anyway, from what I've heard, his contributions were not what the Party needs to hear at this point in our history"

Eamon swallowed hard on hearing this. He wanted

to stand up and defend himself but the Senator placed his hand on his shoulder to restrain him

"The boy is a gift to the Party," the Chairman said emotionally. "He's just like his grandfather. We're losing too many intelligent young people to the Coalition mob."

"They're better off in Labour," growled Allingham. "I think all the young delegates should pay their fair share of expenses—as laid down in the guide for the weekend. And if that's not done all the other young delegates should have their contributions refunded."

"Financial contributions is what you mean, I suppose," the Senator remarked in a droll manner. "Young Eamon was the only delegate from our county who made any other kind of contribution."

"Of course I mean financial."

Ned tapped his pipe on the wooden desk. "No need to be getting hot under the collar about this...it can be ironed out later." He didn't want a full-scale row to break out. There was already enough trouble at the surface for any reporter to start biting. Although he was drifting in and out of the grey world of serious illness, Ned still worried about the Party's troubles being revealed in the cruel light of the printed word. Meanwhile Eamon was ablaze with fury and embarrassment. He had been insulted in public for the first time. He was being accused dishonestly and, worse still, of abusing his position as a Senator's nephew. But his uncle's hand was still pressed firmly

on his shoulder. Although he felt a fool, he couldn't move. Obviously, his uncle felt that it wasn't the right moment to hit at Allingham. Later, perhaps, later.

When Ned tapped the desk with his pipe a second time red ash leapt across the table-top. "Maybe you'd like to give us your impressions of the youth weekend," he asked Eamon. "It's a pity that none of the other delegates saw fit to come here tonight. It would be good for us to hear what ye thought about the whole thing." He smiled at the youngster.

But before Eamon had a chance to speak Condolences stood up. "I'd like to say that I offer my services free to the Party. I haven't yet received a penny in payment for my work." He sat down again, looking like a man who had been betrayed. It was clear from their response that Conory or Allingham hadn't expected this uncharacteristic burst of generosity.

"Condolences must be paid, that's only fair," Allingham said. "It's very kind of him to offer his services free. But we can't have that. A man must be repaid for expenses incurred."

"I agree," the Senator nodded.

"No, no! I don't want a penny of the Party's money!" Condolences shook his head vigorously, raising his hands in the air. "I don't want a penny of yeer money."

"Come off it, Condolences. You must be paid,"

Conory said.

"Not a penny," Condolences repeated. He raised his head in a gesture of suffering defiance. He fended off all offers of comfort.

The Chairman said that it was going to be impossible to settle this matter if Condolences insisted on not being paid. Would he consider a revision of the estimate and acceptance of a smaller sum? That question was nearly an insult: the Chairman was losing his diplomatic touch.

"Not a penny, ever."

"I don't know what we'll do," Ned sighed.

The Senator turned to Ned. "I know what we'll do."

"What?"

"I think we should put the whole question of expenses aside until the next meeting. Chairman, if you could come to some arrangement with Condolences you could let the committee know of your decision. We could ratify a private arrangement... I think that's the best thing. Condolences is a bit upset at the moment."

"I feel insulted, not merely upset," Condolences said, staring at Allingham.

"No insults intended."

The Chairman raised his eyes to the assembled meeting. He received nods of approval. "What about you, Councillor Allingham?" Allingham replied that there was nothing else to be done, that a man

couldn't refuse to be reimbursed. Such a stand would set a complicated precedent. Everybody would feel guilty about claiming expenses. Allingham didn't want Condolences to appear like a martyr in front of the two reporters.

Then the Senator spoke. "We should listen to what Eamon has to say about the weekend."

"Right." There was a bored reply from Conory who had begun to gather his unused papers and his fresh copy of the *Evening Press*. He would have to wait for his public victory over the Senator's clique. Eamon stood up apprehensively. Before he opened his mouth the two reporters stood up and made their way to the door. They were in no mood to report on the sayings of a young brat.

"Scuts," the Senator said loudly when they had left the room.

Eamon's speech lasted nearly ten minutes. Amid cries of "Good lad," and "That's the spirit," he said that he was proud of the Republican traditions of the Party. He ended the speech by thanking the Party for sending him, saying that he had learned things that he never knew before.

"Good man," the Chairman said to him when he sat down. Eamon noticed that there were tears in Ned's eyes: he wondered if they were brought about by his love for the Party, his illness or his tobacco smoke. He would never know.

# NINETEEN

A week later, despite all his protests, Condolences accepted the full amount owed to him by the Party. He phoned Councillor Allingham to say that he'd cash the cheque. Allingham, quick-witted, replied that the Party had to pay all of its debts for the sake of strict financial procedure, but that if Condolences still felt morally obliged to refuse the cheque he could make a donation to the general fund. This infuriated Condolences. He threw down the telephone in a rage and stormed out of the house. "What's wrong with you, what's wrong with you?" his wife shouted after him. But he walked away quickly; walked on until he came to the little square at the centre of the village. He sat on the green bench that was covered with damp red leaves. At that time of day the square was empty; so he had all the solitude he needed to curse and brood.

Other people were having money problems too. The left-wing ministers in the Coalition introduced a new wealth tax. Many rich people felt that that was the thin edge of the Communist wedge. A number took fright and made plans to leave Ireland. As a result of this the local shop-keepers and tradesmen,

small builders, plumbers and gardeners, became even more angry with the Coalition. Those migrant wealthy people were good customers: their arrival into their Irish residences every summer had become a profitable ritual that excited and vitalised the sleepy riverside towns.

Three weeks before Christmas the local co-op creamery announced that it would be closing down. That busy creamery and its ancillary stores employed twenty-six people, including Condolences Dineen. Over half the workforce were members of the Party. The announcement of closure caused a sensation. The local people couldn't believe that a seventy-year-old business connected with agriculture could close down. But the country had joined the EEC. The land now faced the economic consequences of becoming truly "European" and the word "rationalisation" had begun to blow across the Irish landscape, destroying small business and quenching the minute pockets of native confidence.

The Party was very disturbed by the closure announcement because it had such a high proportion of the workforce among its membership. The Senator phoned the senior management with the creameries group and he contacted local deputies and the Parliamentary Secretary to the Minister for Agriculture. The Secretary was unmoved, even hostile. The Senator felt that it would have been better if a local Coalition politician had phoned on behalf of the workforce—

but no Coalition deputies were available. They had probably known in advance about the closure, and were sensible enough to stay outside the constituency until the worst anger had died down. Condolences was distraught. He had never been unemployed in his life: the idea that he might run short of money filled him with terror. Mrs Dineen was frightened too.

The Senator visited the Dineen household to offer support and sympathy. He hoped that the Chairman could accompany him, but Ned had returned to hospital for further treatment. Most people feared the worst at this stage, but their concern remained unspoken. But Rebecca said that she would accompany the Senator, and Eamon was the third member of the group. It was on a Tuesday evening, a time of cold grey mists and insidious showers, that the little deputation called to the Dineen house.

"We thought we'd say hello." Rebecca was the first to speak.

"Is Condolences inside?" the Senator asked, attempting to look over Mrs Dineen's shoulders.

"He is, and Jennifer." She was disturbed by the Senator's lack of good manners. "You shouldn't have taken the trouble to call," she said coldly.

The Senator replied that they just wanted to have a chat, to show the Party's concern and solidarity. The Party was worried about all the workers who had lost their jobs, but Condolences was considered to

be a special case, because he had been such a good friend of the Party. The Party, he said, wanted to see what could be done.

"What can ye do?" asked Mrs Dineen in an exasperated tone. "The Party's not in government, and ye've lost the majorities on all the council committees since Labour joined up with the other crowd. Myself and Condolences have been over this again and again."

"We'll come in anyway, ma'am," the Senator said.

"Do. Come in from that drizzle...Ye'll have a cup of tea?"

When they reached the sitting-room Condolences switched off the television and then returned to his seat by the fire. Jennifer was sitting on the edge of a large brown sofa, still wearing her green school uniform. The movement of so many feet on the old floor-boards rattled the garish ornaments on the television set; even Condolences' two small silver and plastic cups won in an open-road bowling competition vibrated on their wooden stand.

"No luck, Senator?" Condolences asked half-heartedly. He didn't shake anyone's hand or offer any other sign of greeting.

"No luck." The Senator sat down before he was asked, and before the two women had found seats.

"Make room for me there, Gerald," Rebecca said. The Senator pressed closer to Jennifer to make room. The others had to find seats for themselves. Only

Eamon was left standing. He didn't dare to take Mrs Dineen's seat while she went to make tea; that was too close to Jennifer. Instead, he leaned against the chimney-piece and watched while the others spoke. The sight of his girl in her home environment caused his mind to drift. The adults' conversation, interrogation and pleas, empathy and solidarity, seemed to come from a distance like the whine and release of a faraway chain-saw. His eyes focused on Jennifer but she glanced at him rarely, as if she feared their subterfuge. Then he realised that she had just been crying; her eyes were red, swollen. Perhaps she had been crying because of her father's imminent unemployment. Eamon wanted to kiss her mouth, her face. But he couldn't muster up enough courage, or madness, to make that move. He had to look and daydream and feel useless and impractical.

"Mrs Dineen asked you if you'd like tea." Rebecca's strong voice broke through his private mist.

"I won't thanks. No."

"You said you would, at the door. Make up your mind."

"OK. With a lot of milk. No sugar. Thanks, Mrs Dineen." He turned from Rebecca to Jennifer's mother. He wanted to make a good impression.

"You're a good boy," Mrs Dineen said seriously, handing him a frail, translucent cup. "I wish my daughter had some of your steadiness."

"Thanks."

Over tea they discussed the practicalities of finding another job. If Condolences was unemployed over a long period he would lose some status within the community. This would effect the prestige of the Party. People would say that the Party couldn't look after its own; that the Coalition had broken the back of the Party's power. Only the Socialists in the Coalition could use unemployed people to gain a moral advantage. Frugal comfort and even mild manifestations of wealth were the moral status symbols within the Party. They all agreed that something practical must be done, for the Party as well as for Condolences. Mrs Dineen was convinced that there should be a protest on behalf of all the workers in the creamery. "They have families and houses too," she said. The Senator agreed that there should be some kind of protest: a march on the county council offices or the offices of the National Manpower Services, or a campaign of letter-writing.

"Fuck letter-writing," Condolences said. "A protest march is the only thing worthwhile."

Rebecca agreed. She said that marching always made people feel that they were achieving something. That in itself was good.

"It takes people out of themselves, anyway," Mrs Dineen added. "People can become very depressed around Christmas."

"What do you think?" the Senator addressed Condolences again.

Condolences was delighted. "If only Ned were here," he said. "The Chairman could organise anything." Rebecca said they shouldn't dwell on the absence of Ned. They would have to learn to work on their own now. Everyone was surprised when she said that. They expected her to say more. She didn't. Then Jennifer said that she would make some posters for their protest march. The art teacher in school would help.

"I'll help there too," Eamon said. "I can draw straight lines."

"He can," the Senator noted. He said that he would contact all the other councillors. The Party people, maybe even some of the Coalition councillors, wouldn't want to miss the opportunity of taking part in the protest. Condolences said that they shouldn't bother bringing in the other councillors. They were only publicity seekers, he said. But the Senator reminded him that they were all that way inclined.

For several days after that, between the night of their meeting in Dineens' house and the Party's protest march, the Senator waged a private campaign to find another job for Condolences. The managers of the neighbouring creameries had nothing to offer. The two smaller ones expected to be rationalised within a year. They told the Senator in confidence that there would be no hope of finding a job for someone of Condolences' age. The Senator then visited the major hardware outlets in the local towns,

accompanied by a local Party councillor or committee man. Nobody had a job to spare.

"Afraid we're thinking of letting people go," one hardware merchant said.

"A year ago ye were planning to expand."

"That's right. But six months ago we lost our two biggest supply contracts. The hospital and orphans' home."

"The Party lost its majority on those committees."

"I'm not blaming the Party." The man addressed the local official.

"That's the way things are. Now that we're out in the cold."

"You needn't tell me," the merchant sighed.

Between creameries and hardware stores the Senator tried thirty-four potential employers. All of them were thinking of trimming-down rather than expansion. The whole country was trimming down. He felt bitter because of all his wasted efforts, and because of the Party's loss of power. The Party couldn't find the simplest job for one of its members. What would his father say now: his dead father who had built the Party up from the shambles of Sinn Féin and the despondent agricultural sector of the old Labour Party? What would Ned say? He knew what Ned would say. He would say that they hadn't tried hard enough, that they were getting soft. It was an old story. The prospect of having to report to Ned was the bleakest thing.

The day of their protest meeting coincided with the busiest shopping day before Christmas. It also coincided with an afternoon of torrential rain. Water spun off the rooftops of the county council buildings and fell with deadly force onto the flooded pavements. Ill-humoured and determined shoppers barged insultingly through the little group of protesters. Burdened with dripping placards, they were forced off the footpaths and had to stand in the tidal asphalt of the roads. Over fifty people had turned out: half the workers with their wives, a few shopkeepers' wives from the village and a small number of Party officers. The other half of the creamery workforce refused to attend the protest; they were members of a trade union and had been warned off by the Labour people in the Coalition. They still believed that something would be done to save their jobs. There were no major politicians present, no deputies or senior councillors.

They waited for over an hour in the rain before an official from the council would accept their letter of protest. "We have no jurisdiction in these matters, as you know, Senator," he said. "It's a matter that the farmers control; they are the stock-holders."

"Did ye know we were going to lose our jobs?"

"Of course we didn't know."

"Ye did sure. Weren't ye having trouble about the payment of rates?" Condolences shouted. "It's the only thing we have in our parish, the only real

employer."

"Too true! The little town will be crippled without that creamery." The new vet's wife, Mrs Heaphy, moved forward to protest. She was sheltering under a pink Cinzano umbrella that matched her un-smudged lipstick. She was a strong-willed woman and believed deeply in pulling her weight in the community.

"Mrs Heaphy's right, we'll all be crippled!" Condolences shouted.

"I am sorry." The official tried to look sad. Then, as if suddenly inspired, he said, "I must go back inside now. It's still my lunch-break. Flexi-time, you know. Thank you."

"Thank you, Mr Cutin." Councillor Allingham stepped out to the front of the crowd and curtsied to the retiring official. Mr Cutin slipped inside and sealed the chamber doors. He did it neatly and silently, like folding an envelope.

"He said nothing. We got nothing from him!" Mrs Dineen complained. "You shouldn't have left him off like that." By then the water had penetrated through her scuffed leather shoes and her feet were soaking in a pool of cold December rain. She embodied the bad humour and crestfallen nature of the group. "None of the local newspapers turned up. Why didn't they come?"

The Senator, who had been standing on the steps of the council office, walked down to her level. He

offered the shelter of his umbrella. But it was Councillor Allingham who spoke. "It was a bad time to hold a protest march. Most of the people who matter—the people ye could have hit at—are already on holidays. Only the poor local government officials have to work until Christmas Eve. I've been in contact with some newspapers. There will be some coverage in the New Year. It was the best I could do."

"That's my job," the Senator reminded him.

"You didn't do it very well, did you?" Mrs Dineen asked angrily. She removed herself from the shelter of his umbrella.

"It was going to be done later this afternoon."

"The newspaper offices close at four."

The Senator climbed back up the steps to gain some authority. From his perch, the protesters all looked like fat, grey beetles. The weight of the rain pressed down the fabric of their umbrellas and emphasised the frailty of the frames. Only Condolences' face was visible. He never wore a hat and as he refused the effeminate consolations of an umbrella his head was covered with a blue-striped handkerchief knotted at each corner. The Senator himself was well sealed in hat, mackintosh and wellies. He felt slightly ashamed of his cautious dress. As he looked down he knew that they were all waiting for his word of release. Even Allingham had no real interest in an argument. The rain had diminished their drive, diluting and quenching the

fight within. Their hopelessness spread across the afternoon like a terrible squall. He thought of the Coalition ministers in Dublin, and the deputies; their urban, clubbish comforts. They were so far away from all this, the pathetic drenched protest. The Senator wondered if there was any other public representative, any other senator, as far removed from the centre of power as he. He felt that he was forgotten and withering. Rain slipped down the shaft of the umbrella, collecting on his purple hand before stealing under the cuff of his mackintosh. The homely annoyance of the rain made him feel middle-aged and desolate.

"We should get to a warm place," he said finally. "There's not much point in getting pneumonia for Christmas."

# TWENTY

"He's been out of work for seven weeks now." Mrs Dineen cleared her nose, blowing specks of blood on the piece of blue toilet-paper that served as a handkerchief. "I think I must be getting TB. I've had a running nose since Christmas." She was, to use her own expression, nearly destroyed with the flu.

"Those are only the tiny blood vessels in your nose. They bleed when you blow too hard, or over a long period," the young Welfare Officer explained. Fair-haired, with a long purple scar earned in a two-car pile up, he tried to fight his own weariness. He was pale despite two hours of roasting against a two-bar electric fire. The little window of his cubicle was steamed up from the asthmatic electric heat. Beyond the tinted glass a persistent late snow fell. Mrs Dineen had hitched eleven miles in the snow. She had got a lift from a man in a Ford van who was travelling to Waterford to look at some greyhounds, and from another man, a truck-driver in a tall Volvo cab who said that she was a madwoman to venture out into the bleak white day.

"So you're a bit of a doctor as well?" She stared at the Welfare Officer.

"It's just that I've heard it said...about the blood vessels." He chose to ignore her tone. He didn't want to get her going again.

"Pure stupidness," she said.

The tired young man wondered how he could get out of this. He had spent twenty minutes already, side-stepping Mrs Dineen's demands and insults. She was in a terrible state. He understood that perfectly but he had no intention of forgiving her rudeness. Her husband had been out of work since the week after Christmas. He had been made redundant while he was still in bed with the flu. The creamery had folded without warning and without ceremony. In any other organisation there would have been discussions about redundancy pay; but it was the farmers who were the directors of the co-op and they had no time for something as compassionate as redundancy money. The farmers had a long memory. Ever since the farmers' association had broken the labour unions in 1923 they had treated labourers like the scum of the earth. It was an old story, another old story. As far as the Welfare Officer could see Mr Dineen was receiving pay-related unemployment benefit. That wouldn't last long, a few months. But Mrs Dineen felt that she should be getting more—a supplementary allowance, food vouchers, anything—because he was still ill. The official had seen this before. It was the panic of anticipation, an almost bourgeois reaction to unemployment. For the

social services it was worse than real poverty because the applicants were still angry and petulant. Only the passage of time would make them passive. Time and destitution.

"Well?"

"What is it, Mrs Dineen?"

"You fancy yourself as a bit of a doctor then?"

"Just an observation."

"Did you get Deputy Ryan's letter, and Senator Glenville's?" She moved back to the object of her visit.

"They're all here in the file." He reopened the small brown folder. One letter, brief and officious, was typed on cheap Oireachtas paper. The other one, five times as long but containing the same request, was written in the copperplate of a schoolmaster.

"Solicitations like these make no difference." His voice acquired a sudden note of authority. "They don't alter people's entitlements or allow people to jump a queue. They just make our work more difficult in a desperate time."

"A desperate time."

"Yes, a terrible time for us all. But solicitations change nothing. They mean that we have to open all our files again. To do our sums. I don't want to sound cruel, Mrs Dineen, but my union has started a campaign to stop political canvassing of every kind. It creates inefficiency."

"For God's sake, child, politicians are there to help

us." Mrs Dineen shifted unhappily in her chair.

"I'm telling you, they just create trouble. We're living in new times now; there's a different government in power, and we're all Europeans now. We'll have to do things the right way."

"Are you accusing me of canvassing for something I'm not entitled to?" She raised her voice angrily.

"Nothing like that," he said. "You misunderstand what I'm saying. What's happening is this—my union has begun a campaign to tell people to come directly to us with their problems. Not to be bothering politicians who should be getting on with the governing of the country. If you canvass politicians they merely carry the message to us. Like these." He lifted the two letters like a physician raising X-rays to the light.

"Are you saying I must canvass the union so?"

"No. Just us."

"Are you a Communist, son?" Mrs Dineen asked suddenly.

The young man was taken aback. Where had that question come from? He looked at her husband's file as if searching for inspiration there. Then he looked at the anguished woman. He decided to be assertive. "If you must know, I'm a member of the Labour Party."

Mrs Dineen burst into laughter on hearing this, a wild peasant hysterical laugh. She rode on the hard chair as laughter spread across her girth. "Sure God

love you," she said when she caught her breath, "and what has the Labour Party ever done for you?"

"It's the oldest party in this country."

"It doesn't look it," she said. "It's more like a babe in arms. It gets spanked every day by the other crowd in the Coalition."

"The Government is doing its best to pull together. It's what the rest of the country should be doing." He spoke calmly, slowly. He wondered if the woman was having a mild nervous breakdown. He needed to get rid of her: there was still a long queue in the waiting-room, a whole morning's work of battered wives and deserted girls, and lately redundant middle-aged men who hated life for having deposited them in the beggars' place. The men were especially angry because their wives had refused to do the waiting for them. "This will get us nowhere," he said.

"Wasn't it the Labour Party that cut the old age pensions forty years ago?"

"That had nothing to do with Labour. That's all in the past anyway." He began to tidy his desk.

"It may be history to you, child," she replied, "but my grandmother was trying to raise my mother and six other children, without a father."

"I'm sorry, ma'am."

"You are. Tell us another one. Only the Party will look after us." She blew her nose again. The intense and moist winter heat of the electric fire had clogged her nasal passages. While she was blowing the young

official summoned up enough strength to dismiss her. He pointed at the door. "There's a long queue and the day is not getting better...I'm afraid I have to tell you that there's still nothing we can do. Your circumstances haven't changed. I'm sorry that Mr Dineen is still in bed with the flu. But that does not alter the fact that as far as all the rules are concerned he's still just unemployed, not incapacitated. Please God, he'll be up and about in no time."

"Up and about for what? For what? Tell me!" Mrs Dineen yelled at him.

"He has a marvellous record of employment. There will be other jobs. You'll see." He spoke to her in a tone that lacked all conviction.

"Blast ye and yeer Coalition." She rose from the chair and started to button her coat. She pulled a damp pink scarf from her pocket and wrapped it around her head. Its pinkness merged with the high colour of her face; face and scarf seemed like human echoes, satellites, of the radiant electric fire. "Ye'll be out before this year is over. Fancy talk and no money—I've never known a Coalition to be any different." She let out her angry parting shots; showing her anger in the manner of simple people, by ruining her case. She was lost.

"Thank you, Mrs Dineen." The young man's gratitude coincided with her slamming the door, which was made from shaky hardboard. He clipped her application for assistance and the letters from the

Deputy and Senator together, then returned them to the wooden oblivion of the kneehole desk. "Next," he said quietly, as if he were a victim.

Outside, Mrs Dineen made hardly any progress against the snow-laden wind. She had left home without the belt of her coat so that her clothes mushroomed outwards and upwards with every gust of wind. The snow wanted to penetrate to her very soul. Its needles tested her everywhere, its torture nearly defeated her. She wished that she had eaten a large breakfast. But her soul, her memory, had already left the world of pain: it had come to rest in the destitute landscape of her mother's life and her grandmother's house. She relived the suffocating, matt twilight of those who have to live off the state. She hated it. The Party had come to her family in its destitute time, when the Party was young. The family had risen out of its misery with the Party. Her soul hated the young Welfare Officer and his educated attitudes, his hateful Coalition dispassion. This hatred filled her with grief but made her feel warm too, warm with the superiority of those who are despised and left out in the cold, like Mary, the Mother of Jesus. In order not to cry, not to disgrace herself in the hostile county town, she started to say the rosary.

After fifteen minutes she reached the outskirts of the town. Her feet were soaked with melted snow and the calves of her legs had grown numb and hard from the piercing wind. That part of the town was

bleak and alien; the old cottages that stood there had been levelled to make way for an industrial estate. In the Siberian wastes of the unused ground and empty advance factories the snow-laden wind had room to chase and torture the passer-by. She decided to stop for a while to catch her breath and to thumb a lift. Few cars passed by, and those that did were only returning home to the suburban bungalows a few hundred yards away. She decided that she would wait for ten more minutes: if nothing turned up she would go into the new creamery and see if any milk-truck would be driving towards her home. She knew it was unlikely because there was a danger that the roads would freeze. There was no bus service or railway line in that part of the county. All public transport had been withdrawn during an efficiency drive in the mid-1960s.

Ten minutes went by. She already turned back towards the town when a car pulled to a halt at the other side of the road. At first she thought it was someone who had got lost in the snow; then when the driver stuck his head through the window, she saw that is was the Senator.

"Mrs Dineen, what are you doing out in weather like this!" he shouted in anger. But she felt saved. The Party had come for her. She had prayed for that.

"I went to see the Welfare Officer. I thought I could get something. He had your letter."

"Come into the car quickly! Quick!" He pushed

the passenger door open and she got in. "Woman, you're saturated with the snow. You'll get pneumonia."

"I don't care." She removed her drenched pink scarf and placed it at her feet where she felt hot air from the car heater. "The little bastard wouldn't give me anything. He told me to stop asking politicians for help."

"He didn't."

"He did, the little tramp." She placed her hands along the air-vent near the windscreen. "That's better. Did you know that he's a member of the Labour Party?"

"Who?"

"The young Welfare Officer."

"They all are," the Senator said. "All the youngsters who come out of university are Socialists."

"They're no more Socialist than the Queen of England. They hate parting with money."

"I've good news, all the same," the Senator announced. "Great news, in fact."

"Thanks be to God," she said. "You're getting married. Ye've got engaged."

"Ah, not that!" he replied, embarrassed and annoyed.

"What could be good so?"

"I think Condolences has a job. A new job. Isn't that good?" The Senator didn't want to sound too excited. He wanted the pleasure to be Mrs Dineen's.

It might save her from pneumonia. She was silent for a long time, registering the force of the news. Then she said, "Thanks be to God. My prayers." Then she wept, crying openly. The day, the awful numbing day, and the months of her husband's uselessness had been too much.

"It's Mr Winslow," the Senator explained. "When the Chairman heard that Condolences had no job he wrote to Mr Winslow. The Chairman is always lending his car to the Winslows. The American said he'd give Condolences a farm job, beginning next month. They have forty milkers and horses too."

"I thought all the rich people were leaving Ireland because of Red Richie and the Coalition. Aren't the Winslows leaving?" The news was too good to be true. To believe it without making sure would bring bad luck—Mr Winslow would die, he would be divorced, he would leave Ireland, he would become poor. All things would come between her husband and his job. "I don't believe it," she repeated.

"Mr Winslow will be in Ireland for many more years. He visited the Chairman in hospital and told him that."

"I just don't think it's true. These foreigners are always making promises."

"You'd bedder believe it, honey," the Senator said, feebly attempting an American accent.

# TWENTY-ONE

During the second week in March the Senator received a large package from Party headquarters. It contained a series of florid and idealistic documents on health and welfare, published as a result of the Party youth committee meetings in Dublin. The Senator, like every minor politician in every constituency was expected to organise a discussion group within his area to deal with the new ideas. He would have to make a report or appoint someone to make a report to the General Secretary, giving an assessment of the delegates' reactions to the documents. In the old days he would have rejected this paperwork, but now he took it seriously because of the renewed tensions within the Party. The Senator was aware that the young General Secretary was trying to fight off the challenge of potentially violent and ignorant men within the Party. Part of his strategy was to blitz the constituency organisations with discussion papers about everything except Ulster and Republicanism. In forcing Party members to discuss social issues at local level the General Secretary hoped to expose the intellectual poverty of a certain Republican caucus within the organisation.

The Senator had long ago decided for himself who were the violent men within his own constituency. He looked forward to challenging them in terms of health and welfare where he was more articulate and in the know. He got in touch with all the councillors and deputies and asked them to inform their people locally. In fact, the two deputies were missing—one was on a fact-finding tour of the iron-works in Germany, while the other was in Dublin trying to save his property company that had gone into receivership. Their wives, as usual, were holding the fort: they would be delighted to attend. The councillors, on the other hand, spent their lives sitting by their phones.

"Is that you, Councillor Allingham?"

"Who else do you think it is?" Allingham replied sourly. His voice came over the phone like the voice of one shouting through a long metal tube. The Senator told him about the discussion papers. Allingham wanted to know if a committee was being formed. The Senator pointed out that there was no need for a committee. That proved to be a great disappointment. "There'll be no voting so?"

"No."

"Damn!" Allingham's voice skated and somersaulted across the vile electrodes of the post office. "What's the point in going to a meeting when there's no voting? It won't matter a damn what we say if there's no vote."

"Don't come so..."

"Oh, I will. I will of course. I've some sense of public duty, you know."

"Thanks, Councillor. I'm much obliged."

That evening the Senator called on Condolences and Mrs Dineen to enlist their support. Condolences' reaction was the same as Allingham's. "What! No voting? How will you get anyone to go to a meeting that has no voting?"

"It's important to discuss things, Condolences. The trouble with you is that you look on voting as a kind of sport, like scoring goals. There will be hundreds of changes in health and welfare regulations as a result of our EEC membership. We'll have to decide very quickly what we want for ourselves, before we're swamped by foreign regulations. Don't you see?" The Senator looked at Mrs Dineen, begging with his eyes for moral support. She didn't disappoint him.

"I think you're dead right. We haven't been doing enough thinking about the future." She blew her nose.

"Have you still got that cold? You had that at Christmas."

"It's a different cold. It's clearing up anyway. But forget about that—will you listen to what I have to say! We should be planning for the future."

"Good woman...Do you hear that, Condolences? Your wife is ahead of you."

Mrs Dineen promised that Jennifer would come too, in case the crowd was small. Eamon had already been roped in by his uncle and surprisingly, his dour fifty-three year old father had agreed to come as well. Although he hated politics, especially the populist politics of the Party, Eamon's father needed periodic bouts of verbal immersion. The prospect of a discussion on a discussion document was too much to miss.

Mrs Dineen had instinctively reached for the teapot when the Senator arrived. When she was pouring the tea there was the sound of footsteps in the hallway. It was the Chairman. He had returned from the cancer ward. Behind him walked Rebecca, beaming with pride as if she had just raised her husband from the dead. "Good day all."

"Jesus, Mary and Joseph," Mrs Dineen exclaimed. "Where did you come from, Ned? When did they let you out? Sit down." Ned was already exhausted from the effort of walking and standing. Rebecca spooned him into the nearest chair, and he settled down heavily, smiling. He was pleased to be back, to be among his cronies.

"Heard ye got the first batch of the discussion papers, Gerald. About time too. Mrs Cassidy in the shop told us that you were here."

The Senator studied the Chairman's face before speaking. Illness had taken away large chunks of flesh, leaving white and grey pouches of skin: there

his body stored the secrets of its little victories over certain death. His eyes had little or no lustre left; they were colourless and tired from too much fluorescent light. His hair had moved away too. "Bloody hell, I'm amazed," he said.

"Well, if you are...think how amazed I am." Rebecca replied.

"It's quiet before the storm," the Chairman said. "There's no getting away from it." He spoke in a matter of fact way, resigned.

Rebecca tapped the back of his head affectionately. "No need to say that."

"Well, it is."

With the Chairman back in action the Senator felt like a commander who has been restored to his staff. He looked forward to the discussion meeting with even greater hopefulness and ease. He went around telling everyone that Ned was back, that Ned would be at the meeting. He knew that many more people would come because of that: the Party's instinct for nostalgia was all-powerful. The faithful would come just to meet Ned, to shake his dying hand: to save that handshake for future reference like spare coins. Ned dying was a powerful asset.

On the night of the meeting the Senator was surprised to see that a huge number of women had arrived. He was sure that he hadn't invited all of them: maybe he had invited their husbands or brothers? He didn't know. However, Mrs Dineen

seemed to know all of them. Rebecca too sat in the centre of the female crowd, chatting and laughing. The Senator was disappointed that nobody seemed to need his company. He looked around to see if the Chairman or Condolences had come. As he moved further into the interior of the hotel, he realised that it was he himself who needed a friend.

"A lonely man is an egotist. That's what I always say." He overheard Rebecca speaking. Surely they weren't discussing him? She turned around quickly to greet him. "Ned's already here," she said. "He's over there," She pointed to the alcove near the television set, a corner filled with mirrors and clubbish men. He wondered, then, if Rebecca hated him because he was single and would live. He never thought of her as someone capable of hatred. He decided to make a gesture. He made a quick calculation. There were eight women around Rebecca's table; he guessed that they were all drinking minerals. He took a chance.

"Would ye all like a refill?"

"Naw. No thanks." A woman he didn't know gave a bored reply.

"We will of course, girl." Mrs Dineen sprang to life when she saw that it was the Senator who'd offered. She thumped the other woman playfully. "Drinks on the Senator," she shouted.

"Orange? Lemonade? Coke?"

"Gin and tonic would be grand," the woman he

didn't know said.

"Same here."

"Seeing that you're so kind, I wouldn't mind a rum and blackcurrant. Bacardi would do," the woman who sat beside Mrs Dineen smiled up at him freshly.

Even before he had finished taking their order he knew that he was being stung. Badly burned, as they say. There was no way out of it. He called out to Eamon who was sitting on the same bench as Councillor Allingham. What was he doing there anyway? "Help me with this, will you? I've a lot of drinks to get and it's nearly time for the meeting."

"Have something yourself, love." The well dressed Bacardi woman spoke to him again. Then she turned to Rebecca. "Honestly now, isn't he very nice?" she said in a strong Dublin accent. She was the new vet's wife, a committed woman. He decided to escape to the bar.

"I've never seen so many women at a meeting before. What's up?' he whispered cautiously to Eamon. "What do they want?"

"Nothing," replied Eamon. "Mrs Dineen and Rebecca did a very good job, that's all. They told everyone that the meeting was about children's allowances and things like that..."

"I suppose it's no lie." The Senator elbowed his way from the bar. "Isn't if a fright, though...come here, I don't want to shout...isn't it a frightful thing to see so many women drinking alcohol?" Eamon

didn't reply to this, but he smiled broadly. He enjoyed witnessing the little sting. Sometimes, he felt that his uncle wasn't born for the real world at all.

After another half-hour of expensive drinking the meeting began. The Saharan wastes of the function room filled up slowly as people transferred their attention from the smoke-filled lounge to the business at hand. After a long, painful pause the groups finally settled down. The Chairman and Councillor Allingham sat beside the Senator; Councillor Conory beside Rebecca and Mrs Dineen.

"I think it's stupid having no votes. Who ever heard of having a meeting without somebody getting elected?" Jim O'Callaghan, a young county council labourer who had obviously been primed by Allingham's crowd, shot his bolt prematurely. The Senator stared at O'Callaghan, then looked at Councillor Allingham who cleared his throat in embarrassment. The young labourer was nervous and dead drunk.

"Shut up, Jim," a young woman said bravely.

"Who the fuck do you think you are?" he replied.

"Shut up or go home. You're pissed drunk," the young woman said calmly. She could hold her rum.

"Thanks, miss, that's enough," the Senator said. "Right, we'll start again."

The young man sat down, staring arrogantly at the woman as he dropped into his seat. The Senator

explained why the meeting had been called. He told Eamon to distribute copies of the discussion papers. The crowd was twice as big as the Party had anticipated so there weren't enough to go around. "As ye can see, the green paper is about childcare and welfare and the white paper is about health matters generally." When Eamon had finished his distribution the Senator noticed that, apart from Councillor Allingham, Conory and Eamon's father, all the pamphlets were being held by the women. He wondered if this was because a number of men were still holding their pints or because of their general lack of interest. Then it occurred to him that a few male members of the Party were illiterate: that was one of the reasons they hated anything being written down.

"I'm sorry about the shortage of copies..."

"Don't worry your little head about that," a boozy patronising voice replied, creating a mild stir of laughter. It was O'Callaghan again. He perforated the serious classroom atmosphere within which the Senator like to work.

"These should have been distributed long before the meeting." It was Eamon's father who spoke. The Senator never expected any favours from his brother.

"It couldn't be done. It would have been unfair. A lot of people here tonight wouldn't have seen the documents."

"Are these the Party's policies now?" Mrs Heaphy,

the vet's wife, asked. "Or are they just proposals? I mean...could we change them?"

"That's it exactly," he said, pleased. "If we can come up with any better proposals we can send them to the General Secretary."

"A lot of good that'll do," Allingham said cynically. In a raised voice he told them that in the Dublin offices they would never listen to what the country people had to say. Anyway, the General Secretary would soon be out on his ears. A new regime was coming into the Party.

"That's silly defeatism," Mrs Heaphy said angrily.

"What?"

"That's stupid defeatism," she repeated. "Giving up before we've even begun."

Allingham didn't pursue the matter because he didn't want to start a fight with a strange woman, especially one with a Dublin accent. She might know important people. This gave the Senator the opportunity to outline the main points in the documents. He reminded them that some of the proposals couldn't be changed because they were in line with new EEC laws.

It was the proposals on the reorganisation of the health boards that worried most people. Dr Forrestal, who had been quietly nursing his drink in the corner, stood up and spoke. He said that he knew of specific plans to move the local general hospital out of the constituency altogether. He said that those

plans were part of the reorganisation of the new boards. If the constituency lost its general hospital it would have terrible implications for the health of women in particular. There would be no natal unit left in the entire county. This stirred Mrs Hogan, the blacksmith's wife, into saying that the Party should resist the reorganisation.

"Here, here!" Councillor Allingham shouted, "but fighting will have to be done locally. Ye need strong public men."

"Remember, they're not final proposals. They are a mixture of national plans, EEC regulations and youth committee ideas."

"But if Dr Forrestal says we're going to lose our hospital...surely that's serious?" Mrs Hogan appealed to the Senator.

"Where could the new general hospital go? The county hospital in the city is strangled for lack of space."

"I've had plenty of opportunities to think about the county hospital," the Chairman said. "I've been looking out through its windows on and off for the past few months. There is plenty of room for expansion. There's a disused railway-yard that could be taken over by any health board. After all it's owned by a bloody state company."

"That's sensible talk," Allingham said.

"Write that down." Mrs Heaphy addressed the Senator.

"Right."

Then another woman whom the Senator didn't know stood up. "Forget about those big plans," she said. "With all due respects, Dr Forrestal, I think the decision about a new hospital has already been made by more powerful forces. What I resent about this document is its proposal to pay children's allowance by tax-rebate to the father, instead of the mother! I think that's very dangerous. If it becomes a tax-rebate you can be sure that most women will never see the colour of that money. Never."

The Senator was impressed by this woman's fluency and he could see from the expressions on the other women's faces that they were delighted with her contribution. The men, on the other hand, had to struggle to readjust their brains: most of them had been thinking how much a site big enough for a general hospital would be worth. The woman continued to speak: she said that children's allowances were often the only source of financial discretion for women. With those few shillings the state recognised that women existed.

"How true, girl," Mrs Dineen said.

"But isn't it a matter of efficiency?" Allingham asked. "Isn't it simpler to take the payment into account when doing a man's tax allowance. It saves his wife the trouble of visiting the post office."

"That's not the point."

"What about people on the dole? They don't get

any tax allowances," Rebecca said.

"The allowance can be added to the dole money."

"Over my dead body," one woman said.

"Mine too."

None of the other men wanted to get involved in this controversy. The women felt too strongly about the issue; it was frightening. The men were sorry for Allingham, who had become cornered. Condolences—who was still thinking in terms of scoring or losing political points—was delighted that Allingham had stumbled upon a nest of motivated women. "What were your proposals again?" he asked Councillor Allingham.

"The good ladies don't agree with my point of view."

"Should I write down that we're against this proposal so?" the Senator asked, his pen poised for action. He was hiding behind it.

"Do, do, Christ, do," Allingham said.

"Have ye got any other ideas on that line?" the Senator addressed the women.

"Bastards." The vet's wife spoke again.

Ned, Allingham and the Senator braced themselves for a full assault. "Pardon, ma'am?"

"The concept of illegitimacy," the vet's wife went on. "It should be put right." She explained that an illegitimate child still had no rights over the father's property. The Party should change that. After all, she said, the laws of ancient Ireland protected the rights

of bastards. She fidgeted with a strange blue carton of cigarettes while she spoke. She put a cigarette in her mouth and lit it with a match struck off her finger-nail. Condolences' eyes popped when this happened. He had seen matches lit in this way in cowboy films, but he'd never seen it done in the flesh. After taking a few drags of her cigarette the woman proposed a form of wording.

"Should he write this down?" Ned interrupted the woman, pointing to the Senator.

"Sure."

"Will we vote? We'll have a vote on this!" Jim O'Callaghan, who had remained miraculously quiet for so long, shouted.

"Right, we'll have a vote. This is controversial stuff," Condolences butted in.

"You mean to say there are members of this Party who would go against our proposal!" Mrs Heaphy exclaimed. "Disgraceful!" She shouted at Condolences. He withered in his seat.

"Not at all, ma'am, I wasn't saying that. I just thought that we should vote for the record; to make it unanimous."

"You're a fool. These things are too important for votes. Do you know that...You're a fool."

"Shame on you," another woman said.

"We have to be careful about the farmers. They don't like the laws of ownership to be changed. Can anyone name a farmer that doesn't have a bastard

somewhere?" Allingham asked. Most of the men laughed at that.

"Oh, shame on you all! Ye're as tight-fisted as hell." Young Jennifer spoke up.

"Sit down, you little hussy," Condolences said. Most of them laughed at his embarrassment. To be insulted by one's own daughter. Some of the men gained confidence from the leathery volume of their laughter. But the women had already won the day. Before the meeting came to a close they suggested eighteen further proposals and amendments. The Senator wrote furiously in order to keep up with their momentous creativity. After the tenth proposal half the men left the room and adjourned to the bar. The women insisted on unanimous decisions; it was a form of political conduct unknown in the Party. Many of the men had hoped for a showdown between Allingham and Ned or the Senator. Others had come merely to see Ned, knowing that it would be his last constituency meeting. The women, on the other hand, had come to pursue their interests. Their attention to detail, their eloquence, their unwillingness to be softened or patronised, left the men with no room to manoeuvre. The meeting had become what it was meant to be—a discussion about certain policies. But the men felt that they had been robbed of their platform, their regular Party charade.

"Where did ye all come from?" asked Ned.

"Eamon says that Mrs Dineen and Rebecca asked

them all. She thought that I was worried about a small crowd," the Senator replied.

"Were you worried?"

"I was."

"I've never seen so many women so excited. I think it's because of the new Gay Byrne show on the radio. That's what it is. He's got all the women in the country going around airing their problems."

"Eamon thinks it's because of the charismatic movement. Women have got used to crowds and to giving their views in public."

"The women are really tough when they get going," Condolences noted. "I mean, if we were clever enough we'd pay more attention to what they say. Wouldn't it be a good idea to place a few women out front. You know, as councillors or even Dáil candidates. A good female candidate would draw a lot of attention towards the Party."

"If we managed them right there would be a spin-off benefit for the male candidates," the Senator suggested.

"Ye think about it," the Chairman said. "There's a new kind of enthusiasm there. It's a new thing. There's a good future for the Party in that."

# TWENTY-TWO

The Winslows' vegetable garden, cut out of a steep and fertile southern slope, was protected from the harsh northern winds by a thick copse of old oak trees. The high woodland drained into Mr Winslow's acres and spilled into the broad tidal river below, so that the garden was an acidic oasis in a land of temperate limestone. For that reason Condolences had to relearn many of his habits of cultivation. At the same time, Mr Winslow was taught to abandon the use of technical terms like "ph-level."

"Is it acid or isn't it; is it lime or horse-dung you want there?" Condolences had said in exasperation one day.

The amused American got the message. "Plenty of lime, plenty of lime," he said.

They were standing in the artichoke patch, listening to the sound of the angelus bells from the village below, when Mrs Winslow entered the garden through the stable-yard gate. Condolences knew that she had been checking on her two ponies. He had cleared out their pens earlier that morning. But while doing so he had stepped on and smashed an old painted sign on a panel of wood which read *Chien*

*Méchant.*

"Everything OK, ma'am?" he asked apprehensively.

"Perfect, Condolences." She stepped gingerly between two rows of blackcurrant bushes. She didn't want to stain her clothes with chlorophyll. In her expensive Donegal cardigan and tweed skirt she looked very chic and urbane. As far as Condolences was concerned she looked like someone who had no intention of doing any work. She stepped out of the grass margin and into the artichoke bed. Mr Winslow reached out to take her hand, in case she lost her balance. She was frail.

"The grass is becoming terribly long. We've spent so much having those lawns redone. This oil crisis is terrible."

"The garage in the village has done its best. They just can't give us any more."

She looked at Condolences. "The lawns are nearly ruined now...If your Party was in power we wouldn't have this trouble. Would we?"

"That's the story we're sticking to," Condolences replied. He rammed the sharp spade deeply into the white roots.

"Where are they going?"

"We're putting them along that line, see," her husband pointed to the line of creosoted cord. "And I've promised some roots to Julie Phelan for her father's garden. I saw her at the garage yesterday."

"The Senator's girl?"

"Yes, very pretty, very Irish looking."

"He's still a rogue, Condolences," Mrs Winslow joked.

That afternoon, and it was late afternoon because Maura had set the white table on the veranda for tea, Condolences hosed the large bald patch around the hydrangeas. He worked slowly, ruminating playfully between the bushes in order to stretch his working day towards its close. The slow pace of his new job was something he had to get used to. Most of the other workers from the creamery were still unemployed. Even Mary Kearney, the lab technician, was still searching for a new job. The only thing that worried Condolences was that Mr Winslow had no standing in the world of the Party. Saying to Party members that one worked for a Mr Winslow meant absolutely nothing. Being a creamery employee had meant something: it meant that one was inside the fold of a larger organisation, that one was part of its protective air. Now Condolences wasn't a member of any workforce, and he felt chilled and vulnerable in the face of an uncertain future. Also, he realised that the Chairman was dying, and with him all the familial, personal certainties of the Party. He didn't count on the Senator's future; he didn't see any permanence there. The Senator was so incompetent that he hadn't yet developed any brokerage of protection and patronage. Condolences was also worried about the petrol shortage and its effect on

Party schedules. It would also have an effect on Ned's fleet of buses. He was worried about the Chairman's incapacity to deal with such things. Would Rebecca survive, would she be able to carry on? He was thinking about these things when he heard Mr Winslow shouting. "Condolences! Condolences, where did we put the bag with the artichoke roots? Julie's come for the artichokes!"

Mr Winslow came bounding towards him; he was always excited by visitors. "The Senator has come too."

He reminded his boss that they had stored the roots in the stable-yard, so Mr Winslow turned and went off in that direction. Meanwhile, the Senator and Julie were bending over the patchy and ragged sprays of a late forsythia bush. Condolences thought that they looked very happy together, as if they had finally resolved their differences and decided to get married. Maybe they'd finally become engaged. He was sure that they were holding hands while they waited for the American to return from the stable-yard. Their affection excited him because he looked forward to telling his wife about it. It was the kind of detail that she loved to hear.

The high central window of the Winslows' drawing-room had been opened wide. Condolences noticed Mrs Winslow setting up a record-player. When she placed a record on the turntable the sweet tight voice of Ella Fitzgerald sounded out above the

drone of the afternoon noises. *A tisket, a tasket;* the brown scat-singing blew across the crisp April afternoon. After greeting the loving couple, Condolences tried to slip away into a corner where he couldn't be seen; a corner where he could listen to the foreign music.

"Where's Condolences?" he heard Mr Winslow asking. But he didn't move. He heard the rattle of tea-things and the music.

"You'll both have a cup of tea?" he heard Mrs Winslow asking the Senator and Julie. Then it occurred to him that it was an unhappy thing to be a gardener, to have to see others having a good time. The Senator is really a big-shot now, he thought, hob-nobbing with rich people. He doesn't need the Party. It was as if he had been deliberately put there, in Mr Winslow's garden, in order that his loss of faith in the Senator should be complete.

# TWENTY-THREE

Julie's apparent happiness in Mr Winslow's garden was due to the element of certainly that had come into her life. She had decided to go away. When she told the Senator about this he flew into a rage. It was one of the few occasions on which she'd seen him really angry. She was unimpressed; it was too late. She had admitted to herself that this vague love had repressed her; that somehow he had turned her into an object unsuited to love.

When she saw advertisements in *The Irish Times* for administrative assistants in Brussels she tore out the page and saved it. A job in Brussels was a ticket out of the grey and dreary landscape. She carried the page of the newspaper around in her handbag for weeks while weighing up the pros and cons of going away. Then the letters from Helen Doocey began to arrive. She knew that her family would be furious, and that the Senator would panic—at least he needed her that much. But the promise of new things, new streets, new names, new friends, drew her away from the pious future of staying put. She wrote away for the application form and completed it. Months later, after she had dismissed the application as a failure,

she was called to an interview in Dublin. She got the job without much trouble. Her fluent German and mediocre French had carried the day. The fact that she worked for a German company was a powerful recommendation. How to tell the Senator, that had been her problem. She decided to be blunt. "I'm going away to Brussels. I've got a job. I must take it within the next two months..."

"What will your father do?"

"He accepts it. He says he'll be fine without me. He says I'm right not to waste my life."

"I suppose he means our relationship."

"The lack of one. Be honest, Gerald, we're almost strangers to each other now." She resented the fact that he would use her father to make her feel guilty.

"Your father is an old man."

"And I'll soon to be an old woman. That would never occur to you, of course. You always suited yourself..."

It was then he flew into a rage. He said that he had never wanted another woman, that he had always looked upon her as the only one for him. She said that she believed him, but that feelings weren't enough. "Is it blood you want?" he asked. But she wasn't afraid of getting into a fight.

"I'm bored by this whole fucking place," she said. "Even the Party's gone to the dogs—yes, the dogs—and nobody gives a damn. Nobody will come out into the open and say what they feel, even about

that, about politics. It's all subterfuge, innuendo, gossip. Allingham and Conory are just waiting around for the Chairman to die. Everyone can see that. Then they'll be on top of us all like vultures. I'm sick of it." She turned away from the Senator then, and wished that she had spoken about herself. The Party had become a metaphor for too much.

"Glad to see you worried about the Party," he replied sarcastically. "You're a great help, buzzing off to Brussels." While he spoke he was wringing his hands like a perished clerk.

They were standing near her car outside the school-yard. It was nearly tea-time on a cool evening; the street was wet and deserted. She decided to get into her car. "This isn't good, Julie," he said. "You don't realise how things will change, how much I will need you..." He looked stricken with grief, and she was momentarily sorry. Moist March wind had drained the colour from his hands.

"That's right, I'll never know how much you'll need me." She opened the window so that they didn't have to shout.

"This is brinkmanship," he whispered. Then he thought how daft and impersonal that word must sound. He regretted using it. But she was glad: it proved something.

"I'll phone you. Later." She drove away.

It would have been easier to end a relationship that had been violent and lustful and strong. She

knew that she would have to wean the Senator away from her slowly. She felt that they had been beached together without passion because they were educated above the general level of the other adults in the countryside. Their relationship had smouldered away; there had been no great heights and troughs, just a mediocre plateau of companionship. She couldn't recall any moments of overpowering, citric intensity or acute feelings of desire, to dispel the sluggishness of their situation. It was for that reason that he clung to her. He didn't want any drastic changes; he wanted to have all his options open endlessly. She knew that there were possibilities for contentment within their relationship: but she needed more. She would abandon the mediocre.

Meetings, phone-calls, car journeys. Weeks went by. Julie worked her way out of the Senator's system. It was difficult. They met in her employer's office, they had tea in her father's house, they sat in the little pub near Ballyduff. The Senator tried every trick he knew in an effort to make her stay. But she was adamant. By the time Mr Winslow's offer of artichoke roots came round they were amicably separated. They could even hold hands together again because they had achieved something together, a definite end. It was something they could share—like a secret engagement. There was only one day in their long therapy when the Senator suffered a complete relapse of dependence. It was on the day that they had to

take the Chairman back into hospital. The doctor said that he should go into the little cottage hospital that had once served as a county home. There were no treatment facilities there, so that everyone knew he was going there to die. The Chairman was ashen and thin, so weak from his low blood count that he slipped in and out of consciousness.

"Stay awhile," he managed to say from the hospital bed. They came closer and laid their hands on his left hand that had become purple from the intravenous drip. "Stay awhile." They stayed: Julie, Rebecca, the Senator. The Chairman breathed heavily. Although his eyes were closed and he didn't try to speak again, they felt that he was aware of their presence.

It was an hour later, when they were returning home, that the Senator tried to recapture Julie. "How can you go away? Ned is nearly dead. He'll die when you leave. Why can't you stay and help us? Help me."

Julie broke down. The tears that came were bitter, salty. As if a dam had given way under the strong pressure. She rocked and trembled with the awful force of her lost, wasted love. The Senator said nothing. He thought he had won, that he had made her too sad to go. But he was a fool. She wasn't weeping for him or the Party or Ned. She was crying after her own lost happiness. Two weeks later she drove over the mountains, through the ugly little

villages of Tipperary, to Shannon. There, with her new clothes, her new handbag, her new shoes, her new hairstyle, her new watch, her new bracelet, her new novel to read, her new future, with a restrained and polite kiss on the mouth, she said goodbye. The Senator was left with the full burden of his own decisions and his potentially brilliant, but solitary, future.

The weeks went by slowly after that. The Chairman lingered. Official letters from the Party and from the Senate accumulated on the Senator's desk and were left untouched. A debate on education was planned for the upper house to which he would be expected to contribute. He let it pass, although he had already arranged for leave of absence from school. He would cancel everything. In those weeks it occurred to him most forcefully that he wasn't a politician; that he found no joy in exercising the minute powers of a part-time Senator. It was for his father's sake that he had started into politics. He was his father's third choice, he knew that too. His eldest brother had been killed in 1943 and his second brother—young Eamon's father—had opted out in silence. Gerald was the baby of the family, having been born nineteen years after the brother who was killed. The second brother had sold the family business and now lived on a rapidly dwindling reserve of capital. The responsibility to carry on had fallen upon Gerald, who took it up in suffering silence. That had been

his major weakness; that sinned-against silence which has no energy and no capacity for love. He felt sometimes that silence was a genetic weakness of the family; a social and emotional passivity that rendered them ineffective. How strange, therefore, that his father had chosen politics. Still, that had been in the childhood days of the Party when even the most simple men found strength in it.

She had given him her Brussels address. He cleared his desk top of the ominous brown envelopes and placed them on the floor.

*Dearest Julie,*

*I hope you are settled in. Then again I hope you're not! I've been looking forward to a letter from you. I suppose in the excitement of Brussels you've forgotten the lot of us. I've no mind for work and no will left to stay in politics, even in a minor way, now that you are gone. There are several debates going on in the House but I've decided to skip the lot. This will get me into trouble with the teachers in the Party—but I have no intention of seeking re-election to the Senate...*

He went on to describe the Chairman's state of health, and the state of health of Condolences, Mrs Dineen, Eamon and the hostile local clergy. He told her that he was bored with his schoolwork. It was the end of April, that time of year when every teacher longs for the release of June. He was about to say that

he felt he shouldn't have been a teacher, but he thought that this would make him sound too pathetic. He said that he was looking forward to the holidays...

*I know that everything would be easier if you were here. That's the truth. I could really look forward to the summer then. Maybe I should visit you in Brussels? Will I do that; could you put me up? For God's sake, write soon. I want to know how you're feeling.*

A few weeks later he got a reply. He didn't open her letter immediately, but took it to school so that he could halve its impact, if necessary, with the distractions of the class-room.

"*Cead amach!*" A pupil asked to go to the toilet, using the colloquial, abbreviated version of the Irish. That always annoyed the Senator.

"*Cad tá ort, Ó Faoláin*?" he asked.

The child got the message: "*Bhfuil cead agam dul amach go dtí an leithreas, a Mháistir*?" he said slowly.

The Senator told him to hurry. Then he opened her letter. There was silence in the classroom, an expectant silence, because they knew that the master was on edge. Julie had written on strange grey, grainy paper; *papier recyclé* was embossed on the bottom of the first page. It was a long letter, four leaves with the writing on both sides. He was glad. He thought that she must be feeling lonely to write at such length. But when he read on he realised that she had written fluently because she had so much to tell. She had been surprised to find that the city was old, very

old with beautiful streets, markets and cafés. She had been misled by the popular pictures of Brussels on the television, pictures of skyscrapers and endless expanses of glass. She was sharing an apartment with two other girls; a wild girl from Athlone and a timid Protestant girl from Antrim who was a brilliant cook. She didn't say that she was happy—she said that she was "very well settled." It meant that she was happy, he thought. By the time he reached the end of the letter he felt that Brussels had beaten him.

*Don't come here yet. Wait until I'm home in August and we'll talk then. I would feel uneasy about meeting you. I don't feel like talking about anything for some time. I'm getting into the city. I would like to see you here at some stage. It's so full of life. Write again when you get time. Au Revoir.*

While he was tucking the letter back into its envelope he heard a noise coming from the direction of the toilets. It occurred to him that Ó Faoláin was taking his time about answering the call of nature. He got up from his desk and walked across the classroom. A wave of expectation washed across the class. From the door the Senator could see as far as the entrance to the toilets. There was the sound of voices, but something else, the sound of a radio or tape-recorder.

"*Buachaillí!*" he shouted angrily.

One of the boys responded by walking out. He was joined by another; they were two juniors from

Mrs Hussey's class. They slouched towards him sheepishly, but they didn't stop. They made straight for the safety of Mrs Hussey's room.

"Is Ó Faoláin in there?"

"He is."

"He's taking his time."

"He's doing the hard stuff, sir," Nealan replied, tittering.

The cheeky little bastard, I'll give him a kick up the arse, thought the Senator. "Don't be vulgar, Nealan. I'm disappointed in you."

He went into the toilet. The sound of a chain being pulled. "Come out, Ó Faoláin."

"It's my stomach, sir."

"Come out."

"Alright." There was a shuffle, panic. Then something fell to the ground, something metallic. The Senator bent down to look. Ó Faoláin had been listening to a Sony radio. The evidence was on the wet floor.

Ó Faoláin came out. "Sorry, sir. I'm really, sir."

"Really what?"

"Really sorry. I was listening to the results, the card at Newmarket, sir."

"Jesus, child, what are you talking about?"

"We had five pounds on Wednesday's Child, sir. Nearly all Fitzpatrick's communion money. It was an eight-to-one chance."

The Senator laughed. Gamblers, he was teaching

a school of gamblers. "Any luck?"

"Divil a bit, sir. He fell. He took My Princess with him. Fitzpatrick will kill me."

"He probably will," the Senator said with satisfaction. "You deserve a good hiding, Ó Faoláin. Using a junior lad's money."

"Wednesday's Child was a dead cert. A dead cert, sir."

"Who placed the bet for you?"

"My uncle, my mother's brother, Mr Dineen."

"Condolences?"

"Yes, sir. Condolences Dineen."

# PART IV

# THE LOST PARTY

# TWENTY-FOUR

The long white windowsill of the school science room was cluttered with the paraphernalia of spring. Jars of frogspawn, cuttings of slowly budding yellow twigs, broom, forsythia, bean seed on wet blotting paper, and two boxes of striped late crocus occupied habitual places of honour. The bottom half of each window had been made opaque with sheets of ugly plastic adhesive; yellow sunlight that streamed through seemed to come from a rotating source because of the shifting shadows made by new trees planted outside the window. It was four-thirty. After class-hours the science room became Eamon's personal domain because he was supposed to be working on a project for the young scientists' exhibition in Dublin. During the summer months he had got the idea for a portable hydro generator, one that could harness the power of a small mountain stream to generate electricity for holiday homes or isolated cottages.

Now his work-bench was littered with the entrails of a disembowelled 1kw Pelton-wheel. An electrical project kit was also scattered about. He had reached the stage when he couldn't be sure which screws and

armatures and coils belonged to which box. But he wasn't worried—a little methodical exploration would get everything back in its proper place. He stared at the Pelton coil with his dark, intelligent eyes. He was pleased with the way things were going. He felt that he had a future, despite all the rumours about youth unemployment. He was, after all, a tyro-scientist learning to dismember some of the working parts of the world. He had reached a stage in life where his confidence had been consolidated, untested by any familial trouble or hiccoughs in love. His mother had died while he was an infant, yet he had never felt deprived of her love. He moved now with profound ease through all the adolescent territories.

As he stared at the coils and electrodes, at their sweet mathematical predictability, he thought about his uncle, the Senator, and the troubles of the adult Party. He remembered clearly the night of his uncle's humiliation at the hands of Conory and Allingham. He had some sympathy for the two arrogant councillors because they had drive and an energetic ability to make trouble. They were negative energies, he thought, but all energy leads to some creation. He was thinking, also, about one of the ministers in the Coalition, a man who had been an intellectual and a diplomat, a moral kind of person who had been driven into writing history books. The Party hated that man with an ugly, meditated hatred. But Eamon admired him for his capacity to retain facts like a

scientist, and for his public daring in making unpopular judgements. Eamon had kept this admiration secret—only Jennifer knew—in order not to upset his uncle or give cause for scandal.

He knew that it would be difficult to make a useful quantity of power; the ratio of water to wattage was terrifying, even allowing for the fine efficiency of a Pelton-drive and the operation of gears and coils. Eamon's plan was to build a frame of tubular steel, folded like the frames of two bicycles welded together. He surveyed the mess he had made. Somewhere within there was a key design. He felt this deeply, and this feeling filled his afternoon. The silence of the science room was immense, monastic. Its immensity was emphasised by the methodical, faraway drip of a work-bench tap, hidden from his view by a large micro-projector, an exquisite, fragile instrument. Sometimes he felt that the micro-projector had a life of its own, that it breathed and listened from its own molecular world under the grey dust-cover.

He was startled by the sound of someone trying to open the door. The handle was depressed and shaken. He had locked himself in. Then there was a gentle tapping; silence; then four distinct taps. It was Jennifer's code. She had stolen away from her study. He opened the door. "I thought you wouldn't come," he lied. He hadn't thought about her arrival at all.

"Did you know that you were put on the list to

play tennis at four? I was waiting for you down there. You were supposed to play Snotty Ollie in doubles. Everybody kept teasing me. They kept saying 'Where have you hidden Eamon. Where have you hidden him?' I nearly died." Then she said, as an afterthought, "I wasn't at study at all."

He loved the way she said, "I nearly died." She said it in a superior way, like the doctor's wife at the hairdresser's. When he locked the door again they were protected by the shadows of the doorway, out of the range of the long window. Her blonde hair was braided and tied back, revealing the whiteness of her neck. He thought that her hair looked like a drawing of water by Leonardo da Vinci, water falling in slow-motion. She had removed her school tie and opened the two top buttons of her blouse because she had been running. Her opened blouse revealed a patch of red nakedness that matched the high colour of her cheeks. For a split second he smelled the odour of her toilet soap, intensified by the heat of her body. Its simple perfume astonished him, and made him agitated with desire. He fought the feeling.

"I'm still working on the dynamo," he said. "I was trying to sort out a good armature. Whether the things works or not will depend on a strong armature. The coils and things are a secondary matter...Come over to the bench." He took her hand and they walked across the room, through the hazard area of tubes and tanks where the junior school were trying

to grow freshwater shellfish. He was often tempted to drop a cyanide compound or some other deadly gift into the water to put a stop to their intrusive experiments. Then he discovered that in time the shellfish would produce enough poisons to kill themselves. He was delighted with that: he wanted all of the science room to himself.

"Your desk is a mess," she whispered. "What would Mr Mellerick say if he saw that mess? He'd kill you."

"So what?"

"And how do you know which things belong to the school kits and which things belong to yourself?" she went on, after looking at the labyrinth of coils, wires, bolts and armatures.

"Leave that to me, OK? If you're going to interrogate me, you can feck off, now." Then he regretted saying it. She might go away. He had come to depend on her visits: they had strengthened his ambition with an erotic cement. "Ah, I don't mean that...don't take any notice."

"Apologies accepted." She pouted, mock-hurt. "Show me the peroxide thing again." She moved to the chemicals cupboard. "It's in here, isn't it?" She tried to open the cupboard but it was locked. "Shit."

"It's locked," he said.

"I know it's locked." She pulled violently at the door of the press. Then she saw that he was smiling.

"You have the key!" she roared. "You selfish

bastard!"

"Sssh. Shut..." he gestured furiously. The room became quiet again. They heard the sound of footsteps outside the window, the sound of someone tapping a racquet-press against the wall. "It must be Snooty Ollie...and Miss Jennings," he whispered. "Keep down!" Jennifer, in a painful kneeling position, froze against the cupboard. They'd both be in deep trouble if she was caught with Eamon in the science room. There was a knock on the door.

"Oh shit." He knew that he'd have to open it. If he didn't, Miss Jennings would check the teachers' room for the science keys. He would be accused of carrying them around in his pocket: a mortal sin.

"Yes?" he said loudly.

"Is that you, Eamon Glenville?" a sharp, arrogant voice asked. Miss Jennings was a sour bitch, who felt that the Principal had given Eamon too much freedom. "Have you seen Jennifer Dineen?"

"No, miss. No."

"Well, would you kindly open this door?"

Jennifer was trapped. She crouched even lower behind the work bench. Eamon opened the door to confront the neanderthal stare of Miss Jennings. Snotty Ollie stood beside her, holding the damaged windmill of a tennis racquet. "You were supposed to be in the court playing a doubles match. Have you any idea of the amount of trouble you've caused the other people? What kind of a selfish person are you?"

"Sorry, miss. Mr Mellerick told me to keep working on the project. He said that I was to skip the game."

"What project? I suppose we are all expected to keep a day-to-day interest in what you're doing?"

"This." He pointed to the mound of electrical gadgets on the distant work-bench. He hoped that she would be satisfied to see the project from afar. She was, she disliked him that much. "Well, kindly inform us all when you want to alter everybody's day in the future...I want those keys as well. We need them to take chairs out of the boiler room."

He handed over the keys, relieved. Then she asked him how he proposed to lock the science room. He said that he'd wait for her to return.

"Even if it takes until five o'clock?"

"Even until then." She was satisfied with that and went away briskly. He closed the door and listened. When he could no longer hear her footsteps he said, "She must be in a hurry. Otherwise she'd have been much more of a bitch." He walked back around the work-bench towards the chemical cupboard. Jennifer was still crouched low, in a painful position. "I'm all pins and needles," she said, "right up to my thighs."

"Try to lie down and I'll rub you. It will make the blood flow."

"I will not lie down. You're supposed to stand up and walk in order to get the circulation going." She raised herself slowly, painfully, and sat on a tall bench.

"One kiss," he said. He touched her lips gently before she could turn away. It was one kiss only, but open-mouthed: they tasted each other. Meanwhile his hand stroked the insides of her aching thighs. His hand travelled until it met a silky, warm resistance. It rested there.

"We'll be murdered," she said, "if we're ever caught."

"We won't. But I'd be banished from this room. That's for sure."

"You are always thinking of yourself."

"I'm not, that's a lousy accusation. This school has never produced a 'young scientist.' I'd like to be the first..."

"You needn't go over that again," she said with resignation. "You must try to finish it. I'm proud..."

"I'm proud of you too..."

She saw this as an opportune moment. She enveloped his bold hand with her thighs, tightening around him until she almost hurt his knuckles. "Are you really proud?" she asked girlishly. "Of me, I mean." She filled her question with a strong coquettish confidence.

"Christ, girl, of course I'm proud." He moved to kiss her again.

"Stop. I want to ask you something."

"What?" Was she pregnant? O God! His stomach tightened with fear. His desire withered.

"Do you think I'm beautiful? Not just good-

looking. I know I'm good-looking. But beautiful?" It was what she really wanted to know. She wanted to be sure, scientifically. This need for certainty had become all-important to her because another girl in her class had spent the last two weeks boasting about her own beauty. That girl, Veronica Hallie, from a nearby village, had won a beauty competition, and had been crowned at some crossroads dancehall. That was too much for Jennifer, who wanted to be the most beautiful girl in the school because Eamon was the brightest pupil. She was determined to have equal status in another sphere.

"You are the most beautiful person in the school." He offered her his judgement.

"I'm going to enter the beauty competition at the spring fair. Would you be annoyed with me?"

He said that he wouldn't. He was relieved: for a few minutes his future had flashed before him; a pregnant girl-friend, an embarrassed father, a disgraced family, a savage Condolences, an end to his hopes of university...He was relieved for Jennifer's sake too, but that relief was secondary. He wondered if she would still want him if he had no bright future. It was the prospect of a brilliant future that gave their relationship its intensity and phosphorescence. They had mortgaged from its strength and happiness in order to bear up under the strain of parental supervision and the pressure of exams.

"Wouldn't you feel belittled," he asked, "like a

cow or a champion pony?"

"Not if I beat Veronica Hallie. Just to shut her up."

"But isn't your class against these things on principle?"

"I want to win. That's principle enough. I'll go back to principles after I've won the bloody thing." Everyone in her class wanted her to enter, to put Veronica in her place. The principle had been waived.

"You don't have to ask my permission. I don't own you."

"Oh, you do! Say you do!" she insisted, kissing him.

There was the sound of footsteps again. Danger. Miss Jennings was returning with the keys, much earlier than she had said. Eamon moved to the door quickly to intercept her. Jennifer hid again below the tall work-bench. What a miserable bitch you are, Eamon thought as he took the keys from the teacher. She had opened the door without knocking. It was her right, he didn't own the science room. "When you lock up here bring the keys back to me," she said. She turned and left him standing there, annoyed. She hated the odours of the science room, the way the ammonia-cleansed sinks and the lack of ventilation created a nauseating stench.

"Big J is gone," he whispered.

Jennifer reappeared, brushing her gymslip with her hands. She had had enough. She walked to the door and exited smartly. Without touching him

again. Miss Jennings spooked her. He noticed that her blouse had been fully rebuttoned. A long strand of hair had come undone from her da Vinci waterfall.

"Win," he whispered, as she turned and winked outside the cloakroom door.

## TWENTY-FIVE

In the dancehall, the Senator watched the cleaning woman as she sprinkled star-dust across the polished ribs of the floor. It occurred to him that she was only about fifty years old, although she looked much older. He knew that she had always voted for the Party, despite the influence of her husband who was a Coalitionite. She still insisted on spreading star-dust, though the young people laughed at her. Youngsters preferred a bald room, as if their urge to dance had returned to an era before star-dust, to a more lustful and primitive time. The woman shook the pink glitter box to make sure that nothing was wasted. A lump of damp crystals fell onto her shoe. "Blast," he heard her say as she kicked and broadcast the annoying pulp.

It had been a good day for the Senator, this Spring Festival Saturday. He had moved around the display field, unencumbered and cheerful. In the old days—not so long ago—he would have strolled about with Julie linked to his arm. He would have had the luxury of a private day because Julie's presence would have been the public sign of his right to a private life. In her absence the people didn't feel embarrassed to fall

into step with him and share their troubles. He welcomed their complaints about the condition of some minor road, a lack of pressure in the town's water supply, trouble over a non-contributory pension. He head was soon filled with the discomforts of rural life: annoyances which are one source of political power. By the time he finished walking in the festival grounds he knew he had held the most successful clinic of his career. He was renewed and strengthened by the evidence of his own usefulness. He felt that he might be able to deal with things on his own, without the Chairman, without Julie. Perhaps it was the surge of spring. He had even noticed the fresh loveliness of women, the way they had unfolded in whorls of yellow skirts and blouses, in pastel dresses and hats. Their fine legs, their bare arms, still white from the winter, stunned his gut and made his thoughts erect. It must be spring, he felt. Is this what abandoned meant? What he didn't know was that the day was only a chink of light, a remission, in the long illness of his personal life.

"Hello Senator! It's great to see you here. By God, you must be bulling for a woman tonight!" The cleaning-woman was a jovial sort. She didn't stop to chat, though, because small groups of people had already gathered. She knew that she was too domestic an image; she would spoil the romance of her own carefully polished floor.

"Well, Maggie..." the Senator said. That was all he

had time to say before she disappeared. He heard the metal blinds of the bar being opened and he walked across the floor to buy an orange juice. A large knot of seemingly under-age drinkers had beaten him to the counter. He had to wait this turn: in a dancehall there are no privileges allowed, not even to members of the Senate.

Outside, the rain had begun to fall softly, filling the landscape with a metallic blue light. Jennifer and Eamon arrived with a large rowdy mob of school friends. The entire senior cycles of the local schools had decided on a final night out, a final fling, before the sensuous deprivation of summer exams. The youngsters were banked at the door, pushing and screaming. "Stop it, Michael! Give over, Christy! It's me you're pinching, Maura! Bitch!"

"What the fuck's the hold-up? It's raining here," one big fellow said.

The second door of the entrance was opened to lessen the crush. When Eamon saw who the ticket-seller was he nearly fainted. It was Condolences, who craned his neck and shouted into the crowd, "If there's any more bad language, ye can all piss off home! And that includes my own daughter." Some of the boys jeered. "I'm dead serious," Condolences emphasised. He turned back into the ticket booth.

There was silence then, but enough of a background murmur to drown the panicking interchange between Jennifer and Eamon. Jennifer

had no money. How could she get past her father without him discovering that Eamon was treating her to this night? Eamon had only a ten-pound note. He turned quickly while the mob pushed forward. "Change," he whispered. "Change, for Chrissake!" Four of the boys from his class pooled their money in haste. They took the large note and gave him singles and a fiver. "I'll pay for the others," Christy said. When her turn came to pay, Jennifer handed her father a fiver.

"Where did you get this money?" he asked like a fat-faced Nazi commandant.

"My mother. Mama." She knew that he couldn't be sure.

He didn't believe her. But he could do nothing. People might think that his own daughter was a thief. How could he live down that shame? "Your mother should have more sense," he said grudgingly. He handed her the three pounds change. Eamon felt such a wave of relief that he forgot to hand up his own money. He passed the booth. "Hey, you! Eamon! Trying to get away, are ya?" Condolences shouted. The others laughed.

"Sorry, Condolences. Mr Dineen." He handed up the two pounds.

"It's all right. We won't shoot a member of the Party." Condolences' friendly tone embarrassed him. He didn't want to be known as a member of the Party. It made him seem square, middle-aged. He

could sense the unspoken derision of his companions. He didn't want to be set apart: but he was, and he hated it.

"Thanks." He followed Jennifer into the hall. "Does your father ever stop making money?" he asked loudly, joking.

"Some people have to work for their living. They haven't money in the bank," she said, embarrassed.

"Sorry. I'm sorry."

When he said that she looked back over his shoulder to make sure that they were beyond her father's supervision, then she kissed him, deeply.

"Wowee!" one of her friends exclaimed. Most of them longed to be as forthright in love.

On stage the band tuned up. The usual clatter of drums when the drummer became bored or self-conscious; a vocalist with shoulder-length hair tested a microphone; a guitarist stumbled over a ground-level amplifier and fell backwards against the drums. Everyone laughed. Eventually a recognisable, danceable tune was gathered together and blared out over the loudspeakers. People moved away from the stage as the sound acquired its predictable piercing intensity. The hall filled very quickly, veteran dance-goers mingled with the occasional visitors who had come in from the mountains for the festival. They all moved around with a studied but over-dressed indifference.

At twelve o'clock the vocalist announced the six

contestants who had been short-listed for the title Queen of the Festival. Beads of sweat glistening in the heat of the spotlights, the vocalist named the girls for whom most votes had been cast. "The first contestant is Veronica Bateman, then Helen Broderick, then Veronica Hallie, and Jennifer Dineen."

"Oh God, I don't think I can face it!" Jennifer clutched Eamon's shoulder.

"Of course you can, you nut."

"No."

"You owe it to the girls," he said. "They all took the trouble to support you in the first round."

But she was so tense that she didn't know what the other girls did or said on stage. When her turn came she climbed the side steps of the stage, her face frozen into a terrified smile. The seniors from her school cheered wildly, happily, and their cheers helped her. The superiority of her beauty attracted immediate attention: even the smooth vocalist seemed taken aback by the maturity of her figure. She was wearing a short red cotton dress and a large necklace of white costume pearls, as well as a white bangle on her bare arm. The vocalist asked her the usual questions. In her terror they seemed very original and she tried to reply as best she could. After what seemed like an eternity she was released. She left the stage while the band played Presley's "Wooden Heart."

"You were great!" Veronica Bateman said. She was

always very courteous.

"I know you have it." Eamon grabbed her. "I know you have!"

"I'd love a drink." She was still trembling. "Vodka and orange, please."

"I'll ask my uncle to buy the vodka. I think your father is somewhere in the district still." Eamon moved towards the bar.

It was nearly one o'clock in the morning when Jennifer received the crown of tinfoil and cardboard. Her nerves were more steady this time: she walked onto the stage in a slow, deliberate manner. The vodka was a perfect anaesthetic. The vocalist, who presented her with the crown and a hundred pound cheque, held her tightly, placing his hand searchingly at the top of her dress as he gave her a long kiss of congratulations. She was too excited to feel disgust. The spotlight followed her down the steps, through the rows of cheering dancers, into the safety of Eamon's friends.

"Can I take this yoke off now?" She began to remove the clips that held her crown.

"Oh no! You must wear it for the rest of the night. Until the dance is over!" one of the girls shouted at her.

"It's to show how meaningful the title is..." One of her classmates lurched forward, drunk, unafraid to show her plain distaste. The girl had a crush on Eamon.

"Ah, piss off, Mary Quinn," Michael, Eamon's friend, intervened. He caught the girl as she tried to brush the tinfoil from Jennifer's head.

"Piss off, yourself," the unhappy girl said.

# TWENTY-SIX

"Wake up!"

"He's dead." His father stood by the bedside holding a mug of steaming tea. "Drink this. You'd better get up and go to your uncle's house. He might need help to telephone people in the Party."

He had been dreaming about the night before. The dreams were so fresh, so vivid. It was the effect of alcohol. He wondered if Jennifer had got to bed safely after the dance, if she had run the gauntlet of her fretting mother. Condolences would have arrived home before two, carrier of good news. Tolling for her beauty. They might have stayed up to see their Festival Queen. He should have walked with her to the door. He should have gone inside, had a cup of tea. A night-thief, he felt that he was pilfering their daughter's virtue.

His father stood between his bed and the large east-facing window. In his half-sleep he could feel the energy of the morning sun. It burst through, inquisitive, insatiable. Light curved around his father's frame, bringing with it the blinding discomfort of the late May morning.

He glanced at the clock. Eight-thirty.

"When did he die?"

"At five this morning. Rebecca was with him, and his younger brother. The one in the special branch in Cork. I think Mrs Dineen was there too."

Poor Mrs Dineen, who would have only had two hours sleep. His heart was softened by the lasting effect of alcohol. Headache. The poor woman ran a hard path, between her awkward daughter and her dying peers. He was sorry.

"Poor Ned." He wanted to cry, but he didn't want his father to think him an idiot.

"He hadn't a chance. He's better off dead; more peaceful that way. Cancer in the gut is a rotten thing."

"I suppose so." He took a swig of the mug of tea. The hot liquid tore through his guts. In his dreams he had confused Jennifer with Julie Phelan. He had dreamt that the Senator danced with Jennifer. He himself had stroked Julie's hair and touched her tanned, grainy skin. He had unbuttoned her blouse and cupped her right breast while she talked excitedly about Brussels and the European Community. He must tell Jennifer about his dream, just to see her becoming jealous.

"Get dressed now," his father interrupted his reveries. "I'm frying stuff below. Do you want an egg?"

"No." Even the thought of an egg made him feel sick.

When his father left the room, he leaped out of bed. He wanted to overcome the nausea in his system with will-power. He opened the window wide to freshen the room. He loved the crisp air of this time of day. The scent of geraniums floated through the window from the neglected flower-boxes. A moist geranium scent was the essence of late spring. Through the window he could hear the sound of his father's geese; eight muddy pests, his father's pets. They gaggled and complained below in the whitewashed yard while the dogs growled at them. While he dressed he listened to the dogs barking, the hiss of his father's frying-pan, a faint hiss. And his father whistling "The Wild Colonial Boy" slowly, with sentimental relish.

"Eamon! Come on!"

"Coming now, Dad!" he shouted. He bounded down the stairs, his will-power winning, until he reached the cavern of the kitchen. It wasn't until he left the stairs that he felt his headache again. The smell of fried food made him feel sick. But he knew he'd have to eat. His father would see to that; it was part of the punishment. Penance for the night of illegal drinking, penance for his illicit dreams. Sometimes he thought that his father could read his mind.

# TWENTY-SEVEN

Saturday morning. He hadn't gone to school on Friday, but stayed at home to do the Senator's work. He had made twenty-seven phone calls, contacting all the Party men in the constituency; all the senior men, that is, the deputies, senators, councillors and chairmen of electoral areas. The senior men in the eastern part of the constituency weren't sure if they would attend the Chairman's removal. A small factory, a subsidiary of Dunlops, had just closed down, making twenty-six women and ten men redundant. It had happened because of EEC membership and the removal of tariff protection. The Party men in the city wanted to stay put to draft a statement for the press and to meet officers from the National Manpower Service. They wanted to appear to be doing something. Eamon was bright enough to understand this. "I'll tell the Senator," he had said, "and I'll give Rebecca your sympathy."

His father had risen early again that morning to wake him from his sleep. They were expecting people to call to the house. Although his father took no part in politics, hated politics, their house remained a focus for the Party. It was as if his grandfather,

Deputy Glenville, had trained the simple men of the Party to act like homing pigeons. It had become an instinct, a reflex that endured even after thirty years. They had just sat down to breakfast when the Senator and his followers arrived. Eamon was determined to stay put; he had done enough work yesterday. Let his father greet them.

His father rose from the breakfast table. When he opened the door there was a rumble of voices in the hallway. Then, the sound of laughter, his father's laughter, and then the sound of footsteps on the stairway. They were heading for his father's library, the ivory tower where a coal fire already blazed. They can't be soliciting donations for the funeral fund already, Eamon thought. He knew that his father's cheque-book was kept in the heavy oak writing-bureau in the hallway. He wondered what was wrong, but he was too lazy to investigate. He could hear Condolences' voice.

"Thanks, Mr Glenville. Thanks, we're very grateful."

And his father's educated voice. "Steady now, gents. It's delicate."

He got back to his toast. He glanced at the two newspapers on the table, Friday's and Saturday's issues of the *Cork Examiner*. He took up Friday's edition because he hadn't time to see it the previous day. The paper was full of the recent political tensions. More than tension: a crisis—POWER-SHARING CRUX

FACING REES.

The experimental assembly in Ulster had collapsed. It had been killed off by a long and brilliantly organised strike of the reactionary Protestant workers' councils. The paper was full of angry Protestant voices, Mr Paisley, Mr Craig and Mr West: "We won't have power-sharing in any way." Across the front page, flanked by a photograph of a happy British Secretary of State shaking hands with the leader of the dead assembly, there was an account—a brief account—of the Party Leader's speech. The Party Leader had given a speech about the intransigence of Unionists, and their foolish unwillingness to consent to a unified Ireland. The Leader had said "as long as Britain continues the kind of guarantees contained in successive legislation—the Government of Ireland Act, 1949 and the Constitution Act, 1973—and continues military and financial support, that consent is unlikely to be forthcoming." It was an ancient point of view, fundamental within the Party's code, yet it was unusual to hear the Party Leader (who had the reputation of being afraid of the British) stating this point of view in public at such a critical time. Had he been stampeded into saying it, Eamon wondered. Had the Republicans, the hawks, moved a little closer to his throat? He had heard the Senator talking about this with Party workers. The workers had insisted that the Leader's reign was over, that he wasn't capable of handling the great historical

decisions that would have to be made in the near future. And he had heard the Senator say, "Such as what?"

"Such as a final go at the Unionists," the Party workers replied. He had sensed the Senator's disgust, his horror at such a hopeless future.

On the same page of the newspaper, in an item of only eight lines, there was a report that more British witnesses would be called to fight the Irish government's allegations of torture in Ulster. Fat chance they have of winning that, Eamon thought. The British invented law. But his eyes were drawn to a much more interesting item, a report on a statement by a British peer who had said he hated the Irish. The peer had received hundreds of letters from all over England. Eamon took a large draft of tea and bit off a chunk of toast while his eyes fed on the nobleman's words.

"I loathe and detest the miserable bastards."

The peer's words were a reminder of the political necessity of the Party, a reminder that the Party's chauvinism was a response to such blind racism. As long as there was political tension between England and Ireland the English would hate the Irish. When all the political tensions passed away the English would begin to love Ireland in the patronising, perhaps doting, way that they loved other little countries like "little Belgium."

He threw down Friday's *Examiner* and took up

Saturday's edition. But he didn't read beyond the headline: COMMONS NORTH SPLIT THREATENS. He looked at the weather forecast. Today was the last day of May, so that ninety-nine per cent of the population would be anxious about the weather for the June weekend. The paper said that it would be cloudy, with sunny spells, but with some rain and showers. A normal enough forecast, predicting everything except snow.

He heard footsteps on the stairs. He jumped up immediately to plug in the kettle to make fresh tea for his father. He felt a little ashamed that he hadn't answered the door. "Thanks, Mr Glenville. See you this evening," he heard Condolences say. He expected the Senator to come into the kitchen to say hello, but when the door opened he saw that it was his father.

"Thanks for all the help. Plug in the kettle, that tea will be stone cold."

"It's plugged in."

"Good man." His father went to the sideboard and cut a fresh slice of bread. He pushed it into the toaster. "Where have you put the *Examiner*?"

"Here. It's on the back of my chair."

"Did you see Thursday's one? On the book page there's a review of a book by Jim Irwin, the astronaut. It's all about the Apollo mission. You should read it. Talk about triumphant technology..."

"Which reminds me..." his father became serious,

"you're spending far too many nights out gallivanting. When I was your age I was in bed at ten-thirty."

"When you were young there was a war on. Sure ye had nothing to do."

"Don't be smart. We were in bed because we were disciplined."

Eamon needed to change this conversation. His father might get on to the subject of Jennifer Dineen. He must know at this stage. "What did the Party deputation want?" he cast the decoy.

"You'll never guess." His father was taken in.

"Wouldn't they take a cheque?"

"It wasn't money at all. They wanted the loan of the photograph of your grandmother with de Valera."

"The one above the fireplace?"

"Well, what other one have we got in the house?" his father asked impatiently.

The photograph was a family icon. It was a sepia-tinted picture of his father's mother as a young woman presenting a bunch of arum lilies to a young and hungry looking de Valera. It was taken in the early twenties at some country crossroads, while The Chief was still on the run; hunted like a fox from townland to townland. Although it was only fifty years old it had been darkened and matured by turf-smoke and coal-dust from the library fire so that it now looked like an early Victorian carbon print. It was a precious gift that radiated a primitive, holy energy and established the Republican pedigree of

the family. It had called three generations of local voters to the Glenville household, helping the family to produce one deputy, one senator and seven councillors in a period of forty years. A powerful treasure.

"What did they want with it?"

"To put it on the Chairman's coffin!"

"What!" Eamon screamed in disbelief. It sounded ridiculous.

"According to Condolences it was the Chairman's wish. It sounds a bit primitive, right enough. But Ned said that he'd like to have that picture on his coffin when they took it from the chapel to the graveyard. It was on your grandmother's coffin too. I suppose that's why Ned wanted it. He was very close to my father."

"I think it's amazing, kind of daft."

"It may be laughable, but you know Condolences. He gets very emotional, and he promised Ned." His father leafed through the newspaper, folding it neatly when he found the racing pages. "Leopard-stown today. Should be light going."

He knew that his father knew little about horses, but he liked to give the impression that he loved sport as much as books.

"There's racing at Tramore as well," Eamon spluttered through his masticated toast. "The last on the card, the Holiday Plate, is at half past five. Do you think that the traffic will affect the Chairman's

funeral."

"Probably." His father didn't sound very worried. "I wouldn't be worried." He lifted his eyes from the paper and stared through the kitchen window. After a few seconds he said, "Petrol rationing. Have we got enough petrol? Condolences said that some petrol stations were opening for two hours this morning. I should go down to Codey's to see if I can get some." He took a drink of tea from his wide white porcelain cup. "This cursed government; they've left us short of everything."

"I thought you were all in favour of the intellectuals in the Coalition?"

"No harm in having a few brainy people in government. Trouble is they don't get the chance to use their heads..." Then he fell silent again as he went back to reading his paper, laboriously now because his eyes were weak. Eamon tinkered with Friday's paper, his father's cast-off. Their conversations always ended like this. A subject would be broached, touched upon, like the Party, his uncle, staying out late, electronics and its future, the lack of integrity in politics; then the subject would be abandoned after a few sentences. He wished that his father had staying-power. He wished that his father could be really roused by something because his openings were always interesting. He felt that his father had a fine mind, a clear brain like his own. If his father was his own age, he thought, one could say that he

was a lad of great promise. But one requires more than promise in middle age. He was hard on his father.

After breakfast his father did go to the garage to see if he could get some petrol. Eamon went upstairs to rekindle the fire. He was standing by the library window watching the milkman from Dungarvan stacking empty crates when his father returned.

"Any luck?"

"Got four gallons. Not bad for an old father? Eh?"

"Very satisfactory."

His father laughed at the expression. Then he took up the book that he'd been reading all week from the sideboard by the door. It was the second volume of Harold Nicolson's *Diaries and Letters* edited by his son. The book was hugely in vogue and had been reviewed by all the important English Sunday papers. Eamon could see the bulge in the book where his father saved and folded all the Sunday reviews. A true bookman, his father loved to create an aura of commentary around every book he read. The reviews were saved and reread as an alternative to literary friendships; they were a symbol of his father's intellectual loneliness. His father walked across the fireplace to put his backside to the heat. His wide frame hid the blank space from where the sepia-tinted photograph of Dev had been removed. Eamon knew that his father wanted to be alone; he was searching the Englishman's book in the hope of

discovering some higher, more civilised form of politics. Anything to escape from the Party's dead weight.

His father spoke again when he made a move towards the door—spoke loftily, sternly, as if he had just learned from Harold Nicolson's perfect diction. "All this corruption, petty squabbling, your uncle's lack of thrust, dare I say it, trust, it springs from a lack of real politics. Look at Condolences. God help him, he's floundering about in a sea of political pieties. He's like a pious old woman; in the absence of real belief he falls back on the medals and icons...You should have seen his pathetic pleading for the Dev picture. Pathetic."

Eamon was tempted to reply, to say something in Condolences' defence. What about Condolences' loyalty, his belief in the Party? His capacity for work on behalf of the organisation? Politically, Condolences was worth a thousand well-read superior intellectuals. Condolences had an infinite capacity to take pains on behalf of the Party. "The infinite capacity to take pains." Eamon knew that that was a definition of genius.

By the time he had gathered enough words to say in poor Condolences' favour his father had retreated to the world of books. It was easier to leave him there. There were too many unsolved arguments. Anyway, this talk of Condolences brought Jennifer into his mind. He would see her at the removal to

the chapel tonight, and again at the burial. After the funeral they could meet and chat in Rebecca's parlour.

"See you later, Dad."

"Where are you off to now?"

"The Senator's house...there's work to do. Can't spend the whole day moping around in the library." That was a parting shot. He ran off before his father could reply.

# TWENTY-EIGHT

Eamon sat with his father, just behind the front seat of mourners that included Rebecca, the Chairman's two brothers and Rebecca's two sisters. Although he couldn't see her face, he knew from the spasms that rocked her shoulders that Rebecca had begun to cry again. One of her sisters whispered into her ear. He could hear what she said. "Don't be upset, now. Don't be upset." It was useless. The moment had almost arrived when they would prepare the coffin for its final journey to the graveyard.

Eamon thought about the last time he saw the Chairman alive. It was in the small hospital where they had sent him to die as comfortably as possible. It was in a dingy room with glossy mauve walls, the colour of arterial blood. The room had a small corner window that faced northwards towards the black mountains. A bleak place. "Welcome. Good lad." The Chairman was delighted to see him. The Senator, who had brought him there, was standing in the doorway, out of Ned's vision. "Where's your uncle? Has he abandoned me already?" His uncle stepped forward then, and all three of them laughed. Eamon was shocked when he saw how frail the Chairman

looked. Illness had eaten away at all his spare resources, so that his face was reduced to skin and bone. Even the purple patch on his left hand where they had inserted a drip needle was like a piece of withered blotting paper.

"Scrub up a bit of tobacco for me, will you?" the Chairman gestured to his uncle. The Senator took the tobacco pouch and began to scrape away large flakes, while Eamon searched around for a chair. "Sit on the bed," suggested Ned weakly. Eamon sat down. Ned wanted to offer advice, but first he felt that he had to make a lengthy preamble. He told Eamon about the exploits of his grandfather, Deputy Glenville: about his grandfather's thoroughness during the troubled times of the old IRA and the Irregulars. He had been a brave and honest man: his honesty had made him invulnerable and untouchable. "It is characters like him who made the soul of the Party. Why we exist," the Chairman said laboriously. Eamon remained silent; he feared that if he spoke he would betray his lack of interest in the past. He had inherited his father's scepticism, an immunity to the feverish stories of the Party's history. When the Chairman paused for breath, Eamon noticed a grey-white mucus dribbling from his mouth. The Senator came over and wiped it away with a towel.

"Stick with the Party, lad." Ned took a few drags from his pipe, then handed it back to the Senator

who had remained in the background like a footman. "These neo-Republicans, Allingham, Conory. They're not in the Party tradition. We have our own country now. We must make it work first. Stay with the Party, the Party gave us everything we have." It was an old plea, he knew. Even as the Chairman spoke Eamon felt that he had failed the Party, because he couldn't believe everything about the Party's past. Nor could he believe in the way the Party had legitimised certain aspects of the Republican past, while condemning other aspects. The new Republicans, the hawks in the Party, could claim a rival legitimacy. He felt that the onslaught of the future, the very force of things unfolding, would make both versions of the past irrelevant.

"I'm listening, Ned." That was all he could say. He loved the dying man because he had become part of the family, he had protected the Senator and sponsored him, even in awkward and hostile situations. And there was no denying Ned's love for the Glenvilles; it was a kind of feudal thing. The Chairman gripped his hand, held it tightly, painfully. He wanted to say more but he couldn't find the energy or the words. While he summoned up more energy with all his will-power they sat silently. It seemed that a merciless, daemonic vapour invaded the room while they watched Ned taking short, hungry gasps. The pink venetian blinds chatted against the small window-frame. It was a death-

rattle, as if death were a moth attached to the edge of the Chairman's life.

"Move in a bit," his father nudged him. Two Party men from Tipperary had arrived just in time. Canon Hayes left the altar to don his funeral attire. The Party men took the opportunity to leave their seat again to sympathise with Rebecca. A number of other people gained confidence from this move and did likewise. They didn't want to delay after the funeral: they were all heading off to a football match in Dungarvan.

The Chairman's coffin was decked with wreaths, mounds of plastic flowers in perspex cases. There were wreaths from Allingham, Conory, from the local youth club and rowing club (Ned had always lent them one of his minibuses) and from the local GAA. The coffin was draped in the tricolour, and the photograph of Eamon's grandmother with Dev rose triumphantly above the wreaths to proclaim the Chairman's deepest allegiance. There was one beautiful wreath of real flowers, of laurel and camellia leaves and early roses. Eamon guessed that it had come from the local Protestant supermarket-owner. Only a Protestant would have shown such good taste. Six large candles in tall brass holders surrounded the casket, but their funereal effect was cancelled by the bright light of early June that streamed through the chapel windows.

Eamon noticed too that his uncle and Condolences

had seated themselves strategically beside the coffin. Because of the ill-feeling in the constituency between Allingham's Republicans and the Senator's doves they hadn't come to any agreement about who should shoulder the coffin out of the chapel for the two-mile journey to the graveyard by the river. The family had no say in this: a body, because it was emotive and symbolic, belonged to the local Party. The Senator and Condolences were determined that they would get under the coffin. That they would triumph at the opportune moment.

When the Canon emerged from the sacristy the congregation stood in prayer. The priest proceeded quickly to the coffin and stood before it mournfully, surrounded by altar-boys. Just then the sacristan opened the door at the side of the altar and began to gesticulate furiously. Finally, one of the altar boys left his place by the coffin and attended to the sacristan. There was a note for the Canon. When it was delivered the Canon glanced at it. He spoke. What the congregation thought was "Dominus Vobiscum" was, in fact, "Dawn Lass at Epsom." Dawn Lass had cantered home, the clincher in the Canon's treble chance that was worth £600. He looked up and gazed at his altar boys with an almost mystical love. All six acolytes were from the sixth class of the Senator's school; the tip had come from them. What the Canon didn't know was that the information had originated with Condolences. Now

he returned, good humoured, to the matter of the dead.

He gestured to the smallest acolyte who handed him a silver vessel filled with incense. He put two spoonfuls of the mixture into the thurible and began to anoint the coffin with a sweet, ethereal smoke. He worked his way around the casket, muttering prayers that were drowned by the clicking sound of the thurible. When the casket was covered in a dense cloud of incense the canon returned to his starting-point and handed the thurible to one of the altar-boys. He then sprinkled holy water. Then two of the altar-boys removed the six heavy candlesticks and placed them along the front row of seats where the Senator and Condolences were waiting: in doing so the altar-boys blocked the exit. Condolences moved forward noisily to let the acolyte know what had happened, but the young lad took no notice of him and returned to his safe haven by the Canon's side. Before the two had time to scramble around the other side Allingham and Conory and the two Party men from Tipperary had placed themselves under the coffin. They bore it down the aisle. The Senator and Condolences were furious. Condolences wanted to scream, he wanted to throw something, but the candlesticks were church property.

"Poor organisation, what did I tell you?" his father said. He had noticed what happened, and was excited and amused.

"It's an insult to Rebecca. Ned hated those fellows," Eamon replied angrily. He was sorry for his uncle who had been like a son to Ned. But he had seen his uncle outwitted, yet again. There was no stopping the likes of Allingham.

"Rebecca will be very upset."

"Too late now."

As they walked out of the chapel Eamon felt that there was little hope for his poor uncle. In fact, his only hope was being borne away in a casket. "Jennifer Dineen just waved at you," his father said. While they walked behind the coffin—it would be a long walk—a fresh wind had blown low cloud across the valley. Raindrops were spitting lightly.

"Where?"

"You should look where you're going. Notice things. Don't be day-dreaming."

"Where is she? For God's sake!"

"Well, well, we're very interested...look....the girl in the brown dress."

He looked across the advancing crowd. He saw her and stared for a long time. She didn't look back. She was with her family and being good. "If you keep looking across like that your head will get stuck. You'll have to walk sideways for the rest of your life. Leave the girl alone." His father stared ahead and tried not to laugh.

When they reached the graveyard they moved up closer to the mourners. Eamon could smell the damp

laurel leaves of the Protestant wreath. Scents were being released by the agitations of light rain.

"The rain," he said. "Will the portrait of Dev and Gran be damaged by the rain?"

"They're covered with a bit of plastic, there on the wreath-rack." His father pointed to the mound of plastic wreaths. From where he stood he could see an exposed corner of the heirloom. He wasn't going to worry about it. If his father didn't worry, why should he?

"I won't worry about it so."

"Don't."

While they stood around at the entrance he could hear a group of Party men talking at the other side of the hearse. They were discussing Ulster, excitedly, the fall of the assembly and the collapse of the Sunningdale Agreement.

"Did you see that Blaney was roasting the Taoiseach at question time last Wednesday?"

"I didn't see."

"He asked Cosgrave if there would be a plebiscite on the agreement. When Cosgrave said that there wouldn't be one he stood up and asked him if he would admit that the whole Sunningdale debacle was ballyhoo from first to last."

"What did Cosgrave say?"

"What did he say? Feck all. That man has horse-trading in his blood."

"The Protestant workers have made sure that it'll

be a débâcle anyway," one man interjected. "This week it's the end of the assembly...That's the end of power-sharing for the next ten years. You can be sure of that..."

"I blame Edward Heath, the last Prime Minister over there. He wasn't rough enough with the Unionists. He should have shown the bastards the bayonet."

"No," another man said. "I think Heath acted in good faith. I think Heath will be written into the history books as the first Englishman who really tried to find out what was going on up there. He was a friend of Ireland, he was."

"And where did that get him?"

"True enough, he lost his job."

They continued to talk like that, moving from praise of the lost English Prime Minister to criticism of the Coalition leader. They praised the courage of Blaney and of Boland, a Party minister who had displayed old-fashioned honesty and integrity when he resigned from government. They said that one final push was all that was needed to make a united Ireland. Now that the assembly had collapsed everything was open and malleable. They cursed the intransigent Unionists, saying that they didn't know how happy they'd be in a united Ireland. "Look at our Southern Unionists," one man pointed out. "Aren't they the finest and happiest group of people in the world? And isn't every one of them prospering?"

Eamon then noticed the small group of Protestant people who were waiting at a slight remove from the rest of the mourners. They were the poorer Protestants, a milkman, a farm-worker, a gardener, who had no Catholic servants to deliver flowers to the chapel like Mr Winslow or General Whyte. In their poverty and lack of cosmopolitan experience they had been afraid to enter the local Catholic church to put their own flowers on the Chairman's coffin. Eamon wondered if they were really happy. They didn't look happy. None of them supported the Party, which made them double outsiders in a rural area that was a Party stronghold. But they knew and liked Rebecca. Still, the Coalition was now in Government, Eamon thought. Protestants were always happier during periods of Coalition.

Inside the graveyard the June afternoon exhaled a moist pungent aroma of young laurel leaves, freshly cut nettles and mown grass. That moist aroma competed with the suave mildness of the rain. While they waited for the Canon to begin prayers they heard the church bells still tolling on the other side of the river. A shower of sparrows in the hedgerow, the chatter of a wisp of snipe on the disused railway-line, the crunch of mourners' feet on the gravel paths: all those sounds were sucked towards the open grave to compress the corpse and push it even more urgently towards its natural end. The Canon was waiting for the arrival of the ex-

Minister for Local Government, who had found it difficult to park his large white Volvo. After eight minutes of annoyed silence the politician arrived. The Canon began...

"In the name of the Father, the Son and the Holy Ghost..."

When the blessings and invocations were over they lowered the Chairman into the pool of brown water at the bottom of the grave. Rebecca sighed and heaved with grief. Her sister and Mrs Dineen moved to comfort her.

"Now, love. Now girl," Mrs Dineen petted her in the simplest way. As Mrs Dineen moved closer to Rebecca, Jennifer stepped into the vacated space. Her head was bowed and her hands joined in prayer. Eamon faced her across the open grave. He lifted his head sternly, boldly, to prove that he wasn't weeping. Eventually, she looked across the grave, her eyes swollen. Her swollen eyes made him feel tough, like a man. He was delighted.

Then his father shook him, impatiently. "Take that photograph off the ground!"

He saw the portrait of his grandmother and Dev lying on the mound of red earth by the graveside. It had been cast there casually by the undertaker, who had no political connections. Eamon moved nimbly along the edge of the grave to rescue the photograph from its vulgar company of plastic wreaths. He wiped the muddy glass with his woollen

coat-sleeve. He returned to his father's side and stood with the portrait under his arm while they said a decade of the rosary. It was during those moments, when he stood with his agnostic father and protected a party treasure from the elements, that the power of the tribe died within him. He saw the Party as comfortless and meaningless as his father's agnostic prayers. He looked around at the faces of the mourners. He watched his uncle praying. His uncle's thirty-six-year-old face was wizened with grief. Ned had been his political mentor, his political father. In losing Ned he had become orphaned.

Eamon thought of Julie's letter. Sensing the nearness of the Chairman's death, she had written from Brussels on the twentieth of May. She was worried about his uncle, about his ability to retain his vocational senatorship, about his inability to move upward in the Party. "Stick with your uncle. Stay with the party," she had said. Almost the dead Chairman's words. She lived in hope too. "Take care of your uncle for me." Did that mean that she loved the Senator, that she would come back? Or did she merely pity him? Whatever about his uncle, Eamon was happy that Julie was busy in Europe. She was delighted with the bright lights and the frenzy of activity. She had escaped from the darkness, the solitude of their rural place. Such a beautiful woman, clever, he thought. He remembered his lecherous dream.

"It is lovely to hear a man praying with a firm voice." Canon Hayes addressed his father who never went to Mass.

"I pray all the time, Canon," his father said cockily.

"Isn't that good. We'd love to see you below in the chapel." Like all clergymen, the Canon became very confident when standing at an open grave.

"There's more spirituality in my absence than in the company of bawling babies. I read the Bible at least once a week."

"Our version, I hope."

"Both versions," his father replied. "God's beauty is in one, and His clarity is in the other."

"Ah well." The Canon felt that he had lost ground. Eamon's father had a way with words. It would take more than post-graduate training in divinity to bring him around.

The Canon walked on ahead of them towards his car. There was the usual after-funeral chaos. But the chaos was made more acute by the ex-Minister's Volvo that had been double-parked. There was an angry bottleneck: many of the Party officials and minor politicians were in a hurry to get to the Munster senior football championship in Dungarvan. Because of Ned's funeral they had already missed the minor game. From the gate of the graveyard, Eamon noticed some of the poorer children of the parish running their fingers along the metallic paintwork

of the Volvo. Some of them peered through the tinted glass to view the document-cases and umbrellas of a satisfied life. When the ex-Minister emerged from the graveyard he was flanked by his own particular cronies, election-time helpmates and a fringe of councillors and town commissioners. Because of the falling rain, and the fact that so many people had postponed their Sunday lunch to attend the burial, the graveyard emptied very quickly.

"Another new car," Eamon's father said. "I see he has a new Volvo. He must have sold that land in Dublin; the big parcel that he had re-zoned. Do you remember that scandal?"

While his father spoke the wind changed to a north-westerly, driving the mist and skimming the mildness from the light rainfall. His father never wore a cap, claiming that it made a man bald. His hair was now drenched with rain, and the water was beading down the side of his face.

"Don't talk about him. He's right behind us."

"Let him hear me, the bloody racketeer."

"Mr Glenville! Get in, for God's sake!" It was Canon Hayes. He opened the window of his black and silver Escort to offer shelter. He wouldn't accept a refusal. Dismissing all protests, he opened the passenger door of the car. "Get in! Get in!"

Canon Hayes already had one passenger, as Eamon discovered to his surprise. "We saw the two of ye getting drenched," the Canon laughed, making

Jennifer feel at home. She had taken a back seat so that the Canon could offer further largesse to a few stranded parish members.

"Where's your mother?" Eamon asked as he climbed into the back seat.

"Jennifer's mother is well able to look after herself," the Canon suggested.

"She stayed behind with Rebecca. Rebecca's very upset. She wanted to stay on at the graveside."

"Very foolish," Eamon's father said.

"Foolish, but understandable," replied the Canon. Eamon and Jennifer were left to themselves after that, while the Canon and Mr Glenville drifted into a middle-aged conversation. While the windscreen wipers swept across the broad expanse of glass, trying to part the impossible mist, the two elders became lost in a fruitless, contented chat. Their opinions were made generous by the memory of the recently dead.

Eamon pressed his damp leg against Jennifer's thigh. The back seat was full of a limited but delightful possibility. Jennifer responded by moving closer. His damp trouser legs and her damp tights set up a kind of electrostatic tension between their bodies, making them feel nakedly close to each other. Eamon hoped that the priest had no telepathic powers. In the heat of the car, serenaded by the rhythmic sound of the wipers, Eamon thought again about his uncle. Ever since he had witnessed the

defeat of the Senator by Allingham's caucus he had lost faith in the certainty of things. There was no mathematical comfort in politics, no certainty. But at one time, he knew, the Party had promised something that was very close to political certainty, almost an eternal life of electoral loyalties. What he did believe in—and he shared this belief with his father—was that he would live to see the withering away of Party political machines. The needs of Europe, of the EEC, would produce a higher breed of politician. There would be an end to bogmen and gombeen politics.

"Nearly there," the Canon said.

"Very few people around." His father sounded disappointed.

When they reached the outskirts of the town they saw the ex-Minister's car parked outside a pub. The man had stopped to do business. But most of the Party men had skipped off to the football match. They had made their choice.

Eamon squeezed Jennifer's hand. In reply she pressed her thigh more crushingly against his. Her stored-up desire was a bright, liberating force. Meanwhile, the rain pelted westwards, filling their desire with its metallic sound. It filled them with a lurid hopefulness.

"Do you think the Party will survive Ned's going, Dad? Do you think all the fighting will start again, like after the Arms' Trial?"

"Ah, the Party'll survive. People love a fight, that's why they're in politics."

"Aren't we a serious young man," the Canon said, avuncular, patronising.

"I do my best, Canon," Eamon replied savagely. "I try not to think too much."

The Canon didn't reply.

"Good man," his father said. "Good man."

Ollscoil na hÉireann, Gaillimh
3 1111 40039 3805